STUDIES IN ARCHITECTURE

EDITED BY ANTHONY BLUNT AND RUDOLF WITTKOWER

VOLUME XI

SALOMON DE BROSSE

ROSALYS COOPE

SALOMON DE BROSSE

and the Development of the
Classical Style in French Architecture
from 1565 to 1630

ROSALYS COOPE

The Pennsylvania State University Press

University Park and London

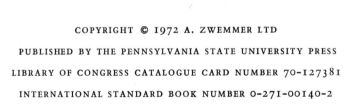

PUBLISHED BY THE PENNSYLVANIA STATE UNIVERSITY PRESS
LIBRARY OF CONGRESS CATALOGUE CARD NUMBER 70-127381
INTERNATIONAL STANDARD BOOK NUMBER 0-271-00140-2
MADE AND PRINTED IN GREAT BRITAIN
BY ROBERT STOCKWELL LTD, LONDON SEI

To Clare and Helena

Contents

Catalogue

List of Plates

Only drawings which are not included in the Catalogue of Works (for example some of those by Jacques I du Cerceau), have their whereabouts indicated in the List of Plates. To assist the reader to correlate them with the text certain plates of Blérancourt and Coulommiers are captioned 'Bib. Nat. Drawing'. Buildings for which no architect's name is given are by Salomon de Brosse.

List of Text Illustrations

List of Abbreviations

B.S.H.A.F.	Bulletin de la société de l'histoire de l'art français
Bull. Mon.	Bulletin Monumental
Bull. Soc. Hist. Prot. Fr.	Bulletin de la société de l'histoire du Protestantisme français
Burl. Mag.	Burlington Magazine
F. (followed by a catalogue no.)	Faucheux, Catalogue de l'Oeuvre d'Israël Silvestre, Paris, 1857
G.d.B.A.	Gazette des Beaux-Arts
Grand Marot	L'architecture françoise ou recueil des plans elévations coupes et profils des églises, palais, hôtels et maisons particulières de Paris et des châteaux et maisons de campagne . . . des environs et de plusieurs autres endroits de France, à Paris, chez Jean Mariette, 1727 (2nd edition)
Mém. Soc. Ant. Fr.	Mémoires de la société des antiquaires de France
Petit Marot	Recueil des plans, profils et élevations de plusieurs palais, chasteaux, églises, sépultures, grotes et hostels . . . dans Paris et aux environs . . . Paris, n.d. (*c.* 1654–1660). The 2nd edition, published by Mariette (*c.* 1738), is sometimes referred to in the text or Catalogue and this is then clearly indicated; otherwise all references are to the 1st edition
P.M.MS.	Pierpont Morgan MS. (Album by Jacques I du Cerceau)

Acknowledgements

The drawing on Pl. 26 is reproduced by gracious permission of H.M. The Queen.

The drawing of the Pitti Palace on Pl. 145 is reproduced by permission of the Provost and Fellows of Worcester College, Oxford, the drawings by Jacques Gentilhâtre on Pls 42 and 57 by permission of The Royal Institute of British Architects and the design for a ceiling on Pl. 167 by permission of The National Trust, Waddesdon Manor. The du Cerceau drawing on Pl. 192 is reproduced by kind permission of Mr Philip Hofer, from the album deposited by him in the Houghton Library, Harvard University.

The photographs for Pls 53, 54, 61, 85–87, 123–125 and 149 were provided by the Musée du Louvre, Paris, who have permitted the publication of the drawings reproduced. Photographs for Pls 30, 83, 107, 115, 118, 126, 127, 134, 139, 140, 169, 189, 210 and 215 were supplied by the Bibliothèque Nationale, Paris, those for Pls 39, 41, 74, 81 and 82 by the Archives Nationales, Paris, and those for Pls 10, 130, 154, 176, 182 and 190 by the Caisse Nationale des Monuments Historiques. The Ecole des Beaux-Arts, Paris, provided the photograph for Pl. 36 and gave permission for the reproduction of this du Cerceau drawing. The Musée Franco–Americain, Blérancourt, supplied the photograph for Pl. 94. The photographs of the plans of Verneuil in the Musée Condé at Chantilly were kindly lent to me by M. Raymond Cazelles. The Nationalmuseum, Stockholm, provided the photographs for Pls 63 and 75 and gave permission for their reproduction. The du Cerceau drawings on Pls 11, 24, 90 and 111 are reproduced by courtesy of the Pierpont Morgan Library, New York, which supplied the photographs. The Cooper Union Museum, New York, photographed for me and permitted the reproduction of the drawing on Pl. 21.

The Staff of the Photographic Department of the Courtauld Institute of Art supplied the photographs for Pls 1, 3, 4, (by permission of the Trustees of the British Museum), 5–10, 12, 14, 15, 18, 19, 20–23, 25–28, 35, 37, 38, 44, 73, 76, 78, 79, 88, 91, 92, 103, 136–138, 141–145, 151, 158–160, 173, 175, 214 and 216.

Acknowledgement is made to the following who allowed me to use their photographs: Professor Sir Anthony Blunt, Pls 2, 185, 202, Fig 2 and Fig 4; M. Philippe Boudon, Pls 158 and 159; Mr Terry Friedman, Pls 146 and 147; Mme Christine Sajou, Pl. 13; Dr Peter Smith, Pls 89, 98–101, 104, 132, 135, 150, 155, 161, 178, 209 and 211; Mrs Mary Whiteley, Pl. 133; and Dr George Zarnecki, Pls 103 and 109.

The publishers also wish to make the following acknowledgements: Bulloz, Paris, Pls 191 and 194; Country Life, Pl. 164; Editions Gaby, Phot. Artauld,

Nantes, Pls 204, 208; Photo Viollet, Paris, Pl. 195, and Studio Ménant, Rennes, Pls 196–198, 200, 205 and 206.

Pl. 40 was drawn by Mrs June Radford, Pls 77, 97, and Fig 3 by Dr Peter Smith, and Pl. 93 by Mrs June Radford and Dr Peter Smith.

Preface

I WAS assisted in the preparation of this book by a grant made to me in 1965 from the Central Research Fund of the University of London. The work has necessitated many visits to France, and I would like to thank all my French friends for the kindness and hospitality they have extended to me on these occasions. I am especially indebted to M. and Mme Bernard Peyrot des Gachons of Montceaux and M. and Mme Raymond Cornon of Rennes, with whom I have so often stayed. M. Cornon, formerly architect-in-charge of the Palais de Justice in Rennes, has helped me greatly with advice on technical questions concerning the building.

I have received help of various kinds from many people in England, France and the United States, from individuals and from those in charge of Archives, Libraries, Print Rooms and other Museum Departments and their staffs; lack of space prevents me from naming all of them, but I sincerely thank them all. Some, for their particular assistance, I must however mention. Four young French scholars, Mmes Françoise Boudon, Hélène Titeux-Derottleur and Françoise Hamon, and Mlle Hélène Couzy, have always been willing to check references, send me information, answer queries by post and take or obtain for me photographs and photocopies. By so doing they have made it very much easier for me to complete the book in England, and their friendly interest and enthusiasm has been invaluable to me. Mme Jestaz of the Département des Estampes of the Bibliothèque Nationale in Paris has also helped me a great deal over identifying and obtaining photographs. M. Jean-Pierre Babelon of the Archives Nationales and M. Michel Gallet of the Musée Carnavalet have been most helpful in discussion of problems concerning public buildings and private houses in Paris.

I owe my introduction to the Minutier Central and my initiation into the mysteries of its workings to Dr Allan Braham and Dr Peter Smith and I am extremely grateful for their help in the early stages of my work there. M. Henri Collard answered my endless requests for help in deciphering documents with the invariable courtesy, patience and interest so well-known to readers who have worked in the Minutier.

M. E.-J. Ciprut, who for many years made a special study of documents in the Minutier relating to sixteenth- and seventeenth-century architects and sculptors, communicated to me all those he found which were relevant to my work. Many of these he had not yet published when he told me of their contents; some of them he was still preparing for the press when he died, in October 1970. After his death all his manuscripts and notes, the fruit of twenty years' work, were tragically destroyed. So it is with an added sense of loss that I acknowledge with profound gratitude the generosity with which he shared his knowledge. He was a good friend and one who will be sadly missed by all his English colleagues.

Dr Margaret Whinney, a friend since my student days under her tutorship, has given me guidance which has been of the greatest help in planning this book. Professor Sir Anthony Blunt, who first suggested that I undertake the work, has supervised it from its inception, helped me at every stage of its preparation and has read, corrected and commented upon the manuscript. But my greatest debt of all to him is that he first taught me French architectural history and suggested that I specialize in the period covered by this study of de Brosse.

I know that I could never have finished this book had it not been for my family's interest and encouragement. To Mrs Anthea Trenchard, who typed and re-typed it all, I am deeply grateful. So should the reader be, for through her vigilance he is spared some notable lapses of grammar and style.

The book is divided into two main sections: the Text and the Catalogue of Works. The latter contains a Chronology of the career and works of de Brosse, with notes on the sources. After that, the works are catalogued alphabetically; buildings in Paris are listed alphabetically under 'Paris'. Entries are divided into four sections: Original Documents; Published Sources; Plans and Elevations (subdivided into drawings and engravings); Chronology and Notes. Where drawings or engravings are illustrated in the book their plate numbers are given. Where some of these sources are lacking, the entries are made in shortened form. Uncertain attributions are discussed in the Appendix to the Catalogue.

A detailed bibliography given for each work, in the Catalogue. A brief General Bibliography is on p. 287. Except in the case where there is more than one title by an author, the author's name only is given in references to his book, followed by the volume, page number etc. as appropriate.

Introduction

THE period comprised within the sub-title of this book is one of the most difficult and confusing for the study of architecture in post-medieval France. The Wars of Religion and the consequent social upheaval affected not only the style of architecture but also, naturally, the number of important building-schemes which were embarked upon. From the mid-1580s until peace was achieved under Henri IV, almost nothing was built, but a great many buildings – and a great many records – were destroyed. Nor was the first decade of the seventeenth century entirely propitious politically for extensive building, and the most significant ventures were in the hands of the King: the continuation of the Louvre, extensions at Fontainebleau and the town-planning schemes in Paris. Such châteaux as were built were mainly those of the King, his Queen or his mistresses.

By the second decade of the new century, growing confidence in the social order began to be reflected in increased building activity among civic and religious authorities and private patrons, and it is to this period that Salomon de Brosse's important works nearly all belong. His contribution to the development of the classical style in French architecture is the main subject of this study, but it has also been necessary to make a fairly extensive analysis of certain aspects of the work of late sixteenth-century architects. Only by such an analysis can de Brosse's own career be properly understood and appreciated. This book is in no way intended as a comprehensive history of French architecture within the period covered, but only as an assessment of certain architectural developments and of de Brosse's significance in relation to them.

For historical reasons the buildings discussed are almost all to be found in Paris and the Ile-de-France. It was in this region that, after the stabilisation in Paris of a formerly peripatetic Court and Administration, most of the important new building, public and private, was done, and it was here that de Brosse almost exclusively worked. (see p. xxiv).

During recent years more emphasis has been placed, in the study of French architecture, upon documentary evidence, mainly in the form of contracts, and particularly upon that available in the Minutier Central of the Archives Nationales in Paris. Here, by law, are now deposited the records kept by the notaries of Paris. These notaries were, in many cases, the direct predecessors of firms still in practice who have inherited their files and day-books, some of which go back to the Middle Ages. Among them are to

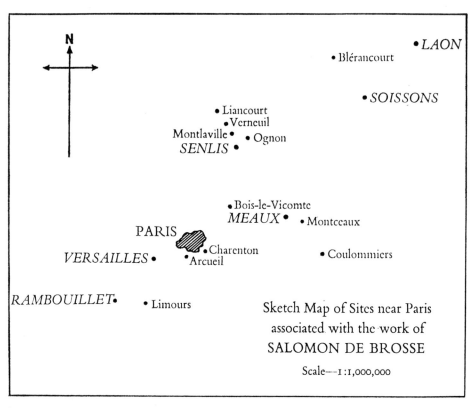

N

•*LAON*

• Blérancourt

•*SOISSONS*

• Liancourt
•Verneuil
Montlaville • • Ognon
SENLIS •

• Bois-le-Vicomte
MEAUX • • Montceaux

PARIS
•Charenton
VERSAILLES • •Arcueil

• Coulommiers

RAMBOUILLET• • Limours

Sketch Map of Sites near Paris
associated with the work of
SALOMON DE BROSSE

Scale—1:1,000,000

be found the contracts for buildings whose history it has previously been impossible to unravel. In addition, the files of the Minutier Central make it possible to trace wills, marriage contracts, inventories and family agreements of various kinds which supply us with concrete facts and dates as a basis for architectural history. Some of this vast collection of material has not as yet been examined or classified and, as this task proceeds, it is obvious that new documents concerning de Brosse and many other architects will eventually be discovered.

There are other valuable records concerning buildings in the main Archives, but these have been known and used for rather longer than those in the Minutier. In particular, the plans of Paris such as the *Terrier du Roy*, the *Censive de l'Archevêché* and the *Atlas Cadastral* have been invaluable for the study of the private houses in the city.

All these sources have led to a much greater knowledge of what de Brosse actually built and, almost equally important in the case of the written sources, have provided a firm basis for the rejection of certain attributions to him which were stylistically confusing or illogically presumptive. A much clearer picture now emerges of de Brosse's career and its real importance.

CHAPTER I

Salomon de Brosse

SALOMON DE BROSSE was born in the early 1570s; the date 1571, now generally accepted for his birth, is supported by such scanty evidence as we have about his early life and work.[1] Philibert de l'Orme, the greatest French architect of the sixteenth century, died in 1570, and it seems peculiarly fitting that de Brosse should have entered the world almost at the same time as de l'Orme left it. De Brosse, though de l'Orme's equal neither in intellect nor in inventiveness, was none the less in many ways his spiritual heir. He was the first outstanding classical architect of the seventeenth century and the vital link between de l'Orme and François Mansart, in whose work the French classical spirit was to find its finest expression in the decades following de Brosse's death in 1626. It was de Brosse's particular achievement to pave the way for Mansart by restoring order and coherence to French architecture, and by freeing it from the influence of the irrational and over-decorated manner of the late sixteenth century.

For this reason de Brosse is a key figure in the development of French classicism, but until recently the part he played has not been properly appreciated. In his own day and for some time after, he was highly esteemed, but his reputation suffered later, not least from such academic criticism as Blondel's strictures on the faults of the Luxembourg Palace. By the end of the eighteenth century many of his buildings had been demolished, and during the nineteenth century, when still fewer survived, he had become little more than a name. Even this name, through some mistake perpetuated by a series of writers, was changed from Salomon to Jacques de Brosse.

Apart from the few remaining works attributed to him, almost nothing was known about this shadowy figure. Even now no portrait of him has been convincingly identified; no letters from him have been found; we possess only one certain specimen of his handwriting; the one set of drawings which can so far be securely attributed to him, the plans of the Palais du Parlement at Rennes, drawn and inscribed by him in 1619, were lost at some

1. Cf. Chronology and Notes, preceding the Catalogue of Works, p. 197.

time subsequent to 1911. The album of drawings in the Louvre always
attributed to him cannot be proved to contain anything from his hand, and
is probably the work of Charles du Ry.[2]

In all these respects the case of Salomon de Brosse is very different from
that of de l'Orme and Mansart, whose characters, ideas, prejudices and
methods of work are well documented, and whose appearance is recorded
in portraits. Contemporary references to de Brosse are comparatively rare,
but some of them if only by implication are revealing, and taken all together
they do help us gain an impression of his character and his methods of work
which is confirmed by the history of several of his projects.

In 1911 two books were published which went some way towards
reinstating de Brosse's reputation: the Pasteur Pannier's *Un Architecte
Français au commencement du XVIIe siècle, Salomon de Brosse*, and Reginald
Blomfield's *History of French Architecture 1494–1661*.

Blomfield's short study of de Brosse in his second volume is inaccurate
over biographical details, and, like Blondel whom he quotes, he has strong
academic prejudices against the deficiencies of style and proportion which he
finds in de Brosse's buildings. Pannier, particularly in his early chapters,
relies to a large extent on the articles and manuscript notes of Charles Read,
a Frenchman who spent twenty-five years collecting information about
de Brosse, but only published one very short monograph in 1881. Thanks to
Read's researches, Pannier's book contains invaluable information concerning de Brosse's family and background. Both Pannier and Read were
Protestants, and as such were particularly interested in de Brosse who was
also a Protestant. In Pannier's case this interest caused him to give de Brosse
greater credit as an architect than the documents justify. He attributed to
him, on the scantiest evidence or on none at all, any notable early seventeenth-
century building which caught his attention and which had no architect's
name firmly attached to it. But, although much of his book is misleading,
its lists of references are extremely valuable, as also are the appendices
containing transcriptions of documents.

In recent years more documents have been discovered, a few of which
have already been published; there have also been sympathetic studies of
de Brosse in books and articles. This study is an attempt to collate all the old
material and all the new information available, and to present a study of
de Brosse's work as a whole which will establish his proper position in the
history of French architecture. At the same time I hope that his personality

---

2. Pannier mistakenly confirmed the attribution; cf. Cat. pp. 219-220.

may emerge a little more clearly than hitherto, so that we can know him better not only as an architect but as a man.

Salomon de Brosse, the son of Jehan de Brosse and Julienne, daughter of the famous architect and engraver, Jacques I Androuet du Cerceau, was probably born at Verneuil-sur-Oise where his father seems to have settled in the late 1560s.[3] In 1568 du Cerceau had begun to build the great château at Verneuil for Philippe de Boulainvilliers, and he probably called in de Brosse as an assistant; later Jehan may have gone to Paris to work for Marguerite de Valois, for the name 'Jehan de Brosse, architecte et secrétaire' appears in her accounts for the years 1578, 1579 and 1582, but otherwise we know nothing about him. He died before 1585, for a document of that year refers to Julienne du Cerceau as a widow, living at Verneuil with her children, all of whom were still minors.[4] Julienne's father died also about 1585, but since her two brothers, Baptiste and Jacques II du Cerceau, were both architects they no doubt assumed responsibility for training the young Salomon de Brosse. Baptiste was dead by 1590, but Jacques II[5] lived until 1614, and since Salomon later maintained a close relationship both family and professional with him, this uncle was probably his principal teacher. His training would have been mainly received at Verneuil itself, where the château provided a constant source of employment for nearly two decades.

The first-known reference to de Brosse's professional life is in 1598, when he was employed with his uncle at the château of Montceaux-en-Brie, which the King had given to his mistress, Gabrielle d'Estrées. An inventory of papers drawn up at Montceaux after Gabrielle's death in 1599 mentions two receipts: '... Item ... une liasse dans laquelle sont enfillés les acquits et papiers qui ensuyvent ... à M. du Cerceau du VII avril dudict an (1598) de la somme de VI escus ... autre de Salomon de Brosse, neveu du Sr. du Cerceau XXI may la somme de X escus ...'. The work for which these payments were made is not recorded, but it may be of some significance that of two small sums de Brosse received the larger.

Only two documents have so far been discovered concerning de Brosse's life between 1598 and 1608, both marriage contracts which he witnessed. The first, in 1600, between Hugues de la Fond and Elisabeth Coupel, a niece of Jacques I du Cerceau, is signed by him, 'Salomon Brosse, ingénieur de la

---

3. Cf. Chronology and Notes, first entry p. 197. There is no reason to suppose with Blomfield (I, p. 146) that Jehan de Brosse and not Jacques I du Cerceau was the designer of Verneuil.

4. That is, under twenty-five years old. For the age of majority, cf. ibid. third entry.

5. Cf. Geymüller, p. 26 ff., and Hautecoeur, I, p. 501.

Reyne de France', and the second, in 1602, between his uncle Jacques II du Cerceau and Marie Malapert, is signed by him as 'architecte de la Reine'.[6]

During the period 1600 to 1608 de Brosse made designs for the completion of the château at Verneuil which Henri IV had presented to Henriette d'Entragues in 1600; his work for her there was almost certainly begun soon after this date, but the record of his employment by Henriette occurs only at a much later period when he was appealing to her for payment.

In 1608 the King provided Marie de Médicis with money to launch a new building programme at Montceaux. For the next nine or ten years de Brosse was to be responsible for all the building done at the château.

We do not know where else besides Verneuil and Montceaux de Brosse may have worked during these years, but by 1608 he must have been very well established, since in that year not only did he become the Queen's architect at Montceaux, but he was commissioned by Sully to design all the public buildings and the various types of houses for the new town of Henrichemont near Bourges. It is probable that his uncle Jacques II du Cerceau promoted de Brosse's interest in the right quarters, just as de Brosse himself was later to do for his own son Paul.

From about 1610 onwards de Brosse's name is connected with important commissions in Paris. He may have designed the Collège de France, begun in 1610;[7] and at the Hôtel de Soissons, for Charles de Soissons who died in 1612, he built the celebrated *porte-cochère* giving on to the Rue des Deux-Ecus.

Between 1612 and 1614 de Brosse lived in various lodgings in Paris, so as to be near whatever work he had in hand. He undertook important extensions to the Hôtel de Bouillon in the Rue de Seine, in the contract for which he is described as 'architecte du Roy et de la Royne', and as living in the Rue Saint-Honoré. When he signed a contract for work at the Hôtel de Bullion in 1614 he had moved to the Rue des Viels-Augustins; but in the next month a contract for the Hôtel Bénigne Bernard shows that he had moved again (this time permanently) to the Faubourg Saint-Germain, and his address is given as the Rue de Vaugirard. The same year he received by far the most important commission of his career, the new palace of the Luxembourg for Marie de Médicis, who laid the first stone in April 1615.

6. I am obliged to M. Ciprut who told me of the existence of these marriage contracts, which he intended to publish in a study on Jacques I Androuet du Cerceau; cf. Chronology and Notes p. 197.
7. Cf. Cat. Appendix p. 284.

Connected with the work at the Luxembourg was the Aqueduc d'Arcueil, which de Brosse may have designed, and which was begun in 1613.

Meanwhile, outside Paris de Brosse had undertaken commissions for the two most important châteaux built during the first years of the seventeenth century, Blérancourt in Picardy, begun in 1612, and Coulommiers-en-Brie, where the first stone was laid in 1613.

In September 1614 Jacques II du Cerceau died in Paris, and de Brosse inherited his position and pension on the royal pay-roll. The place must already have been assured for him at his uncle's request, for about three weeks before du Cerceau's death de Brosse signed an undertaking to the effect that he would assign half this pension each year to his cousin Jean du Cerceau, Baptiste's son.[8] He also undertook the guardianship of all this uncle's children who were still minors at the time of their father's death.

The years 1615 to 1618 mark the high point in de Brosse's career. The commission for the Luxembourg had established his position as the leading architect of the day. In 1616 the churchwardens of Saint Gervais decided to add a classical façade to their late-Gothic church, and according to a well-founded tradition[9] they invited de Brosse to provide the design. In 1617 the exiled Queen Marie de Médicis ordered him to plan a pavilion for her at Blois, which was later demolished by her son, Gaston d'Orléans. Between 1615 and 1619 a serious attempt was also made to complete the château at Montceaux.

In 1618 de Brosse received two of his most important non-royal commissions; the rebuilding of the Salle des Pas Perdus in the Palais de Justice in Paris, and the design for the Palais du Parlement at Rennes which had been begun in 1614 but about which the authorities were dissatisfied.

From this time de Brosse's health, possibly never robust, seems to have begun to deteriorate, and by 1622 we know that he was often ailing. He accepted few new commissions during the last years of his life and none of great importance. In 1619 Marie de Médicis' Intendant, Antoine Feydeau, bought the château of Bois-le-Vicomte, and for this de Brosse designed a new forecourt and other buildings. A doubtful attribution has been made to him of the château of Liancourt, a more plausible one of work at the château of Ognon, near Verneuil, and he worked at the château of Limours for Cardinal Richelieu in 1623.[10] His last commission was for the second Protestant

8. Cf. Chronology and Notes, p. 198, entry for this date.

9. Cf. below, pp. 137-138 and pp. 136 and 137, nn. 8 and 9.

10. Cf. Blois, Cat. p. 208; Liancourt, Cat. Appendix p. 280; Ognon, Cat. p. 282; and Limours, Cat. p. 225.

Temple at Charenton, for which the contracts were signed in June 1623.

About 1622 de Brosse collaborated with Michel Lasne to produce an engraving in honour of Pope Gregory XV (1621–1624), which bears the inscription, 'Salomon de Brosse Inve. Miael Asinius Sculp.'. As far as is known, this is the only occasion on which de Brosse produced a design for an engraving, though he is supposed to have collaborated in 1619 in the re-edition of Jean Bullant's *Reigle Générale d'Architecture*.[11]

From April to December 1622 de Brosse's name appears frequently in the letters of Peiresc, Rubens' agent in Paris. Rubens had asked Peiresc to obtain from de Brosse the measurements of the Long Gallery at the Luxembourg, together with drawings of projected fireplaces, doorcases, etc., to enable the artist to plan the dimensions of his paintings of the life of Marie de Médicis destined for the gallery. After repeated efforts, frustrated by de Brosse's vagueness and procrastination, Peiresc succeeded in obtaining what was wanted. Thanks to these letters this period of de Brosse's life is better documented than any other, and they give us the first intimations of the troubles threatening the architect in connection with his work at the Luxembourg. The Queen Mother had spent three weeks in February going into the whole progress and finances of the project, and she was not satisfied because there was serious overspending. On 26 June 1623 a 'Procès Verbal et Expertise des Travaux' was carried out which lasted two months. A difference of 188,476 livres 9 sols was found against de Brosse. The final document concerning this case is lost, but it appears that in the end the major discrepancy concerned the amount spent on the roof-timbering.[12] De Brosse had to pay to the carpenter the difference of 83,700 livres and the debt, still unpaid at his death, was to remain a charge on his heirs.

In spite of these findings, there does not seem to have been any scandal, nor was there talk of the architect's disgrace. On 14 March 1624, de Brosse signed the contract for the building of the East Gallery of the Palace; but ten days later he resigned the 'entreprise générale' of the work at the Luxembourg to Marin de la Vallée, and this resignation included the withdrawal of Paul de Brosse and Jean du Cerceau as sub-contractors.

De Brosse remained on the list of architects 'de la maison du Roy' until he died two years later. In April 1624 he was asked, together with Rémy

11. First published in 1568; cf. Pannier, p. 144 *et seq*. This extremely rare edition is so appallingly badly produced that it is to be hoped that de Brosse actually had no hand in it. There is no evidence to support Pannier's assertion that de Brosse re-drew the very coarse illustrations.
12. Probably the affair was never satisfactorily concluded and more than one of the documents concerning it may have been lost; cf. Cat. pp. 263-264.

Collin and Clément Métezeau, to recommend masons to submit estimates for the continuation of Lescot's wing at the Louvre.

During this time de Brosse was in correspondence with the authorities of the Cathedral of Sainte Croix at Orléans,[13] with whom he had been engaged since 1618 on the project for the restoration and completion of the building. In March 1625 the commissioners sent to Paris to enquire whether de Brosse would visit them and provide plans and drawings for the building of the Cathedral transepts. They received no satisfactory reply, and asked again in April that he should either come, or send the drawings. In June they reported that, owing to his illness, he seemed unlikely ever to come, and in July they reluctantly decided to look elsewhere for an architect. Paul de Brosse and Jean du Cerceau went to Orléans in August, and so, later, did other contestants. All the competitors' designs were sent to Salomon de Brosse in Paris. In April 1626 de Brosse sent all the designs back with adverse comments, adding further designs of his own to the collection. In the end the Commissioners chose a Gothic design by Martellange.

This is the last we hear of de Brosse's activities as an architect. He died at his lodging at the Luxembourg on 8 December 1626, aged fifty-five.

This recital of facts provides some clues to de Brosse's character, his way of life, his manner of working and also to the esteem in which he was held by his contemporaries.

The fact that he was born at Verneuil is significant because the château was an important centre of building activity dominated by the du Cerceau 'workshop'. The town was moreover important as a Protestant centre. De Brosse's parents, his maternal grandfather, Jacques I Androuet du Cerceau, his du Cerceau uncles and the members of other local families to whom he was related, or to whom he became related by marriage, were Protestants. Towards the end of the sixteenth century the Protestants of Verneuil were tolerated and had access to a place of worship, the Temple on the outskirts of Aumont near Senlis.[14] Many of them were masons, carpenters and artisans of various kinds who had gathered at Verneuil because of the employment available at the château.

In 1584 religious persecution broke out with renewed violence after the Edict of Nemours. De Brosse's uncle Baptiste, who had just built himself a fine house in Paris,[15] had to flee, 'aimant mieux quitter ses biens que retourner

13. Cf. Cat. p. 235.
14. Pannier, p. 22.
15. Ibid., p. 28. The house was on a piece of land between the Rue Visconti, the Rue des Petits-Augustins and the Rue Jacob.

à la messe',[16] and his new house was badly damaged by rioters. In 1588 Jacques II du Cerceau also had to retire, to Tours, where he came under the protection of the powerful Duc d'Alençon. De Brosse, however, remained at Verneuil. Between the years 1588 and 1592 his name appears, together with those of various other known Protestants, in the baptismal registers of Verneuil Parish Church, where he is recorded several times as a godfather. This is no indication that he, or they, temporarily changed their faith in a time of persecution. Lacking a local Temple[17] or pastor, the Protestants were obliged to take their children to be baptised at the local parish church, since a law of 1559 had laid down that entry in the Baptismal Register was necessary for legal citizenship.[18]

It is not possible to assess whether or not his religious beliefs much affected de Brosse's character and outlook.[19] He seems to have been attached to his faith, for he brought up his seven children as Protestants, and saw most of them make Protestant marriages, and it was not until after his death that one or two of them turned Catholic. Like most members of a minority group, religious or otherwise, he was clannish; the community at Verneuil to which he belonged was a close-knit one, held together by a common religion as well as by the ties of profession and marriage. But it is not possible to say whether, apart from his own family and relations, he especially favoured employing his co-religionists, and he certainly had no scruples whatsoever in working for Catholic patrons or the Catholic Church itself.

Although he did not leave Verneuil, and was able to survive there in peace, the Wars of the Ligue in the 1580s and early 1590s came at an unfortunate time for de Brosse. At the château work dwindled after the deaths of its second patron, the Duc de Nemours, and of the architect, Jacques I du Cerceau.[20] Troubled times did not encourage the widowed Duchess to continue building on any large scale. In 1589, when the last savage phase of the wars broke out, de Brosse was still under twenty, and the years in which he would normally have been establishing himself as an independent architect must have been spent in largely idle seclusion at Verneuil. It is not only because of the absence

16. L'Estoile, *Régistre Journal du règne de Henri III*, éd. Michaud 1964, p. 193.
17. Access to Aumont obviously being impossible.
18. Hence 'Etat Catholique' for what became, after the Revolution, 'Etat Civil', i.e. the record of birth, marriage and death, kept only by the Church under the *ancien régime*.
19. Some ambivalence in his religious attitude may be indicated by the following: '... nous mentionnerons encore un "Obit" fondé par l'architecte à l'Eglise de Verneuil, sans doute pour le repos de l'âme de ses parents'. (J.-P. Babelon, 'Documents inédits concernant Salomon de Brosse', *B.S.H.A.F.*, 1962, p. 154).
20. Du Cerceau's death-date is not absolutely certain, but he is believed to have gone to Geneva and to have died there about 1585; he certainly worked no more after that date.

of relevant documents that we have no information about de Brosse's work before he was twenty-seven years old; there was in fact little work for architects, except in military projects. Jacques II du Cerceau was fortunate in being appointed 'conducteur des plans et ouvrages de fortifications' for the municipality of Tours.[21]

De Brosse was therefore a late beginner; moreover, he only lived for twenty-eight years after he first appears at work with his uncle at Montceaux in 1598.[22] The short span of his working life, further reduced by illness and and virtual retirement about four years before his death, must be recognized as an important factor when we try to assess his achievement.

No personal details can be gleaned about de Brosse between 1592 and 1613. He seems to have married soon after 1592;[23] his wife was Florence Métivier, sister of Antoine Métivier, another architect at Verneuil.[24] Through this marriage de Brosse became connected with the master-mason Charles du Ry, who was to be his chief collaborator and *entrepreneur*.[25]

In 1613 de Brosse is described in a legal document as 'Sieur des fiefs de Royaumont et de Colombier sis à Verneuil-sur-Oyse'. These lands were probably recently acquired, and formed part of the considerable property which de Brosse held in and around Verneuil,[26] of which the most important were the fief of Saint-Quentin at Montlaville-sous-Verneuil, and the Seigneurie of du Plessis-Pommeraye, just south of Creil. The latter estate de Brosse received in 1616 from Henriette d'Entragues in lieu of the money long

21. Cf. J.-P. Babelon, *Demeures parisiennes sous Henri IV et Louis XIII*, 1965, p. 241.

22. Although the only mention of Jacques II du Cerceau and de Brosse is made in 1598, the work at Montceaux began in July 1597, and the two were almost certainly employed there from the start.

23. His eldest son Paul was an architect in the King's employment in 1615.

24. Florence appears under her maiden name as a godmother in the Verneuil register for 1592; there is no record of the date of her marriage.

25. Charles du Ry married Camille Métivier. From what can be deduced from the known facts about the Métiviers, it seems clear that she was sister to Florence, and that by these marriages the two men became brothers-in-law. The du Ry family, which was Scottish in origin, had moved from Normandy to Verneuil at about the same time as the de Brosse, and Charles was born there about 1570. Among the marriages of his children and grandchildren the names du Cerceau, de la Fonds, le Blanc de Beaulieu and Aubert occur as frequently as among the family of de Brosse himself, so that the descendants of Charles du Ry (and particularly of his son Mathurin, a later 'architecte du Roy') could count among their forebears not only du Ry and de Brosse but Jacques I du Cerceau. Of these descendants, some later emigrated to Cassel in Germany where they became architects to the Court (cf. Chap. VIII, note 9), and one, Théodore, emigrated to England, where he became military engineer to William III (in the tradition of his great-great-uncle, Jacques II du Cerceau) and founded the English family 'Dury'. I am indebted for this information to Mr A. W. D. Mitton, the noted genealogist, himself a descendant of the Durys.

26. Pannier gives some of these, but J.-P. Babelon has recently furnished many more and more exact details (op. cit. above, n. 19; p. 150 *et seq.*).

overdue which she owed him for the work he had done for her at the château of Verneuil.

Pannier[27] repeats local tradition that the 'hôtel seigneurial' of Saint-Quentin at Montlaville was built by de Brosse, and was his family home. Its description in a document which he quotes, dated 1642, gives it '. . . grand' et petitte porte, cour, ung grand corps-de-logis construit en thuille, et un pavillon couvert d'ardouaize, cave et cuisine; rang d'estable et rang d'écurie, pigeonnier, poullier, jardin', also 'un clos dans lequel il y a un vivier à poissons . . .'. De Brosse bought the fief and 'hostel de Sainct-Quantin' in 1613, as we now know from a recently discovered *Acte de Vente*,[28] so there was already a house on the site. However the building, which still in part survives, has details so typical of de Brosse at a date near 1613 that it can be supposed that the architect replaced the original dwelling with one of his own design. The pavilion 'couvert d'ardouaize', despite later alterations to the windows, is still imposing (Pl. 108).

The lodging in the Rue de Vaugirard, to which de Brosse finally moved in 1614, was presumably provided for him by Marie de Médicis as one of the perquisites of the architect of her new palace. His rooms were in part of the old Hôtel de Luxembourg which the Queen had bought and which gave its name to the palace. De Brosse shared them for the rest of his life with his son Paul and his nephew Jean, son of Baptiste du Cerceau. These two worked with him at the Luxembourg and elsewhere, and the three of them jointly owned a quarry near Saint-Germain-des-Prés which provided much of the stone for the palace.

This dwelling near the Luxembourg was simple and certainly not spacious; we know of its interior arrangements from the inventory made just after de Brosse died there in 1626. The kitchen, for instance, was nothing but 'ung petit bouge au dessus de la porte servant de cuisine', and there appear to have been only two decent-sized rooms and another tiny alcove or 'bouge' '. . . . à costé de la chambre où est déceddé ledict deffunct'. So that, although at the time of her husband's death, his wife was living there, it is more probable that she and their numerous children passed most of their time at Verneuil. The rooms were merely a professional pied-à-terre for the three architects. In a document of 1627 concerning repayment of a debt from de Brosse's estate, Jean du Cerceau declared that he and de Brosse had always lived in a very friendly way together, '. . . qu'ilz auroient vescu famillièrement en mesme

27. p. 115; pièce II, p. 256, and illustration, p. 15.
28. J.-P. Babelon, op. cit., above n. 26; p. 151, n. 1: 'Jean Brosse avait déjà acheté 17 verges de terre en 1568 . . . qui, en 1585, étaient occupées par une maison, une grange, des étables et un jardin au hameau de Montlaville'.

logis et en bonne intelligence et amictyé . . .'.[29] The youthful Paul de Brosse,
who had caused some trouble in March 1616, rioting in an inn and fighting
in the street, was taken to court, and in the indictment is described as living
'en la maison de son Père qui est en l'hostel du Lucenbor'.[30]

De Brosse and his wife owned a small house in the Rue des Saints-Pères
which was let, and 'une grande place et fonds de terre' just beside it. Nearby
was the quarry owned jointly by de Brosse, his son Paul, his nephew Jean du
Cerceau, his brother-in-law Charles du Ry and his godson Salomon de
la Fonds.[31] Thus, although towards the end of his life he fell into financial
troubles, he was a man of some substance.

De Brosse was certainly instructed beyond the mere necessities of his
profession. Indeed, his handwriting and signature are those of an educated
person of the period; the handwriting is particularly distinctive and competent. When writing about de Brosse to Rubens, Peiresc may complain
about his difficulties in dealing with the architect, but he always speaks of him
with respect. He conveys the impression that he considers de Brosse an equal,
and assumes that the painter does so, too. In 1623 Peiresc mentioned to Rubens
a collection of Antique medals which were for sale in Paris; Rubens was a
possible purchaser; so was de Brosse, which indicates some community of
cultivated interests. Rubens sent de Brosse one of the first two copies of his
Palazzi di Genova to come into France, a fact of some significance in the
history of architecture. This gift was intended as an incentive to the architect
to comply with the painter's request about the Luxembourg gallery.

There is no evidence at all that de Brosse ever travelled abroad, and it is
fairly certain that had he done so some reference to the fact would have
survived. His knowledge of Italian architecture, especially that of the sixteenth
century, seems to have been gained from books and, more importantly, from
drawings and descriptions brought back by contemporaries.

The dedication of Nicolas Piloust's 1619 edition of Jean Bullant's *Reigle
Générale d'Architecture*, already referred to, speaks of 'cette oeuvre de feu Sieur
Bulant à présent revue, corrigée, augmentée et mise en meilleur ordre
qu'auparavant par Monsieur de Brosse, architecte du Roy'. In the epistle to
the reader, Piloust says he himself corrected the text, but he asked de Brosse
to help him with the illustrations, '. . . qui n'estoient nullement selon leur
ordre, aucunes estant meslées . . . j'ay prié Monsieur de Brosse, architecte du

29. E.-J. Ciprut, 'Notes sur un grand architecte parisien; Jean Androuet du Cerceau', *Bull.
Soc. Hist. Prot. Fr.*, CXIII, April–June 1967, p. 166.

30. Pannier, p. 110 *et seq.*

31. E.-J. Ciprut, op. cit., pp. 164–165.

Roy, et l'un des plus beaux esprits de ceux qui se meslent à présent de l'Architecture, de vouloir prendre la peine de revoir et corriger le deffaut qui y pouvoit estre et le rendre en estat digne d'estre offert; ce que sa courtoisie m'ayant accordé je puis dire que je te l'offre comme en sa perfection'.

Even allowing for the specious flattery common in such addresses, it is evident that the publisher considered that de Brosse's name would give his book prestige; and he presented him to the reader as a learned architect; 'un des beaux esprits' implies more than just technical excellence.

De Brosse's professional advice was evidently valued; he had been called on to help with the works at Orléans Cathedral and the Parlement at Rennes; he was also consulted about the new stone bridge which it was proposed to build at Rouen, and between 1619 and 1622 meetings to discuss this were held at his lodgings or at those of Rémy Collin. Several architects, including Jacques Lemercier, were involved in this project, which however was not carried out.[32]

In 1624 de Brosse was asked to recommend masons for work on the Louvre; the 'association' of masons who undertook the contract consisted of Paul de Brosse, Jean Androuet du Cerceau, Charles du Ry and Salomon de la Fonds – all de Brosse's relations and all, except du Ry, giving his house as their address.[33] These are the recorded occasions when his advice was sought; there were no doubt others.

It seems that de Brosse paid some attention to establishing himself and his family socially. His daughters mostly married rather well, and outside the small circle of architects and master-masons.[34] His accumulations of land at Verneuil and the building of a solid family house were probably part of this aim, as well as being sound investments. Some idea of his social standing is given by the papers which survive concerning his visit to Rennes in 1618. He was accompanied on his journey by his son-in-law, Pierre le Blanc de Beaulieu, 'avocat au Parlement de Paris', who no doubt helped him to treat with the commissioners. The bill survives for his accommodation at their expense at an inn, together with le Blanc, two servants, an 'homme-de-chambre' and a lackey, a coachman and four horses.

The most important source which we have for our knowledge of de Brosse personally is the letters of Peiresc, already referred to. These letters were

32. Cf. E.-J. Ciprut, 'Oeuvres inconnues de François Mansart', *G.d.B.A.*, LXV, 1965, pp. 39–50.
33. Cf. Dumolin, 'Le Louvre de Lemercier et de Le Vau', *G.d.B.A.*, XVIII, 1928, pp. 128–148. The work was never carried out.
34. Pannier, pp. 270–271, who gives the family tree.

written when de Brosse was fifty-one and nearing the end of his life. He is seen as ailing and difficult to deal with because of his vagueness and procrastination. This impression is confirmed by the letters of the Cathedral authorities at Orléans. We do not know whether de Brosse had only recently become ill, or whether his ill-health was of long standing; Peiresc's letters imply that by 1622 at any rate de Brosse, physically a sick man, was also somewhat neurotic, and found it difficult to concentrate for long on anything.

De Brosse probably did not develop these tendencies late in life, but a naturally neurotic disposition may have become intensified as his health declined. The history of many of his projects supports this idea. It also suggests that all his life de Brosse was neglectful of detail because he was not interested in the minutiae of his undertakings. What appears to have seized his imagination was the initial design, the general conception of a building, its effect as a mass or as a composition of various masses juxtaposed. Once a scheme was off the drawing-board he seems to have lost interest, unless he was kept at it by a powerful patron, as he was at the Luxembourg, and even then disaster was not averted. The history of the château of Coulommiers will serve as an example.

Coulommiers, one of his early works, was commissioned by the immensely wealthy Catherine de Gonzague de Clèves, Duchesse de Longueville. Early left a widow by Henri, Duc de Longueville, she never re-married but devoted her life to the upbringing of her son, Henri II, Duc de Longueville, and the building of her château.

The Seigneurie of Coulommiers had formed part of Catherine's dowry; but as the house belonging to it was dilapidated she decided not to rebuild it, but to purchase land below the town to the south-west on which to build a château and lay out extensive gardens.

The land which she bought was laboriously acquired piece by piece from various owners, not all of them willing to part with their portions. Unfortunately the site, so deliberately chosen, was low lying, threaded by several good-sized streams, marshy, unhealthy, plagued by mists and generally unsuitable for building. Good stone was also lacking in the neighbourhood, and such as was available was highly susceptible to humidity. Catherine de Gonzague was undoubtedly a formidable patron, determined to exploit her new terrain in the most grandiose manner, but it seems that her chosen architect never even attempted to point out the disadvantages of her site from the technical point of view. De Brosse may have had no choice, his advice may not have been asked, or, if asked, may have been rejected by Mme de

Longueville; tradition, however, does not exonerate him. A writer of 1699[35] tells the following tale of Coulommiers: 'Les architectes, pour engager Catherine de Gonzague dans cette entreprise luy firent voir le plan de ce château en élévation et promirent de l'exécuter, et de le rendre parfait pour deux cent mil escus. Cette somme se trouva consommée par le premier compte de la dépense qu'on luy en rendit; le bâtiment n'étant qu'au premier cordon. Ce qui luy fait verser des larmes. On tient qu'il a couté deux millions de livres . . .'. The contract, signed on 3 January 1613, specifically names de Brosse as the designer; it was to be built 'suivant le plan paraphé . . . en élévation que le Sieur de Brosse en a faict . . .'. This bears out the story of the 'plan de ce château en élévation'.

De Brosse was present with Charles du Ry and others ('les architectes') in March 1613 when the surveying was done for the foundations, but after that, and having provided the general designs, he handed the whole enterprise over to du Ry, and as far as we know never troubled himself further about the project. So completely did du Ry take charge that in later local tradition he became known as the sole architect of the château, and indeed he made important modifications to de Brosse's original designs. Work went on slowly and expenses soon got out of hand; in 1629, when Catherine died, the château was far from complete. It was said that there was only one window which had by then received its sculptured decoration. Henri II de Longueville toiled on, trying to finish the huge work, but even as new parts were added to the structure the earlier buildings were falling into decay; the stone perished in the damp; the statues fell down; by 1655 it was still unfinished, and remained so until 1738 when it was finally decided to abandon the château and the expense of its upkeep and to demolish the whole crumbling edifice.

When Peiresc wrote to Rubens in 1623 that he feared proceedings were to be taken against de Brosse on account of the Luxembourg '. . . au sujet d'une partie de sa construction pour laquelle il avait mal conseillé, et que la construction de l'autre galerie était en retard . . .', we hear echoes of the Coulommiers story. It is hard not to believe that these troubles could have been averted had the architect been more punctilious and possessed a better head for the business side of his enterprises.

Despite the enormous sums spent on Coulommiers, there does not seem to have been any dishonesty involved in de Brosse's procedures. The evidence points simply to his being vague about money. For when in 1623 Richelieu,

35. Phélypeaux de Pontchartrain, *Mémoires de la Généralité de Paris*, 1699, publ. *Mémoires pour servir à l'histoire de France*, 1887, Série 2, 631, fol. 279.

writing to Marie de Médicis' treasurer, d'Argouges, to ask why the building of the Luxembourg was proceeding so slowly, voiced doubts as to the architect's probity, d'Argouges replied that there was a shortage of money, but added 'J'ay veu la distribution par le même (de Brosse) de deux mil livres que je luy fournis et je vous assure qu'il ne met rien à sa bourse'.

De Brosse seems to have been an amiable man (in contrast to Mansart, who was very difficult indeed), and, as we have seen, Jean du Cerceau found that living in cramped quarters with his cousin did not impair their 'bonne intelligence et amyctié'.

By the end of his life de Brosse was seriously ill and in great pain, and Peiresc speaks of the gout 'qui lui donne de grands tourments'. The Orléans authorities gave up hoping for his visit because of his 'grande incommodité', but although Peiresc complains in his letters of de Brosse's dilatoriness and unpredictable absences, he never mentions discourtesy or irritability, the usual results of gout, even when the architect was in such pain that he could not sleep at night.

A final glimpse of de Brosse's way of life in his Paris apartments is afforded by the inventory made after his death.[36] It shows that he lived in extremely simple circumstances which probably became even more austere after the adverse conclusion of the Luxembourg investigation which put him heavily in debt. At the same time it must be remembered that the inventory takes no account of his houses, land and other possessions at Verneuil. De Brosse died in his rather shabby room in his great bed, 'une grande couche de bois de noyer à pilliers tournez'. Nearby was 'une petite table de bois servant à mectre devant le feu (et) une petite chaire servant de fauteuil de mesme bois . . .'. There were not many objects of value: '. . . Trois medailles d'or en l'une desquelles est gravé le Roy à présent reignant, en l'aultre la Reyne sa Mère, et en l'autre Monsieur de Nevers . . . une chaine d'or à grosse maille . . .', some rings, '. . . trois bourses de velours' (apparently empty). There was in the room 'un petit carrosse', presumably a wheel-chair for the sick man. Finally, '. . . une Bible en français de l'impression de Genève in-folio relié en veau rouge . . . un nouveau Testament in-octavo, trois livres d'architecture couverts de parchemyn . . .'. It would be interesting to know what these three books of architecture were; perhaps one was Rubens' gift, *I Palazzi di Genova*.

36. J.-P. Babelon, op. cit., above n. 28, p. 146 ff. It is interesting to compare this inventory with 'the one made of Louis Métezeau's possessions in 1615. Métezeau, who enjoyed much the same status as de Brosse in the royal employ, died a wealthy man; cf. Pierre du Colombier, 'Autour des Métezeau', *Bibliothèque d'Humanisme et Renaissance*, III, 1953, pp. 182–183.

From this inventory we can visualize the place which de Brosse inhabited
for so many years and the room in which he died. The objects listed some-
how succeed in bringing this elusive man nearer to us; we see him among
his little treasures, his medals and chain, Geneva Bible and Testament, the
three architectural books; his personal furniture, the wheelchair, the table
and chair in which he could sit by the fire. Lastly, we find a sign of his
calling in his room: '. . . Quattre petits morceaux de plomb avec une
eschasse de fer servant à monter pierres à des bastimens'.

As the law enjoined for Protestants, de Brosse was buried very quietly with
no ceremony in the Protestant Cemetery in the Rue des Saints-Pères near
Saint Germain-des-Prés. The burial was recorded in the registers of the
Consistory of the Reformed Church in Paris, 'Salomon de Brosse, nati(f)
de Verneuil, ingénieur, architecte des bastimens du roy, a ésté enterré le
maircredi 9e jour de désembre mil VI c 26 assisté de deux archers du guet'.[37]

37. Pannier, p. 107.

CHAPTER II

The Sixteenth-Century Background and the du Cerceau Family, 1540-1614

B Y birth as well as by training de Brosse belonged to the du Cerceau circle, and so inherited in a particularly personal way the tradition of their school, which he later developed and combined with other influences to form his own style. To understand the architecture of this circle it is necessary to place it in relation to the works of other sixteenth-century architects who also influenced de Brosse, among the first of whom must be counted Philibert de l'Orme.

It is often less easy to point out the direct influence of Philibert de l'Orme upon Salomon de Brosse than that of other sixteenth-century architects; at the same time we can assert that de l'Orme's approach to architecture must have made a deep impression on de Brosse.

De l'Orme attempted the task of fusing the influence of classical antiquity and Renaissance Italy with the vigorous medieval tradition still flourishing in France. To this task he brought such outstanding qualities that any failures are far outweighed by the success of the solutions which he found for most of the problems he tackled. He was a man of extreme ingenuity and inventiveness, technically brilliant, a scholar, theorist, mathematician, humanist and friend of learned men, and, as Professor Blunt has written, 'the first Frenchman to claim and deserve the name of architect in the modern sense'.[1] De l'Orme's classicism was fundamental and not a matter of embroidering essentially gothic structures with classical motifs. His architecture is not always easy to understand or to accept. His approach was experimental and even when his buildings are not entirely satisfactory they are never dull. His writings illustrate his approach; they are at once theoretical and practical, and they are also enlivened by a very engaging style. De Brosse would have done well to heed de l'Orme's practical advice, especially on the preparation and conduct of his works and on the relationship between architect and patron.[2] Neglect

1. A. F. Blunt, *Philibert de l'Orme*, 1958, p. 2.
2. Summarized by Blunt, ibid., pp. 8–13.

of it did much to contribute to his troubles at the Luxembourg and to the unsatisfactory state of affairs at Coulommiers.

Most of de l'Orme's buildings have disappeared. At his château of Anet the chapel and the entrance-gate survive without much alteration, but the frontispiece to the main *corps-de-logis* has been removed to the courtyard of the Ecole des Beaux-Arts in Paris, and the rest of the château was largely destroyed at the Revolution. One other structure at Anet of great importance for its influence on de Brosse has partially survived, namely the crypto-porticus beneath the terrace on the garden side (Pls 1 and 2).

Of the work which he did at the châteaux of Saint-Maur, Saint-Léger, Montceaux and Limours nothing now remains; a few fragments, widely scattered, survive from the Tuileries;[3] the Château-Neuf and the chapel at Saint Germain and the chapel at Villers-Cotterets have all disappeared, so has the outside staircase which he built at Fontainebleau. Fortunately we have drawings and engravings which record the plans and elevations of some of these structures, which were all of the first importance in the history of French architecture. The tomb which de l'Orme designed for François Ier survives in Saint Denis, and the *jubé* of Saint-Etienne-du-Mont has been attributed to him.[4]

De l'Orme's contemporary, Pierre Lescot, began building the west wing of the Square Court of the Louvre in 1546. It is an astonishingly classical design for its date, and was to have a very marked influence on two of de Brosse's châteaux, Coulommiers and Blérancourt (Pls 3, 4). Lescot also almost certainly designed the château of Valléry, begun in 1556, the impressively rusticated exterior of which must have influenced Jacques I du Cerceau, who surely recalled it when he came to design the château of Verneuil about 1567.[5]

Lescot does not appear to have visited Italy until after his career as an architect was over, so that when he designed his wing at the Louvre and the château at Valléry he only knew the architecture of Classical Antiquity and of Renaissance Italy at second-hand. He seems to have been an educated amateur rather than a professional architect, with an extraordinary ability to translate the foreign prototypes available to him into a personal and entirely French idiom. It was this achievement of Lescot's which, nearly seventy years later, impressed de Brosse when he too was searching for a French interpretation of classical and Italian models.

---

3. Ibid., pp. 99–100; pls 60a and b, 61a and b.
4. Ibid., pp. 26 and 77–79; pl. 52.
5. For the history and attribution of Valléry, see Pierre du Colombier, 'L'énigme de Valléry' in *Humanisme et Renaissance*, IV, 1937, pp. 7 ff.

Three Italians came to France in 1540–1541 to work for François I at Fontainebleau and elsewhere; Sebastiano Serlio, Francesco Primaticcio and Giacomo Barozzi da Vignola.[6] Primaticcio's name as an architect is chiefly associated in France with the building of the Valois Mausoleum at Saint Denis (Pls 5–7). This was commissioned by Catherine de Médicis to contain the tombs of her husband, herself and her children. It was begun in 1563 to Primaticcio's designs, and continued by Jean Bullant (1570–1578), who may have contributed some new details. On Bullant's death in 1578, Baptiste du Cerceau was put in charge of the work, but the building was left unfinished and was abandoned in 1585. It was finally pulled down in the early eighteenth century. The most Italianate building in France, with superimposed orders and a circular plan going back to Bramante, Michelangelo and Sangallo, it was to be a source of inspiration to de Brosse for two of his most important designs.

Serlio's actual buildings in France, the château of Ancy-le-Franc and the house of the Cardinal of Ferrara at Fontainebleau ('le Grand Ferrare') (Pls 8, 9) were exceedingly important, and so were his designs for other buildings in France never carried out, but it was for his engravings and drawings that he was best known.

His influence on French architecture of the sixteenth and early seventeenth centuries was far more profound and far-reaching than Primaticcio's. Serlio's writings and engraved designs became for many French builders their principal introduction to the antiquities of Rome and to the ideas of the Italian High Renaissance. De l'Orme, Jacques I du Cerceau and others certainly knew not only his published work but also many of his unpublished designs, and in particular the body of drawings and their accompanying text in manuscript which were to have formed what has come to be known as the 'True Sixth Book' of the *Architettura et Prospettiva*. This manuscript left France in 1550 and was not published until very recently.[7] A detailed analysis

6. Little is known of Vignola's activities in France, where he was not employed as an architect. One statement occurs in an inventory of paintings in the *Cabinet des peintures* at Fontainebleau in 1642, viz. 'un grand tableau de perspective de Vignole'. Nothing further is known to support the attribution; however cf. Herbet, *Le Château de Fontainebleau*, Paris, 1937, pp. 93 and 94, quoting le Père Dan, *Trésor des Merveilles de la Maison Royale de Fontainebleau*, 1642. Vignola may also have been asked to submit a design for a palace to François I, cf. A. Chastel, 'La Demeure Royale au XVIe Siècle et le Nouveau Louvre', in *Studies in Renaissance and Baroque Art presented to Anthony Blunt*, Phaidon, 1967, p. 80. These indications are important in view of Vignola's influence on de Brosse.

7. The drawings were bought by Jacopo Strada from Serlio in Lyons in 1550 and went to the Library of the Duke of Bavaria. They are still in the State Library at Munich, and were published in facsimile in Milan in 1966. Professor Rosci tells the history of these drawings and analyses them

of the influence of the drawings for the 'True Sixth Book' on the leading architects of the sixteenth century has yet to be made; in this present study we shall only be able to examine their impact as it affected the elder du Cerceau and through him de Brosse.

By the 1550s a new generation of architects had come to maturity in France, and their style, which as time went on became increasingly disturbed and exaggerated, reflects the tensions produced by the religious and social upheavals of the period. The leading figures of this generation were Jean Bullant and Jacques Androuet du Cerceau the elder.

Bullant, whose date of birth is unknown, is first referred to as an architect in 1556. He had been to Rome in the 1540s and he incorporated what he had learned there into his book, the *Reigle Générale d'Architecture*, published in 1563. He was much influenced by Philibert de l'Orme in the earlier part of his career, and to the end of his life the exquisite classical detail of his buildings reflects this influence and his Roman studies. His later work, however, shows a highly original and anti-classical development and makes a deliberate departure from de l'Orme's sense of scale. The most striking examples are the south frontispiece at Ecouen, where he used a colossal order copied from the Pantheon in Rome, and the gallery and it's entrance at La Fère-en-Tardenois,[8] built between 1552 and 1562 (Pl. 10). Bullant's late works and particularly this gallery had an important influence on the even more exaggerated style of Jacques I du Cerceau.

Jacques I du Cerceau was probably born about 1520. His fame has always rested more upon his engravings and drawings than upon his architecture, and rightly so. All the same, his rôle as an architect has been underestimated, and his influence on the architects who followed him has been somewhat misunderstood. Du Cerceau has really suffered from being at once too well-known and yet not properly known at all. Since he had such a profound effect on de Brosse, it is necessary to correct these misunderstandings, especially as new evidence has come to light which greatly helps a re-assessment.

It is not surprising that du Cerceau has not been taken very seriously as an architect, for all traces of the only two buildings we know to have been commissioned from him, the châteaux of Charleval and of Verneuil, have

---

in his *Il Trattato di Architettura di Sebastiano Serlio*, ed. Brizio, Milan, 1966. Another collection of drawings, many of them variations on the Munich collection, but considered to be earlier in date, are in the Library of the University of Columbia in America. Some of these have been published by W. Dinsmoor, 'The Literary Remains of Sebastiano Serlio', *Art Bulletin*, XXIV, 1942. pp. 54–91 and pp. 115–154.

8. Cf. Blomfield, p. 98 and pl. LIV; Blunt, *Art and Architecture*, p. 78 and pl. 59A.

long since disappeared.[9] Unfortunately, even his reputation as a graphic artist rests in part on indiscriminate attributions. Until very recently any drawing of a certain type has been labelled 'du Cerceau', and indeed this is not to be wondered at, since so little scholarly research has been devoted to analysing his oeuvre.[10]

It would be interesting to examine the whole of his output as a draughtsman, but for the present purpose it will only be necessary to isolate his late drawings, that is to say those dating from about 1560 to 1580. Among these, the most important are certain drawings in the British Museum, an album in the Vatican and another in the Pierpont Morgan Library in New York.[11]

Du Cerceau, like de l'Orme and Lescot, went to Rome, probably in the 1540s, and what he saw there made an equally deep impression upon him; but his reaction was quite different. His early engravings, published between 1549 and 1559, show an extreme freedom in the representation of antiquity. Of course, du Cerceau was not the only artist to 're-create' the Antiquities of Rome in a more or less fanciful manner; indeed this kind of architectural fantasy became exceedingly popular in the later sixteenth century. In Rome, for example, Pirro Ligorio (c. 1520–1580) produced many such 'reconstructions'.[12]

These 'dream buildings', remotely based on classical models, reflect a totally anti-classical and indeed an anti-architectural approach to architecture. Their essentially decorative, fantastic and two-dimensional characteristics are to be found in many of du Cerceau's designs for contemporary buildings.

In 1559 du Cerceau published the first of his three Books of Architecture.

9. There are still writers who doubt that du Cerceau was the architect of Charleval and Verneuil, and who do not consider the evidence adduced to be sufficient to justify the claim; cf. Naomi Miller, 'A Volume of Architectural Drawings ascribed to Jacques Androuet du Cerceau the Elder, in the Morgan Library, New York', *Marsyas*, XI, 1962–1964, p. 36 and n. 9, and p. 37, n. 13. Admittedly, final proofs, such as a contract with a reference to du Cerceau or a record of payment to him, are lacking, but the weight of evidence contained in his own *Les Plus Excellents Bastiments* is enough to support the attribution to him of the designs for these châteaux. Professor Blunt, in *Art and Architecture*, p. 83 and p. 260, n. 28 accepts du Cerceau as the designer of both châteaux.

10. The chief source-book is still Henri de Geymüller's *Les du Cerceau, leur vie et leur oeuvre*, published in 1887, which, although in many ways invaluable, is misleading in both its attributions and its dating of drawings.

11. Some notes on these drawings and the dates proposed for them will be found in the Appendix, p. 193.

12. For Pirro Ligorio, cf. his *Libro di Pyrrho Ligorio Napoletano delle antichità di Roma*, publ. in Venice in 1553, and his book on the Baths of Diocletian publ. in Rome in 1558. His drawings of the Antique are discussed by Erna Mandowsky and Charles Mitchell in 'Pirro Ligorio's Roman Antiquities', in *Studies of the Warburg Institute*, vol. 28, 1963. Montanus, whose drawings were for a long time accepted as genuine records of antique buildings, is now thought not to have produced them until about 1600, in which case they could not have influenced du Cerceau.

Until this date his engraved books had dealt only with Antiquity, Decoration
and Perspective.[13] The *Livre d'Architecture* ('The First Book') of 1559 is
different; it is intended to have a very practical application: 'contenant les
plans & dessaings de cinquante bastimens tous differens; pour instruire ceux
qui desirent bastir soient de petit, moyen ou grand estat . . .'. When the *Livre
d'Architecture* was published, Serlio's treatise, of which the first complete
edition had appeared in 1556, was the only really practical handbook available
to French architects, since de l'Orme's *Nouvelles Inventions* and *Premier Tome
d'Architecture* were not published until 1561 and 1567 respectively.

Du Cerceau's *Livre d'Architecture* is clearly influenced by Serlio's engraved
work and, more importantly, by his unpublished drawings for the 'True
Sixth Book'. Du Cerceau therefore must have known these drawings before
they left France.[14]

Serlio's influence particularly affected du Cerceau's later work, which will
be discussed in some detail because it shows many interesting developments
which have perhaps not been sufficiently noticed hitherto. Some of these
developments are also important for their influence upon Salomon de Brosse.

In 1561 du Cerceau published his *Second Livre d'Architecture*, which does not
deal with buildings but with details such as doors, windows and miscellaneous
small works such as tombs, wells and fountains. For the larger fountains and
the pavilions which housed some of the smaller ones he includes plans which
are centralized and linked with important Italian prototypes of the fifteenth
and sixteenth centuries.[15] One plan which du Cerceau repeats three times
with slight variations is close to that of de l'Orme's chapel at Anet.[16] Centrally-
planned garden-pavilions such as du Cerceau shows in this book became
popular in France in the sixteenth and early seventeenth centuries; de l'Orme,
for instance, built two circular *tempietti* on the west terrace at Montceaux,
recorded and sketched by Scamozzi in his diary of 1600.[17]

13. *Arcs*, 1549; *Temples, Grotesques* and *Fragments Antiques*, 1550; *Vues d'Optique* and *Compositions
d'Architecture*, 1551.

14. Fig. XXVI of du Cerceau's First Book is clearly derived from Serlio's unpublished projects
for Ancy-le-Franc of which there are two versions, one in the Munich and one in the Columbia
MS. of the 'True Sixth Book'. Cf. Rosci/Brizio, op. cit., p. 70; W. Dinsmoor, op. cit., and Blunt,
Art and Architecture., pp. 42–43. These authors trace the history and the changes in the design of this
château which do not directly concern us here.

15. Some of these, deriving from Peruzzi and others, are included in Serlio's Third Book,
Delle Antichità.

16. And, through the chapel at Anet, with Palladio's chapel at Maser. Cf. Blunt, *Philibert de
l'Orme*, pp. 44–46. The plan is repeated by du Cerceau in figs. III, IV, and V of this section of the
Second Book.

17. Cf. Cat. p. 230.

As time went on du Cerceau incorporated an increasing variety of geometrical forms into his plans for buildings great and small, real or imaginary.
The fountain and pavilion plans of the Second Book are an indication of this
trend absent from the First Book.

His late drawings and engravings all demonstrate this preoccupation, of
which the chief source of inspiration was probably the Roman palaces,
thermae, theatres and amphitheatres of Serlio's Third Book. It is also significant that in 1570, while du Cerceau was actively engaged with his two great
châteaux, Verneuil and Charleval, and was finally preparing the *Plus Excellents
Bastiments* for publication, Palladio published his *Quattro Libri*. His Second
Book contains several plans of buildings, notably that of the Palazzo Thiene
in Vicenza, which had been deeply influenced by the architect's visit to
Rome in 1541, where he made a special study of Roman *thermae* and of
Hadrian's Villa at Tivoli.[18]

The idea that du Cerceau was interested in Palladio is strengthened by the
inclusion in the Morgan Library album of six drawings of his villas and their
plans, from the Second Book.[19] In France at that time there was no great
interest in Palladio's book, and he never subsequently exercised much
influence on French architecture.[20] It is all the more surprising, therefore, to
find these drawings in the Morgan Library album.[21] The plans which du
Cerceau copied contain elements of drama in their general lay-out and complicated geometrical forms for the principal rooms, which evidently com-
mended themselves to the French architect's attention. The plans of the
Villa Trissino at Meledo and the Villa Rotonda near Vicenza, which du
Cerceau copied, both have a large circular *sala* as a central feature. This

18. Cf. R. Wittkower, *Architectural Principles in the Age of Humanism*, 1949, p. 72 and J. S.
Ackerman, *Palladio*, 1966, pp. 94–98. Wittkower, op. cit., pls 26b and c, compares the plan of the
Palazzo Thiene with Palladio's reconstruction of a Roman house for J. Barbaro's 1556 edition of
Vitruvius.

19. Palladio, II, p. 60, Villa in Cicogna for Odoardo and Theodoro Thiene, cf. Pierpont Morgan
MS. fol. 103 verso; Palladio, II, p. 76, Villa Mocenigo, cf. P.M.MS. fol. 104 recto; Palladio, II,
p. 53, Villa Emo at Fanzolo, cf. P.M.MS. fol. 105 verso(a); Palladio, II, p. 58, Villa Trissino at
Meledo, cf. P.M.MS. fol. 105 verso(b); Palladio, II, p. 56, Villa Pogliana, cf. P.M.MS. fol. 106
recto(a); Palladio, II, p. 61, Villa Angarano, cf. P.M.MS. fol. 106 recto(b).

20. In contrast to his immense influence elsewhere and especially in England, Palladio's lack
of influence in France is discussed by Professor Blunt in 'Palladio e l'Architettura Francese', *Bollettino del Centro Internazionale di Studi d'Architettura*, 'Andrea Palladio', II, 1960, pp. 14–18.

21. N. Miller, op. cit., p. 36, had discussed these drawings and suggests that they may not be
by the same hand as the remainder of the album. A re-examination of the originals would be
necessary before offering a further opinion on this, but no great difference in handling was observed
by myself. However, the drawings, even if not by du Cerceau, must come from his immediate
circle, which is in itself significant.

arrangement probably influenced designs for 'bastiments à plaisir' in the Morgan Library album, and also in du Cerceau's Third Book, published in 1582 with which the album is closely linked.[22]

One such 'bastiment à plaisir', the grandest design in the Third Book[23] (Pl. 11), has a large circular courtyard in the centre which is probably connected not only with Palladio's villa-plans but with other important prototypes, two of which du Cerceau had seen on his visit to Rome.

Du Cerceau's design in elevation, with its series of disconnected units, may seem a far cry from the High Renaissance conception of the circular courtyard as expressed in the Villa Madama in Rome, at Caprarola or in Charles V's palace at Granada. Yet its plan is connected with all these in their attempt to recreate the grand setting of the Antique Roman house. Nearer home, Serlio in his palace-designs for the 'True Sixth Book' had been similarly pre-occupied.[24]

Four out of the six villa-plans copied from Palladio's book into the album make use of quadrant-sections of the circle, forms which occur often in du Cerceau's later designs. He particularly favoured the hemicycle, the prime source of inspiration for which was Bramante's Belvedere niche in the Vatican, and the semi-circular façades engraved in Serlio's Seventh Book.[25]

Many of du Cerceau's designs are for quite small buildings with semi-circular façades flanked by taller pavilions. In 1557 Philibert de l'Orme had planned a structure beneath one of the terraces at Montceaux, a grotto with a semi-circular façade between two pavilions. This, judging from the surviving contract, was similar in type to, and may have inspired, some of du Cerceau's designs of this kind.[26] As far as we know du Cerceau himself never built any of his semi-circular façades, but one of his most striking compositions of this type, the sixth 'bastiment à plaisir' of the Third Book, obviously inspired the Château of Grosbois begun by the master-mason, Florent Fournier in 1597 (Pls 12, 13).

22. The Third Book contains plans and elevations for '. . . Seigneurs, Gentilshommes et autres qui voudront bastir aux champs . . .'.

23. Design XX of the Third Book and fols. 101 verso and 102 recto of the Morgan Library album.

24. Bramante's proposed setting for the Tempietto in San Pietro in Montorio engraved in Serlio's Third Book (1540). For a comment on Palladio's intentions at Meledo, cf. J. S. Ackerman, op. cit., p. 75. Du Cerceau undoubtedly sought to give his designs 'antique' authenticity, frequently marking the rooms with their Roman names.

25. Also the Villa Giulia and the courtyard at Caprarola.

26. E.-J. Ciprut published the text of the contract which includes notes in de l'Orme's own hand, in 'Documents inédits sur quelques châteaux de l'Ile-de-France', *Mémoires publiés par la Fédération des Sociétés Historiques et Archéologiques et de l'Ile-de-France*, Tomes XVI-XVII, 1965-1966, pp. 131-136.

The oval is another form which occurs in many of du Cerceau's plans. The architectural implications of its use had been studied by Leonardo, Peruzzi, Vignola and, in a limited way, by Palladio, who incorporated oval staircases in some of his plans. Serlio, having inherited Peruzzi's relevant drawings, made his own versions of them, which were du Cerceau's source of inspiration.[27] Du Cerceau used the oval in one of the projects in his Third Book and, on a grand scale, for his proposed completion of de l'Orme's palace of the Tuileries.[28] He also incorporated it on a smaller scale into several of his other designs. In France the only prototype for the use of the oval were de l'Orme's unfinished staircase at the Tuileries and his terrace-steps at Anet, which are an oval version of Bramante's circular steps at the Belvedere.[29]

In his First and Third Books, and in the Morgan Library album, du Cerceau presents designs for houses or châteaux of modest scale. The plans of these are unusually compact for their date in France, and are obviously influenced by designs from Serlio's 'True Sixth Book'; they may also owe something to Palladio's Second Book. But while Serlio's and Palladio's plans are vertical in axis, du Cerceau's are strongly horizontal (Pl. 90). This change of emphasis is accounted for by the necessity to plan French houses round the French *appartement* consisting of one large and two smaller rooms and a closet; an *appartement* or a group of *appartements* were separated and approached by one or more anterooms or saloons. This domestic arrangement was not in use in contemporary Italy, although it had originally been imported from Italy into France.[30]

De Brosse was unquestionably influenced by some of the plans by du Cerceau just mentioned (and particularly by those making use of the circle or sections of the circle), the importance of which has generally been overlooked by art historians who have concentrated on his designs for elevations and decorative features. These have met with severe criticism, and their

27. For an exhaustive discussion of the oval form and church-planning, cf. W. Lotz, 'Die Ovalen Kirchenräume des Cinquecento', in *Römisches Jahrbuch für Kunstgeschichte*, 1955, VII, pp. 7–99; also Rosci/Brizio, op. cit., p. 13.

28. Blunt, *Philibert de l'Orme*, p. 93, has suggested, and it has been generally accepted, that the schemes for the Tuileries and for the château of Chenonceau engraved in the *Plus Excellents Bastiments* contain many inventions by du Cerceau himself.

29. Professor Blunt has pointed out that here de l'Orme has made a deliberate and mannerist distortion of the perfectly circular plan of the original. Cf., for the steps at Anet, Blunt, op. cit., p. 50. Also A. Chastel, 'Palladio et l'escalier à double mouvement inversé', *Bollettino del Centro Internazionale di Studi di Architettura*, 'Andrea Palladio', II, 1960, pp. 34 ff. For the Tuileries staircase, see Blunt, op. cit., p. 142 ff. and pls 62a–d.

30. Blunt, *Art and Architecture*, p. 12, discusses the introduction of the *appartement* into the château of Chambord by Domenico da Cortona.

unfortunate effect on French architecture for nearly five decades has been justifiably, though perhaps excessively, emphasized. Writers have been led to neglect the fact that du Cerceau could, and often did, design perfectly sober buildings. This criticism also distracts attention from his awareness of serious contemporary developments in France and Italy, which was far greater than is usually admitted. This awareness was to have important results for his successors and especially for de Brosse.

We must now turn from du Cerceau's 'bastiments à plaisir' and his imaginary designs to the two châteaux which he was actually commissioned to build, Verneuil, first begun in 1568, and Charleval, begun in 1570.

The *First Design* for Verneuil was made for Philippe de Boulainvilliers and was an ambitious project.[31] Du Cerceau engraved plates of it in the first volume of the *Plus Excellents Bastiments*, and the preparatory drawings for all these are in the British Museum. Another plan, obviously connected with Verneuil, is in the Vatican album, and may represent an alternative, possibly an earlier design.

The *First Design* plan (Pl. 14) with its doubled angle-pavilions is impressive, and its interest at first tends to disguise the incoherence and eccentricity of some of its internal arrangements. The entrance-pavilion is oval in plan, an idea without precedent, and its form is complex, being divided in the interior into four curved bays with re-entrant angles and having four large niches on the exterior.[32] The first floor of this entrance-pavilion was intended to contain a chapel.

At the other end of the building the main entrance to the *corps-de-logis* gives access to three vestibules of diminishing size which, passing under the mezzanine landing of the great staircase, lead directly out on to the terrace. The stair itself is only directly approached by the doors on each side of the main entrance. This arrangement may to some extent reflect that of the lower part of de l'Orme's staircase at the Tuileries, which gave direct access to the

31. For a full discussion of Verneuil, see R. Coope, 'History and Architecture of the Château of Verneuil-sur-Oise', *G.d.B.A.*, LIX, May–June 1962, pp. 291–318. See also Catalogue pp. 274-277, where, although only the last stages of the work are by de Brosse, the whole chronology has been included, since it is such an important building for the study of his development as an architect.

32. It is just possible that du Cerceau knew by report of Palladio's design, not published until 1570, of the house 'dell'Atrio di quattro Colonne', *Libro Secondo*, Cap. V, where the oval space is marked 'Loggia per il quale si entra all'Atrio'. It has been suggested that Palladio's drawing for his book were known to a limited circle before publication and by implication to certain architects in France, cf. N. Miller, op. cit., p. 34, n. 3. In *Architectural Principles in the Age of Humanism*, p. 58, n. 1, Professor Wittkower says that the book was a long time preparing for the press.

garden by way of shallow flights of steps under the main stair.[33] The right-hand flight of the staircase at Verneuil curves downwards, joining another short straight flight leading to the great saloon which lies under the terrace whose semi-circular façade, flanked by pavilions containing oval staircases, gives on to the second terrace. This second terrace is semi-circular, and in obvious allusion to the Antique is inscribed as 'en théâtre'. There is also a probable reference in the whole idea of this saloon beneath the terrace to de l'Orme's *cryptoporticus* at Anet, and to his courtyard for theatrical displays at the Château-Neuf at Saint Germain.

From this point two further terraces led downwards to the water-gardens at the foot of the steep hill upon which the château was built. It is likely that the whole conception of the garden lay-out and terrace-architecture at Verneuil reflected contemporary developments in Italy, such as those at Caprarola and the Villa d'Este at Tivoli, where steeply-sloping sites were used.

Du Cerceau's elevations for the *First Design* were in parts extremely elaborate and sometimes fantastic (Pls 18, 19), and nowhere more so than in his engraving for the semi-circular façade of the saloon beneath the terrace with its riot of ornament and vast statuary. It recalls Serlio's dictum, '. . . it is a splendid thing if an architect is abundant in innovations, because of the consequent diversity of things that will happen in the structure'.[34] As with so many of du Cerceau's elevations, one feels that altogether too many things have happened. Oddly enough, this strange façade does not appear in du Cerceau's bird's-eye elevation of the whole Verneuil scheme, where the exterior of the terrace-saloon is a strongly rusticated but quite sober building.

In 1570, two years after Verneuil, du Cerceau's vast project for the château of Charleval, near Fleury in Normandy, was begun for King Charles IX[35] (Pl. 28). When the King died in 1574, the building, which had scarcely risen above the foundations and that only in the main forecourt, was totally abandoned. Charleval was a colossal undertaking, a palace in the country rather than a château in the usual sense, just as Versailles was later to be. Indeed, one of du Cerceau's sources of inspiration for his plan was the projects for royal palaces from Serlio's 'True Sixth Book', one of which was, it is

33. Cf. Blunt, *Philibert de l'Orme*, p. 104 ff. Professor Blunt traces the connection of de l'Orme's Tuileries staircase with Michelangelo's steps in the Biblioteca Laurenziana. Complaints were made of the darkness of the lower part of de l'Orme's stair, and this could probably have been said of the two smaller vestibules at Verneuil.

34. Translated and quoted by J. Shearman, *Mannerism*, 1967, p. 202.

35. Cf. Mme René Lemaire, 'Quelques précisions sur le domaine royal de Charleval', *B.S.H.A.F.*, 1952, p. 7.

thought, intended for the Louvre (and later influenced Richelieu when he built the great château which bore his name).

It is easier to imagine the King and the royal entourage progressing in state around such buildings than actually living in them. The plan of Charleval, like Serlio's plans, is in fact conceived as an expression of the royal power, and as a setting, a *mise-en-scène* in a theatrical sense, for the royal life, 'la vie d'apparat'. Charleval thus takes its place among other sixteenth-century palaces which were embodiments of the same spirit, and which were rivals for pre-eminence among European rulers: Philip II's Escorial, Henry VIII's Nonesuch, and Charles V's palace at Granada, that extraordinary, romantic and unfinished re-creation of Imperial Roman grandeur. Du Cerceau's own projects for the completion of the Tuileries and the château of Chenonceau embodied the same mystique.[36]

The association of these ideas with the palaces of Imperial Rome was natural enough, and had been further influenced by the publication in 1556 of Barbaro's edition of Vitruvius. To this Palladio had contributed the reconstruction of a Roman house, and in his own book he published several such reconstructions, one of them on a palatial scale.

At Charleval the château proper and the complex of courts surrounding it were completely contained within a vast rectangle. The whole plan is severely symmetrical and contained; no undue accentuation of any part of the façades is allowed to break the regularity of outline. Though there are two centralized chapel buildings in the smaller side-courts, and four interesting centrally-planned rooms in the wings leading off the terrace facing the garden, the rooms of the château itself show no variety of planning; only two oval staircases break the series of squares and rectangles. All is in fact subordinated to the dramatic focal point of the entire progression of buildings and courtyards, the enormous vestibule at the far end of the main courtyard.

The regularity of the Charleval plan, and several of its details, are clearly Italianate in character, but there is no necessity to suppose that any Italian

36. For this aspect of Charleval, cf. Rosci/Brizio, op. cit., p. 82. In a very important passage the whole question of the palace-theme and the 'Vitruvian revival' of the sixteenth century is analysed. Cf. also A. Chastel, op. cit. above, n. 6, p. 78 ff. The whole of this article is very important for the understanding of the Charleval project. A further example of this type of architectural thinking is provided by Francisco de Ollanda's remarkable designs in his *Da fabrica que falece á cidade de Lisboa* (1571). Ollanda travelled in Italy and in France, and French influence, notably that of Jacques I du Cerceau, is evident. A startling example is the gate-design (Lam. VI) which is discussed later, cf. Chap. III, n. 15. For the text of Ollanda's book, cf. *Archivo Español de Arte*, V, 1929, p. 209 ff.

collaborator helped du Cerceau to create his scheme. The sources already mentioned were available to guide him, and a further influence has been rightly suggested, Leonardo's drawings for the château of Romorantin (Pls 26, 27).[37] There is nothing severe or Italianate, however, about the elevations of Charleval, which are among the most fantastic of du Cerceau's whole *oeuvre*. He recorded five of them himself, together with the plan in *Les Plus Excellents Bastiments*. Only one façade appears actually to have been begun, and that was in the forecourt, not the main château. Other drawings made early in the seventeenth century by Jacques Gentilhâtre[38] are possibly copied from or based on other du Cerceau projects for the château. If all the façades of this vast complex of buildings were to have been decorated in an equally unrestrained manner, what the total effect would have been is painful to contemplate (Pl. 29).[39]

In the four years during which work went on at Charleval, it was carried out by Claude Foucques and Guillaume le Marchant, master-masons, supervised almost certainly by Baptiste du Cerceau, who in one document is named as 'architecte à Charleval'.[40]

Meanwhile at Verneuil du Cerceau's project was not going well. The *First Design* was proving too costly, and had to be modified. Philippe de Boulain-villiers, falling into financial difficulties, sold the entire estate to the Duc de Nemours in 1575.[41] For Nemours du Cerceau made a new and more modest project, incorporating the north wing with its sculptured figures of Assyrian Kings which was fairly near completion. Three engravings of this *Second Design* are in the *Plus Excellents Bastiments* (Pls 15, 20). Though the plan, which is drawn at first-floor level, is much larger in scale than that of the *First Design*, it is much more compact and coherent. The unity of the whole design is much increased by the suppression of the doubled angle-pavilions. The entrance-pavilion has been entirely altered, being slightly larger and having an octagonal not an oval ground-plan. The chapel, shown here on the first floor, has a plan which is on a tiny scale an adaptation of one of Michel-

37. Cf. Rosci/Brizio, op. cit., p. 43. M. Adhémar suggests that Italian collaboration is indicated by documents now in the Bibliothèque Nationale, which contain the names of various Italian artisans on the King's pay-roll, one or two of them specifically in connection with Charleval. Some Italians made 'ung portrait au vif sur carte' of the château, others models in wood, but the evidence is not sufficient to establish any of them as the architect of the project. Cf. J. Adhémar, 'Sur le Château de Charleval', *G.d.B.A.*, LVIII, October 1961, pp. 243 ff.

38. R.I.B.A. Drawings Library, London.

39. Curiously, the engraved façade of the forecourt, inscribed 'Face commancée dedans la basse court' does not correspond with any part of the engraved plan.

40. Cf. Lemaire, op. cit., pp. 9 and 11.

41. In my article on Verneuil, I erred in transposing this date to 1576 N.S.

angelo's projects for San Giovanni dei Fiorentini in Rome (1559), which du Cerceau must have known through drawings brought from Italy, for it was not engraved until 1609. Access to the chapel was from the two angle-pavilions along a terrace running above the entrance-screen.

The great saloon beyond the *corps-de-logis* now lies directly below the terrace, its façade in line with the substructure, and not built out from it or 'en théâtre' as in the *First Design* (Pl. 14). It is flanked by two anterooms, and this arrangement, it has been suggested, foreshadows the disposition of the Galerie des Glaces, the Salon de la Paix and the Salon de la Guerre at Versailles.[42]

The elevations of the *Second Design* are far more architectural in feeling and less decorative in character than those of the *First* (Pls 18, 20). They are simpler, with a stronger sense of mass and greater restraint in detail. Curiously, they seem closer to the elevations shown in the bird's-eye view of the *First Design*, which gives a sturdier and more sober impression, comparable to the *Second Design*, and does not correspond to the larger and fantastically elaborate engravings of the *First Design* façades.

The four angle-pavilions each have three storeys, as in the *First Design* but the top storey is no longer set back, so that the square dome directly covers the whole pavilion. The domes at Verneuil have a kind of horizontal ridging, and are of a type which became widespread in early seventeenth-century architecture, especially in the work of de Brosse. The decoration of the outer wall-surface has disappeared except for plain panels flanking the windows, while practically all the sculptured decoration is kept above cornice-level. The entrance-façade and pavilion have been a good deal simplified; the coupled columns are replaced by rusticated strips, the niches and statues by rectangular openings with heavy *voussoirs*, and the Corinthian columns of the *First Design* are here limited to eight in number and confined to the entrance-pavilion, of which the lower and the upper parts are now much more unified.

The architecture of the three main façades on the court side does not appear to have been altered from the *First Design*. This was to some extent dictated by the already nearly-completed north wing, but it is perfectly consistent with the contemporary notion that the exterior of a building should be severe and strong, while the inner façades could be lighter and more decorative.

It may be that the changes at Verneuil made after 1575 were due to financial considerations only, but it seems more probable that a greater economy went hand in hand with a change of taste as well as a change of patron. Du Cerceau's

42. L. Hautecoeur, I, p. 353.

description of the château in the *Plus Excellents Bastiments* suggests that the changes were in part due to the Duc de Nemours himself, and that there was some collaboration between patron and architect. Whatever the extent of this collaboration may have been, Verneuil emerged radically changed.

To understand the significance of this change it is sufficient to compare the engraved plans and façades of the *First* and *Second Designs* with the almost exactly contemporary designs for the forecourt of Charleval. These engravings show du Cerceau's move away, during the years 1568 to 1575, from a fantastic, decorative kind of mannerism to a far greater grasp of architectural design and to a real feeling for three-dimensional composition. The changes represented by the progression of the Verneuil project from the *First* to the *Second Design* can be said to have opened the way to some of the most important developments of the early seventeenth century.

There is another drawing of Verneuil, in elevation, in the Cooper Union Museum in New York (Pl. 21) which, though it is not by du Cerceau,[43] certainly came from his atelier at Verneuil, probably in the last years of the sixteenth century.[44] Curiously enough at this late stage, the spade-shaped bastions of the substructure have re-appeared in this new proposal for the entrance-front, which had yet to be built. In this project the screen and entrance-pavilion have been further simplified. The screen is still more restrained than the one proposed in the *Second Design*, and in the entrance-pavilion a great rusticated arch, running in an unbroken line right up from the ground to well above the cornice, has at last succeeded in imposing a satisfactory and dramatic unity between the lower and the upper parts of the structure. The Corinthian columns have been retained, but the base on which they stand has been reduced in height so as to follow the line of the base of the screen.

This final design for Verneuil is extremely important; it differs from the *Second Design* elevation only in comparatively small details and yet these details result in a design more sophisticated than any which du Cerceau attained, and they change the whole feeling of the entrance-front. It has become more monumental; it is also simpler and more logical. The name of the architect who made this design cannot as yet be determined, but it is certain

43. Geymüller, op. cit., knew this drawing when it formed part of the Destailleur collection, and attributed it to du Cerceau. Since I wrote my study on Verneuil, I have seen the drawing, and do not believe it to be by him.

44. The armorial bearings on it are those of the Duc de Nemours, so that the date is apparently prior to 1600 when the château passed out of the possession of that family.

that it came from the workshop at Verneuil where de Brosse was trained and where he was working until 1598.[45]

In 1585 work at Verneuil stopped. The Duke died, the wars broke out again, du Cerceau left and died soon after. The widowed Duchess could do little more building in the prevailing circumstances. Verneuil remained unfinished until de Brosse came back to complete his grandfather's château.

Jacques I du Cerceau died about 1585, leaving his atelier to be carried on by his two sons, Baptiste and Jacques II. Baptiste probably died about 1590 when Salomon de Brosse was nineteen, and it seems likely from the few records we have of his career that he worked chiefly in Paris and at Charleval, not at Verneuil. Through Baptiste's appointment in 1578 to succeed Jean Bullant as architect in charge of the Valois chapel at Saint Denis,[46] de Brosse may, whilst still a boy, have become familiar with Primaticcio's original drawings for the chapel, and with subsequent ones by Bullant. The du Cerceau connection with the Valois chapel is doubly important; Bullant influenced all three of the Cerceau, and the chapel had a great influence on de Brosse.

The Hôtel d'Angoulême, (now Lamoignon) in Paris was begun in 1584 for Diane de France, Duchesse d'Angoulême, and is usually attributed to Baptiste du Cerceau.[47] It stands on the corner of the Rue des Francs-Bourgeois and the Rue Pavée, and consisted originally of a *corps-de-logis* flanked on both the court and the garden sides by pavilions which projected only for the length of one bay. The garden front, now completely denuded of all its original articulation and decoration, is only known to us from an engraving by Chastillon, but the court front survives almost intact. In 1620 the house was completed by the addition of a gallery which runs from the northern pavilion along the Rue des Francs-Bourgeois (and which is supported by a celebrated *trompe* on the Rue Pavée). The only plan of the original building is to be found on a drawing by Robert de Cotte,[48] and though it is overlaid by de Cotte's many proposed alterations and extensions, the original design is still visible. Although the interior disposition is quite different, the plan may be based on the sixth design of Jacques I du Cerceau's First Book. It consists of

---

45. In the present state of knowledge about de Brosse's drawings, it is not possible to discuss the possible attribution of this drawing to him. The grounds for believing the drawing to be the last of the series for Verneuil are stylistic. Were it not for the presence of the Nemours arms, it could be placed in the early seventeenth century, not only because of draughtsmanship, but for the architectural details such as those described and the gate-house in front of the moat. Its relationship with a set of later plans of the château, only recently discovered, will be discussed in Chapter III.

46. Blunt, *Art and Architecture*, p. 56.

47. Ibid., p. 83.

48. De Cotte No. 331, B.N. Estampes Va442.

a block with two projecting wings on each side, and such a scheme is very rare; no other executed town-house on this plan of an earlier date survives (Pl. 30).

In elevation the Hôtel d'Angoulême is remarkably tall for the comparatively small area which it occupies, and an impression of overbearing height and weight is imposed by the colossal order, the tall pedimented dormers which rise through the entablature, the heavy broken pediment over the central bay, and the attic storey of the pavilions surmounted on each face by an enormous segmental pediment. The attic storeys, like those of the *First Design* for Verneuil, form an almost separate unit above the cornice surmounting the two main floors. The sense of discomfort produced in the spectator by the odd proportions and top-heavy decoration of the façades was certainly intended by the architect and is in the mannerist tradition (Pls 31–33).

Late drawings and engravings by Jacques I du Cerceau[49] provide prototypes for three of the most striking features of the Hôtel d'Angoulême: the curious heavy pavilions forming the cross-pieces of an I-shaped building; the three enormous segmental pediments surmounting them; and the use of the colossal order. The pediments particularly are characteristic of several of these late designs.

The colossal order, authorized by Michelangelo on the Capitol in Rome in 1547, was known in France through the treatise of de l'Orme, engravings in Serlio's Seventh Book and notably through drawings for his 'True Sixth Book'. De l'Orme had proposed it for a wing which he was commissioned to build at Fontainebleau in 1558,[50] but which was never executed. Even earlier, before 1546, a Serliesque adaptation had been made at the château of Joinville, and in the 1550s a more naïve version had appeared at Fleury-en-Bière. Jacques I du Cerceau in his later work was obviously much interested in the colossal order, which he intended to use extensively at Charleval. Nevertheless, the façades of the Hôtel d'Angoulême are nearer in spirit to the work of Jean Bullant than to du Cerceau or any other architect. The central bay of the Châtelet at Chantilly (*c.* 1560) and the entrance to the gallery at La Fère-en-Tardenois (1552–1562) may well have suggested to Baptiste the form of the central bay at the hôtel, with its wide triangular pediment broken at the base.

This type of pediment appears on the sixteenth-century façades of the château of Ormesson, which was begun about 1578.[51] Though there is no

49. Principally in the Morgan Library album (notably fol. 52 recto).
50. Blunt, *Philibert de l'Orme*, p. 58 ff.
51. The right-hand side of the château was extended in the eighteenth century.

evidence that Baptiste designed it, there is a connection with the du Cerceau circle; the small château, with its four angle-pavilions, standing in a lake, is designed as a symmetrical free-standing block, as was the Hôtel d'Angoulême.[52]

Too little is known of Baptiste du Cerceau for any clear summary to be made of his style or of its importance. The Hôtel d'Angoulême alone, however, shows him to have been a powerful architect and original in the use he made of his various sources. Nor was he by any means entirely dependent here upon his famous father; a comparison between this hôtel and the elevations designed for Charleval is enough to point the difference in outlook. Both father and son felt the influence of Bullant, but it is certainly fair to say that Baptiste had a better grasp of what Bullant was trying to express.

When Henri IV entered Paris in 1594 and the war ended, Baptiste's younger brother Jacques II du Cerceau came back to the capital from Tours and entered the King's service, working on the new building programme at the Louvre. In 1595 the Grande Galerie was begun, to join the Louvre to the Tuileries on the river side. Jacques II is generally believed to have been the architect of its western section, of the Pavillon de Flore begun about 1607, and of the Petite Galerie des Tuileries, begun about 1608, which joined the Pavillon de Flore to Bullant's pavilion on the west front of the Tuileries (Pls 34, 35, 37, 44).

Jacques II's design for the Grande Galerie, with its colossal order of coupled Corinthian pilasters supporting giant pediments goes back in inspiration to his brother Baptiste's Hôtel d'Angoulême, to his father's late drawings and engravings and, through both, to the influence of Bullant.

Among the elder Jacques du Cerceau's designs there is one which is particularly interesting in connection with the Grande Galerie. This drawing was never engraved and is not in any of the albums[53] (Pl. 36). The frontispieces at each end of the entrance-wings of the palace depicted[54] are an almost direct prototype for those bays of the Grande Galerie which have segmental pediments.

When, later on, Jacques II built the Pavillon de Flore, he united it with the

52. The conception goes back to de l'Orme's design for the free-standing Château-Neuf at Saint Germain (cf. Blunt, op. cit., p. 67, fig. 19). But Jacques I du Cerceau had himself made several designs for small free-standing buildings, and one or two others on a larger scale. One of the latter, in the Third Book, is quite close to Ormesson. Ormesson is illustrated by E. Ganay in *Châteaux et Manoirs de France (Ile-de-France)*, vol. II, 1938, pls 301 *et seq.*

53. Paris, Ecole des Beaux-Arts (Masson, Ornements 3286).

54. This building is yet another version of the palace-château with a grand circular courtyard discussed earlier.

Grande Galerie by introducing the colossal order up to the level of the first cornice, but used single, not double pilasters. In the Petite Galerie des Tuileries he returns to the double-pilaster rhythm; much of the rest of the detail in the Petite Galerie des Tuileries is derived from Lescot's wing in the courtyard of the Louvre. In the staircase pavilions at each end (removed after Le Vau's alterations), the doors are directly copied from Lescot, but the type of pavilion, with a ridged dome, and the way in which the door is placed within it, is typical of the du Cerceau family and can be found in innumerable designs by the elder Jacques.

All the buildings erected at the Louvre and the Tuileries by Jacques II have disappeared or been altered, and it is not wise to judge their details entirely from drawings and engravings, since these were perhaps made after the original buildings had been modified.[55] The general appearance of his buildings at these two palaces is, however, sufficiently good evidence for the attribution to Jacques II du Cerceau of Henri IV's alterations and extensions to the château of Montceaux-en-Brie, an attribution for which there is some traditional and documentary evidence. This work is of great importance in the present context because it provides the first firm date in Salomon de Brosse's architectural career.[56]

Montceaux, near Meaux (Pl. 38), was begun by Philibert de l'Orme in 1547 for Catherine de Médicis.[57] After the Queen's death the château passed into the hands of her creditors, from whom it was purchased in 1596 by Henri IV for his mistress, Gabrielle d'Estrées.[58] In the next year the King

55. Cf. L. Batiffol, *Les Travaux du Louvre sous Henri IV*, Paris, 1912, p. 172 ff. and p. 415 ff; Jacques Hillairet, *Le Palais Royal et Impérial des Tuileries*, Paris, 1965, pp. 24 and 25, figs 1–7; Y. Christ, *Le Louvre et les Tuileries*, Paris, 1949, p. 34.

56. The connection of the name du Cerceau with Montceaux goes back at least to the eighteenth century. Of course nobody at that time was clear which du Cerceau he was referring to, for the family had become one conglomerate personage, 'du Cerceau', who, to judge by the attributions made to him, must have lived for about a hundred and fifty years. In his *Description de Paris*, 1742, pp. 368–370, Piganiol de la Force attributes the Hôtel Séguier to 'du Cerceau'. This hôtel, formerly de Soissons and then de Bellegarde, had a long and complicated history, but in 1613 it was bought by the Duc de Bellegarde from the Comte de Soissons, and rebuilt. Piganiol says the Duc employed du Cerceau '... comme alors il n'y avait point d'architecte qui eut plus de nom que du Cerceau car c'était lui qui avoit conduit les Châteaux de Montceaux et de Verneuil ...'. The association of Verneuil, Montceaux and the hôtel is interesting. Sauval, *Histoire et Recherches des Antiquités de la Ville de Paris*, 1724, I, p. 127, supports Piganiol in this: '... Roger de Saint-Lary, duc de Bellegarde ... acheta en 1612 ... l'hôtel, placé rue de Grenelle, qu'il fit ruiner de fond en comble et rebâtir ... par du Cerceau le plus renommé architecte de son temps ...'.

57. For the full history of Montceaux, cf. R. Coope, 'The Château of Montceaux-en-Brie', *Journal of the Warburg and Courtauld Institutes*, XXII, 1959, p. 71, and cf. also Cat. pp. 226-234.

58. He presented it to her in 1594 when strictly speaking it was not his, and only bought it officially in 1596.

decided to complete the unfinished building. Early in 1599 Gabrielle died, but the work went on slowly up to and after the turn of the century.

De l'Orme's château was to have consisted of a *corps-de-logis* with a central staircase pavilion, single angle-pavilions and long narrow wings; and we may presume that he intended to close the court on the entrance-side either with another wing or with a screen and entrance-pavilion. Of this scheme, only the *corps-de-logis*, the north-west pavilion and the north wing were carried out. The only record we have of de l'Orme's work is a plan of the foundations,[59] and a drawing made by Scamozzi in 1600 which shows the north wing before alteration, and the circular pavilions on the west terrace, which he calls 'due rottonde assai ornate'.[60]

Henri IV decided to widen the staircase-pavilion of the *corps-de-logis* by one bay at each side; to enlarge the north-west pavilion by one bay on its inner side; to build the south-west pavilion; and to add a long, narrow south wing to match de l'Orme's northern one.[61] A pavilion was to be built at the end of each wing, linked by a screen with an entrance-pavilion in the centre. (His project for this completion and extension of de l'Orme's existing château can be deduced from a comparison of the plans of the cellars and the ground-floor.)

De l'Orme's elevations were re-faced; the plain walls were articulated by a colossal order with single Ionic pilasters between each window-bay; the frontispieces of the *corps-de-logis* on the court and garden sides were, as Scamozzi shows, given prominence by four attached columns.[62] De l'Orme's north-west pavilion received new dormers with decorations including the entwined cipher H & G, to bring it into line with the three pavilions to be built.[63] The new pavilion-design can be seen in the ruins and in one of the drawings by Jacques Gentilhâtre a master-mason who was for a time associated with the du Cerceau workshop[64] (Pls 42, 43).

59. The *Second Design* for Verneuil (pl. 15) may well have been modelled on de l'Orme's original plan for Montceaux, although for the entrance-pavilion and screen (about the earlier designs for which at Montceaux we know nothing) it cannot be suggested as a prototype.

60. Cf. Cat. pp. 227, 230.

61. The extension southwards of the central part of the south wing was a later modification, and the original foundations of the wing can be traced in the plan of the cellars which is illustrated in Coope, op. cit. above, n. 57.

62. In my article on Montceaux I supposed the columns of the *corps-de-logis* to have been added after 1609. This was a mistake, as was shown by the subsequent publication of Scamozzi's *Journal* and his sketch of the château.

63. The pavilions were all completed, as the eighteenth-century descriptions state that all were decorated with 'H & G' ciphers in the attic storey.

64. The florid decoration suggested by Gentilhâtre for the attic storey of the *corps-de-logis* may have been in this case largely his own invention. The real quality of the sixteenth-century decora-

The lay-out of Montceaux as actually executed was of course governed by the existance of de l'Orme's foundations, and there is nothing particularly notable about it, except for the plan of the entrance-pavilion which derives directly from the entrance-pavilion of the *First Design* for Verneuil (Pls 14, 41). The screen was originally designed as a single, pierced wall, the ground-floor plan proving that the inner arcade was not added until later (Pls 39, 41). At this stage, therefore, the first floor of the pavilion was not intended to contain a chapel or a room of any importance, since the only access to it would have been by narrow newel-staircases in the thickness of the wall.

The plan of Montceaux, despite the link with Verneuil in the entrance-pavilion, gives us no firm clue as to the identity of the architect, but the elevations are more revealing. If we compare the angle-pavilions at Monceaux with the Pavillon de Flore (Pls 42, 44), and consider that Montceaux preceded the latter by eleven years, it would be reasonable to assume that the same architect designed both, even were there no documentary evidence to support the suggestion. The use of a colossal order of pilasters for the façades is in a tradition which runs right through the work of the du Cerceau family down to Jacques II du Cerceau's Grande Galerie at the Louvre, begun in 1594 only three years before the King's buildings at Montceaux. The Ionic order is an innovation in the du Cerceau circle, but may have been influenced by de l'Orme's Ionic order at the Tuileries.

The combination of large forms and finely-cut, sharp detail which is conspicuous even in the ruined façades built for Henri IV at Montceaux recalls Bullant, an architect who, as we have seen, deeply influenced the du Cerceau family. If Marot's engravings and the surviving evidence about the Pavillon de Flore are to be trusted, the treatment of du Cerceau's buildings at the Tuileries was the same, and that of the Grande Galerie was certainly comparable. A feature at Montceaux, condemned by Scamozzi on his visit, was the height and narrowness of the windows flanking the entrance to the *corps-de-logis*, and the windows of the Pavillon de Flore had the same characteristics.

One further feature of the sixteenth-century designs for Montceaux links the buildings with the du Cerceau tradition. The fragments which remain around the main court are numerous enough to indicate that their size and decoration were disproportionate to the comparatively small area which they enclosed. The effect of the surrounding façades with their colossal order,

---

tion at Montceaux is better indicated by the surviving fragments of the ruined façades. (For Gentil-hâtre, cf. Cat. p. 230 and above, p. 29 and n. 38).

decorated dormers and high-pitched roofs must have been somewhat over-whelming when seen either from the court or from the terrace, which is a good deal narrower than it appears in the engravings. Montceaux in this respect is close to Baptiste du Cerceau's Hôtel d'Angoulême, which dominates its courtyard in such an uncomfortably impressive way. As at the Hôtel d'Angoulême, so at Monceaux there was a conflict between the desire to create an impression of size and weight, and a tendency to nullify this by broken lines and by thin, precise decoration, which despite its accomplish-ment is monotonous. If this is noticeable to some extent at the hôtel it must have been overpowering on the long repetitive façades of the château. Common to both buildings also is a strong stress on the vertical, underlined by the tall narrow windows.

Henri IV's remodelling of Montceaux, although it was begun only just before the turn of the century, looks firmly back to the 1580s. Paradoxically, it is perhaps most noteworthy for its lack of influence on de Brosse, who from the first chose to stress those aspects of his grandfather's work at Verneuil – a much earlier building – which looked forward to the archi-tectural developments of the new century.

CHAPTER III

Verneuil, Henrichemont and Montceaux, 1600–1620

I N 1600 Henri IV was concerned to find a suitable residence for Henriette d'Entragues, Gabrielle's far less amiable successor as *maîtresse-en-titre*. He chose Verneuil, bought it from the dowager Duchesse de Nemours, and gave it to Henriette together with the title of Marquise de Verneuil. Henriette's career as a favourite had its dramatic ups and downs, lasting with stormy interludes until 1608. But even as early as 1604, as Sully noted in his memoirs, there were times when the King and his mistress 'seldom met but to quarrel', and in 1608 her disgrace was total; she retired from court and lived for the rest of her life at Verneuil, took to good works and was perpetually short of money until her death in 1633.

Henriette was responsible for the completion of Verneuil;[1] she finished the entrance-pavilion, built the screen, added a forecourt, and surrounded the entire estate with a wall pierced by arched gateways. All this work was probably planned before 1608, although it was only paid for (in land and not in money) in 1616.

The appearance of Verneuil is recorded in engraved views by Aveline and Poilly, and the ruins were drawn and engraved by Dupont in 1776 (Pls 22, 23). Two descriptions of the château exist, the first dated 1615, the second 1705.[2] These are a useful check upon the accuracy of the engravings, since all the buildings have disappeared.

The 1615 description occurs in a declaration of her possessions at Verneuil made by Henriette to Louis XIII. There were still two châteaux on the estate, as there had been when du Cerceau made his engravings for the *Plus Excellent Bastiments* some thirty years earlier; and the description reads as follows: '. . . deulx chasteaux lun assis sur la crouppe de la montagne continue des bastiments par ladicte dame y ayant ung beau portail, deulx pavillons

1. See Cat. pp. 274, 277; cf. also Sauval, II, p. 311; also R. Coope, 'History and Architecture of the Château of Verneuil', *G.d.B.A.*, LIX, 1962, p. 315.

2. Cf. Cat. p. 274.

magniffiques le pourtour de lavant cour revestu de boulingrins et balustres à lentour du chasteau composé en carré de quatre pavillons fort richement elaborés estant sa structure et architecture très belle pour la rareté de ses ediffices . . .'.

The grammar of the phrase, 'lun assis sur la crouppe de la montagne continue des bastiments par ladicte dame', is peculiar and is not helped in its context by the almost total lack of punctuation in the original document. However, it presumably indicates that the buildings of the new château were continued by Henriette.

In 1705 the then owner of Verneuil, the Prince de Condé, made a similar declaration to Louis XIV. This is more specific about the various parts of the 'new' château: '. . . plusieurs corps de logis et bastiments, sçavoir un grand corps de logis et quatre gros pavillons appliquez en plusieurs offices . . . quatre petits pavillons de pierre à costé des deux fossez, portes, grande cour, une grande porte pour y entrer faisant fasse au dict chasteau, une chapelle et deux grands pavillons aux costez . . . une avant cour et une porte à pont-levis pour entrer avec deux petits pavillons de pierre aux costez . . .'.

Until recently visual evidence for de Brosse's contribution to Verneuil depended mainly upon the seventeenth and eighteenth-century engravings of the elevations. Now a pair of plans has been discovered in the Archives at Chantilly,[3] which suggest further interesting possibilities. The exact date and provenance of these plans is not known, nor, for lack of external evidence, can their relationship to the Cooper Union drawing be established, but if, as has been suggested,[4] they date from the early part of the seventeenth century, we can reasonably assume some connection (Pls 16, 17).

We cannot compare the Chantilly ground-plan of Verneuil with that of du Cerceau's proposed arrangement, for unfortunately he only engraved the first-floor plan of his *Second Design* in the *Plus Excellents Bastiments*. But, if we compare du Cerceau's *Second Design* first-floor plan (Pl. 15) with the one at Chantilly, we find three modifications in the latter. The gallery in the north wing has been extended into the north-west angle-pavilion, cutting out a large part of the original *appartement*. On the other side of the château a corridor has been inserted down the full length of the south wing.[5]

3. By Raymond Cazelles, publ. *G.d.B.A.*, 1969, cf. Cat. p. 275.

4. By M. Cazelles in his article, on the evidence of the majority of the inscriptions. Stylistically, however, the plans are puzzling and a date much later in the century may be possible for them.

5. The inscriptions 'Gallerie' in the N. wing and 'Corridor' in the S. wing are in a different and, according to M. Cazelles, a later hand than most of those denoting the use of the rest of the rooms etc. This hand, however, also occurs on the Salle des Gardes and the screen-terrace, both undoubtedly part of the early seventeenth-century structure. The gallery, and particularly the

More important than either of these alterations is the change in the design of the upper floor of the entrance-pavilion. (Incidentally, in this Chantilly plan we have the first definite statement that the chapel occupied this space; du Cerceau's plan is not so inscribed, and the 1705 description is not specific). Du Cerceau's miniature adaptation of Michelangelo's plan for San Giovanni dei Fiorentini has been abandoned and is replaced by a chapel which resembles the one designed by de Brosse (*c.* 1615) for the upper floor of the entrance-pavilion at Montceaux (Pl. 40), though the handling of the space and the play of curves at Verneuil are simpler than at Montceaux.

The Chantilly ground-plan is in some ways puzzling. We know, for example, that the north wing was the first to be built,[6] and du Cerceau shows it in the plan and elevation of the *First Design* as having a loggia on the ground floor. The Chantilly plan shows that at some later stage the loggia was replaced by a suite of rooms with a central vestibule leading out to a semi-circular *perron*; this *perron* and the inscription 'parterre' beyond the wing indicate that du Cerceau's arrangement of moat and terrace had here been modified. Elsewhere the ground-plan is more ambiguous over levels and is difficult to read in this respect.[7]

The most interesting feature of the plan[8] is the central element in the south wing. Three steps lead up to the entrance from the court, beyond which lies a pair of oval vestibules cut into by a square central space on either side of which flights of steps lead up to the rooms beyond.[9] The far vestibule gives access to the eastern part of the wing and also, by means of rectangular *perron*, to the garden.

Unfortunately we cannot be certain whether or not this ingenious arrangement of space into contrasting curved and square elements formed part of

---

corridor alteration, might date from the late seventeenth or early eighteenth century if the original plan could have been altered at this point by erasion. M. Cazelles does not specify whether they are in ink or pencil, and the photographs are no help in the matter.

6. Cf. Chap. II, p. 30.

7. For example, the N. wing is shown as having its ground floor at ground level. The *corps-de-logis* and N.E. pavilion, which it adjoins, are six steps above ground level, yet no steps are shown rising between the wing and the N.E. pavilion. Similarly, the passage-way through the vestibule of the staircase-pavilion from the court to the E. terrace is shown, correctly, at ground level, but so also is the entrance from this passage-way to the staircase-vestibules, which is impossible. Du Cerceau's ground-plan of the *First Design* shows the correct arrangement with steps up from the passage-way to the staircase-vestibules.

8. The equally interesting principal staircase is part of du Cerceau's *First Design* and has been discussed, cf. Chap. II, pp. 26, 27; and R. Coope, op. cit. on Verneuil.

9. The total number of steps in the change of level between this wing and the court is eight, three from the court and five in each of the flights from the vestibule. This compares with six from the court to the staircase-vestibule in the *corps-de-logis* adjoining it to the east.

du Cerceau's original ground-plan for the *Second Design*. On balance it seems unlikely, for although du Cerceau made considerable play with geometrical shapes both in his theoretical designs and in his plans for Charleval and Verneuil itself, they are not as lucidly thought out as this is.[10] Nevertheless, his authorship cannot be discounted on such negative evidence alone. On the other hand, de Brosse's interest in curved geometrical forms, stimulated by Serlio's and du Cerceau's designs, may be reflected in this vestibule as well as in the chapel shown on the first-floor Chantilly plan. But the vestible seems somewhat advanced for de Brosse in the period 1600–1608, and if it is his work he may have designed it at some later period before 1616 when Henriette d'Entragues made her apparently final settlement with him for work done.[11]

The engravings by Aveline and Poilly show the principal façade and the forecourt of the château as they were completed by de Brosse. The most remarkable feature of the façade is the screen, consisting of an arcade on each side of the pavilion.[12] Like the previous screens designed for Verneuil, it was double and had a terrace-walk above it, but in all other respects it differs from its predecessors.

All the engravings show the entrance-pavilion without the columns of the Cooper Union drawing (Pl. 21), but the Chantilly ground-plan includes them,[13] and it is probable that the pavilion itself was built according to the Cooper Union design; the lower part certainly dates from the period before Henriette acquired the château.[14] The use of a colossal order of fluted Corinthian columns is paralleled in de Brosse's almost contemporary design for the entrance-pavilion at Montceaux (Pl. 69).

The rustication of the screen and the entrance-pavilion and the comparatively austere treatment of the latter would have given an air of grandeur and strength to the façade; the whole effect anticipates de Brosse's design for

10. In the Plan of Verneuil in the Vatican Library (cf. Cat. p. 275) this space is occupied by an oval staircase and a pillared oval vestibule in the stair-well, a design du Cerceau was unlikely to have been capable of carrying out.

11. Unless further evidence comes to light of building activity between 1616 and 1735, when the château was demolished, it seems very unlikely that the vestibule was created after de Brosse's death. But it is just conceivable that Henriette had it built between 1616 and her own death in 1633.

12. Aveline shows four openings in the arcade, Poilly four, and Dupont space for three only. The Chantilly plans now prove Aveline and Poilly to have been correct.

13. The fact that the Chantilly first-floor plan does not is probably explicable by the fact that they did not run up the whole height of the upper-floor of the entrance-pavilion.

14. The Cooper Union drawing and Dupont's engravings show arms with the Nemours supporters; cf. R. Coope, op. cit. p. 311.

the monumental entrance-front at Coulommiers. There is a complete contrast between this approach and that of the architect of the late sixteenth century entrance-screen at Montceaux (Pl. 42), where the surface is broken up with decorative panels, relief-sculpture, mannerist *voussoirs* and the like.

Henriette's decision to add a forecourt to the château must have enormously increased the impressiveness of the approach to the main buildings. The gates and pavilions of this court were designed to harmonize with the style of the entrance-façade of the château, the detached pavilions and the gatehouses with their arches having some plain surfaces but a good deal of strong rustication. It is worth noting that one of the descriptions quoted suggests that brick was not used, at any rate in the moat pavilions, '. . . quatre petits pavillons de pierre aux costez des deux fossez . . .'.

The gate-houses and gate on the south side of the forecourt, which are shown still standing in Dupont's engraving of this front, are close in type to the drawbridge-gate of the Cooper Union drawing, and both are in a style which was to become very characteristic of de Brosse's work. The arches are based on an identifiable du Cerceau model;[15] the gate-houses too are close to du Cerceau; yet both are more restrained and better articulated than their prototypes.

Unfortunately the moat-pavilions had disappeared by 1776, so Dupont's engraving gives us no record of them. Aveline shows them with square domes, Poilly with pointed roofs and lanterns. In this case Aveline is possibly more exact, as we know from Dupont that the square domes designed for the château itself were executed, and it seems likely that the little pavilions repeated the pattern. There are several features in the moat-pavilions which anticipate similar later work by de Brosse, and in general, apart from the roofs, the seventeenth-century engravings are probably fairly accurate. Dupont also shows that the forecourt stood upon a substructure rusticated in the same fashion as that of the Cooper Union drawing, de Brosse having simply extended the moat westwards to accommodate the new courtyard and buildings. In fact, it is clear that the Cooper Union drawing, whoever made it, was the starting point for de Brosse's completion of Verneuil.

Until it was destroyed during the Second World War, one of the gates which de Brosse built in the estate-wall at Verneuil still stood in a good state

---

15. Pierpont Morgan Library Album, fol. 4 recto; there is a curious relationship between this type of gate by du Cerceau and one of the illustrations to Francisco de'Ollanda's *Da Fabrica que falece á cidade de Lisboa*, 1571, Lam. VI (cf. Chap. II, n. 36). A further relationship, through the du Cerceau influence common to both, can be seen between de'Ollanda's gate in Lam. VI and de Brosse's Porte Henri IV (cf. below, p. 44) at Verneuil.

of preservation, and was known locally as the 'Porte Henri IV'. As with the
forecourt-gates, the relationship to and the differences from a du Cerceau
prototype are interesting (Pls 24, 25). If we can judge from the Cooper Union
drawing and the Dupont engraving, the rustication used by de Brosse in the
screen and entrance-pavilion at Verneuil was of a fairly heavy and prominent
type, and it would have been similar to that he later used in the forecourt at
Montceaux (Pl. 65). The rustication of the Porte Henri IV arch is different;
shallower, more incisive and rather more sophisticated in its handling. In
fact it shows signs of the influence upon de Brosse, soon to be all-important,
of Vignola's doors and the so-called 'Porte di Michelangelo' from his *Regola
delle Cinque Ordini*. There is also a certain resemblance to the Porta Faulle
at Viterbo. The fact that de Brosse himself had not seen the gate at Viterbo
would not eliminate the Italian building as an influence, since, as we shall see
later, he was in contact with travellers who could have described or made
drawings of it. Admittedly, the Verneuil gate is a little naïve and tentative,
but it is extremely interesting and also a useful work against which to measure
future attributions.

During the period when de Brosse was working at Verneuil, he became
involved in an interesting project which was being set in hand many miles
away to the south. In 1605 Maximilien de Béthune, Duc de Sully, Henri IV's
celebrated minister, had bought from the Duc de Nevers the fief of Boisbelle,
near Bourges. This domain was small, Boisbelle itself being merely a village,
but it was nevertheless a principality, and since the title of Prince de Boisbelle
went with the land, it meant added prestige for Sully's family. He planned to
abandon Boisbelle and transfer the seat of the principality to a new town to be
created for him and named Henrichemont in honour of the King (Pls 45, 46).
Personal and family aggrandisement were among Sully's motives in founding
Henrichemont, but he had others as well. He was inspired by Henri IV's
ventures in town-planning in Paris at the Place Royale (des Vosges), the
Place Dauphine and the Place de France, and he was no doubt also aware of
what was being planned for Charleville, the town which Charles de Gonzague,
that same Duc de Nevers from whom he had bought Boisbelle, was planning
in Normandy.[16]

There is evidence that Sully intended the town to be settled by his fellow-
Protestants, for freedom of worship was ensured by the provision of 'une

16. The Place des Vosges was begun in 1605; the Place Dauphine was opened in 1607; Charleville and Henrichemont were both begun in 1608. Although the Place de France was not begun
until 1610 (and soon abandoned), its design was no doubt a subject of discussion long before that
date.

église . . . (et) . . . ung Temple'; and he hoped to attract industrious traders and artisans. Unfortunately, Henrichemont (like the Cardinal's town of Richelieu later on) was pre-destined to failure as a centre for anything, and was a totally uneconomic venture. As an agricultural town it had well-established rivals nearby; for trade, industry and mercantile enterprise it lacked almost every pre-requisite. Even the local building-material was extremely poor, and stone of any quality was sadly lacking. Henrichemont had indeed 'la situation la plus ingrate du monde'.[17]

Towns like Henrichemont and Charleville followed a tradition of planning which, in France, dated back to the Middle Ages and of which the town of Vitry-le-François, founded in 1545, had been a continuation and development.[18] Symmetrical town-plans also reflected ideas proposed by Leonardo, Alberti, Filarete, Cataneo and other Italians,[19] and by the Frenchmen Bernard Palissy and Jacques Perret.[20]

In addition to their symmetrical plans, Henri IV's projects for the *places* of Paris and Nevers' and Sully's towns of Charleville and Henrichemont were intended to contain houses which were also subjected to strict rules of symmetry; all the houses round a square or along a street being built according to pre-determined designs.

The plan of Henrichemont was probably made by the military engineer and canal builder, Hugues Cosnier of Paris; the architect called in to make the design for all the buildings, public and private, from which no contractor or private builder was to deviate,[21] was de Brosse, who presumably had his drawings made by 1608 when the town was begun.

There is no evidence that de Brosse ever went to Henrichemont. He probably made the drawings, handed them over to the Paris contractors, Cosnier and Gobelin, and left them to their work. His lack of concern with his projects once they were off the drawing-board may have appeared for the first time in

17. Hippolyte Boyer, *La fondation de la ville de Henrichemont*, Bourges, 1873.

18. Hautecoeur, I, p. 356 *et seq.*

19. Leonardo, notes in the *Codex Atlanticus*, 'concerning houses forming cities'; Alberti, *De Re Aedificatoria*, 1485; Filarete, project for the ideal city of Sforzinda in his treatise on architecture, written *c.* 1457–1464, and widely circulated in manuscript, but not published until the nineteenth century; Pietro Cataneo, *Quattro Primi Libri di Architettura*.

20. Palissy, *Recepte veritable par laquelle les hommes de la France pourront apprendre à multiplier et augmenter leurs Tresors*, 1563; Palissy, among his practical 'receipts', includes some Italianate theoretical ones, 'le jardin delectable' and 'la Ville de Forteresse'; cf. also J. Perret, *Des fortifications et artifices d'architecture et perspective*, 1601. For summaries of the development of town-planning and the influences, cf. Hautecoeur, I, p. 578; Blunt, *Art and Architecture*, p. 98 and p. 262 n. 5, where the Sforza town of Vigevano, near Milan (*c.* 1550), is referred to as an expression of Alberti's ideas; See also J. Summerson *Inigo Jones*, Harmondsworth, 1966, pp. 85–86.

21. Cf. Cat., p. 223.

relation to this commission. He may not have been informed by the contractors of the difficulty in obtaining good building-materials; even if he did
know of the problem, as he did later with regard to similar conditions at
Coulommiers, he is unlikely to have worried about it much. Nevertheless,
if de Brosse ever did visit the site after some of his buildings were finished,
even he could scarcely have remained unmoved by the sight of what local
talent, working with local materials and inadequate guidance, could do with
his designs (Pl. 47).

Despite their naïve decoration the houses round the Place Henri IV, called
in the contract 'les huit pavillons de la Grande Place',[22] though most of them
are very much altered, still have a feeling of monumentality, achieved by their
simple solidity, their high massive roofs and good proportions (Pl. 46). They
were based on good models, for the contracts stipulated that their *portes-
cochères* should be measured according to those of the 'Place Roialle' (des
Vosges) in Paris, and that their windows should be the same as those of Sully's
Arsenal.

The so-called 'Maison du Procurateur Fiscal'[23] in one of the streets of the
town has been well restored (Pl. 48), and recent repair-work in one of the
houses on the Place Henri IV revealed details of original masonry in a powerful
style reminiscent of de Brosse's work in the forecourts at Verneuil and
Montceaux.[24] However, the houses at Henrichemont cannot be said to add a
great deal to de Brosse's stature as an architect except in so far as they show
in an early work his feeling for buildings with dignity and presence, and a
well-developed sense of composition revealed by the type and grouping of the
'pavillons' designed for the Place Henri IV.

Between 1600 and 1608 de Brosse's activities were unlikely to have been
confined to Verneuil and his work for Henriette, but we know very little
about his career at this time, although he may have been concerned with
Henri IV's and Sully's project for the Collège de France in Paris.[25] It is
probable that during this period he continued his connection with Montceaux,
either alone or in continued collaboration with his uncle, Jacques I du Cerceau,

22. Ibid.

23. Near this house is another, the so-called 'Hôtel des Monnaies', which is built to the same
design. In the nineteenth century a reconstruction-drawing was made of the houses of the Place
Henri IV, using the Maison du Procurateur-Fiscal and the Hôtel des Monnaies as a basis. The
design of the houses of the *Place* differed, however, from those in the streets, notably in having
no pilasters and in having *portes-cochères*.

24. This has unfortunately been covered over again. The Hôtel des Monnaies, mentioned in
n. 23 above, has also had its façade plastered over, hiding the original work.

25. Cf. Chap I, p. 4 and Cat. Appendix, p. 284.

for when Gabrielle died early in 1597 work at the château did not cease. In 1601 Henri acquired the estate from his children by Gabrielle, César and Henriette de Vendôme, and gave it to the new Queen, Marie de Médicis. For a long time he did not pay for it, still less did he provide funds for extensive building operations; nevertheless, work continued slowly. Sully recounts how, one day in 1602, the King was 'detained a little time at Montceaux by a fever, occasioned by a cold he got when walking late in the evening to see his masons at work'.[26] In 1600 and 1602 de Brosse signed documents with the title 'architecte' or 'ingénieur de la Reine', and in 1605 the Queen herself wrote of him as 'architecte de nos bâtiments', though she does not specifically mention Montceaux.[27]

It would certainly be rash to attribute any particular building at Montceaux to the period 1600–1608, since there is no certain documentary evidence to support either authorship or date. But two of the remaining parts of the château show an interesting mixture of late sixteenth-century and early seventeenth-century features, which suggests that they date from the earliest years of the new century. These are the portico and door of the south wing and the ground-floor of the north-east moat-pavilion.

The south-wing portico has two banded fluted columns which immediately recall Philibert de l'Orme's 'French Order' (Pl. 49). They are certainly derived from this, but if we compare the columns at Montceaux with any of those designed by de l'Orme, we can see that they are very different in detail. Indeed, the interlacing pattern of the bands on the columns at Montceaux is a motif which was to become widespread all through the first half of the seventeenth century. It seems to have originated in du Cerceau's engravings, but here at Montceaux it is not a flat linear decoration, and in contrast with de l'Orme's columns at the Tuileries it has a simpler theme and a more sculptural treatment (Pl. 50). Although the masonry of the upper part of the columns is badly eroded, there appears to have been a curious 'frill' at the top, above the final band and below the capital. It is as hard to judge what this motif was as to find any precedent to explain its appearance.

The door between the banded columns seems, at first glance, to be not unlike that of the *corps-de-logis* which is unfinished (Pls 51, 52). But there are some interesting differences. The composition of the *corps-de-logis* door derives directly from Lescot; the south-wing door, with its tympanum above,

26. Sully, *Mémoires*; cf. Cat. p. 228.
27. Cf. Cat. Chronology and Notes, p. 197, entry for 1605.

has no parallel in Lescot's work, nor indeed is it easy to find any exact sixteenth-century prototype for this composition.[28] Silvestre's drawings of the château, in which something of the court-façades can be seen (Pl. 53), show that above the banded columns and the main cornice there were, over the doors from the court to the wings, large square *tablettes*, apparently flanked by pilasters and surmounted by a semi-circular pediment. This is very close indeed to de Brosse's style, but it may belong to a later date than the rest of the frontispiece. The lintel of the door is made to protrude beyond the consoles with their foliage 'drops', and the profiles of the door-mouldings are more rounded, less thin and sharp, than the door and windows of the *corps-de-logis*, or the north-west pavilion. In the same way, the foliage-decoration of the consoles and the bean-pod motif in the side-scrolls are much more fleshy and sculptural in their treatment than the thin incisive decoration of the door and the windows of the *corps-de-logis* and the north-west pavilion. This difference is seen more clearly on the site, for, despite the perishing of much of the stone, some details remain remarkably clear; they are not, however, easy to photograph.

The moat-pavilions at Montceaux were designed before 1600, as is proved by a Gentilhâtre drawing which shows the H & G cipher above the door.[29] (Pl 57).The original form of these pavilions is best shown by Silvestre and Rigaud (Pls 54, 55); the first of them to be built, the so-called 'Pavillon Conti', survives and is the one in Silvestre's drawing. The first-floor, cornice and roof existing to-day are eighteenth-century work, and new windows were cut in the north and east walls at the same date. Otherwise the ground-floor is all original, although modern plaster rendering covers the brickwork of the entrance side (Pl. 56).

The pavilion as Silvestre shows it is of a type associated with de Brosse's later châteaux, and even the roof, which might be thought to be much later, is derived directly from du Cerceau's Third Book. The dormer windows, as a drawing by Gentilhâtre shows clearly, and as Silvestre and Rigaud indicate, had *tablettes* with curved pediments above the cornice, another motif familiar in de Brosse's later work; these dormers had large *oeils-de-boeuf*

28. Those which come to mind, but of which none is a door, are: certain Italian Renaissance tombs, such as that of Pius II in St Peter's, Rome; Bullant's gate at Ecouen; and the entrance-pavilion and N. wing Frontispiece of the *First Design* for Verneuil.

29. For dating of Gentilhâtre's drawings, in the R.I.B.A. Drawings Libary, cf. Cat. p. 230. The pavilion discussed here, the Pavilion Conti, was certainly the first built. In 1600 the *tempietti* of Philibert de l'Orme were still *in situ* on the W. terrace; later they were destroyed to make way for the new moat-pavilions. The S.E. pavilion was not commissioned until 1622; it survives in part with the stone panels awaiting decoration still uncut.

between them. The most interesting feature of the Pavillon Conti is the door shown in Gentilhâtre's drawing where, however, it is more decorated than in the executed work (Pls 57, 58, 60). The most noticeable difference is in the *voussoirs*, which as executed are quite plain; the lower ones on each side being 'bent round' and made to pass, as it were, behind the consoles, emerging to form part of the vertical rustication running down the side of the door. This emergence of the *voussoir* on the other side of the console is reminiscent of the treatment of the lintel in the south-wing door (Pl. 51). The keystone in the actual door does not, as in Gentilhâtre's drawing, protrude into the semicircular motif beneath. This semi-circular motif, which again recalls the form of the opening over the south-wing door, is copied from one of the fireplaces at Verneuil, engraved by du Cerceau. The mouldings are strong, the principal one emphatically rounded in profile and beautifully cut. Instead of the indeterminate strapwork decoration within the semi-circle shown by Gentilhâtre, there is a shell which, before it became worn away, would have added to the three-dimensional effect. In contrast to the door drawn by Gentilhâtre, the executed door is clear and unambiguous in treatment – and it is quite unlike any known work by Jacques II du Cerceau.

The sculptured decoration of the consoles of this door are very worn, but it is clear from the cutting of the decorative panel beside the door that it and the door-consoles were done by the same hand as the decoration of the south-wing door (Pls 51, 59). It is interesting that the photograph of the Porte Henri IV at Verneuil (Pl. 25) suggests that the decoration in the keystone and the pediment was close to this work at Montceaux.

From 1608 onwards the exact chronology of the buildings at Montceaux is as difficult to establish as what went on there between 1600 and 1608, but the attribution of the work presents no problem.

On 7 September 1608 the Queen wrote to her overseer at Montceaux, M. de Verdilly, referring to '. . . les bastimens et eddiffices auquelz nous faisons continuellement travailler . . .'. In 1609 she appointed a concierge for the forecourt, '. . . la grande bassecour qui se construit à présent audict Montceaux', and wrote of Salomon de Brosse as 'mon architecte . . . de mes officiers servans à Montceaux'. By 1610 she could tell Marguerite de Valois, '. . . vous trouverez à Montceaux tant de changemens depuis que vous n'y êtes venue que vous ne le recognoistrez plus . . .'. Work had begun again at the château on a really large scale and de Brosse was in charge. In the building estimates for 1613 he is described as 'spécialement affecté à Montceaux'.

The King had at last paid Gabrielle's children for Montceaux, and agreed to provide the Queen with money for building there. The occasion for this generosity was the birth of their third son, and Sully was asked to find the money; '(the King) allowed at the request of this Princess that ten or twelve thousand crowns should be expended on the buildings at Montceaux and sent me orders to that purpose . . . This . . . he repeated when the Master Builder, who had undertaken the work, informed him that he had been obliged, through want of money, to dismiss his men . . . the King sent me orders . . . to advance the Master Builder the money . . .'.[30]

The forecourt was never completed, and today only half the south range remains, very much altered (Pls 61, 67). Silvestre's engraving (Pl. 62) shows what was actually built; the rest was never even begun (though some pirated versions of Silvestre's engravings show it complete).

Save for its size and symmetry the plan of the court is unremarkable. The contemporary Cour des Offices at Fontainebleau (1606–1609) by Rémy Collin (who worked at Montceaux in 1597–1599) has a far more interesting lay-out on plan.[31] A comparison of the elevations, however, shows that de Brosse had more skill in the composition of various buildings grouped round a large area; a talent he had already exercised in the Place Henri IV at Henrichemont. His use of detail also is more in keeping with the scale than Collin's. The buildings at Montceaux, like those at Henrichemont, could dominate the great space they enclosed, because they were kept massive and simple. To give the façade more interest, the central window-bays of each *corps-de-batiment* were placed in groups of three, as Silvestre shows (Pls 61, 62). The triple window-bays were separated from each other and from the single bays at the ends of each block by narrow stone strips which divided the brick facing into panels, two narrow and three wide, echoing the verticals of the pilasters on the two end-pavilions. Unfortunately this arrangement was broken up in the nineteenth century, when the remaining wing was converted into a dwelling.

There were to be three great entrance-arches leading into the court, the grandest feature of the composition, but only one was built, most of which remains (Pl. 65). These arches were in pavilions separated from the main ranges, and were themselves flanked by low pavilions, of which a part survives. The whole composition can be seen in miniature in Silvestre's view. In this arrangement of the arch-within-an-arch de Brosse has repeated the ideas worked out for the entrance-pavilion at Verneuil.

There is another interesting comparison between the Montceaux forecourt and Collin's Court at Fontainebleau. At Montceaux the entrance loses

30. Sully, *Mémoires*; cf. Cat. p. 228.
31. This will be discussed by the author in a forthcoming publication.

nothing of its dignity and impact through extraneous ornament, and the sturdy widely-spaced rustication is used with logic and restraint to enhance the monumentality of the structure. The entrance-niche of the Cour des Offices (Pl. 64) is equally monumental, if sheer size alone is considered, but its dramatic quality is lessened by the fussy treatment of the rustication which is applied in bits and pieces, not logically, and solely as decoration. It distracts the eye and breaks up the plane surface in an irritating manner. De Brosse knew when to leave well alone, whereas Collin did not.

These two courts, so close in date, have been spoken of together to show how far de Brosse had succeeded by 1609 in breaking away from a decorative and two-dimensional approach to architecture, and in eliminating the inessential. Collin produced a striking design at Fontainebleau, but his treatment of it reveals that he had not gone far beyond the conventions of the late sixteenth century. Nevertheless, in fairness to Collin as well as further to stress de Brosse's achievement, one can compare both these courts of 1609 with the range of buildings designed for Henri IV for the château of Blois about 1595 (Pl. 63). This design, which embodies all that was worst in the mannerism of the late sixteenth century, shows that Collin had made considerable strides, and that de Brosse's advance was truly remarkable.[32]

One of the pavilions, with which it was intended to terminate the long wings of the court to north and south, was actually built at Montceaux, and still exists almost in its original condition (Pls 67, 68). It contained, and still contains, the chapel meant for the use of those accommodated in the forecourt. The façade is original; the side-windows are eighteenth-century, and were probably given their present form when the chapel was 'beautified' for the Prince de Conti, to whom Louis XVI gave Montceaux in 1783. The masonry of the exterior apse also clearly belongs to a different period from the body of the chapel (Pl. 66), but it is probably simply a reconstruction, since an apse appears on the plan of Montceaux made in 1724 and the interior proportions would have been peculiar had the chapel been contained in a square box-like pavilion.[33]

The façade of the chapel, like the Porte Henri IV at Verneuil, shows Vignola's influence – in this case in a curiously direct way. It seems scarcely

32. The proposed buildings at Fontainebleau which he dates 1594–1597 are discussed by F. Lesueur, 'Projets inconnus pour la reconstruction du Château de Blois', *G.d.B.A.*, LIX, March 1962, pp. 129–142.

33. The 1724 plan shows that the projection southwards of the chapel including the apse is only fractionally greater than that of the square pavilion at the far end of the wing. Had the chapel also been square, its lesser projection would have been definitely noticeable, and made the S. façade asymmetrical.

possible that the resemblance between de Brosse's façade and that of the Vignolesque church of Santa Maria del Piano at Capranica in Italy[34] can be purely coincidental. Both are ultimately derived from Serlio's 'Tempio a Tivoli', but resemble each other more than either resembles the Serlio engraving. This may be another example of the influence upon de Brosse of a drawing brought back from his travels by an admirer of Vignola.

Instead of the Corinthian order of Serlio's 'Tempio', and the Ionic of Santa Maria del Piano, de Brosse has used the Doric, which he was always to prefer. The proportions of his façade forced him to omit the proper Doric frieze, leaving only a vestigial remainder over each pilaster.[35] Nevertheless, as an essay in classicism this façade is well in advance of the work of any of his contemporaries. It is also less flat and linear than the one at Capranica, the niches are larger, and more sweeping, which gives a satisfying sculptural effect to the whole composition. It is interesting to compare this treatment with the sculptural effect achieved by de l'Orme in the *cryptoporticus* at Anet (Pl. 2), a comparison which is even more relevant when we come to look at the interior of the chapel which de Brosse built in the entrance pavilion of the château itself (Pl. 72).

If we may assume that the reconstructed exterior apse followed de Brosse's original design, one characteristic of his handling of the applied orders, which remained consistent all his life, is seen for the first time in the façade and the apse of this chapel;[36] the pilasters stop just short of the corners of the building which therefore show through (Pl. 66). This break is followed up through the mouldings of the entablature and the cornice, and the effect of the whole undeniably weakens the impact of a part of the structure whose strength should be emphasized. At Ancy-le-Franc Serlio had brought the pilasters right up to the corner on each face, an arrangement which poses no problems where the Doric order is used, as at Montceaux (Pl. 9).

In the main château at Montceaux de Brosse doubled the entrance-screen, making a terrace-walk along it; he enlarged the entrance-pavilion and built a chapel on the first floor to which the screen-terrace gave access. He widened the centre of the south wing to accommodate a Salle des Spectacles, and built a big semi-circular staircase between this and the south-east pavilion. He also built the three great bridges over the moat, which still exist, their gates

34. The church at Capranica is illustrated by M. Walcher-Casotti, *Il Vignola*, 1960; II, fig. 170. She does not consider it sufficiently well-documented for a direct attribution to Vignola.

35. The width of the frieze does not allow for the correct spacing of triglyphs and metopes. The uncut stones in the frieze suggest that he intended some other form of decoration.

36. If we discount the Maison du Procurateur-Fiscal at Henrichemont, where no doubt the local builder had misunderstood most things.

and guard-houses; he erected a large *jeu-de-paume* near the second terrace, and was responsible for other outlying buildings.

It is, however, difficult to assign any of this work to an exact date. The accounts of Marie de Médicis' treasurer, Florent d'Argouges, for 1616–1620, which concern work at Montceaux survive, but the only important building for which they give a date is the completion of the interior of the entrance-pavilion in 1617. There is to be found no record of new buildings, apart from the *jeu-de-paume*, so that de Brosse's work at Montceaux must have been nearly all planned well before 1616.

It is possible that Marie de Médicis decided to install her apartments and state rooms at the eastern end of the south range, which would have given her easy access to the Salle des Spectacles and to the first-floor rooms of the south-east pavilion, by way of the new great staircase (Pls 39–41). This semi-circular stair is, as far as we know, unique in de Brosse's work. It may have been inspired by some of the staircase designs of Serlio and Jacques I du Cerceau, though none is exactly like this.[37] There was not to be another example of such a staircase in France until 1652, when Antoine le Pautre published one in his designs for châteaux.[38]

If the Queen's apartments were in the south-east pavilion,[39] she would then have been able to pass easily along the screen-terrace to the chapel-royal in the entrance-pavilion.

In the nineteenth century two fairly complete bays of the inner arcade of the screen survived and were recorded. From a drawing made in 1883[40] and from the little which remains of them today, we can see that the arcade was a later addition to the court side of the entrance-front. On the plan it cuts right across an earlier flight of steps to the north-east angle-pavilion.

The arcade had sharply rusticated arches, contrasting with the rounded bosses of the piers, which were decorated with brick panels (Pl. 70). It was probably modelled on the one which doubled the screen in the *Second Design* for Verneuil, though it appears to have been sturdier and simpler. On all the evidence it seems to date from the period after 1609.

Traces of the original entrance-pavilion of 1597–1599 can be seen among

37. Closest is Serlio, 'True Sixth Book', Plan XVII.

38. This staircase was never executed. I am obliged for this information to Mrs Mary Whiteley. It is possible that the Montceaux stair is a later addition and not de Brosse's work, but in view of the building-history of the château this seems very unlikely.

39. In the eighteenth-century descriptions of Montceaux, the *corps-de-logis* was described as unfinished (as its main door still is) and with its chimneys unblackened by smoke. Marie de Médicis presumably, therefore, never used it.

40. Cf. Cat. p. 230.

the ruins of the present structure, notably where the arcade, the screen-terrace and the later entrances to the chapel in the re-designed first floor cut across the earlier pilasters (once decorated with brick panels) on the side of the pavilion. The entrances to the chapel rise from the screen-terrace, flanked by massive rusticated piers and, near these, in the angles, can be seen thin strips and roundels of brick-inlay, probably part of the unfinished first-floor of the 1590s.

The original entrance-pavilion was enlarged on the court and forecourt sides by the addition of a frontispiece (Pl. 69). The central entrance-arch, with the large chapel-window over it and the niches which flanked it, were framed by four colossal Corinthian columns. Among the decorative devices of these frontispieces were the royal crown and the interlaced double-M cipher of Marie de Médicis.

De Brosse may have been inspired here by Bullant's gallery at La Fère (Pl. 10) and his south-wing portico at Ecouen, as well as by the du Cerceau tradition of monumental columned entrances such as we have seen in the designs for Verneuil. Another possible source may be the designs for triumphal entrances in the first part of de l'Orme's Eighth Book. De Brosse never used the colossal order in this way again, but at Montceaux he needed it to balance the existing columned frontispiece of the *corps-de-logis* across the courtyard (Pl. 71). The great columns of de Brosse's pavilion have a type of fluting with convex fillings which, though not infrequently used in Italy and in France for the lower part of a column, was rarely carried all the way up as it is here.

All the upper part of the entrance-pavilion has gone, but Silvestre's drawing shows the cornice, the segmental pediments over the chapel doors and the big *oeil-de-boeuf*, the curve of which, breaking up through the balustrade above the chapel-window, was repeated by a concentric rusticated frame surmounted by a typical de Brosse motif, a *tablette* with scroll-supports and segmental pediment. The vertically-ribbed dome was crowned by a double lantern (Pl. 53).

Although its brick-and-stone decorative detail was not particularly original or distinguished, the entrance-pavilion was very successful as a composition. The engravings and drawings of it, though not accurate in all details, justly convey the sense of solid grandeur achieved here by de Brosse.

Within the pavilion, the chapel occupied a space slightly smaller than the room beneath. This reduction in size enabled de Brosse to use the extra thickness of masonry to describe within the oval plan (Pl. 40) a series of six shallow sweeping curves, four of which had large niches hollowed out of them. This manipulation of space within the comparatively small chapel must have been singularly impressive, and even today in its ruined state one can see how accomplished it was and how beautiful were the swinging curving lines (Pl. 72). The niches, over which were heavy consoles and garlands, show the sculptural treatment already noticed in the forecourt-chapel façade.

The interior of the chapel dates from 1617, as d'Argouges' accounts reveal, and it is more advanced in style and far more accomplished than anything else at Montceaux. It was probably influenced not only by the oval plans of Serlio and the elder du Cerceau, but also by de l'Orme's chapel at Anet and the interior elevation of the chapels in the Valois Mausoleum at Saint Denis (Pl. 7); its position, form and decoration were all later to influence François Mansart.[41]

Of the great Salle des Spectacles in the south wing we know nothing, save that it was large and 'voutée en calotte'. But its plan (Pl. 39), of seven bays, suggests that it may have been a forerunner of the seven-bayed Grand' Salle of the Palais du Parlement at Rennes. Rigaud's engraving (Pl. 55) shows de Brosse's extension to the south wing in which this Salle was contained. He also shows, better than Silvestre, the octaganol *guérites*, or guard-houses, at each side of the bridge-gates, which are a development of the gate-houses and the Porte Henri IV at Verneuil (Pls 23, 25). The gates themselves belong to the next chapter, where a very important sequence of designs made by de Brosse between about 1609 and 1614 will be discussed.

Montceaux was never really finished, and by 1656 it was tumbling down, for by then it was considered too old-fashioned and inconvenient to repair or use. When the King gave it to the Prince de Conti in 1783, the buildings of the main court, which the villagers had been using as grain-stores, were converted into kennels for hunting dogs. During the Revolution the château was confiscated and, save for the forecourt, pulled down. There is a local tradition that the villagers and the demolition-contractor decided to leave enough fragments standing on each side of the court to show how splendid the buildings had been. It is fortunate that what was left remains today, preserved and cared for, and also that we have adequate written and graphic records to enable us to make a fair reconstruction of Montceaux as it was completed by de Brosse. For his buildings, with their combination of old and new influences, mark an important stage in his career, and in the development of early seventeenth-century classicism in France.

41. The whole question of de Brosse's influence upon Mansart, will be dealt with by Dr Peter Smith and Dr Allan Braham in their forthcoming book on the architect.

CHAPTER IV

Private Houses in Paris, 1608–1618

BETWEEN 1608 and 1618 de Brosse received commissions to work on six hôtels in Paris – and there may have been more – but as far as we know he never had the opportunity to build an entirely new one. The times were still not yet tranquil enough for the encouragement of large private building enterprises in the capital; the great era of hôtel-building did not begin until after de Brosse's death. Meanwhile, the nobility and the wealthier members of the *noblesse de robe* sought to restore town-houses which had fallen into disrepair or had been damaged during the Wars of Religion. This also provided an opportunity for alterations and extensions.

All the hôtels upon which de Brosse is known to have worked, save two, lay within a short distance of one another in the streets west of Saint Eustache[1] (Pl. 73); the exceptions, the Hôtel de Bouillon (later Liancourt) and the Hôtel de Fresne were respectively in the Rue de Seine, across the river opposite the Louvre, and in the Rue Saint-Honoré. All six have totally disappeared,[2] and even before they were demolished they were undoubtedly much altered and modified as successive owners sought to adapt them to fashion or convenience.

Fortunately a few engravings and some descriptions of these buildings survive, and in recent years various contracts and records of payment have been discovered. Thus we can to some extent trace de Brosse's contribution to them, but our knowledge is still sadly incomplete.[3] Nevertheless these

1. Now part of the Quartier des Halles, an extensive topographical and historical study of which is in preparation in France under the direction of Professor André Chastel.

2. The late Dr Constance Tooth (cf. below n. 15) believed that part of a building visible within an hôtel on the north side of the Rue des Beaux-Arts was a relic of the Hôtel de Liancourt, but this has not been verified, and it is in any case inaccessible.

3. See Catalogue: Hôtel Bénigne Bernard, p. 238, Hôtel de Bouillon, p. 241, Hôtel de Bullion, p. 245, Hôtel de Fresne, p. 248, Hôtel du Lude, p. 249, Hôtel de Soissons, p. 251. The Hôtel de Fresne was, until now, entirely unknown either as a building or as a work of de Brosse. The contract for it was communicated to me (by Mme F. Boudon) after the completion of the final draft of this chapter and notes. No sources, therefore, are quoted in the notes, but those relevant to the owner, Forget de Fresne, will be found in the Catalogue entry, together with the reference to the contract. Cf. Cat, p. 248 for Fauvelet du Toc's book, referred to below, p. 59, in connection with the Hôtel de Fresne.

scanty records are important, for they help to fill a serious gap in our knowledge of developments in hôtel-design before 1627, in which year François Mansart probably began work on his first town-house, the Hôtel de l'Aubespine.[4]

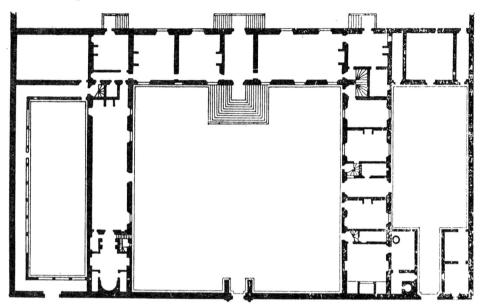

Fig. 1.   Serlio. Fontainebleau. The Grand Ferrare. Plan

The general pattern for the French town-house had been set by the Grand Ferrare, built by Serlio at Fontainebleau in 1544–1546 (Fig. 1). The scheme of this house was basically a château-plan adapted to an urban setting: a *corps-de-logis* at the end of a courtyard, wings on either side, and an entrance-screen pierced by a large gateway. To one side of this lay the *basse-cour*, and behind the *corps-de-logis* was normally the garden, though this is sometimes found on the other side of the courtyard, balancing the *basse-cour*. Upon this basic arrangement variants were introduced, and in de Brosse's day ideas were still evolving which contributed to the form of the typical mid-seventeenth-century hôtel.

Before he came to France Serlio had spent some fourteen years in Venice and the Veneto, an environment which greatly influenced his *Fourth Book* (the first to be published). Among other things, he had been impressed by

4. I am indebted for information on the hôtels of this period and of the later sixteenth century to Dr Peter Smith's *François Mansart as a designer of Hôtels*, a thesis in the University of London, 1965.

the large rusticated doorways which led from the streets into the courtyards
of important town-houses in the Veneto: 'Come in molti luoghi d'Italia si
vede lungo le strade al dirimpetto di alcuna nobil casa per serraglio del cortile;
perciochè simili danno gran presenza a tai luoghi'.[5] This admiration and
recommendation is reflected in the large rusticated entrance set in a screen at
the Grand Ferrare, and it was to exert a considerable influence upon de Brosse.
(Pl. 8). It must also have influenced the entrance built about 1548 to the
Hôtel de Ligneris (later Carnavalet) in Paris, attributed to Lescot and decorated
by Goujon. But although an imposing entrance on to the street was becoming
fashionable for the important town-house in the later sixteenth century, it
was usually not very well set apart or distinguishable from the buildings
which crowded in on either side along the street.[6] An example of a fine
entrance from the first years of the seventeenth century is the still-surviving
entrance of the Hôtel d'Almeyras in the Rue des Francs-Bourgeois.[7] But
neither at the Hôtel de Ligneris nor at the Hôtel d'Almeyras does the doorway
rise through two storeys.

Sauval was right therefore when he said, describing the door which de
Brosse built at the Hôtel de Soissons: 'jusques là personne en France ne s'étoit
avisé de parer les entrées des Palais de Portaux d'une grandeur si extraordinaire
et si majesteuse, car celui est le premier'. He also recognized that it was through
de Brosse's work that such *portes-cochères* became widely popular, and more
and more of a prominent feature, set apart as much as possible from neighbouring buildings as a focus of admiration and an indication of the owner's
status. It was, however, not merely the size but the style of de Brosse's doors
which was important for the future development of this feature of the French
town-house.

The earliest record of a private house upon which de Brosse worked is a
contract for the Hôtel de Fresne in the Rue Saint Honoré. It has not yet been
possible to determine its position in this street, but it may have stood in the
short stretch of it which lies north-east of the Louvre. No representation of
it has so far been identified and, until the recent discovery of the contract,
all record of it had been lost.

Pierre Forget de Fresne, who in 1608 commissioned de Brosse to design
considerable extensions to his town-house, was one of Henri IV's four
Secrétaires d'Etat. He was also a patron of men of letters and held literary

5. IV, p. 132, *molti luoghi d'Italia* can be confined to the Veneto, where such doors had been
in use since the later Quattrocento. Cf. Rosci/Brizio, op. cit., p. 42.
6. Cf. J.-P. Babelon, *Demeures parisiennes sous Henri IV et Louis XIII*, Paris, 1965, p. 140 ff.
7. Illustrated ibid., pl. p. 147.

meetings at his house. In the 1590s the King had made him Intendant of the Bâtiments Royals for a particular, and for us, very interesting reason. Fauvelet du Toc, historian of the Secretaries of State, writing in 1668, says, '. . . le Roy l'honora de la charge d'Intendant de ses bastiments et luy donna en cette qualité la conduite du magnifique chasteau de Monceaux, comme il estoit allié de celle qui en portoit le nom et qui possedoit le plus absoluement les bonnes graces de Sa Majesté . . .' (the person referred to as bearing the title of the Montceaux is, of course, Gabrielle d'Estrées).

Forget de Fresne, as Secrétaire d'Etat, was responsible for drafting the Edict of Nantes in 1598, and during the remainder of his tenure of office he dealt with all Protestant affairs in France. Although himself a Catholic, as all holders of his office had to be, he understood the aims and problems of the Protestants and was always active in obtaining peace and justice for them.

After a long and honourable career Forget sought retirement in 1608, and in this year he was negotiating the sale of his office to Charles de l'Aubespine for 60,000 écus. Marie de Médicis, however, opposed this and put forward her own candidate, Phélypaux de Pontchartrain, who obtained the post after Henri IV's death. Forget de Fresne survived his master by only two months and died in June 1610.

In 1608, therefore, when de Brosse started work on his hôtel, de Fresne expected soon to receive a large sum of money from de l'Aubespine, and presumably intended to use part of this to prepare his house for the years of his retirement. His choice of de Brosse as his architect indicates that he had been favourably impressed by him at Montceaux in the 1590s. He would presumably also have seen the designs which de Brosse was making for Marie de Médicis' *basse-cour* at the château. Whether or not de Brosse had already been employed at the Hôtel de Soissons we do not know, for the extent and the date of his work there is uncertain. However, if he had, Forget may also have been influenced by what de Brosse had done for Charles de Soissons.

The 1608 contract for the Hôtel de Fresne is signed by Claude Pouillet, master-mason of Paris. In the last paragraph it is stipulated that Pouillet shall only receive such payment as is authorized by the patron and the architect: '. . . de faire tous les ouvrages dont il ne sera payé aucune chose sans l'ordonnance expresse, signée de la main dudict seigneur et du Sieur de Brosse, architecte qui a fait le devis'.

The contract is for an extension, thirty-three feet long, to the existing *corps-de-logis*, part of which was to be demolished. It is expressly laid down that the roof-line of the old and new buildings is to be unified, '. . . sous le même toit ou comble'. The style was to continue that of the former building with plinth, window-bays, 'chaines faisant parement en forme de pilastre', and entablature, all of stone, presumably on brick, '. . . comme il est ja faict et aussy porté par le desaing'. But in one respect the new building is to improve on the old; it is to have a correct type of cornice: '. . . Et d'autant qu'il n'y a poinct de corniches au viel logis mais est levé en pignon, se fera une corniche de belle ordonnance avec des modillons convenables . . . comme est porté par le desaing'. This cornice is then to be extended along the old *corps-de-logis*. New stone *lucarnes* are to be placed over the cornice and are also catered for in the 'desaing'. The façade on to the stable-court behind the building is to be astylar, with a plinth, string-courses and cornice of stone.

In the centre of the newly-constituted *corps-de-logis* large doorways, eight feet wide, are to be built leading into a passage which led from the main to the stable-court, '. . . pour entrer les carrosses et harnois'. *Portes-cochères*, in fact, whose position also indicates that at the Hôtel de Fresne the staircase was not placed in the centre of the main block. These *portes-cochères* were not designed to project and do not appear to have been particularly interesting in design.

The contract mentions a 'desaing' for the staircase, but does not specify where it is to be built, nor of what type it is to be.

In addition to the *corps-de-logis* de Brosse designed a small building with a passage through the centre of it from the stable-court to the street beyond, and with an exterior newel-staircase leading to a little gallery and rooms over the stables. Two more stone *portes-cochères* were to be built for the passage to the street.

The disposition and appearance of the Hôtel de Fresne, which are clearly set out in this contract, have been dealt with in some detail, not only because they are all the evidence we have about this building by de Brosse, but to make identification easier if any plan or elevation should in future come to light.

In the first years of the seventeenth century, Charles de Bourbon, Comte de Soissons, lived in an hôtel which stood opposite the gardens of the great town-house which Jean Bullant had built for Catherine de Médicis near the church of Saint Eustache. Catherine's hôtel later belonged to Henri IV's widowed sister, the Duchesse de Bar, who died in 1604. The Comte de Soissons had wished to marry Madame de Bar, but was forbidden to do so by Henri IV on political and religious grounds. In 1605 he bought her house, out of sentiment it was said, and sold his old hôtel to the Duc de Montpensier. The house built for Catherine de Médicis became thenceforward the Hôtel de Soissons, and the former Hôtel de Soissons eventually became the Hôtel Séguier.[8] Soissons lived only eight years in his new house, dying in 1612, but he undertook some building there, the exact nature and extent of which is not, however, known. He is believed to have renovated, or rebuilt, the *cour carrée*, the courtyard in which stood Bullant's famous observatory column.[9]

The *cour-carrée* opened on the Rue des Deux-Ecus (Pl. 74), and it was probably here that de Brosse built the *porte-cochère* referred to by Sauval. A drawing of it is in the Nationalmuseum, Stockholm, and its date is confirmed by the presence on the panels of the door of the cipher of Charles de Soissons and of his wife Anne de Montafié (Pl. 75). What else de Brosse may have done at the hôtel we do not know, and Sauval's remark that the door harmonized with the buildings around it is not much help as an indication whether or not these buildings were by de Brosse.[10]

Sauval's description of the door is worth quoting here at length because it contains some important details: '. . . On y entre par un portail aussi grand que superbe, et quoique' imité de celui du Palais Farnèse à Caprarolle, il passe néanmoins pour un des chefs-d'oeuvres de Salomon de Brosse l'un des meilleurs Architectes de notre temps.[11] Il est simple, rustique, fort haut, fort large et très bien proportionné à l'étendue, aussi-bien qu'à l'ordonnance du logis . . . tout ce qui lui manque, est de n'être pas dressé dans une rue plus large ou vis-à-vis de quelque rue, afin qu'on le vit mieux et qu'il fit ce bel effect qui rend son original si considerable'. He continues, concerning *portails*, '. . . on ne les avoit point encore élevés au-dessus du premier étage; mais celui-ci ne fut pas plutôt achevé qu'il parut si superbe aux yeux des Architectes et si considerable à la face d'une grande maison que ne les ayant d'abord employés qu'aux logis des grands Seigneurs, depuis ils les ont rendus si communs et même ont passés à un tel excès et pour la hauteur et pour la largeur . . . qu'on pourroit dire aujourd'hui de quelques-uns, ce que Diogènes

8. The old Hôtel de Soissons was sold by Montpensier in 1612 to the Duc de Bellegarde, who had it rebuilt by Jacques II du Cerceau. The Chancelier Séguier bought it in 1633. The histories of the successive Hôtels de Soissons have been confused, notably by Hautecoeur in his *Architecture Classique*. In his Index (I, p. 877) all references under Paris, (Hôtels); de Soissons, after p. 541, except the notes on pp. 766, 792 and 803, are really to the Hôtel Séguier. The plate which he publishes on p. 543 is not of the Hôtel de Soissons. For the Hôtel Séguier see below p. 65.

9. I am indebted to Mme H. Dumuis for unpublished information on the Hôtel de Soissons courtyard, in a thesis presented at the Institut d'Art et Archéologie, Paris.

10. Sauval, II, p. 216: 'un portail . . . très-bien proportionné à l'étendue, aussi-bien qu'à l'ordonnance du logis . . .'; (from the passage quoted below).

11. It must be remembered that although Sauval's book was not published until 1724 he actually wrote most of the printed text in *c.* 1649-1652.

dit aux Ninydiens, qui à leurs petites Villes avoient fait de si grandes portes:
Fermez vos portes au plus vite, de crainte que la ville ne sorte.'

The plans and the elevations of the hôtel by Gomboust and others indicate
that the *porte-cochère* at the Hôtel de Soissons was set in a façade and not in a
screen like Serlio's at the Grand Ferrare. Nevertheless, de Brosse's design was
eminently suited to the screen-entrance which later architects were to develop
from this prototype. An interesting example of a door strongly influenced by
de Brosse, and set in a screen, was that of the Hôtel Séguier, built after 1633
by Jean du Cerceau.[12]

'Imité de celui du Palais Farnèse à Caprarole', says Sauval of the Hôtel de
Soissons door. It is in fact a variant of two designs: Vignola's celebrated
door at Caprarola, and the entrance to the Palazzo Grimani, Rome, which
he published in the *Porte di Michelangelo*. So here we meet again, early in
de Brosse's career, the same Vignolesque influence, even stronger and more
specific, that we encountered in the Porte Henri IV at Verneuil and the forecourt-chapel at Montceaux. This influence might not seem surprising, since
Vignola's *Cinque Ordini* and *Porte di Michelangelo* had been in print since 1562,
but the fact remains that until de Brosse began his career these publications had
had a negligible effect upon French architects.

The manner in which de Brosse adapted the two original designs reveals
certain highly personal touches. For instance, he carries the rustication on
behind the pilasters and across the other side in unbroken lines. This logical
treatment of rustication, even in small details, became a characteristic of
his style throughout his life. An order of fluted pilasters is substituted for
the columns of Vignola's door at the Palazzo Grimani, and this makes the
design much thinner and less three-dimensional. While such a transposition
is uncharacteristic of de Brosse in general, it is explained in this context by
the fact that, as Sauval says, the door gave on to a narrow street; it could
not be admired from any distance, and so it would have been unsuitable
to have introduced a deeply-cut or elaborately sculptured design. De Brosse
has also abandoned the heavy modillions of the Caprarola door and substituted dentils in the cornice, possibly on the pattern of another Vignola
door, at the Cancelleria.

Above the cornice de Brosse has adapted the crowning motif of the Palazzo
Grimani door to his own idiom, and this arrangement of a tablet with an
inscription or escutcheon, crowned by a pediment and sometimes supported
by seated figures, recurs repeatedly in de Brosse's own works and in those

12. Two drawings closely connected with this are in the du Ry (so-called 'de Brosse') album
in the Louvre, and the Gentilhâtre album in the R.I.B.A.

of his followers.[13] The Italian ancestry of the design is perfectly clear, but at the same time, de Brosse has transformed the combined composition into something unmistakably French.

In 1610, Henri de la Tour d'Auvergne, Duc de Bouillon and Prince de Sedan, bought the old Hôtel Dauphin in the Rue de Seine near Saint-Germain-des-Prés (Pls 76, 77). This powerful and turbulent member of the Protestant nobility commissioned de Brosse, in 1612, to enlarge the hôtel and to re-model part of the old *corps-de-logis* to conform with the new extensions. Besides the additions to the *corps-de-logis* there were to be two pavilions on the garden side. One, in fact, was already built, presumably by de Brosse, for the contract states 'un pavillon à l'encognure vers ledit meur mitoyen servant de simetrie à l'autre à present levé de neuf'. New chimney-pieces were to be built in various rooms, and the existing staircase continued up to the new second floor of the *corps-de-logis*. Along the garden-front a paved terrace was to be laid out, with a balustrade all along its length, interrupted by a flight of steps leading down into the garden. It is not certain whether this contract covered in detail all the work carried out at this period; it provided for payments totalling 25,000 livres to be paid at intervals. De Brosse was architect and contractor, promising to undertake 'les ouvraiges de maçonnerie . . . declairez au devis cy devant escript en l'hostel dudict sieur duc, . . . selon le plan et desseing de ce faict . . .'.[14]

A great deal must remain conjectural about the Hôtel de Bouillon as far as de Brosse's work there is concerned; the house was later bought by Roger du Plessis, Marquis (later Duc) de Liancourt, who pulled down most of what de Brosse had built.[15]

De Brosse appears to have been responsible for the whole garden-front as shown by Silvestre and Marot (Pl. 78), except for the central triple-arched entrance and balcony (which replaced a new door built by de Brosse and mentioned in the 1612 contract), and the two small *cabinets* supported on *trompes* at either side of the pavilions.[16] The façade of the small *corps-de-logis* giving on to the *basse-cour*, shown in Marot's engraving to the left of the later (principal) staircase, is probably also part of de Brosse's work (Pl. 79).

13. There are many such designs, for example, in both the du Ry ('de Brosse') and the 'Derand' albums in the Louvre, and in the Gentilhâtre album in the R.I.B.A. For these albums cf. Chap. V p. 87 and n. 4; Cat. p. 219, and ibid, p. 230.

14. Cf. J.-P. Babelon, '*Documents inédits concernant Salomon de Brosse*,' B.S.H.A.F., 1962, p. 142 ff.

15. The principal sources of information are *The Private Houses of Louis le Vau*, by the late Dr Constance Tooth (thesis in the University of London, 1961, pp. 149–173) and the notes made on this by Dr Peter Smith in the light of later information. Pl. 77 is by Dr Smith; based on Marot's plan it was originally intended to demonstrate the various building-periods at the hôtel.

16. As Dr Smith has pointed out, these *cabinets* are typical of Lemercier and like those which he introduced on the garden-front of the Château de Richelieu.

Although it is not mentioned in the 1612 contract, it is on stylistic grounds fairly certain that de Brosse built the original entrance-front of the Hôtel de Bouillon which can be seen in the plans and in Marot's section (Pls 77,80), hidden behind Lemercier's later front, which unlike the previous one followed the diagonal line of the street.[17] It is, basically, a screen with a narrow gallery above it, pierced by an entrance-pavilion in the centre. Two vestibules lead off at right-angles to the entrance and on the court side two small pavilions containing staircases are linked to the entrance by quadrant curves hollowed into niches. The introduction by de Brosse in 1613, one year after he began work at this hôtel, of quadrant-arcades in the courtyard at Coulommiers is the strongest reason for the attribution to him of this entrance-front. De Brosse's arrangement was both ingenious and original, and it is unfortunate that we have no more adequate representation of it. The staircases were necessary, for at that date the principal stair was in the *corps-de-logis*, so that these two would give direct access to the wings. Whether de Brosse also built the wings we do not know, but they are not specified in the 1612 contract.[18]

In 1614, Bénigne Bernard, Baron de Beaune, a not particularly prominent member of the *noblesse de robe*, employed de Brosse to enlarge his house in the Rue Coquillière.[19] In the past there has been some doubt about the site of this property,[20] but a sale-contract, recently discovered in the Archives Nationales,

17. The intervention of Lemercier as architect at the Hôtel de Bouillon (Liancourt) is not certainly documented, but there are many hints of it, and the style of the 1630s building supports the theory. Marot's engraving of the entrance-front (not published in *Le Grand Marot* or *Le Petit Marot*) bears the inscription 'Vue et perspective de l'hostel de Liancourt lors qu'il sera parachevé du dessin de Mr Mercier Architecte du Roy'.

18. Unfortunately Gomboust, usually accurate enough, is no help for the appearance of the hôtel in 1652. The garden-front is quite incorrect, there are no quadrants in the court, and the *basse-cour* is omitted altogether. The Abbé Delagrive (Pl. 76) made a more accurate block-plan in 1729.

19. The other patrons who employed de Brosse on their town-houses were more important and distinguished persons who even at that date were justified in using the title 'hôtel' for their houses. Bénigne Bernard had no such pretensions, and though now referred to as 'l'Hôtel Bénigne Bernard', it would not have been so called in his day. It was not until later that the bourgeoisie adopted the name 'hôtel'; Séguier was among the first to do so and was mocked for it. Cf. J.-P. Babelon, *Demeures parisiennes*, p. 117.

20. Ibid., p. 268, Rue Coquillière. Cf. also Dumolin, *Etudes de topographie parisienne*, quoted by Ciprut, *B.S.H.A.F.*, 1956, p. 123 ff. According to this, Bénigne Bernard's house was on the corner of the Rue Coquillère and the Rue Coqhéron. This is not possible because this site was entirely occupied by the Hôtel de Bullion and its dependencies, which Dumolin elsewhere makes quite clear.

makes it possible to fix its position with some certainty.[21] This document was drawn up in 1605, and records the sale by Charles de Soissons to Henri de Bourbon, Duc de Montpensier, of 'ung hostel et maison assize rue de Grenelle . . . tenant d'une part aux heritiers de (Framarin?) et aux maisons et jardins de Rémy (Bazelly?) au Sieur Fétard et à l'hostel de Brosse[22] d'autre part à la maison de Mr. Bénigne Bernard conseiller du Roy, maitre ordinaire en sa chambre des comptes et greffier de la cour des aides et aux maisons du Sr. de (Montesier?) et Robert (Druis?) aboutissant d'un bout par devant sur la rue de Grenelle et par derrière sur la rue du Bouloi'.

This 'hostel et maison' between the Rue de Grenelle and the Rue du Bouloi is in fact none other than the one which later became the Hôtel Séguier and which, as we have seen, the Comte de Soissons sold to the Duc de Montpensier when he moved into Catherine de Médicis' former home. Its site is clearly shown in the *Terrier du Roy* of about 1700 (Pl. 81), where it is marked 'la Douanne' (in other plans also the 'Hôtel des Fermes'), because by that date it had become the headquarters of the tax authority known as 'Les Fermes Générales'. It is immediately apparent from the plan that the only property of any size adjoining 'la Douane' is that occupying 'lotissement no. 41' facing the Rue Coquillière and the Rue de Bouloi.

Sauval,[23] writing about 1650, gives a long description of the entrance-door of a house in the Rue Coquillière: 'la Maison de Nicolas de Mouy de Riberpré, Marquis de Bauve, qui fait partie maintenant de l'hostel Séguier est située dans la rue Coquillière et dans celle du Bouloi'. The only house which could have faced on to both the Rue Coquillière and the Rue du Bouloi and which at the same time could have been incorporated into the Hôtel Séguier (Douane or Hôtel des Fermes) must have occupied 'lotissements 39–41' of the *Terrier* of 1700. (The accompanying census informs us that all three sites had one owner, the Duchesse de Verneuil).

Turgot's plan of 1739[24] shows the corner-site at the junction of the Rue du Bouloi and the Rue Coquillière as occupied by an hôtel which has its entrance in a screen facing the Rue Coquillière. The area facing the Rue du Bouloi is occupied by a tower (in the angle of the streets) and the low wall of a *basse-cour* or garden (Pl. 73). Allowing for buildings either previously on the site or

21. Cf. Cat. p. 238. This document and its topographical significance were kindly communicated to me by Mme Françoise Boudon, assistant to Professor Chastel on the project for the Quartier des Halles (cf. above n. 1). Cf. also F. Hamon, 'L'Hôtel de Hervart au Quartier Saint-Eustache les travaux en 1658' *Revue de l'Art*, No. 6, 1969, pp. 77 and p. 80, n. 4.
22. No connection with the architect.
23. II, p. 198.
24. Gomboust does not show it.

added to it later, the general lay-out is not incompatible with details of the masonry contracts signed by de Brosse and Bénigne Bernard in 1614 and 1616, especially with regard to the garden which lay, not behind, but to one side of the *corps-de-logis* and the west wing of the hôtel.

De Brosse's first contract, of February 1614, was for work costing 16,000 livres, which sum he received in October 1615. In May 1616, he undertook further work, for which the contract is lost, but the nature of which is known from the *quittance* signed by him in January 1618 for 7,000 livres.

The wording of the 1614 contract is not always easy to follow, but it shows that de Brosse was to enlarge one end of a *corps-de-logis* already existing on the site and to insert into this a new staircase with its own entrance-door. He was to pull down and rebuild the flight of steps (*perron*) leading from the courtyard up to the *salle*, presumably in the centre of the façade, and to build a flight of steps down from the *corps-de-logis* into the garden, at its western end.[25] The *lucarnes* of the existing *corps-de-logis* were to be pulled down, and new ones built to match those of the extension and of the new buildings. The façade on to the garden was to be altered, and a wing built between the court and the garden to house kitchens and stables.[26] Finally, a little pavilion was to be built at the corner of the *corps-de-logis* on the garden-side, carried at ground-floor level on arches and brackets ('tasseaux et arcades') and probably containing a cabinet on the first floor and a room over.

The 1616 contract, as we can tell from the *quittance* for it signed by de Brosse in 1618, concerned 'ung petit logis qu'il convient rediffier et reparer de neuf, joignant . . . (le) grand corps de logis'. This was presumably the wing on the other side of the court, but the *quittance* does not go into details. This contract brought the total spent on the hôtel between 1614 and 1618 to 23,000 livres.

If we accept that Sauval's house of M. de Riberpré on the corner of the Rue Coquillière and the Rue du Bouloi, and the Hôtel Bénigne Bernard, are one and the same, then we are furnished with a detailed description and an illustration of what we may presume to be part of de Brosse's work at the hôtel: the entrance-door, of which Sauval says: 'Salomon de Brosse, l'Architecte du portail Saint-Gervais et du Palais d'Orléans (Luxembourg) l'a

---

25. The wording about the steps to the garden is not clear, but implies that this was part of the main staircase-design, viz.: 'plus sera faict ung escalier dans le grand logis au lieu porté par le desseing son partour de maçonnerie jusques à l'aire de la salle. Et les marches dessendans dudit aire au jardin seront de pierre dure . . .'.

26. 'Ung petit corps de logis regardant de face sur la cour . . . lequel sera reculé vers le jardin de quelques quatre pieds ou environ . . .'.

élevé dans la face de cette maison de la rue Coquillière.'[27] Sauval gives as laudatory an account of this door as he had for the one at the Hôtel de Soissons. He stresses its size and grandeur and its skilful construction: '. . . Son entrée est une grande porte quarrée, longue, d'oeuvre rustique, fort simple, mais si haute et si large, qu'encore que présentement on entre dans tous les nouveaux Hôtels par des porteaux d'une extraordinaire grandeur, elle ne laisse pas de paroitre démesurée pour sa hauteur . . . l'ordonnance . . . et la composition . . . est si singulière, que tous ceux du métier l'admirent'. It was all in rusticated stone, with no columns or pilasters; the keystone and the *voussoirs* were very large and so well cut and placed that, despite their size and weight, they stayed in place without cement. At the end of his description of this door, Sauval gives an important clue, comparing it to Michelangelo's work: 'Aussi est-ce une des merveilles de Michel Ange, et de la nouvelle Rome, qui a paru si admirable à Vignole célèbre Architecte d'Italie qu'il lui a donné place dans son livre des cinq ordres d'Architecture . . . Salomon de Brosse n'y a rien ajouté du sien, qu'un grand fronton rond, garni d'un cartouche dans le milieu, qui ne se voit point dans celui que Vignole a dessiné, et mis en lumière; mais qui se voit dans celui du Vignole François in-8° de la traduction de Pierre le Muet'.

The engraving to which Sauval refers is plate 75 of le Muet's rare little book, *Le Vignole Français*, published in 1630 (Pl. 83), and it has not previously been realized that it shows the door by de Brosse, apparently that of the former Hôtel Bénigne Bernard, described by Sauval.[28] The problem is, where in the hôtel was this door situated? It is not mentioned in any contract or receipt, and it cannot have been the door built to give access to the staircase, for the contract specifies that this was to be placed in a space of about four feet, whereas Sauval implies something very much larger.[29] It seems more probable that it was in an entrance screen on the Rue Coquillière; the Turgot plan shows a screen between the two wings of the house on the site described by Sauval, but it cannot be relied upon for so small a detail (Pl. 73).[30]

Whatever the topographical problems however, there is no reason to doubt

27. Cf. J.-P. Babelon, op. cit., p. 265, Rue du Bouloi. He does not, however, note the connection with the Rue Coquillière.

28. The design is not, as Sauval says, one of the *Porte di Michelangelo*, but one from the body of Vignola's book, pl. xxxiiii.

29. The 1614 contract shows the *corps-de-logis* to have had a basement, first floor, second floor and attic. Since the entrance-door to the staircase was to have had one window ('croisée') only over it, it may have been a very tall one.

30. Delagrive, like Gomboust, omits the hôtel from his plan.

Sauval's attribution to de Brosse of the door engraved by le Muet. The attribution of the Hôtel de Soissons door rests entirely on Sauval's evidence and has never been doubted; and the two are strongly linked by their close derivation from Vignola. Both are also connected with gates and doorways designed by de Brosse about this time for buildings outside Paris, such as the drawbridge-gates at Montceaux (derived from the Cancelleria at Rome, but with *voussoirs* reminiscent of Ammannati at the Pitti), and the inner and outer entrance-gates at Blérancourt (the inner one taken almost directly from the Porta Grimani of the *Porte di Michelangelo*). Also possibly by de Brosse, and linked with this series of doors, is the unfinished door beneath the late-Gothic porch of the parish church at Verneuil (Pl. 84). Though it is tentatively attributed by Pannier to one of the du Cerceau family,[31] the gravity of its style and its carefully thought-out rustication are more characteristic of de Brosse. Another pointer to this attribution is the omission of the rustication on the pilasters immediately under the capital and above the base, which also occurs in pilasters at the Luxembourg (Pl. 152).

In the same year in which he began his work for Bénigne Bernard, de Brosse undertook extensions costing 36,000 livres for Claude de Bullion at his newly-acquired hôtel in the Rue Plastrière (now Jean-Jacques Rousseau) (Pl. 82). Bullion, later 'Chancelier et Surintendant des Finances' and a pillar of Richelieu's administration, had bought the house in 1613 from another patron of de Brosse, Henriette d'Entragues, Marquise de Verneuil. On 30 January 1614, de Brosse signed a contract with Bullion to enlarge the existing *corps-de-logis*, to build two wings from it, one on each side of the court, the one beside the *basse-cour* to the north to contain a gallery, and finally to build an entrance-front between the ends of these two wings, to link them up along the street. This front was to be pierced by a *porte-cochère*, '. . . plus sera faicte la muraille de la devanture sur la rue entre les deux pignons desdits logis, laquelle muraille sera aussy fondée à vif fonds . . . dans le mitan et espace dudit meur se fera une porte de quelque jolie ordonnance estant de pierre dure . . .' There was to be another 'grande porte' leading into the *corps-de-logis*.

In addition, although we do not learn of it from this contract, a principal staircase seems to have been built either at one end of the *corps-de-logis* or, more probably, in the north wing adjoining the *corps-de-logis*, possibly in a special pavilion. The presence of the staircase here is indicated by the contract signed by Charles du Ry when he enlarged the *basse-cour* and built a long

31. Op. cit., p. 20.

gallery down the side of the garden for Bullion in 1633.[32] De Brosse was to be paid 3,000 livres at once, and the rest of his money (the sum is not specified in the contract) from time to time as the building progressed.

Unfortunately, we know nothing about the exterior appearance of the Hôtel de Bullion, which later became famous for its interior decoration by Sarrazin, Vouet and Blanchard.[33] Gomboust did not include an elevation of the hôtel in his plan of Paris, and Turgot's elevation of 1739 (Pl. 73) shows the corps-de-logis right on the Rue Plastrière; whereas the Terrier du Roy (Pl. 82) shows it lying between the court and the garden, a position which the 1614 contract surely indicates. However, the Terrier du Roy, Delagrive's plan of 1729, Jaillot's plan of 1713 and the Atlas Cadastral de Paris (1815–1855) all give block-plans of the hôtel at their respective dates, some more accurately than others.[34]

The plan of the entrance-front and the porte-cochère is interesting, and, if the Terrier du Roy and the Plan Cadastral show what de Brosse built and not a later entrance, also important (Pl. 82). The door was set into a large niche, the curves of which were so arranged in relation to it as largely to disguise the fact that the courtyard and buildings of the hôtel did not lie parallel with the street. Although for this reason here treated asymmetrically, the quadrant curves of the Hôtel de Bouillon entrance have, as it were, been turned inside out, and have provided de Brosse with a solution to the problem of the axis of the hôtel in relation to the street.

If the entrance to the Hôtel de Bullion really dates from 1614, it, as well as the quadrants of the Hôtel de Bouillon, may have influenced François Mansart when he built the entrance to the Hôtel de l'Aubespine in the Rue Coquillière nearby (probably begun in 1627). Here a concave curve in the court and a convex one on the street – a composition of great subtlety and complication – served to disguise a similar change of axis between street and court.[35]

An enlargement to the corps-de-logis of the Hôtel de Bullion was to be made by the addition of two pavilions, but the wording of the contract does not

32. Cf. Cat. p. 245.

33. Cf. J.-P. Babelon, op. cit., p. 272, Rue Jean-Jacques Rousseau, and pp. 213–220.

34. Except that Delagrive's does not show the garden-gallery.

35. Cf. P. Smith, Thesis cit., and P. Smith and A. Braham, forthcoming book on François Mansart. The entrance is clearly shown on Gomboust's plan.

make it clear whether one or both were to be on the court side or on the garden-front.[36]

The last of the hôtels on which de Brosse worked was the Hôtel du Lude (later la Reynie) in the Rue du Bouloi, south of the Hôtel Séguier and the Hôtel Bénigne Bernard. This is shown in Turgot's plan, on the extreme right of the section illustrated (Pl. 73). The hôtel immediately next to it was combined with the Hôtel du Lude in 1677, and in later plans such as Delagrive's the joint buildings appear as the Hôtel de la Reynie.[37]

The house which François de Daillon, Comte du Lude, bought in 1609, and which in 1618 he commissioned de Brosse to restore and enlarge, was the reputed birthplace of Richelieu. It is not altogether certain how much de Brosse actually rebuilt, but certainly he was responsible for the *corps-de-logis* on to the street, which was pierced by 'un grand portail' giving access to the court; this door can just be made out in both Gomboust's and Turgot's plans (Pl. 73). In the courtyard de Brosse built an interesting structure, referred to in the contract as 'l'ovalle appelée coppole', and in later documents as 'le dosme'. The function of this building is not specified; possibly it was a chapel; if so, its form is linked with the chapel in the entrance-pavilion at Montceaux and that at Coulommiers, and with the plans by du Cerceau, Serlio and Vignola on which they were based.

De Brosse also built a staircase in one angle of the courtyard, possibly (although nothing is specified in the contract) in a special pavilion set between the *corps-de-logis* 'au fond de la cour' and one of the wings.

Leaving aside the great *portes-cochères* of the Hôtel de Soissons and the Hôtel Bénigne Bernard, we know so little about the appearance of de Brosse's buildings in the five hôtels discussed in this chapter that we can scarcely assess the influence which their style may have had. However, some deductions can be made. If, for example, the main walls of the garden-front and the façade of the *corps-de-logis* on the *basse-cour* of the Hôtel de Bouillon, shown in Marot's and Silvestre's engravings, are de Brosse's work, they represent an important development. The orders are discarded, so is the kind of surface-

---

36. 'Premièrement fault faire un Pavillon adossé contre partie du pignon du Grand logis à présent faict lequel pavillon ... estant appliqué pour faire un grand cabinet et une garderobe en chascun estage. ... Plus sera faict le meur mytoyen entre ledict sieur (Bullion) et la place joignant Monsieur Brandon, ... et entre ledict meur et pavillon qui sera la largeur dudict logement ... se fera un autre cabinet joignant led. pavillon et ayant sa vue sur le jardin ...'.

37. Dumolin, op. cit., II, p. 421; E.-J. Ciprut, *Bull. Soc. Hist. Prot. Fr.*, October–December 1964, p. 253; D. P. O'Connell, *Richelieu*, 1968, p. 2; J.-P. Babelon, op. cit., Rue du Bouloi, p. 116. The Comte du Lude was married to Marie, daughter of Antoine Feydeau for whom de Brosse was at this time working on the château of Bois-le-Vicomte.

decoration seen in late sixteenth-century hôtels such as Baptiste du Cerceau's Hôtel d'Angoulême (Pls 31–33). The walls are instead simply panelled, the windows unpedimented, and over every window-bay there is a pedimented dormer (Pl. 78).

De Brosse's innovations at the Hôtel de Bouillon were not immediately accepted. The entrance-front of the Hôtel de Mayenne, built at about the same date, has superimposed orders, and the dormers on the entrance- and garden-sides are of the clumsy late sixteenth-century type. The Hôtel Sully, built in the 1630s, has a decorative treatment of enormous elaboration, including sculptured reliefs reminiscent of the sixteenth-century façades decorated by Goujon.[38] But, in other hôtels of the earlier part of the century, such as the Hôtel de Chevreuse and the Hôtel Châlons-Luxembourg, the plain or panelled astylar treatment is used to good effect.[39] Later, under the influence of Mansart, the orders were seldom used, even for important houses. It seems plausible that, since de Brosse influenced Mansart and other later hôtel-builders in other ways, his treatment of wall-surfaces was also a source of inspiration.

De Brosse was evidently required to regularize and classicize the old hôtels on which he worked, and to pull them together into as much symmetry as possible. One of the methods of doing this mentioned in the contracts is the rebuilding of old dormers to match those of the new ranges of buildings. The introduction of a pedimented dormer over almost every window-bay became a regular feature of the mid-seventeenth-century hôtel, and here again de Brosse may have exerted an influence. Certainly he would have contributed something to the search for symmetry and order in the elevation so typical of later hôtels, where feats of ingenuity were accomplished in order to regularize awkward sites and disparate buildings.

The influence of de Brosse's Vignolesque type of hôtel-entrance was as immediate and as widespread as Sauval asserts. The drawings of his

38. The Hôtel de Mayenne was rebuilt in 1609 when it was bought by Charles, Duc de Mayenne. In *c.* 1613 his son, Henri, had more work done, probably to the plans of Jacques II du Cerceau (the earlier work was conducted by a mason called Christophe Deschamps). The central screen of the entrance-front had a storey built over it in the 19th century: J.-P. Babelon, op. cit., Rue Saint-Antoine, p. 279 and pls pp. 128 and 141. The Hôtel Sully was built *c.* 1625 for Mesme Gallet, Sieur du Petit-Thouars, and continued (1628–1629) for Roland de Neufbourg. It was then bought by Sully. The design is attributed to Jean du Cerceau; ibid., p. 279 and pls. 158–161.

39. The Hôtel de Chevreuse, attributed to Clément Métezeau, was built after 1622, according to J.-P. Babelon, op. cit., Rue Saint-Thomas-du-Louvre, p. 282. The Hôtel Châlons-Luxembourg (ibid., Rue Geoffroy Lasnier, p. 271) was probably built somewhat later than M. Babelon and the authors whom he cites believe. The dating of this hôtel will be discussed in the forthcoming book on F. Mansart by P. Smith and A. Braham.

collaborator, Charles du Ry,[40] le Muet's *Vignole Français* and Marot's engravings of the seventeenth-century hôtels of Paris all bear witness to this.[41]

The Hôtel de Bouillon provides perhaps the earliest example of a new variation on the basic hôtel-plan. The Hôtel de Ligneris and the house of Philibert de l'Orme are examples of sixteenth-century houses with a *corps-de-logis* (free-standing), having two small pavilions projecting on to the court. At the Hôtel de Bouillon the projecting pavilions are transferred to the garden-front, and this transposition probably influenced the design of the striking garden-front of the Hôtel Châlons-Luxemboug.[42] It must not be forgotten either that as early as 1584 Baptiste du Cerceau had given the Hôtel d'Angoulême small projecting pavilions on to the garden as well as on to the court (Pl. 30).

It is a pity that we have no reliable representation of the entrance-front of the Hôtel de Bullion on the Rue Plastrière. The contract makes no mention of pavilions terminating the side-wings, but despite this, and their absence from the later plans (Pl. 82), we cannot certainly presume their absence from the building of 1614.

This point is important, because there was another, though short-lived, variant on hôtel-design, whereby separately-roofed, projecting pavilions terminated the court-wings, as in château-architecture. This feature occurred in later modifications to the Hôtel de Ligneris, and is well exemplified in the surviving street-fronts of the Hôtel de Mayenne and Hôtel Sully. But, at Métezeau's Hôtel de Chevreuse, for example (about 1624), these pavilions have disappeared, and in the hôtels of Mansart and his contemporaries they were abandoned. It would therefore be interesting to know whether de Brosse encouraged their suppression, by abandoning them also at the Hôtel de Bullion.

Finally, a feature of de Brosse's hôtel-planning which led to important later developments was the positioning of the principal staircase, as exemplified in three of his designs.

The traditional position for the main stair in a grand town-house, as in a château, was in the centre of the *corps-de-logis*, and the most usual type of stair was the tunnel-vaulted single-return flight. Such staircases persisted well

40. In the 'de Brosse' album at the Louvre.
41. Cf. J.-P. Babelon, op. cit., p. 141, Hôtel de Mayenne; p. 143, Hôtel Pelletier de Souzy; p. 145, Hôtel Sully. Outside Paris, cf. the château gates and the main door at Brécy, Calvados (1630s).
42. Cf. above n. 39. For the Hôtel d'Angoulême, cf. above, Chap. II, pp. 32, 33.

into the new century; they can be seen at the Hôtel de Mayenne and at the Hôtel Sully. The position and type was not invariable; at the Hôtel de Ligneris a spiral staircase was set into one of the small pavilions flanking the *corps-de-logis*, and a staircase also occupied one of the projecting pavilions of the Hôtel d'Angoulême.[43] A much more notable exception was the staircase of the Hôtel Zamet[44] in the Rue de la Cerisaie, which was of advanced design and placed in the east wing of the court. But generally, the central position prevailed.

Although we do not know where de Brosse's staircase for the Hôtel de Fresne was placed, we are certain that it did not rise from a vestibule directly within the central entrance of the *corps-de-logis*. The contracts of the Hôtel Bénigne Bernard and the Hôtel du Lude stipulate that new staircases are to be built in the corner of the courtyard, and, as we have seen, the later contract signed by du Ry for the Hôtel de Bullion indicates an existing staircase in the same position. De Brosse's staircases may, as has been suggested, have occupied a special pavilion between the *corps-de-logis* and the wing, and were almost certainly on an open-well plan, similar to that of the staircases at Coulommiers and the Luxembourg,[45] albeit on a smaller scale.[46]

The advantage of siting the principal staircase, as de Brosse did, to one side of the *corps-de-logis* was that it permitted simultaneous access to the *corps-de-logis* and one wing, and a continuous enfilade of important reception rooms on the first floor. The latter arrangement was increasingly prized as the century progressed, and is admirably illustrated in the plan of the Hôtel de Bouillon after it had been remodelled for the Marquis de Liancourt in the 1630s (Pl. 77).

In the years after de Brosse's death, Mansart and Le Vau developed ingenious variations on the hôtel-staircase, but its most popular position remained the one adopted by de Brosse in the three hôtels mentioned. However, the centre

43. It still survives.

44. Built by the Italian financier, Sebastian Zamet, at the very end of the sixteenth century. The staircase is known from a plan by the English architect, John Thorpe, and plans by Robert de Cotte; cf. Sir John Summerson, 'The Book of Architecture of John Thorpe in Sir John Soane's Museum', *Walpole Society*, vol. XL, 1964–1966, p. 90, pl. 78 (T 163). The stair had two flights from the ground to the first floor, with a single flight return to the second floor.

45. Cf. below pp. 104 and 128.

46. The long flight of stairs seen in the right-hand side of the court wing of the Hôtel de Bullion or what remains of it), in the *Plan Cadastral*, is probably not the original one, but may date from du Ry's construction of the garden wing (also absent from the plan) or even later. However, we cannot be certain of this. In connection with the position of de Brosse's hôtel-staircases, it is worth recalling the semi-circular stair he built between the S.E. pavilion and the state-rooms of the S. wing at Montceaux, *c.* 1609–1615. Cf. Pls 40, 41.

of the *corps-de-logis* façade was still often stressed, and a flight of steps might lead up to an entrance-door. At the Hôtel Bénigne Bernard de Brosse built a new and no doubt grander *perron* to replace the old one leading to a central *salle*; later such a *perron* might give access to an imposing vestibule.

Thus, despite scanty records, the disappearance of the buildings and an almost total lack of visual evidence as to their appearance, it has been possible to indicate, though in some cases only tentatively, how the hôtels upon which de Brosse worked may have influenced his successors. Mansart and Le Vau were the supreme hôtel-builders of the succeeding generation, and it in no sense diminishes their achievement to suggest that they may have learnt more than is usually granted from their predecessor, Salomon de Brosse.

CHAPTER V

Blérancourt: The Patrons, the Artists and the Building

O N 11 April 1612 Charles du Ry signed a contract with Charlotte de Vieuxpont, wife of Bernard Potier, for work at the château of Blérancourt.[1] This contract reveals that building was already going on at Blérancourt, though just when it was started is uncertain. The first paragraph stipulates that the foundations for two pavilions must be dug '... sur la face de l'entrée du chasteau lesquelles fondations seront ... de mesme profondeur que celles du logis (dé) jà fondé ...'. The assertion that de Brosse, not du Ry, was Charlotte de Vieuxpont's architect, although his name appears in no surviving contract, is supported both by contemporary references and the style of the building.

No contract for the château survives from a date earlier than 1612.[2] This is particularly unfortunate because recent discoveries indicate that for de Brosse Blérancourt was an immensely important commission, and that his connection with the Potiers and their circle had a great influence upon him. If the project for the château was under discussion by 1611, or possibly even earlier, certain developments already noticed in de Brosse's work at Verneuil, Montceaux and in Paris may well have been encouraged by the Blérancourt connection.

The suggestions put forward in this chapter concerning the importance of Blérancourt and its owners for de Brosse's career are admittedly based upon incomplete evidence, much of which is tantalizingly elusive. All sorts of questions so far remain unanswered. Nevertheless, much new material is now available about the building, and enough can be pieced together to indicate

1. Cf. Cat. pp. 203-207.
2. E. Coyecque, the editor of the official guide to the Musée Franco-Americain at Blérancourt (ed. 1957) says that the château was begun in 1612, but cites no evidence. L. Hautecoeur, op. cit., I, p. 503 and n. 1, gives the date as 1614, basing this on Charles Dessin (wrongly cited as C. Denin), *Le Bourg de Blérancourt*, Laon, 1926. Dessin may have known of the existence of the 1614 contract for the principal staircase.

that the character and ambitions of the patron were of great significance for
the architect.

On 15 May 1600 a notary was summoned to ratify family agreements made
upon the occasion of the marriage of Bernard Potier and Charlotte de
Vieuxpont. The father of the bridegroom, Louis Potier de Gesvres et de
Tresmes, agreed to cede to his son and daughter-in-law his house and lands at
Chaillot and Blérancourt (Bernard is already referred to as 'Seigneur de
Blérancourt'). He stipulated that the couple's chief places of residence should
be Paris and Blérancourt, and for his part Bernard agreed to make improve-
ments at the château of Chaillot and also to 'ladicte maison, terre et seigneurie
de Blérancourt', indicating that a house already stood there. According to
tradition this was not upon the same site as the present château,[3] but this
would appear to be disproved by the contract of 1612, where du Ry
undertakes to demolish two towers in order to build the two new pavilions.
It is possible, however, that these towers were only erected shortly before that
date and then pulled down again.[4] The money for such architectural ventures
was easily forthcoming, for Charlotte brought a good dowry, the Potiers,
descendants of a family of merchant-furriers, were wealthy, and Louis Potier
had been a favourite of Henri IV and held lucrative royal appointments.[5]

Charlotte de Vieuxpont was a woman of decided character and a would-be
'femme-savante', who had her portrait painted 'en Minerve'.[6] Tallement des
Réaux, in his *Historiettes*,[7] poked fun at both Bernard Potier and his wife, but
together with his mocking references to the husband's lack of culture and the
wife's pursuit of it, there are verifiable and important allusions to Blérancourt.
M. de Blérancourt travelled widely, says Tallement, and wrote enough about
his journeys to fill three great volumes, but since he was only concerned to
record the best hostelries of Italy, Spain and Germany, no-one would bother
to publish his work. His wife, Tallement writes, was '. . . une femme qui

3. M. Coyecque notes, 'La Seigneurie de Blérancourt fût acquise en 1595 par Louis Potier de
Gesvres . . . Il la donna au second de ses trois fils, Bernard, qui fit construire le château du 'Marais'
assez loin de l'ancien donjon du 'Colombier' qui se trouvait au bas de la colline de l'église'.
   4. See below, p. 82.
   5. For a summary of the history of the Potier family who subsequently became patrons of
Mansart, see Allan Braham, 'The Château of Gesvres', in 'Mansart Studies', IV, *Burlington Magazine*,
1964, vol. 106.
   6. Michelaut, in his *Voyage de Pierre Bergeron ès Ardennes, Liège et Pays Bas en 1619*, Liège, 1875,
records that Charlotte's portrait was in the Hospice des Orphelins of the Convent of the Feuillants
in Blérancourt, both of which were founded by Bernard Potier in 1614. Cf. M. Pette, 'Le Couvent
des Feuillants et l'Hospice des Orphelins de Blérancourt,' *Bull. Soc. Arch. de Soissons*, XI 2e sér.,
1880.
   7. First publ. ed., quoted here, 1840, IX, pp. 77–80.

s'étoit mise à étudier. Bergeron, chanoine de je ne sais où . . . fut celui dont elle se servit pour s'instruire . . . Bergeron demeura avec elle tout le reste de sa vie . . . Ce fut Madame de Blérancourt qui bâtit la maison de Blérancourt en Picardie. On dit qu'elle la fit quasi toute défaire pour reparer un défaut, de peur qu'on ne dit que Madame de Blérancourt avoit fait une faute . . .'.[8]

It is a great pity that Bernard Potier's journals are lost to us, for even if Tallement's estimate of their contents is correct, they would still be very valuable as an exact record of where he went and, possibly, who went with him. Fortunately Charlotte de Vieuxpont's tutor, Pierre Bergeron, wrote the *Voyage ès Ardennes, Liège et Pays-Bas,*[9] an account of a tour which he made with M. and Mme de Blérancourt in 1619. They visited Blérancourt on the outward and return journeys, and from Bergeron's description of the château it is clear that the building was by then almost finished. At the end of the description he gives the names of the well-known men who worked there, among them 'des Brosses'. Bergeron also says that 'Fremynetz' and 'Tremblans' worked there, a statement confirmed by the recent discovery of a contract, dated 1619, wherein the sculptor Barthélemy Tremblay undertook to carry out 'ouvrages de sculpture et architecture' to the design of 'le Sieur Fremyne' (Fréminet).[10] 'Des Brosses' is undoubtedly de Brosse, and it must be remembered that, as a permanent member of the Potier household, Bergeron, despite his erratic spelling of artists' names was in a position to know what he was talking about concerning Blérancourt, its patrons and the men who worked there.

In the preamble to the *Voyage* of 1619, Bergeron states that he has at various times visited divers parts of Europe and written about these journeys. These works found favour with his well-wishers and '. . . ceulx soubz les auspices et en la compagnie desquelz j'avois eu l'honneur de faire tels voyages . . . tant de voyages entrepris coup sur coup en Italie, Espagne, Allemaigne Angleterre Pais Bas et ailleurs . . .'. This list tallies in part with the countries mentioned by Tallement des Réaux to which Bernard Potier had travelled; and the expression 'with whom I had the honour to make such journeys' strongly suggests that Bergeron was in Potier's company on some, if not all, of his travels. In the *Voyages* he also writes concerning the pentagonal château of Herluin near Montdidier, that it cannot compare with the similarly-shaped '. . . beau palais de Caprarole, que nous avons veu en Italie, près de Viterbe sur

8. See below, pp. 78, 82.
9. See n. 6. Cf. Cat. p. 203.
10. Cf. Cat. p. 203, and below pp. 80-81.

le chemin de Rome . . . (de) . . . l'excellent architecte Vignole'. In the margin
of the ensuing paragraph of Bergeron's MS. is written, perhaps in another
hand, a eulogy of Vignola, 'tant pour son esprit ingénieux et intelligent à
rendre une chose et belle et commode tout ensemble'.

The 'nous' of 'que nous avons veu' cannot, in the context of the 1619
journey, refer to anyone but Potier, and strongly suggests that Charlotte de
Vieuxpont may also have accompanied her husband at least on the journey
to Rome. In any case the reference to, and particular praise of Vignola is
extremely significant. A knowledge of architecture was definitely among the
subjects about which Charlotte required instruction from her tutor.

Charlotte was certainly the moving spirit behind the project for Blérancourt; Tallement's statement that she was the builder of the château is true
in this sense. She signed the 1612 contract alone, and in the 1614 contract
is a note to the effect that her husband authorizes her to deal with the matter.
Tallement's story that she had most of her château pulled down because of a
mistake in architecture may in part be true; it is possible that the two towers
mentioned in 1612 had been built since 1600 when Bernard and Charlotte
had promised to 'improve' Blérancourt, and that later Charlotte, deciding
that they were not in the correct taste, ordered their demolition.[11] Correct
taste would be modelled upon what her tutor and perhaps she herself had seen
in Italy, and influenced by an admiration of Vignola and other sixteenth-
century Italian architects. The 1612 contract breathes a certain air of pedantry
with its unusually meticulous instructions on the proper details suitable to
the orders.

This involvement of Charlotte de Vieuxpont in the work at Blérancourt
is reflected also in the passage from Bergeron's *Voyage* which will be quoted at
the end of this section, where he states that all plans and drawings had to be
submitted to her judgment.

Charlotte's evident preoccupation with architectural sources and style
was of great importance for Blérancourt. Further evidence about the kind
of architecture which appealed to Charlotte and her circle is contained in
an album of drawings now in the Cabinet des Dessins in the Louvre,[12] the
work of a so far unidentified architectural draughtsman of considerable
competence. It is possible that the drawings it contains which were made in
Italy are a record of things seen by the author when travelling with the
Potiers, for there is a link between him and Blérancourt.

The drawings in the album were made between *c.* 1602 and *c.* 1622, and

11. See below p. 82.
12. Cf. Cat. pp. 204-205.

thirteen of them bear the inscription 'Der', which has led to their attribution to Derand, the contemporary Jesuit architect, an attribution which can be completely discounted on both stylistic and chronological grounds.[13] They show buildings of antiquity in Italy, and also fifteenth- and sixteenth-century buildings in Florence, Rome, Naples and elsewhere. There are, for example, measured details of the drum of the dome of St Peter's in Rome, and several pages of measured details from the Medici Chapel and Library in San Lorenzo in Florence. The importance of Vignola for the draughtsman is indicated by the presence of drawings after work by him. The majority of the door-designs in the album are derived from mannerist followers of Vignola, although the influence of Ammanati is also evident in some of them.

There are other drawings obviously made in France, and of these four are inscribed 'à blérancourt' and one 'Dessigné à blérancourt', and bear the dates 1614 or 1615. Only one of these (folio 5 bis) (Pl. 86) could conceivably have any connection with a French château, and that bears the royal arms and a crown in the design, so may have nothing to do with Blérancourt.[14] Even in this, the most French of all the five drawings, the influence of Rome is unmistakable; the trumpet-blowing angels on the pediment are directly derived from a tabernacle in the Sforza Chapel in Santa Maria Maggiore.

The remaining 'Blérancourt' drawings, and especially folios 3, 33 (Pl. 85), and 38, are highly Italianate. Two are strongly influenced by Florentine sixteenth-century architecture, particularly that of Ammanati, and the third shows the door of the Cancelleria in Rome, not as it was engraved, but as it was actually executed.

The author of this album, whoever he was,[15] is therefore an influence to be reckoned with in the Blérancourt circle; a man who had travelled extensively, and possibly with the patrons, in Italy, who brought back a collection of very important drawings, and who was definitely at Blérancourt itself in 1614 and 1615. Alas, so far all efforts to establish his identity have failed.

All the evidence discussed indicates that the architectural ideas of the Potier circle were, for Frenchmen, considerably in advance of the times, and this is particularly instanced by their admiration for Vignola and his work. The de Brosse-'Der'-Blérancourt link is an excellent example of the manner in which French architects who had not themselves been to Italy came into contact with Italian architecture through those who knew about it

13. Ibid.

14. This elevation is made on a plan from fol. 5 which has a scale inscribed 'Palmi Napolitani'.

15. It has been suggested to me by Professor Hamish Miles that the inscription 'Der' is one of ownership, not of authorship, as I have hitherto assumed.

at first hand. It may have been through the unknown author of the Louvre
album that de Brosse knew of the Vignolesque buildings which influenced his
work at Verneuil and Montceaux.

A further proof of the quality of the work commissioned for Blérancourt,
and the stature of the artists whom Charlotte de Vieuxpont employed there
is the contract signed by Barthélemy Tremblay in 1619. Martin Fréminet, on
whose designs Tremblay was to work for interior decoration and for sculpture
on the exterior of the building, was the most distinguished painter and
decorative artist of the first two decades of the seventeenth century in France.
His drawing in the Louvre for the altar of the Chapel of the Trinity at
Fontainebleau (begun 1608) (Pl. 87), and the decoration of the chapel ceiling
itself show the use he made of what he had learned during an apparently
protracted stay in Italy. He was working in Rome in 1589, and possibly also
visited Turin and Venice, before he was called back to France by Henri IV to
work at Fontainebleau in 1602–1603. He remained in the King's employment
until his death in 1622. Whether he actually came to Blérancourt to execute
the ceiling-painting we do not know.

Barthélemy Tremblay collaborated with Fréminet at Fontainebleau from
1613 to 1619,[16] executing the fine plasterwork surrounding Fréminet's
ceiling-paintings (Pl. 88). The form of the ceiling is strongly influenced
by Roman schemes, which Fréminet had seen during his years in Italy, and
some of its details are very advanced for this period in France.[17] Fréminet in
these paintings also shows a grasp of the dramatic use of architecture, of a
most surprisingly grave and classical type, well in advance of his contemporaries. This is demonstrated dramatically in two of the panels of the
Trinity Chapel ceiling and, to a lesser extent, in the architecture of the
altarpiece drawing.

Much of Tremblay's plasterwork at Fontainebleau is strongly influenced by
Florentine mannerists such as Buontalenti. Indeed, Buontalenti was to exercise

16. Cf. S. Béguin, 'Two Projects by Martin Fréminet for the Chapel of the Trinity at Fontaine-
bleau', *Master Drawings*, 1963, no. 3, pp. 30–34; and, by the same author, Cat. no. 163, 'Martin
Fréminet, Projet de décoration d'autel', Catalogue of the Exhibition of Drawings, *Le XVI Siècle
Européen*, Dessins du Louvre, Paris, Musée du Louvre, 1965. In this entry, Mme Béguin gives
Fréminet's death-date as 1619, as does Thieme-Becker, but in the article cited she gives it as 1622.
I am grateful to Professor Hamish Miles for information about Fréminet, some of which is con-
tained in his unpublished thesis on painters of the early seventeenth century. For Tremblay at
Fontainebleau, see Thieme-Becker, *Künstlerlexikon*.

17. Blunt, *Art and Architecture*, p. 106. Professor Blunt's imputation of mediocrity to Fréminet
might now be qualified since the cleaning of the Trinity Chapel ceiling. Cf. also L. Dimier, *Histoire
de la peinture française . . .* 1300 à 1627. Paris 1925, p. 82 ff.

a great influence on decoration in France during de Brosse's lifetime and for a decade after his death. This Italian artist, like Ammanati,[18] had done some of his finest work at Marie de Médicis' childhood home, the Pitti Palace.

The whole decorative scheme produced by Fréminet and Tremblay in the Chapel of the Trinity must have seemed to contemporaries a marvellous revival of the arts at Fontainebleau, and it would have been a matter of self-congratulation for Charlotte de Vieuxpont that she had captured its creators to embellish her country seat.

Among the works listed in the 1619 contract for Blérancourt is a statue of Minerva, '. . . une Minerve de pierre . . .', to be placed over the pediment of the *corps-de-logis* on the garden front. Was this Charlotte in her favourite rôle? However, even if her intellectual pretensions rendered the lady faintly ridiculous in the eyes of her contemporaries, as Tallement des Réaux implies, the importance of her patronage of the arts and her employment at Blérancourt of the best talents of the day is unquestionable. For nearly a decade Blérancourt was a centre for developments, strongly influenced by Italy but as strongly French in character, which were to have a profound effect upon the architecture and the decorative sculpture of the 1620s and 1630s.

Like most writers who lived by patronage and pension in the seventeenth century, Bergeron adopted a very high-flown sycophantic manner when describing the personal qualities or the possessions of his employers. His eulogy of Blérancourt, however, was mainly justified, even if it contained some exaggeration: '. . . superbe et inimitable palais de Blérancourt, qui seroit une oeuvre à part, qui en vouldroit dire tout ce qui en est, et quoy qu'on en die c'est toujours au deça de son mérite; mais je me contenteray de dire qu'en ce seul bastiment se peut voir l'abregé de tous les autres plus beaux et plus excellens qui soient au monde . . . soit pour . . . la hautesse et majesté de l'eslevation de son bastiment, son esquise structure, sa juste symmétrie et proportion, ses divers ordres d'architecture accompagnez de toutes leurs moulures, colonnes, architraves, frises, corniches, entablemens, . . . dômes et amortissemens; soit les diverses figures bien et artistement achevées, . . . soit le dedans . . . ses escaliers à deux rempans, . . . salles, antichambres . . . cabinets et autres logemens; brief, soit en enrichissemens du dedans, en peintures, dorures, sofites et plafonts à figures et ouvrages de relief; peintures esquises; . . . et enfin soit que l'on considère les industrieuses et sçavantes mains des plus excellents ouvriers de ce temps qui y ont travaillé, chacun selon la

18. Cf. A. Venturi, XI, 2, 1939, p. 459 ff., for comprehensive plates illustrating Buontalenti's work; and ibid, pp. 219 ff. for Ammanati's. For Buontalenti, cf. p. 103, n. 28.

perfection et bienséance de son art . . . Que tous les plus grands dessins de ces dignes ouvriers ont passé par le solide jugement et la reigle exacte de ceste belle, sage et vertueuse Dame qui est comme l'âme de ce petit univers . . .'.

When Bergeron passes on to compare the château with Hadrian's Villa at Tivoli, he may be going too far; but his description indicates the intellectual level aspired to in the 'little kingdom' of Blérancourt, presided over by Charlotte de Vieuxpont.

Although we know from the 1612 contract that the new château was already under construction at this date, we cannot, for lack of any earlier contract or other documentary evidence, establish exactly when building operations began.

The two towers which du Ry undertook to demolish and replace by two pavilions adjoining the *corps-de-logis* may have been, as previously suggested, an earlier stage of the new work; they can hardly have been built by de Brosse, since it seems inconceivable that he should ever have proposed a château with towers. All we know is that by 1611 de Brosse must have been involved in the design of anything that was being constructed. This is proved by the presence of du Ry, by this time the principal member of the de Brosse team.

The only representations of the château which are at all well-known are the engravings by Silvestre. These are inaccurate in some details, omit most of the detached buildings, and give an over-simplified classical appearance to the façades (Pls 91, 92).

A late eighteenth-century water-colour by Tavernier de Junquières in the Musée de Blérancourt[19] is somewhat more exact (Pl. 94), though it shows the château with the bulbous domes which replaced the original roofing after the sack of Blérancourt by the Spaniards in 1652. The general impression of the façades in Tavernier's sketch is a good deal less austere than Silvestre's engravings imply, and this impression is borne out by a series of seventeenth-century drawings, hitherto unpublished and recently discovered in the Bibliothèque Nationale[20]. Also in the Bibliothèque Nationale is a plan, probably eighteenth-century, giving the general lay-out of the château and park (Pl. 89). From this plan, the only one of Blérancourt we have, and from the other drawings, a reconstruction of the château in perspective can be made[21] (Pl. 93).

19. The drawing is no. 2 in the Museum Catalogue.
20. By Dr Peter Smith and the author, 1962–1963; cf. Cat. p. 204.
21. Based on a drawing by Dr Peter Smith.

Today almost nothing of the main château survives; there remain only the ground-floor of the south-west angle-pavilion and the western end of the *corps-de-logis*. A replica of these has been built on the old foundations on the south-east side, while a gap remains between old and new where the frontispiece once stood (Pls 95, 96).

The château was free-standing, occupying a moated terrace reached through a 'porte d'honneur' flanked by two pavilions. Two other pavilions at the far end of the terrace, shown by Silvestre, were never completed.[22] The moated terrace was preceded by an open court entered through another gate, very large, flanked by two attached pavilions and from this outer gate radiated several roads on a 'goose-foot' pattern (not seen on the plan), the traces of which can still be followed today, and which evidently formed part of a scheme for the small town.[23]

The eighteenth-century plan shows the main château as consisting of a central block flanked by symmetrical wings, each linked to a pair of pavilions. The use of this type of plan at Blérancourt was a very important step indeed, in the evolution of the classical château as it was later evolved by François Mansart.[24] As a free-standing, symmetrical block, designed to be seen from all sides, it derives ultimately from Italian Renaissance models such as Bramante's House of Raphael. Indeed the direct influence of Roman buildings is likely in view of the Italian travels of the Potier family and Charlotte de Vieuxpont's determination to erect a modern classical building in a 'correct' style. There had, however, been some interesting experiments with the block-plan château in France in the sixteenth century and these are probably more directly linked with Blérancourt.

As early as 1528 François I built the Château of Madrid, where two blocks of paired apartments flank a central saloon, and where there is no courtyard, exterior or interior. This design, revolutionary for its date in France, was strongly influenced by Italy,[25] but although the plan of Madrid gives the impression of a fairly classically proportioned block, the elevation certainly did not.

22. Coyecque (Cat. Blérancourt Museum) says they were suppressed in 1652. He considers the remaining pavilions to have been rebuilt at that date, but cf. below p. 90 and n. 37.

23. The main road to Compiègne and Paris; main local thoroughfares to right and left; these three linked by small paths.

24. Cf. Blunt, *Art and Architecture*, pp. 102–103.

25. For a discussion of the Italian influence on Madrid and on François I's château of Chambord, and the connection of both with the Villa Medici at Poggio a Caiano, cf. Blunt, *Art and Architecture*, pp. 24–27. The hunting lodges which the same king built at La Muette and Challuau were variations on the plan of Madrid.

Philibert de l'Orme carried the idea a stage further in using a central block flanked by double pavilions when he designed the one-storey Château-Neuf at Saint Germain, begun in 1557 (Fig. 2).[26] Although his building was to have been preceded by a walled courtyard, this hardly affected its appearance as a free-standing unit, and the château is an obvious prototype for Blérancourt.

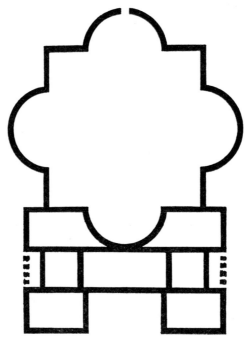

Fig. 2. Philibert de l'Orme. Château-Neuf at Saint Germain. Plan. (*Reconstruction*)

De l'Orme's plan for the Château-Neuf and de Brosse's for Blérancourt may have had a common inspiration in a plan of similar type engraved by Serlio in his Third Book, published seventeen years before de l'Orme began the work at Saint Germain. Describing the advantages of such a plan, Serlio wrote, 'ella non è impedita da nessun late dove i quattro angoli hanno la luce apertissima', a description which also fits Blérancourt.[27]

26. Fig. 2 is reproduced from Professor Blunt's *Philibert de l'Orme*, fig. 10.

27. Cf. for Blérancourt the doubled pavilions introduced by de l'Orme in his second design for Saint Maur, which is an adaptation from his plan for the Château-Neuf. The possible influence of Baptiste du Cerceau's plan of the Hôtel d'Angoulême and some of Jacques I du Cerceau's plans in the Pierpont Morgan Library Album are also relevant. The engraved plan by Serlio referred to is III, fol. 122 verso. Finally, cf. also de l'Orme, *Architecture*, fol. 19, to which Professor Blunt draws attention in connection with this type of plan in *Philibert de l'Orme*, p. 67, n. 2.

Jacques I du Cerceau had been influenced as we have seen by Serlio's small-scale block-plans,[28] and adapted them to accommodate the French *appartement* as the basic unit of planning. He experimented with these plans in some of his designs for free-standing châteaux or country manors; one of them is certainly based on Madrid; another, for a 'bâtiment à plaisir' which we have already seen has, despite its quite different plan and its circular courtyard, an elevation of great interest for Blérancourt (Pl. 11). A third has a compactness of plan and a sobriety and restraint in elevation which seem well in advance of its time. Despite its comparatively small scale, this third design might well have appealed to de Brosse's strong sense of composition in mass[29] (Pl. 90).

The ancestry of the free-standing block-plan used at Blérancourt is thus fairly complex. Direct Italian influence upon it is probable, re-inforced by French prototypes, notably de l'Orme's Château-Neuf.

For the interior planning and appearance of Blérancourt we have no evidence save what can be gleaned from Bergeron's description and from the contracts of 1614 and 1619 for the staircase and decoration. The substructure of the château remains, enclosing the cellars, and this might provide clues which have so far not been followed. According to the usual practice, however, the central block would have contained the principal staircase, the wings to each side of it the state rooms and the four pavilions the *appartements*, one or two to each floor. It is safe to assume that the 'Grand' Salle' decorated by Fréminet and Tremblay was on the first floor, to one side or the other of the staircase, which was presumably approached through the central door in the frontispiece. The fact that the projection of the central block on the garden -side was greater than on the entrance-front was presumably due to the need to accommodate the staircase.[30] One of Silvestre's engravings (Pl. 92) suggests, probably correctly, that there was a clear way through, under the first landing, to the terrace and garden beyond. This arrangement, which we have already seen at Verneuil, was later used by de Brosse at Coulommiers and the Luxembourg. The Blérancourt stair had double ascending flights to the first landing and in this respect was, as far as we know, of a type unique in de Brosse's work; it was a grand feature of the château particularly remarked upon by Bergeron.[31]

28. Cf. above Chap. II p. 25.

29. The château of Grosbois, cf. above Chap. II, p. 24, may originally have been designed without wings, for the present ones were added in 1614. However, Grosbois with its curved entrance-façade and grouped pavilions is designed to be seen not in the round but axially.

30. The asymmetry of the central block at Blérancourt was later adopted by Mansart at Balleroy.

31. The form of the staircase is revealed by the 1614 contract. I am indebted to Mrs Mary Whiteley for her elucidation of the staircase-plan from this document. Bergeron refers to an 'escalier à deux rampans'.

So far the architect's intentions at Blérancourt can be fairly reliably assessed, but a problem arises when we come to study the elevations of the château shown in the newly-discovered drawings.

One set of these drawings shows the frontispieces of the central block on the court and on the garden sides (Pls 97–101). (The presence of the lantern over the pediment in the second set proves that it is the garden-front which is represented, as is shown by the position of this lantern in Tavernier de Junquière's water-colour). We know that the frontispiece on the garden-side was actually built, since the 1619 contract commissioned Tremblay to sculpt a Minerva for the top of the pediment, but its form could not have been as it is shown here.

The measurements of the respective frontispieces, taken from the drawings, are as follows:

Court Side

Ground to Cornice (Doric)	19 pieds	9 pouces
First to Second Cornice (Ionic pilasters)	15 pieds	1 pouces
Attic (Corinthian)	9 pieds	6 pouces
Total	44 pieds	4 pouces

Garden Side

Ground to Cornice (Astylar base)	14 pieds	8 pouces
First to Second Cornice (Corinthian half-columns)	21 pieds	8 pouces
Attic (Corinthian)	9 pieds	6 pouces
Total	45 pieds	4 pouces

(It may help to give an idea of the relatively small size of Blérancourt if it is pointed out that the height to cornice-level of Mansart's frontispiece at Blois (Pl. 164) was sixty feet).

The disparity of the total height of each face is not particularly significant. It may be due to inaccuracies in the original drawing, or in the modern calculations made from it, or it may be explicable by the raised terrace on the court-side shown in Silvestre's engravings and on the general plan.[32] What is disturbing when we compare these two drawings is the difference in heights of the floors on the two fronts and the fact that the first floor is articulated on

32. The greater number of steps to the door of the entrance-front as compared with the door of the garden-front suggests a change of level within the house. Unfortunately, the 1612 contract gives us the measurements for the thickness of the walls of the storeys of the two pavilions of the entrance-front but not their height.

one façade by Ionic pilasters and on the other by Corinthian half-columns.[33]

None of this would matter, were we not considering a free-standing building which we can reasonably assume to have had a single arrangement of superimposed orders carried right round it.

The 1612 contract stipulates that the angle-pavilions are to be of two storeys and an attic; the orders are to be Doric, Ionic and, for the attic, what the document describes as 'little pilasters'. This arrangement is seen in the drawings of the court-side of the central element (Pls 97–99), and the representations of the château by Silvestre and Tavernier de Junquières tally in general with these and with the contract (Pls 91, 92, 94). The surviving part of the château – the ground floors of the south-west angle-pavilion and part of the main block – prove that there, at any rate, the Doric order was carried round as the contract required and as the pictures show.

The only explanation of the discrepancies of arrangement between the court and the garden-fronts of the central block in the drawings is that the one of the garden was not made, as the others seem to have been,[34] from the executed fabric, but represents an unexecuted project by de Brosse.

The contract of 1612 reveals that Blérancourt was to be built entirely of stone; an important stipulation at that period when a combination of brick and stone was predominantly used. This decision was probably made under the influence of the patrons' impressions of Italy; it undoubtedly enhanced the classical appearance of the building for which patron and architect were striving. The detail with which the treatment of the orders is gone into enables us to confirm that most of the decoration of the pavilions corresponded with that of the frontispiece on the court-side, including, in the Ionic order, 'des chiffres de Mondit Sieur et de Ladicte Madame sur chascun pilastre' (Pl. 98).

In the entrance-façade of Blérancourt the horizontals are very strongly emphasized, and in this, his first independent château commission, de Brosse turns his back on the colossal order so beloved of his du Cerceau relatives. Not that the elder du Cerceau neglected superimposed orders, indeed he used them in several of his later drawings (Pl. 11).

As an influence on the treatment of the façades at Blérancourt, however, some of Serlio's engravings and certain of his drawings from the 'True Sixth

33. The attic above had pilasters, as in the court-frontispiece, and as in Lescot's Louvre façade.

34. It is not possible to determine the precise purpose of the B.N. drawings. They all are by the same hand, their character and internal evidence suggest that they are not working-drawings. If one of them represents an unexecuted project, we may assume that it and all the rest were copied from other drawings, or that this project was so copied and the rest made (as they appear to have been) from the fabric itself.

Book' seem more relevant, and even more so does his château of Ancy-le-
Franc (Pl. 9). De l'Orme's frontispiece at Anet and Bullant's portico at
Ecouen are precedents for de Brosse's court-frontispiece at Blérancourt, while
the work of both architects at the Tuileries is an obvious source for the treat-
treatment of the Blérancourt façades. But over and above all these different
influences, Lescot's work at the Louvre stands out as de Brosse's principal
source of inspiration, and much of the detail is distinctly related to it (Pls 3, 4).

The application of the orders on the court-side at Blérancourt is more
correct than Lescot's in its succession of Doric and Ionic. The peculiar type
of capital used for the dwarfed 'pilasters' of the attic-storey, derives both from
the Tuileries and from Lescot's Louvre; de Brosse's version of this theme was
to become almost a hallmark of his work. The mouldings in the window-
friezes on the ground floor of the court-frontispiece are found at theTuileries,
and the window above the entrance is based on a Vignola engraving.[35]
Clearly, the use of large semi-circular pediments on the frontispieces is based
on Lescot's façade; and the military trophies within it (a reference to Bernard
Potier's military office) are yet another reflection of the Louvre.

The ground-floor windows of the angle-pavilions differ from those of the
frontispiece, and derive from Michelangelesque prototypes (Pl. 102).
Windows and doors with flat caps and this particular type of console were
much used in sixteenth-century Italy, notably by Ammanati and followers of
Vignola. Such consoles were used by de l'Orme at Anet, and by the designer
of the screen-doors at Saint Etienne-du-Mont in Paris.[36] The author of the
'Derand' album made neo-Florentine door-designs using this motif, but in
view of de Brosse's extensive use of this kind of window at the Luxembourg,
the influence of Ammanati at the Pitti may have already been at work at
Blérancourt.

In the project for the garden-frontispiece the central window (Pl. 101) is
an adaptation from Lescot, though the curious way in which the frame-
mouldings are carried right down to the first-floor cornice does not occur
at the Louvre. It has a type of drapery in the frieze which was to become a
characteristic motif in de Brosse's buildings. The remainder of the ornament on this front and the niche, are more closely related to Coulommiers,
while the cartouches are reminiscent of Fréminet's and Tremblay's work at
Fontainbleau. This type of cartouche, based on Italian mannerist originals,
and rare at this date in France, became very popular in the 1620s and
1630s.

35. Vignola, *Regole*, XXXV.
36. Possibly designed by de l'Orme; cf. Blunt, *Philibert de l'Orme*, p. 77.

Fig. 3. Blérancourt. Original appearance of the detached Pavilions (Reconstructed from Drawings in the Bibliothèque Nationale, Paris)

This analysis of detail in the drawings of the frontispieces at Blérancourt is made to show the sources of de Brosse's inspiration. We can judge more easily of the effect that the lost entrance-façade would have had when we come to look at the surviving moat-pavilions and the *porte d'honneur*.

Until the discovery of the Bibliothèque Nationale drawings, it was often assumed that the detached pavilions were of a later date than the château itself,[37] an assumption founded mainly on their present roofs, which give them an air of the later seventeenth century. These roofs are modern, based on those put on in 1652.[38] The relevant drawings show the original arrangement of the pavilions[39] (Fig. 3 and Pl. 103).

The south-west pavilion was very much restored in the 1920s, when it was lived in by the founder of the Blérancourt museum. The other one, here illustrated, has much more original work left, although some stone is re-cut and the balustrade is modern.

In their original form these pavilions follow on from those at Verneuil and Montceaux (Pls 22, 55), but are more sophisticated. The horizontally ribbed domes derive from Verneuil, and the surmounting cupolas are characteristic of de Brosse, as are the pedimented *tablettes* above the *oeils-de-boeuf*. The bold way in which the cornice is carried up over the circular opening is an arrangement derived from du Cerceau which de Brosse also used in his own house at Verneuil (Pls 108, 109).

There were no pilasters on the detached pavilions; Tavernier de Junquière's sketch is here misleading; the Bibliothèque Nationale drawing proves that the rustication of the corners, though some of it may be restoration, is part of the original design. The slightly raised panel cut away round the windows and beneath the masks under the *oeils-de-boeuf*, adds interest to the wall-surface and may have influenced Mansart's treatment of the small pavilions which he added, in 1631, to de Brosse's château at Coulommiers. The windows, still somewhat high and narrow, like those of Jacques II du Cerceau, have finely-cut details, of which most of those on the south-east pavilion are original. Particularly striking in these windows is the severe treatment of the leaf-mouldings in the friezes and the decoration of the consoles (Pl. 109).

37. Cf. above n. 22.

38. The post-1652 roofs, shown in Tavernier's sketch, were blown off in the 1914–1918 war. A water-colour in the Musée de Blérancourt by Metouet shows the pavilions roofless, but with the walls not too badly damaged.

39. Another piece of evidence for the early date of these pavilions and their original appearance is provided by a drawing made by Gentilhâtre (fol. 25 verso) about 1620–1625. He has added a great deal of extraneous ornament and rustication, but their form is clearly visible beneath it.

The more florid decorative foliage in the friezes of the pavilions themselves is linked with that on the outer gate at Blérancourt (Pl. 113), and it is also interesting to compare it with the decoration of the pediment and keystone of the Porte Henri IV at Verneuil (Pl. 25).

The inner gate, or *porte d'honneur*, between the pavilions, has already been mentioned in Chapter III as the most impressive of a series of Vignolesque doors and gates designed by de Brosse early in his career (Pls 104–106). It is directly based on the Porta della Vigna Grimani from Vignola's *Porte di Michelangelo*, but in de Brosse's version we find a transformation similar to that which he effected in his treatment of the door at the Hôtel de Soissons (Pl. 75). De Brosse once more demonstrates the gift he shared with Lescot, a particular ability to adapt the Italian idiom to something entirely and unmistakably French.

Looking at the detached pavilions and the *porte d'honneur* together (Pl. 110), and even allowing for the partial restoration of the former, we can gain some idea of what the quality of the stonework on the façades of the château must have been, and of the impression which the classical proportions and fine decoration must have made upon the visitor; an impression which is also partially recaptured by the smallest drawing from the Bibliothèque Nationale series (Pl. 107).

The outer gate also survives, with its adjoining pavilions (Pls 113, 114, 116). Its inspiration is again Vignolesque.[40] The flat, sharp rustication with its unbroken lines is of the same kind as on the inner gate, but more massive in feeling; both gates compare in this with the door of the Hôtel de Soissons and the Porte Henri IV, and also with the surviving basement of the château (Pl. 112). The opening on the inner side of this gate, with the arch so depressed as to be nearly straightened, is most unusual.

It is interesting to compare this gate with a drawing, a far from Italianate design, by Jacques I du Cerceau in the Pierpont Morgan album (Pl. 111). This drawing is placed in the album next to the one cited earlier in the chapter on Verneuil, which probably influenced the Porte Henri IV (Pl. 24).

Du Cerceau is also recalled in the style of the pavilions at each side of the outer gate; they are descendants of the Verneuil pavilions, with their horizontally-ribbed domes, and somewhat more sophisticated versions of the gate-pavilions in the forecourt at Montceaux. An amusing detail of the pavilions was the dog which sat upon the top of each; the drawing shows one of them, but today only the paws remain (Pl. 115).

40. Cf. 'Porte di Michelangelo', xxxiiii, 'Porta della Vigna del Cardinale di Sermoneta'.

This gate is extremely impressive, and together with the *porte d'honneur* helps us to imagine the impact made by the great *portes-cochères*, now destroyed, which de Brosse built in Paris, and which Sauval so much admired.

A further small fragment of Blérancourt remains; one of a pair of gates which led to the stable-yard and the gardens on each side of the outer approach (Pl. 115). This garden-gate curiously resembles in feeling the chapel-façade at Montceaux, and like the chapel-façade it is unfinished and has uncut stones in it; the triglyphs and cartouche are blank. The width of the arched opening in proportion to the rest of the gate is curious, and it is apposite that this fragment at Blérancourt should be reminiscent of two gates in Italy which may well have been seen by the Potiers on their travels, the Roman gate at Rimini and a gate at the Villa Garzoni at Ponte Casale.

There are still many things to be discovered about Blérancourt, but we know enough to be sure that architecturally it is a very important landmark both in de Brosse's own career and for future developments in France. Despite some links in style with de Brosse's preceding work at Verneuil and Montceaux, it marks a great advance on anything he had previously done. This is manifested in the plan, in the handling of classical detail and in the decoration.

It has been important to list all the influences discernible at Blérancourt because an analysis of them shows that at this château de Brosse, though he did not forget the du Cerceau tradition, looked chiefly to de l'Orme, to Bullant, and above all to Lescot and Vignola.

What remains at Blérancourt shows us this combination of influences turned to very happy account. Bergeron was probably not alone in recognizing this building as something exceptional, for here de Brosse had revived and developed a classical spirit not seen in France for over half a century. For this reason the loss of Blérancourt is a tragic one, the preservation of what does remain most fortunate.

CHAPTER VI

The Château of Coulommiers

D E BROSSE's next undertaking was the château of Coulommiers-en-
Brie for the Duchesse de Longueville. Something has already
been said about this château and its inauspicious beginning in
1613.[1] It was a large and important commission, but neither in de Brosse's
own career nor in the architectural history of the period can it be considered
to be of such consequence as Blérancourt; the less so because we now
know that the inception of Blérancourt preceded that of Coulommiers
by at least a year if not longer. In the context of de Brosse's whole
development, this difference of time, small though it may seem, is
significant.

Coulommiers did not depart from the traditional French château-plan;
corps-de-logis 'au fond d'une cour', wings and closing screen. We have three
early plans, two engraved by Marot (of which the one in the *Grand Marot* is
the more accurate), and one plan made at some time after the modifications
to the entrance-front were undertaken in 1631 (Pls 117, 118). The latter
belongs to a series of five drawings recently acquired by the Bibliothèque
Nationale. These plans (as also the elevations) can be checked with an
invaluable, detailed description of the château made in 1714.[2]

At the angles of the court are doubled pavilions, recalling the *First Design*
for Verneuil (Pl. 14), one large one terminating each wing and one 'petit
pavillon hors oeuvre'.[3] The entrance-front of the original design (shown in
the Marot plans) was formed by a screen with a terraced walk above, and a
large entrance-pavilion of two storeys with a chapel in the upper floor,[4]
as at Montceaux and Verneuil. The plan in the *Grand Marot*, some of which
is taken at first-floor level, may show this chapel. The north wing is of one

1. Above, Chap. I, pp. 13-14. For all detailed source-references, see Cat. pp. 214-222.
2. Cf. Cat. p. 215 for this *Procès Verbal* and pp. 217-220 for a full discussion of all the drawings. It is
difficult to date them, but the plan would appear to have been made from the building itself, and
it is accurate, agreeing with the *Procès Verbal* of 1714.
3. Carpentry contract, 1613, Cat. p. 214.
4. Masonry contract, 1613, Cat. p. 214.

thickness only, but the south wing is doubled, and it contained two super-imposed galleries and two chapels, one above the other, leading off them.[5] The *corps-de-logis* at the end of the court is linked to the wings by quadrant arcades, the motif already seen at the Hôtel de Bouillon,[6] an invention which was later to influence Mansart at Berny and Blois (Pls 77, 164).

It is not certain whether the doubling of the south wing was originally intended. On all the plans the north wing (probably the earlier as far as the outer structure was concerned)[7] has nine bays on each side, whereas the south wing has nine on the courtyard and seven only on the outer face (Pls 117, 118).[8] There are many details in the 1714 description which indicate that the south wing had been altered in several ways, internally and externally, during the long period of building at Coulommiers. Also, the fenestration of the smaller pavilions is not the same on each of these fronts (although in the *Petit Marot* the engraver has 'corrected' this).[9]

As there was to be a chapel in the entrance-pavilion, it would scarcely seem necessary to have had two more in the south wing. Catherine's son, Henri II de Longueville, seems to have been responsible for most of the interior arrangements of this wing, and he certainly began, though he never finished, these two chapels.[10] The wing itself, however, was built by Catherine in the 1620s,[11] so the chapels may have been part of de Brosse's original design, or added by him later because no entrance-pavilion chapel was available. Alternatively, they and the whole outer part of the south wing may date only from the moment when the entrance-front was finally abandoned in 1631. Two points about this part of the plan are of interest; the oval chapel-plans are very characteristic of de Brosse; and the idea of the double wing with a chapel leading off it derives from the plan of de l'Orme's château of Anet.

The form of the principal staircase in the *corps-de-logis* was probably inspired to a certain extent by du Cerceau's *First Design* for Verneuil (Pl. 14). The

5. *Procès Verbal*.

6. Cf. above, Chap. IV, p. 64.

7. Masonry contract, 1613; Accounts 1619–1629, Cat. pp. 214-215.

8. The *Procès Verbal* apparently contradicts the plans, '... (la) façade du nord ... est comme l'autre ornée de 7 croisées au rez-de-chaussée et autant au dessus compris 3 grandes croisées cintrées...'. But despite the word 'compris' I believe that the writer intended to indicate nine bays, seven rectangular and three arched.

9. Admittedly the *Grand Marot* plan may show the pavilion at first-floor level, but all the evidence is against any of the pavilions having a fenestration of two-over-one.

10. Hébert and Fleigny MSS; *Procès Verbal*; Accounts 1619–1629; cf. Cat. pp. 215-216.

11. Accounts 1619–1629.

state-rooms were on the first floor of the north wing[12] as at Montceaux; later, in 1631, François Mansart built the large and very interesting staircase which is shown in detail in this wing on the Bibliothèque Nationale plan[13] (Pl. 118). Mansart was probably also responsible for the 'chambre du bain'[14] in the south-west pavilion, the oval pool of which is seen in the Bibliothèque Nationale plan on the right of the entrance-front, and he certainly contrived the ingenious arrangement of the inner façades of the two angle-pavilions at the entrance-end of the court.[15]

Most of the more striking details of the later plan are therefore due to Mansart, but the quadrant arcades were definitely part of the contract of 1613 for which de Brosse provided the drawings.[16] A result of the introduction of these arcades is that the symmetry of the courtyard was arranged on a two-tier system. At ground-floor level the unit was a square, formed by the entrance-screen and by the wings as far as the terrace which lay in front of the *corps-de-logis* and between the arcades. At this level the wings had only nine out of eleven bays visible, and the *corps-de-logis* only seven out of nine, for two bays in each wing and one at each end of the *corps-de-logis* were masked by the arcades. At first-floor level all the bays of the three façades were visible and the symmetry was based on the full rectangle of the court. The door in each wing was placed in the centre of the ground-floor disposition, leading to the apparent asymmetry of Marot's engraving of the south wing on the court-side (Pl. 122).

We are more fortunate at Coulommiers than at Blérancourt in the comprehensiveness of the early representations of the château in elevation which have come down to us. There are the three engravings by Marot (Pls 120–122); two – unreliable – by Silvestre; two coloured drawings in the Bibliothèque Nationale (Pls 126, 127);[17] several drawings in the so-called 'de Brosse' album in the Louvre (Pls 123–125);[18] and a water-colour of the garden-front still in private hands. In addition, there is a representation of the garden-front in the

12. Fleigny and Hébert MSS; *Procès Verbal.*

13. Masonry contract 1631. This is an interesting parallel with Montceaux where de Brosse later added the semi-circular stair to the staterooms of the S. wing. See above, Chap. III p. 53.

14. *Procès Verbal.*

15. Masonry contract 1631. For Mansart's work at Coulommiers, cf. A. Braham and P. Smith, op. cit., in preparation.

16. '. . . . ad(ict) deux terrasses à costé du portail sera faict un appuy sur le premier cornice ionique . . . suivant les desseigns . . .'.

17. Cf. Cat. pp. 217-219. The drawings are eighteenth-century, and are connected with the Hébert MSS. They were certainly made after the demolition of the château and are probably copies of earlier drawings.

18. For a discussion of this album, its problems and importance, cf. Cat. pp. 219-220.

background of a plaster relief decoration of about 1630 in the Capuchin church built by du Ry beside the château (Pl. 119).[19]

It will be necessary to go into the problems posed by the various representations in some detail, because until now it has always been assumed that Coulommiers was as Marot engraved it. The *Procès Verbal* of 1714 and the newly-published drawings show that this was not so. The engraving of the entrance-front is inscribed by Marot, 'Principale entrée du Chasteau de Colombiers comme estoit la pensée de l'architecte', but it was never erected. Presumably Marot had seen either the contract-drawing or some copy of it, for his engraving follows in general the stipulations for the entrance-front laid down in the 1613 contract.

In 1631 all hope of building this front was given up; the cost, on top of the already crippling expenses of the rest of the project was too much. Charles du Ry contracted to build instead two small pavilions and a closing balustrade to Mansart's designs, and the stone for them came from the abandoned foundations of de Brosse's projected buildings.[20]

The supposition that Marot knew de Brosse's original drawings is important when we come to consider his engraving of the exterior of the château (Pl. 120), inscribed 'Le costé de dehors du Chasteau de Colombieres en Brie'. This shows one of the wings (almost certainly the north) and the doubled pavilions, but is not said to represent the 'pensée originale de l'Architecte'; nor, on the other hand, does it show this part of the building as it was actually executed.

The most important difference occurs in the pavilions which flank the wings. Marot, followed by Silvestre, shows them with only two storeys, and this form is apparently also shown in a drawing in the Louvre album (Pl. 125).[21]

The fact that in Marot's engraving the large terminal pavilions are a storey higher than the inner ones has the effect of making the central part of this façade a strongly united horizontal mass, firmly enclosed within the sharp verticals of the terminal pavilions. In the château as it was built, however, all

19. The Capuchin church and convent were founded by Catherine de Gonzague. They figure in the building accounts of 1618–1629. Cf. Dauvergne, *Notice sur le Château Neuf et l'Eglise des Capucins à Coulommiers-en-Brie*, p. 597 ff.

20. '... Plus sera desmoly du massif sur lequel doivent poser les susdits pavillons tout ce qui sera nécessaire pour construire iceulx. Ensemble fondre à neuf au (susdit) massif tout ce qu'il conviendra suivant ledict dessein et semblables materiaulx au susdict massif ...', from masonry contract of 1631.

21. Though, as this stops abruptly at the top, it is impossible to say absolutely that a third floor was not intended. The drawing differs from Marot in having rusticated quoins. Cf. Cat. p. 219, RF 5946, fol. 21 recto.

the pavilions were of equal height, eight of them, each of three storeys and thus they appear in all the representations of the château apart from Marot's and Silvestre's, and are so described in the *Procès Verbal*. In addition all eight originally had high, pointed roofs.[22]

Such a stress on the vertical and on a more broken silhouette seem surprising in a château begun after Blérancourt, which was, as we have seen, strongly horizontal and unified in treatment. The long building history of Coulommiers, and the probably almost immediate delegation of the entire enterprise to Charles du Ry, would suggest that the heightening of the small pavilions was due to the latter.

All the same, although we may grant that Marot's version can be supported by his actually having seen drawings by de Brosse, the decision to make all the pavilions of three storeys must have been taken at a very early date. The masonry contract of 3 January 1613 stipulates, '. . . et lestage atticque estant sur le deux'e cornice des pavillons seulement sera aussy de pierre de taille en son parement et portera ornemens et pilastres . . .', and the carpentry contract (7 December 1613) says, '. . . item; sera faict la charpenterie des planchers des premier et second et troisième estage du petit pavillon hors oeuvre joignant le grand pavillon . . .'.

There is one important feature of the exterior façades of the two wings which is not shown in Marot's elevations, and which only appears in the south wing in his plan. The three central bays of each wing contained large arched windows on each floor. These are shown in the south wing in the perspective (Pl. 127) and are mentioned as existing in both wings in the *Procès Verbal*. The Bibliothèque Nationale plan shows that these windows did not correspond to the interior arrangements in the south wing (Pl. 118). The most westerly window lights the chapel and the other two give light to two small rooms in which they are placed off-centre. In the north wing the corresponding bay lights Mansart's staircase, and the other two open asymmetrically on to small rooms.[23] This suggests that these arched windows were not part of the original design. Moreover, this motif of three arched openings with three more above them is exceedingly unusual before the

22. The drawings contradict each other on this, and possibly the roofs were lowered later, but in the 1630s they were high and pointed. This is proved by the plaster-relief in the Capuchin church. The general accuracy of this representation can be checked by a comparison of it with a drawing from the Louvre album (Pl. 124) which can, in its turn, be checked by the masonry contract of 1613 and the *Procès Verbal* of 1714.

23. Though there is an error in the total number of bays in the N. wing; see above, n. 8. The fact that Marot does not show the three arched openings in the wing he engraved supports the possibility that he shows the N. wing and made his elevation from an earlier design.

1640s. The *Procès Verbal* is quite explicit that the arrangement was repeated in both wings, so it seems likely that it was introduced at the time, after 1631, when Mansart built his staircase in the north wing and possibly designed the chapels for Henri de Longueville in the south wing.

There is no engraving by Marot of the garden-front, but there are various other representations which unfortunately conflict with one another on certain points: a perspective by Silvestre; a drawing by du Ry in the Louvre album (Pl. 124); a water-colour in private hands;[24] and the plaster relief in the church of the Capuchins (Pl. 119). The Louvre drawing and the plaster relief correspond fairly exactly, and in neither is a dome indicated. The absence of a dome seems to be confirmed by the drawing of the *corps-de-logis* in the Bibliothèque Nationale (Pl. 126) and by the absence of any reference to it in the *Procès Verbal* or the carpentry contracts. It seems safe to assume there-fore that Silvestre's engraving, and the perspective view of the Bibliothèque Nationale (Pl. 127) are incorrect on this point. Du Ry's Louvre drawing is almost certainly reliable, and was probably made during the early stages of the building. It differs from the description in the *Procès Verbal* in only one respect, in showing no niches between the columns flanking the arched entrance. On the other hand, these niches, as far as can be made out, are also absent in the plaster relief; the *Procès Verbal* may be at fault, confusing the court- and garden-fronts of the central pavilion of the *corps-de-logis*.

Du Ry's drawing serves a useful purpose as a corrective to Marot's render-ing of the exterior treatment of the château. Marot, working later in the century, has 'classicized' his façades, slightly altering the window-proportions, enlarging the niches, and playing down the strongly-rusticated *voussoirs* and keystones so as to give a more unified and stately effect.

Coulommiers, despite a more correct handling of orders and details than in either of the earlier châteaux, was in spirit a direct descendant of Verneuil and Montceaux, and with the exception of two outstanding features had nothing about it as inventive as Blérancourt. These exceptions were the quadrant arcades of the court and the design for the entrance-front (Pl. 121).

The contract of 1613 lays down for the entrance-front that '. . . les endroitz du portail et ses retours la fonda'on en sera d'espoisseur convenable eu égard à la masse d'Iceluy . . . des murs du dehors portant lesd. terrasses iusques à la haulteur de la corniche sera de pareille pierre de taille portant le même ordre Toscan avec les croisées entre deux et la reste de brique . . . des dosseretz

24. For the water-colour in, or lately in, the Ogier de Baulny collection, which I only saw briefly and cannot illustrate, and for a general discussion of the problems of this collection, cf. Cat. p. 220.

qui porteront des arcs doubles avec des voultes . . . La massonnerie du portail sera ornée de coulonnes et de pilastres tant en ses faces qu'aux retours jusques à la haulteur de la première cornice de l'ordre qui sera advisé par Madame . . . ensemble les grandes portes dentrée entre lesd. coulonnes le tout de pierre de taille . . . Audessus de la cornice sera faict un aticque avec tous ses ornemens et couronnemens et appuy pour servir à la terrasse qui sera aupourtour dud. portail . . . et audessus sera une chapelle par dedans oeuvre et ses entrées et sorties par les terrasses . . . le tout suivant les desseings qu'en seront donnez tant p'or le dehors dud. portail que le dedans servant po'r la chapelle et dosme . . .'.

Then, in the concluding legal paragraph of the contract come the words, referring to the whole château, '. . . suivant le plan paraphé par les notaires soubssignez en elevation que le Sieur de Brosse en a faict lequel plan est demeuré ès mains desdicts entrepreneurs . . .'.

Whether Marot saw this plan 'en élevation', and whether it was this which formed the principal basis for his engravings, is a speculation, but there is no doubt that this was the drawing which is said to have 'deceived' Mme de Longueville.

The wording of the contract is interesting, not only as regards the intended entrance-front, but as an indication of method. 'The drawings will be supplied later . . .'; the order to be used for the central pavilion 'will be advised by Madame', despite the stipulation of the Tuscan order for the screen. It is likely that many of the drawings supplied later were prepared not by de Brosse himself but by du Ry.

The entrance-pavilion which de Brosse intended for Coulommiers was related to those at Verneuil and Montceaux. These too were designed to be of brick and stone, were decorated with an order of columns, contained chapels on the first floor, and were surmounted by domes. But at Coulommiers, the Colossal order used at Verneuil and Montceaux was abandoned in favour of three superimposed orders, and the principal source of inspiration was undoubtedly the Valois mausoleum at Saint Denis (Pl. 6).

Primaticcio's design for the Valois mausoleum was, as we know, inspired by Bramante's Tempietto, so the entrance-pavilion proposed by de Brosse for Coulommiers has an ancestry reaching back to the Italian High Renaissance.

Marot's engraving remains the only visual evidence we have for de Brosse's design of the entrance-front, and it would be unwise to rely on any details which are not vouched for by the 1613 contract. From this contract we have seen that, in its general lines, the engraving is correct, and so too is Marot's representation of the screen with its high arched openings, recalling the screen which de Brosse had built for Henriette d'Entragues at Verneuil (Pl. 22).

The whole entrance-front at Coulommiers was evidently an exercise for a larger and more important design which was already in de Brosse's mind: the entrance-pavilion and screen for the Luxembourg (Pl. 150). As altered by Chalgrin in the early nineteenth century the Luxembourg screen is even closer to Coulommiers than the original, which was not pierced by arcades (Pl. 141). It is fortunate that in this way the most original and impressive part of the Coulommiers design, though it was never realized, is recalled for us by Chalgrin in a part of de Brosse's most celebrated work.

The use of the Tuscan and Doric orders on the exterior walls at Coulommiers is characteristic of de Brosse; he preferred these always, and had used them at Blérancourt. As at Blérancourt also, de Brosse has not carried the pilasters right to the corners of the building and, characteristically, he preferred to stress not the angles but the divisions of the window-bays by coupled pilasters.

The capitals of the 'little pilasters' of the attic-storey in the pavilions and frontispieces appear to have been the same as those used in parts of Blérancourt and the Luxembourg (Pls 99, 154).

Dauvergne, in his 'reconstructions' of Coulommiers made in the nineteenth century,[25] shows curious coupled herms in the attic-storey of the larger pavilions (to which he wrongly allots three window-bays and a Corinthian order on the first floor). These herms may also be seen in the perspective elevation of the Bibliothèque Nationale (Pl. 127), although whether they ever existed or not is uncertain; if they did, they more probably emanated from du Ry than from de Brosse. They, and the statues in the niches shown in the perspective elevation, may be suspect in the light of a declaration by the *Procès Verbal*: '. . . mais comme dans les faces exterieures il n'y a point de colonnes, statues, figures ni autres ouvrages de sculpture en relief en danger d'estre cassées par la chute des pierres . . . desdites Lucarnes . . .'. But even this quotation reads somewhat ambiguously, and it may simply mean that the herms did not project enough to qualify.

The *lucarnes*, alternating with urns on pedestals, are shown in detail in one of the Louvre drawings (Pl. 123). The whole effect above the cornice was ornamental and picturesque, but for this reason also rather old-fashioned.

Before we leave the exterior of the château, it should be stressed again that the whole building was of brick and stone. This is not at all clear either from

25. Cat. p. 220.

Marot's engravings or Dauvergne's 'reconstructions'. But now we have the evidence of the 1613 contract and of the *Procès Verbal*, of the indication 'b' for brique, in the Louvre drawings, and above all of the two elevations in the Bibliothèque Nationale. These, in the original, are very brightly coloured: bright red for the brick, dazzling white for the stone, blue for the slate roofs. They, far more than Marot's sober engravings, and despite incorrect details and proportions, give a true impression of what Coulommiers really looked like (Pls 126, 127). The only brickwork surviving at Coulommiers is on part of a wall remaining behind one of the quadrant arcades.

All that is left of de Brosse's work at Coulommiers are the fragments of the quadrant arcades, one of which has been slightly restored, the other scarcely touched (Pls 128, 130) and the entrance to the main *corps-de-logis* with part of its flanking niches (Pl. 129). The plan of the chapels of the south wing is preserved in gravel and grass.[26]

As the buildings of the courtyard stood, the *corps-de-logis* and the wings were of equal height, of two storeys, and each had an identical frontispiece with an attic-storey surmounted by a large segmental pediment. The frontispieces, with their superimposed orders of full columns, in this case Ionic and Corinthian, are modelled even more closely than those at Blérancourt on the pavilions of Lescot's wing at the Louvre (Pl. 3). But, at Coulommiers, the two superimposed orders of full columns are carried right round the whole court, and not limited to the central feature on each side. This use of columns necessitated deeper breaks in the entablatures which, together with the elaborate decoration of the window-pediments, the sculptured decoration of busts and figures, and the *lucarnes*, urns and statues of the roofline, must have produced a restless and overpowering effect. We are reminded of the over-decorated court-façades at Verneuil shown in du Cerceau's engravings. As if all this were not enough, there was, as at Verneuil, the contrast of brick walls with stone dressing and decoration. How much of this elaboration was de Brosse's own conception, and how much was dictated by the patron, we cannot know, but it is all included in the 1613 contract.

So very little of the original building is left at Coulommiers that it is difficult to judge the scale, but we are helped by the survival of the quadrant arcades, for from them we can tell that the height from the ground-floor to the top of the cornice was approximately 24 feet; the height of the buildings round the court was approximately 48 feet, and the frontispieces were about 56 feet high to the top of the pediments.

26. Blomfield, II, p. 58, gives the measurements of the court, 180×150 feet, which may be compared with the court of the Luxembourg, 210×180 feet.

One difficulty confronts us when we consider the treatment of the court-yard façades. Where the wings joined the angle-pavilions of the entrance-front, there would have been, at ground-floor level, a juxtaposition of Tuscan pilasters with Ionic columns; and at first-floor level of Doric pilasters with Corinthian columns. We do not know what was proposed for the inner side of de Brosse's entrance-screen, which might have solved this difficulty at ground-floor level. But on the first floor the junction would not have been happy. As it was, when Mansart had to design new ground-floor façades on the court-side for the angle-pavilions (after the abandonment of the screen), he could not solve the problem de Brosse had set. All he could do was to substitute Tuscan columns for the pilasters.

This is an example of de Brosse's besetting weakness; he could compose splendidly in mass, and could design fine details, but he so often failed to con-sider the relationship between the details of one part of a building and another.

The quality of the courtyard façades at Coulommiers, so crudely portrayed in the Bibliothèque Nationale drawing, can be assessed to some extent by examination of the still-surviving quadrant arcades, although there was no elaborate decoration on these.

The three frontispieces of the courtyard are very exactly described in the 1613 contract, and, with one exception, the details shown in the Bibliothèque Nationale drawing conform to it (Pl. 126). The exception is interesting: the Coulommiers contract more or less repeats the requirements for the attic storey at Blérancourt, '. . . sera faict un atticque audessus des corps saillans ornez de petitz pillastres garnis de leurs bases chapitaux Cornices & frontons & amortissemens croisées & quadres dans les atticques . . .'. The drawing, however, shows figures which may (the drawing is ambiguous) support the attic-cornice, and the *Procès Verbal* confirms their presence: '. . . Au dessus . . . est un atique, . . . orné de pilastres et corniches avec quatre figures représentant des enfants et une croisée dans le milieu le tout aussy orné de sculptures . . .'.

Whether de Brosse or du Ry decided upon the addition of the figures we cannot tell. They may have been caryatids or they may have stood free of the cornice like the figures which de Brosse later designed for the central pavilion of the *corps-de-logis* at the Luxembourg (Pl. 165). If they were caryatids, it should be noted that they pre-dated by at least ten or fifteen years the caryatids of Lemercier's design for the attic-storey of the Pavillon de l'Horloge at the Louvre. The relationship between Coulommiers and Lemercier's design will be discussed more fully below, in connection with the staircase at the château.[27]

27. See below pp. 107-108.

The windows of the court-façades departed altogether from the Lescot models which inspired de Brosse at Blérancourt; the decoration was much heavier and more deeply cut. The broken pediments contained masks, and beneath them were heavy consoles. Particularly interesting are the friezes of the ground-floor windows, visible in the Bibliothèque Nationale drawing of the *corps-de-logis* (Pl. 126). Here swags of drapery are 'pulled through' a central console. Drapery pulled through a console, or in some cases a loop or ring, is a motif which is often associated with buildings by de Brosse. The drawings show that it occurred at Blérancourt in a not very emphatic way, but here it is more prominent.

The source for this motif is the Florentine sixteenth-century school; the work of Ammanati, Buontalenti and Cigoli,[28] which also inspired the cartouches of the Blérancourt garden-frontispiece. Similar treatment of drapery or swags is found in the drawings of the 'Derand' album in the Louvre, where in one case the drapery is actually pulled up through the cornice; and in the 'de Brosse' album in the Louvre, in a pedestal probably designed for Coulommiers (Pl. 123).

Such details of the sculptured decoration at Coulommiers influenced Mansart not only in the entrance-pavilions he himself built at the château, but in his early Church of the Visitation and later at Maisons-Lafitte (Pls 131, 132). The derivation of Mansart's console-and-swag and garland motifs seems clear, and it is also possible that the eagles and drapery-swags on the façade of the Visitation were influenced by the great eagles in the frontis-piece-pediments at Coulommiers.

There must have been a large team of sculptors working at Coulommiers, and for a long time. If the statues and busts for all the court-façades, as well as the statues for the roof-line and various balustrades, are taken into account, not to mention the relief-sculpture, the total amount of work involved must have been enormous.

Some of the sculptors are identified in the accounts of the 1620s. The names include David de Villiers, a certain 'Timothée', and Pierre Collot, who published a book of designs for doors and chimney-pieces. The château must therefore have been a centre for decorative sculpture in the early part of the century, and others besides Mansart were no doubt influenced by it.

If we compare the quadrant arcades at Coulommiers with the columned entrance-pavilion at Montceaux (Pl. 69), we can see, despite the ruinous

28. Buontalenti had come to France. This is mentioned in a latter from Marie de Médicis to the Grand Duke of Tuscany (quoted by Pannier, who does not give the date but puts it as shortly after 1610). Cf. Pannier, p. 53. Buontalenti died in 1608.

state of both, that the handling of the former is far more sophisticated and that the influence of Vignolesque classicism is much more pronounced. Furthermore, it seems, from the Bibliothèque Nationale drawings and from the ruins themselves, that the arcades were all of stone, and this must have added greatly to their impressiveness.

The extremely weathered fragment which remains of the entrance from the court to the vestibule and staircase in the central pavilion of the *corps-de-logis*, is useful as an indication of scale (Pl. 129). The question of whether or not there was meant to be a dome over this central feature has already been discussed in connection with the garden-front. Coulommiers was in most ways a traditional building, and in one way it would have been strange not to have a dome at this point, but on the other hand de Brosse did not put a dome over the frontispiece and staircase pavilion in the *corps-de-logis* of the Luxembourg (begun just after Coulommiers). The accounts of the 1620s, however, mention the dismantling and replacing of some timbers of the 'dosme', but do not specify which.[29] It may be, therefore, that a dome was originally intended for the staircase pavilion of the *corps-de-logis*, was never completed and was eventually abandoned.[30]

The staircase in the centre of the *corps-de-logis* was considered to be very remarkable. Marot's plans of it are slightly confusing,[31] but are now supplemented by the plan in the Bibliothèque Nationale series of drawings, by the 1613 contract and by the descriptions contained in the *Procès Verbal*, the Hébert and Fleigny MSS. and the *Journal* of Louis Huygens.

The contract provides for the stairs to be supported on vaults, '. . . Et sera continué led. noyau en amont tout de pierre de taille depuis le rez-de-chaussée de la terrasse jusques au dernier estage avec les voultes des deux costez dont les arcs arrestes seront de pierre de taille'.

The *Procès Verbal* reads thus: 'Nous sommes entrés par le portique du milieu de la face du principal *corps-de-logis* dans le vestibule allant de la cour au jardin, dans lequel est le grand et principal escalier conduisant jusqu'au comble, lequel est soutenu par six colonnes représentant sur toutes les faces des femmes plus grandes que nature . . .'.

The Fleigny MS. gives more details: '. . . Trois marches pour entrer dans le

29. '. . . a ésté payé à Simon Bazier, charpentier, sur ce qu'il fault pour avoir estayé le dosme pour abattre et refaire les calés . . .' (1623).
30. There was an internal dome, probably by Mansart, in one of the pavilions; and another *internal* dome, again probably by Mansart, was projected for the upper chapel. Both these are known from the *Procès Verbal*.
31. The stair-well, and by implication the vestibule, are mistakenly shown as oval by Marot in his plan in the *Petit Marot*; but this plan is in any case taken at first-floor level.

vestibule ou l'on trouvait le grand escalier . . . voûté par dessous, soutenu par des figures de femmes qui avaient beaucoup de gorge c'est pourquoi on l'appelait "l'Escalier des Nourrices" . . . Le haut de l'escalier était voûté en calotte au milieu de laquelle étaient les armes de la Maison de Gonzague et celles de Longueville que l'on voyait aisément du bas de l'escalier, c'était une pièce que l'on admirait . . .'.

Hébert's *Mémoire* provides another detail concerning the caryatids; they did not support the staircase on their heads, but their hands: '. . . son bel escalier dont les massifs étaient revêtus de figures colossales de femmes extrêmement bien sculptées qui de leurs mains en soutenaient les rampes . . .'. Louis Huygens admired it too, on his visit to Coulommiers in 1655: '. . . Une pièce fort remarquable dans la maison est le grand escalier . . . il est soutenu au lieu de colonnes par de grandes statues 2 à 2 de pierre de taille qui est fort magnifique à voir . . .'.

These descriptions do not differ materially, save that only the *Procès Verbal* mentions the number of carved figures which, in lieu of columns, supported the stair-vaults.

The rectangular stair-well was open right up to the summit of the vault which covered the whole stair-chamber and in the centre of which were displayed the arms of Longueville and Gonzaga. The stair-chamber had straight sides terminating in quadrant-curves. The influence upon this arrangement of the principal staircase in the *First Design* for Verneuil cannot be doubted; de Brosse has in fact simply added another half to du Cerceau's stair-chamber (Pls 14, 118).

At Coulommiers the visitor, entering the stair-chamber from either the courtyard or the east terrace, found himself in a shallow hall, basically a half-circle. On the court-side, the curves of the walls contrasted with those of the quadrant arcades of the courtyard; on the terrace-side they repeated them. The definition of such relatively confined spaces by graceful shallow-curved walls is yet another example among many of de Brosse's predeliction for a play on semi-circular or oval forms. In the stair-chamber at Coulommiers he was working out ideas later developed at the Luxembourg. If we reverse the staircase-plan, and look at it from the garden-side, we see something very similar to the arrangement of the chapel behind the staircase of the Luxembourg (Pl. 137).

The staircase-well at Coulommiers, as at Verneuil, formed a vestibule through which one passed under the half-landing at the eastern end out on to the terrace overlooking the garden.

The progression of levels approaching and within the staircase-vestibule

I

is easily followed on the Bibliothèque Nationale plan. Four steps led from the courtyard proper up to the terrace which lay before the *corps-de-logis*. From this terrace a flight of five steps gave access to the main entrance. Five steps led down into the vestibule in the stair-well, and four more led from the door at the far end down to the eastern terrace.

The width of the vestibule, little more than a passage, contained within the stair-well, was the same as that of the flights of the staircase. It must have been rather dark, especially at the eastern end where light was obscured by the half-landing. Darkness was a fault we have suspected in the lower part of the staircase proposed for Verneuil in the *First Design*, and the staircase of the Luxembourg was later to be criticized for the same reason.

The conception of a vestibule leading along the main access, through the stair-well and out into the garden, derives as we have seen from Verneuil, and as at Verneuil it is ultimately based on Philibert de l'Orme's staircase at the Tuileries. The arrangement at Coulommiers, however, with its changing levels and the flight of steps within the vestibule itself, is closer than Verneuil to the Tuileries, though a very long way from the complicated and subtle variations introduced there by de l'Orme.[32]

The first flight of stairs rose on the left of the stair-chamber, opposite the courtyard entrance, and led to a half-landing on the garden-side lit by the large window seen in the drawing of the garden-front ascribed to Charles du Ry (Pl. 124). The second half-landing on this side was lit by a segmental-headed opening seen in the same drawing, and the topmost part of the stair-chamber, contained within the attic-storey, received its light from a window on the court-side and an *oeil-de-boeuf* on the garden-side. In this way the upper ranges of the staircase were well-lit, a fact which is confirmed by the Fleigny MS. when it states that the coats-of-arms in the vault could easily be seen from the foot of the stairs.

The five steps seen on the right of the courtyard-entrance in the Bibliothèque Nationale plan presumably represent the beginning of a flight leading down to the basement. They are shown as being divided from the vestibule by a balustrade and by the arches supporting the return-flight of the main stair, not by a solid wall. In this way the almost total obscurity of the descending flight of the Verneuil staircase has been avoided.

There were in all four rising flights at Coulommiers from ground- to attic-level. The total height of the staircase-pavilion was approximately 56 feet; the height occupied by the staircase itself was some 12 feet less, so that the rise of each flight was approximately 11 feet. The flights were covered by

32. Blunt, *Philibert de l'Orme*, p. 100 f.

a gothic type of groined vault, with stone ribs and brick in-filling; the contract specifies, '. . . les voultes . . . dont les arcs arestes seront de pierre de taille et les residus desd. voultes seront massonez de bon mortier et brique'.[33]

These vaults would customarily have been supported on arches carried by columns or piers, as they are, for example, in the staircase of the near-contemporary château of Cormatin near Châlon-sur-Saône (Pl. 133).[34] But at Coulommiers caryatid figures replaced some, if not all, of the more traditional supports of the staircase. If there were, as the *Procès Verbal* states, six of these caryatids (or pairs of caryatids, for Huygens noted 'de Grandes statues 2 à 2 de pierre de taille'), then they presumably carried the staircase only as far as the principal rooms on the first floor. After this, in the flight leading to the attic, columns or piers would have replaced the statues. The drawback to this arrangement would have been an uncomfortable asymmetry at first-floor level, with caryatids facing plain supports across the stair-well. It is possible that the authors of the *Procès Verbal*, describing the staircase as it appeared to them when they stood on the left of the vestibule at the foot of the first flight, only specified the number of statues they could see without crossing to the other side or craning their necks.

Irrespective of their number, however, the introduction of caryatid figures at Coulommiers, possibly in the court-frontispieces and certainly in the staircase, was a very original departure.

There are two obvious sources of inspiration for these caryatids; the Brézé tomb (*c.* 1540) in Rouen Cathedral, where pairs of female caryatids support the cornice on either side of the equestrian figure of Louis de Brézé; and the gallery supported by four single caryatid figures made for the ground-floor *salle* in Lescot's Louvre wing and atrributed to Goujon.[35] Both these early examples were unusual for their time. Later du Cerceau the Elder used caryatids quite frequently in his engraved fireplace designs, and in the drawings of his followers we find them used on façade-designs of great elaboration.[36] The members of the du Cerceau circle were evidently much influenced by the

33. The term 'Arcs arestes' (or 'arêtes') derives from the word for a fishbone. The use of this type of vault, however old-fashioned, persisted well into the seventeenth century, as in the church of Notre-Dame at Vitry-le-François; cf. Hautecoeur, I, p. 675 and fig. 492.

34. No exact date can be given for this château, but it was almost certainly begun in the early years of the seventeenth century for the Marquis d'Uxelles. Some of its exterior features may be of a later date. It figures in the sketchbook of Jacques Gentilhâtre, and also in the notes and sketch-book of an unknown engineer of the early seventeenth century preserved in the Bib. Nat. MS. Fr. 14727.

35. For the history and attribution of the Brézé tomb, cf. Blunt, *Art and Architecture*, pp. 69–70. He illustrates it (pl. 52) and the Goujon gallery (pl. 30A).

36. Notably in the Fitzwilliam sketchbook, see below n. 37.

Roman temple at Bordeaux, now vanished, called the Palais des Tutelles; this building was engraved by Jacques I du Cerceau and appears in three important sketchbooks emanating from the du Cerceau circle which are in the Bodleian Library, the Fitzwilliam Museum and the Ecole des Beaux-Arts in Paris.[37] In each of these it is repeated more than once. The representation in the Bodleian sketchbook shows most clearly the caryatids which supported the entablature of the upper arcade, and the interesting effect of 'double caryatids' made in this drawing, at the junction of the façades of the temple, may have influenced the caryatids of the Coulommiers staircase if the latter were double, as Huygens says.

The Coulommiers caryatids may have acted as a sort of intermediary between the Palais des Tutelles and Lemercier's Pavillon de l'Horloge at the Louvre with its double caryatids by Sarrazin.[38] Lemercier's first design for the Pavillon de l'Horloge is recorded in a medal struck in 1624; it has no caryatids, but in general is close to the design of the frontispieces of the *corps-de-logis* and the wings in the courtyard at Coulommiers. Both are modelled on Lescot's Louvre, but Lemercier's executed design is much later than the medal or any of the work at Coulommiers. The drawings for it in Stockholm are dated 1641, and thus it is possible that Coulommiers, as well as the Palais des Tutelles, influenced Lemercier. A rare engraving by Marot, showing a design in which he proposed a caryatid staircase for the Louvre, provides a further indication of the impact which the Coulommiers stair made on later architects (Pl. 134), as also may Marot's introduction of a staircase with a single caryatid figure supporting the upper landing into his engraving of the Hôtel d'Argouges (later Carnavalet).[39]

How far de Brosse was responsible for the Coulommiers staircase design cannot be known; it was basically rather old-fashioned; only the caryatids

37. Geymüller, p. 165, fig. 80, reproduces one of the engravings. This shows figures which are not caryatids and do not reach the entablature. However, the engravings and the various drawings differ (some show no figures at all), but cf. n. 38 below. The sketchbooks are: Bodleian Library, Oxford, Rawlinson MS. D. 1023; Fitzwilliam Museum, Cambridge, Drawings 904*1; and Ecole des Beaux-Arts, Paris, Coll. Masson 4303. The latter is referred to by Geymüller, pp. 104–121. I am indebted to Mr Luke Herrmann through whose good offices I was enabled to see the MS. in the Bodleian Library.

38. Cf. Blunt, *Art and Architecture*, p. 266, n. 20, for a discussion of the Palais des Tutelles and its possible influence on Lemercier's Pavillon de l'Horloge. The Roman building, which survived into the seventeenth century, is engraved in Claude Perrault's *Les dix livres d'architecture de Vitruve* (219). For Lemercier's Pavillon de l'Horloge and the Stockholm drawings for it, cf. also Blunt, 'Two Unpublished Drawings by Lemercier for the Pavillon de l'Horloge', *Burl. Mag.*, cii, October 1960, pp. 447–448.

39. The engraving is published and discussed by A. Mauban, p. 83 and fig. 15. It is generally agreed that the staircase of the Hôtel d'Argouges is an invention by Marot.

were in any way unusual or advanced. Because of the caryatids, however, the staircase exerted, later in the century, a hitherto unsuspected influence.

When Huygens visited Coulommiers in 1655 it was still unfinished, but 'on y travaille tous les jours'. By the death of Henri II de Longueville in 1663, new building work had virtually ceased; only the endless repairs had to go on, and, as the *Procès Verbal* makes clear, these finally became too much. The château had long been old-fashioned and inconvenient; now it became ruinous, and one hundred and twenty-five years after it was begun, still unfinished, it was pulled down.

CHAPTER VII

The Palace of the Luxembourg

'MA tante. Estant en volonté de faire bastir et accomoder une maison à Paris pour me loger et voulant en quelque chose me regler sur la forme et modelle du Palais de Pitti . . . je vous fais celle cy pour vous dire que Jauray à singulier plaisir que vous m'en faciez faire un plan en son entier avec les élévations et perspectives de bastiments . . .'.

Marie de Médicis, now Regent of France, sent this request to her aunt, the Grand Duchess of Tuscany. She dictated her letter on 6 October 1611 at Fontainebleau, adding a postscript in her own hand: 'Ma tante, vous me feres bien plaisir de menvoyer le plan et les desseings du Palais de Pitty dont ie me veux servir pour l'ordre et ornement de ma maison . . . Marie'.

Eight days later, she decided on more direct action and dispatched a French architect to Florence to make the plans and drawings. She wanted 'une entière intelligence du modelle de lad. maison . . . et des mesures et proportions de toutes les pièces . . . et que pour me servir plus utillement de ce desseing pour la structure et ornement de la mienne . . . je vous ay déspeché ce porteur nommé Métezeau, architecte . . .'.[1]

This was the genesis of the Luxembourg,[2] de Brosse's most celebrated building, of which the first stone was laid in 1615.

During the period 1611–1614, while de Brosse was occupied with Bléran-court and Coulommiers, the Queen was nursing her project for a palace of her own in Paris. As her principal architect, de Brosse could keep himself fully informed about the royal intentions, and he would also have seen the drawings which Louis Métezeau brought back from Florence. The influence of these upon his own work, well before he began the Luxembourg itself, was important, and we have seen its possible effect upon his two châteaux.

De Brosse did not receive the Luxembourg commission outright, there was

---

1. For the full text of both letters, cf. Cat. p. 261-262. Métezeau was back in Paris by the following year when he attended the baptism of his daughter on 17 May 1612 (Pannier pp. 56 n.). It is probable that it was Louis, not Clément, Métezeau who went to Italy (cf. Pannier, op. cit. also E.-J. Ciprut, G.d.B.A., January 1965, vol. LXV, p. 49 ff.).

2. Cf. Cat. pp. 257-265.

a competition. This de Brosse won; he apparently submitted several plans
to the Queen from which she chose the one executed. It is said that before the
building was begun his plan was sent by the Queen to various European
courts for comment.[3]

The plan of the Palazzo Pitti had no influence whatsoever upon de Brosse's
plan for the Luxembourg;[4] he used the traditional château plan, as he had
at Coulommiers (Pls 135–138). The *corps-de-logis* is flanked by doubled
pavilions and approached by a terrace with curved steps,[5] an arrangement
recalling the plan of Blérancourt and having the same antecedents. The
court is flanked by wings terminated by single pavilions, joined by a terraced
screen which gave access to the first floor of the domed entrance-pavilion.
This by now familiar arrangement differed only from Verneuil, Montceaux
and Coulommiers in that the entrance-pavilion contained no chapel.[6]
Instead, there was a circular *salon* on the first floor with a belvedere above.

The Queen had a private oratory in her apartments in the Palace, and she
also founded the Chapel and Convent of the Filles du Calvaire beside the
Luxembourg in 1622.[7] This may explain the relatively small size of the
Palace-chapel which is on the garden-side of the *corps-de-logis*. This chapel,

3. Pannier, p. 57. Sauval, III, p. 7, says 'Le dessin de ce palais a été promené par toute l'Italie
avant que d'être exécuté. Il a passé par les mains des meilleurs Maîtres de l'Europe'. A. N. Dézallier
d'Argenville, *Vie des fameux architectes*, 1787, p. 327, repeats, 'Il fit plusieurs plans. Celui que la
reine préféra fut envoyé par ses ordres en Italie et dans plusieurs autres royaumes d'Europe aux
architectes célèbres dont la princesse souhaitait avoir l'avis'. It is interesting to speculate whether
the English architect John Thorpe saw a copy of the plan in England, for his book in the Soane
Museum contains a plan inscribed 'Queen Mothers Howse fabor Snt Jarmins atte Paris'. It is
clearly based on the Luxembourg, but is, as the inscription further reads, 'altred J. Thorpe'. Cf.
Cat. p. 260, under London, Sir John Soane's Museum.

4. Curiously, however, there appears to be a reminiscence of the Pitti plan (as Ammanati left it)
in the original lay-out of the principal parterre. Some authors have attributed the garden to de
Brosse, cf. Blomfield, II, p. 52. Pannier, p. 191 says Lasteyrie made this attribution in error in his
Paris-Guide of 1897, I, p. 597. The gardens were designed, according to Pannier, by Jacques
Boiceau, a Protestant contemporary of de Brosse, 'gentilhomme ordinaire de la chambre du Roi
et Intendant de ses jardins'. Boiceau wrote a treatise on gardening, published posthumously in
1638.

5. Blomfield, II, p. 54, criticizes the terrace, nearly 50 feet deep, because it would have to have
been traversed on foot in all weathers before reaching the *corps-de-logis*. But such terraces were a
frequent part of châteaux-plans, as at Coulommiers and Montceaux. The Queen's accounts for
building at Montceaux mention that 'les petits carrosses de la Reine' were to be kept under the
vaulted entrance-screen. These were covered wheeled or sedan chairs to convey important personages across the courtyard in inclement weather.

6. Cf. below, p. 130. There is no evidence that it ever did, even in the earliest sources.

7. Cf. Hautecoeur, I, p. 552.

and the vestibule beneath it, were joined to the angle-pavilions of the garden-front by an arcaded terrace-screen of one storey in height. This part of the plan is totally unrecognizable today, for de Brosse's *corps-de-logis* and garden-front were swept away in the nineteenth century.

The double pavilions at the south end of the Palace caused the lateral façades to be asymmetrical. This asymmetry was further stressed when, in the nineteenth century, a third pavilion was added on each side of the *corps-de-logis*, which was itself extended southwards.

Perhaps the most interesting part of the original Luxembourg plan was the arrangement of the staircase, the vestibule and the chapel in the *corps-de-logis* and the placing of the terraced loggia on each side of the chapel as part of the garden-façade. De Brosse has, as it were, created an 'entrance-screen' on the garden-side of the Palace, an inversion of the plans of Verneuil, Montceaux and Coulommiers (Pls 136–138).

The staircase occupied a rectangular well, as at Coulommiers,[8] and again there was a way through from court to garden under the mezzanine-landing, but at the Luxembourg the passage formed by the staircase-well led into a semi-circular niched vestibule flanked by the arcades of the chapel-terrace. The vestibule was preceded on the garden-front by an arched entrance between coupled columns, forming part of the frontispiece containing the chapel (Pl. 136).

The chapel above the vestibule was two storeys high (Pls 137, 138). There was no entrance to it from the staircase-landings or from the vestibule below,[9] so that the only access was from the angle-pavilions along the screen-terrace. The design thus incorporated all the inconveniences of a chapel in an entrance-pavilion of the kind which de Brosse had just designed at Coulommiers.

The chapel had an unusual plan; it was not, as might have been expected, semi-circular like the vestibule beneath it. It really consisted of a large rectangular bay, entered from the screen-terraces, from which quadrant curves led up to the altar and the deep window-embrasure. The masonry was in this way strengthened, presumably to take the thrust of the semi-dome and the lantern which covered this part of the chapel.

The only other part of the Luxembourg plan which is at all remarkable (and which survives only slightly modified in the existing structure) is the

8. Contrary to a tradition at least as early as the eighteenth century (cf. d'Argenville, op. cit., p. 329), de Brosse was responsible for the general design of this staircase. This is proved by the *Procès Verbal* of 1624; cf Cat. pp. 257-258.

9. At Montceaux, for example, spiral staircases led up to the chapel from the Salle des Gardes situated on each side of the ground floor of the entrance-pavilion.

arrangement of the interior of the entrance-pavilion. On the ground and first floors, and on a third floor within the drum of the dome, de Brosse has created three characteristic and interesting variations on a circular ground-plan, the ground and first-floor plans combining a Greek cross with the circular central space (Pls 139, 140). It is possible that he was influenced by the plan of de l'Orme's chapel at Anet, although of course his own interiors were on a very much smaller scale.

Most writers have conceded a link between the Luxembourg and the Pitti Palaces in elevation, but have mainly confined their observations to the use of rustication throughout both buildings. Blomfield, while condemning the rustication, went so far as to surmise that in all other respects Marie de Médicis' wish for her architect to turn to the Pitti for inspiration 'was either a fable or de Brosse must have hoodwinked his employer'.[10] Hautecoeur remarked that de Brosse 's'inspira non pas du Pitti mais de Verneuil'.[11]

Certainly the Queen's letters to her aunt in Florence, asking for such detailed information, and her sending Métezeau to make extensive plans and drawings of the Pitti, seem, at first sight of the Luxembourg, to have been a waste of time. If what she wanted was an Italian palazzo, what she got was a French château[12] which certainly owed a good deal to Verneuil and still more to Coulommiers. Yet despite this, the influence of the Pitti is more pervasive than might at first appear.[13] What de Brosse adopted and what he rejected from Métezeau's drawings give a further insight into his methods of dealing with foreign models.

The only part of the Palazzo Pitti relevant to the Luxembourg is the court-yard built by Ammanati during the period 1558–1570,[14] which was surrounded on three sides by buildings three storeys in height (Pls 145, 146). Ammanati's treatment of the Pitti façades is very strong, in parts almost brutal. De Brosse uses the much lighter, more incised, Vignolesque rustication we have already seen at Verneuil and Blérancourt (Pls 25, 113). Yet the rustica-tion of the entire building was in itself a direct reference to the Pitti, and there are certain passages at the Luxembourg where de Brosse has sought to emulate

10. Blomfield, II, p. 52.

11. Hautecoeur, I, p. 525.

12. It must be recalled that in the early seventeenth century the Faubourg Saint-Germain was well on the outskirts of the city, very countrified, with extensive private gardens, so that de Brosse was quite justified in producing the traditional château-plan for the Luxembourg.

13. Pannier, p. 177 ff. saw this, and remarked upon it, and although some of the parallels which he drew are inaccurate, his general observations are sensible.

14. Cf. P. J. Murray, *The Architecture of the Italian Renaissance*, 1963, p. 215; and J. Shearman, *Mannerism*, 1967, p. 110 and fig. 57.

the massive, vigorous and sculptural effects achieved by Ammanati, with their possibilities for dramatic manipulation of light and shadow (Pls 147, 148). He recognized, however, that in his own building the wall-surfaces must, on the whole, be modified to suit the northern climate and the northern light.

Some of de Brosse's windows and arched openings are surrounded by a rusticated frame which is derived directly from Ammanati, and is perhaps one of the most striking motifs of the Pitti courtyard. The manner in which de Brosse carries the rustication over the pilasters and columns of his Doric order also derives from Ammanati. These similarities between the Pitti and the Luxembourg can be seen together in the upper part of de Brosse's entrance-pavilion (Pl. 151).

The composition of the Luxembourg as a whole cannot be judged satis-factorily from the elevation of the building as it now stands; we must rely upon representations of it made before the alterations of the nineteenth century. We have the perspective views of the seventeenth-century plans of Paris; Marot's, Silvestre's and Blondel's engravings (Pls 141–144), and a drawing which may be by de Brosse himself considerably elaborated in parts, and in one or two details not corresponding to the executed building.

Although we cannot be sure that the drawing is by de Brosse or even that it necessarily precedes the execution of the building,[15] we are immediately aware of its intensely three-dimensional approach. The sense of solidity and mass is heightened by the graduated effects of light and shade, defining the separate blocks and their individual details. The drawing is notably different in style from those of Charles du Ry contained in the album in the Louvre traditionally attributed to de Brosse.

The draughtsman is evidently pre-occupied by the composition 'la fer-meté de ses masses', as one writer well expresses it,[16] and the effect of their juxtaposition. He seeks to convey a satisfactory balance of one block against another, and at the same time an underlying unity. To achieve this, he stresses the horizontals, and the continuity of the surface-treatment which can also be seen in the engraved section (Pl. 142). There is no unity of roof line, but stress on horizontality, which recalls the treatment of Blérancourt, is followed through in the type of roofs used. This has been more or less preserved through the vicissitudes of alteration and restoration, except in the *corps-de-logis* (Pl. 163), which has a travesty of its original covering. Characteristically

15. Cf. Cat. p. 260. The reason for using Blondel's plates, published 1752-3, rather than those from the *Petit Marot* of *circa* 1654, to illustrate the Luxembourg, is discussed in the Cat. p. 261, and cf. below, n. 38.

16. Vaudoyer, *Histoire de l'architecture*, 1846, quoted by Pannier, p. 172.

(and this is more obvious in the building itself), there is a certain carelessness in detail, in the juxtaposition of various parts of the building which will be discussed later.

Apart from the segmental pediments of the *corps-de-logis* and the triangular ones of the pavilions, there was nothing to break the line of the cornices and balustrades, above which the roofs rose almost uninterrupted by openings, for many of the ugly dormers and louvres now spoiling this unbroken line are modern additions. Gone are the *oeils-de-boeuf* and dormers of Blérancourt, and the almost Gothic elaboration of the roof-line at Coulommiers. The pediments themselves are kept well within bounds; too well, perhaps, in the case of the *corps-de-logis*, where the proportions seem rather mean in relation to the pitch of the original roof; even the addition of the reclining figures above, now gone, did not restore the balance (Pls 149, 165, 166).

THE ENTRANCE FRONT (ANGLE PAVILIONS AND SCREEN)

Engravings of the entrance-front of the Luxembourg have one great advantage over photographs; they can show the whole (Pl. 141), whereas owing to the confined approach to the building up the Rue de Tournon no photographer can achieve this, however widely-angled his lens. On this front the lateral pavilions are of three storeys, the uppermost an attic, and for this reason their roofs are, and always have been, pointed, to bring them level with the flattened tops of the doubled pavilions at the other end of the building. De Brosse however clearly conceived of these pavilions are separate entities, and as fulfilling a different function from the double ones flanking the *corps-de-logis*. They are there to terminate the wings, and to add to the dramatic effect of the entrance itself. They make their chief impact, as he surely meant them to do, when looked at diagonally across the Rue de Vaugirard. They have, from this angle, a powerful aspect; they mark off uncompromisingly the beginning and end of the Palace proper as you approach it along the parallel street; they are strong, four-square and highly sculptural in treatment (Pls 153, 155).

Characteristically de Brosse has ignored the fact that the asymmetry, and indeed slight imbalance, of the lateral façades of the palace, caused by the use of single pavilions at one end and doubled ones at the other, is even further stressed by the different proportions of the pavilions at the entrance end and the different treatment of their upper storeys.

The pilasters of the attic storey of the single angle-pavilions (Pl. 155) are squat, with curious, almost cabbage-like, acanthus capitals familiar to us from Blérancourt and Coulommiers (Pls 99, 124). The omission of the rusticated band from the upper or lower extremities of the pilasters, or both, is characteristic. It occured in the original attic storey of the *corps-de-logis* on the garden side and is seen in the drum of the dome (Pls 152, 154).[17] The attic windows between the pilasters have a frieze of a type used before, at Bléran-court on the ground floor of the court frontispiece (Pls 98, 155). The foliage-decoration in the attic-frieze is similar to that used in the Blérancourt frontispiece drawings. All these details, which in the angle-pavilions are largely restored and re-cut, can be seen in a presumably quite unrestored state in part of the original garden-front of the Palace now masked by the nineteenth-century additions (Pl. 154).[18] The figures between the window-bays on the attic-façades facing towards the entrance-pavilion are a much later addition to the decoration of this storey.

The rustication of the Doric pilasters of the first floor and the rusticated framing, derived from Ammanati at the Pitti, which surrounds the window-bays (Pls 151, 155), have already been discussed. The windows themselves are like those of the angle-pavilions at Blérancourt (Pl. 102), and have the same origin. These first-floor windows, together with all those on this level on the exterior and interior façades of the building, have been lengthened downwards and provided with balustrades. This has upset the original proportions, but the result is not inelegant.

The introduction of a boldly-rusticated niche on this floor between the window-bays adds to the sculptural feeling of the pavilions. The engraving shows statues in the niches (Pl. 141), but whether or not they were intended or executed, they are gone now, and the niches are undeniably more effective left unoccupied.

The ground-floor of the pavilions (Pls 141, 150) has a Tuscan order of double pilasters between which are rusticated arched openings, and set behind these are windows with segmental tops and lugged mouldings. This arrangement of win-dows within arched openings may possibly refer, though somewhat remotely, to the street-façade of the Pitti. Much closer prototypes, however, are Lescot's court-façade at the Louvre (Pl. 3) and the garden-façade at the Tuileries.

The segmental-headed windows themselves are of a type uncommon in the late sixteenth and earlier seventeenth centuries, even in Italy. Lescot had used them at the Louvre on his interior and exterior façades, and such windows occur in Serlio,[19] but very rarely, and then only in the form of a

17. Cf. above, Chap. IV, p. 68, for the connection of this motif with the church door at Verneuil.
18. This is part of the attic of the original *corps-de-logis* on the garden side, with one window of the return round the attic of the frontispiece containing the vestibule and chapel.
19. In several drawings in the 'True Sixth Book' and engraved in Book VII, Caps. 42 and 58.

half-window above a rectangular one. Du Cerceau proposed windows like Lescot's for the *First Design* of Verneuil (Pl. 18), and de Brosse himself had introduced them into the attic-storey at Blérancourt while either he or du Ry used the segmental half-window at Coulommiers (Pl. 124).

The Louvre drawing of the Luxembourg and the engravings show ground-floor windows with a decorative motif between the consoles supporting the sill (Pls 141, 149), but none of these was apparently executed, or all have since been removed during restoration.

The original screen joining the angle-pavilions to the entrance-pavilion was closed (Pl. 141). It had large panels surrounded by the same 'Ammanati' frames as the first-floor bays of the pavilions and the entrance-pavilion. In the centre of each plain panel was a further raised panel, also without decoration.[20] The four bays of the screen on each side of the entrance were separated by coupled Tuscan pilasters, which carried through the order of the ground floor of the angle-pavilions (and of the whole palace) to the entrance-pavilion where it was continued.

This screen achieved its effect by its solidity, its sobriety, and by the variation of surface introduced by the massive raised panels, while the unity of the whole front was ensured by the coupled Tuscan pilasters carried on over the pavilion. The whole effect was changed by the piercing of the screen-arcades by Chalgrin in the early nineteenth century (Pls 150, 151). The present screen is neither ugly nor ineffective, but it produces an effect opposite to that intended by de Brosse. Chalgrin's arched openings continue those on the ground floor of the pavilion and destroy the subtle contrast in de Brosse's design. In sacrificing de Brosse's variety Chalgrin came near to monotony.

The original Luxembourg screen was de Brosse's final answer to a problem which was first tackled by his grandfather at Verneuil, and on which he himself had been working at Verneuil and Coulommiers. It undoubtedly had a great and lasting influence upon the screens of Paris hôtels, particularly on those of François Mansart, but also on architects of the late seventeenth century, and even the eighteenth century.[21] It is a measure of de Brosse's development by 1615, and of the maturity of his style, to compare this screen

20. The engravings show plain panels in the blank bay between the windows, in the attic storey of the angle-pavilions, but it is difficult to tell if these were actually executed. This space is now rusticated and, as has been said, a statue introduced on the east- and west-facing sides. If the plain panels were ever proposed, de Brosse may have meant to use them as a link between the decoration of the pavilions and that of the screen.

21. De Brosse may, of course, have designed similar screens for the hôtels on which he worked in Paris, but if so we know nothing about their appearance. Cf. above, Chap. IV.

with the one designed eighteen years before by his uncle Jacques II du Cerceau
when they were working together at Montceaux (Pl. 42).

THE ENTRANCE PAVILION

The entrance-pavilion which de Brosse had designed two years earlier
for Coulommiers was certainly in the nature of a preparatory exercise for the
one at the Luxembourg (Pl. 121). Indeed, the whole of the rusticated exterior
of Coulommiers was a kind of preliminary experiment for the more important
commission already in the wind. The Coulommiers entrance-pavilion is
greater in diameter than that of the Luxembourg, and has an extra bay flanked
by pilasters on each side of the projecting columns. It is nearer in feeling to the
common protoype, the Valois chapel. The Coulommiers pavilion also had,
to judge from the engravings, little or none of the variety of surface treatment which adds interest and dramatic impact to the Luxembourg design.

The exterior of the Luxembourg entrance-pavilion remains today almost
completely unaltered[22] (Pls 150, 151). There is the massive arched entrance
with its slightly dropped keystone, flanked by Tuscan columns; above, the
four arched openings of the *salon* on the first floor are set in their
'Ammanati' frames and flanked by Doric columns. The derivations from
Ammanati's Pitti courtyard, used with such effect by de Brosse on this floor
of the entrance-pavilion, are not alone in creating the special link which the
pavilion seems to have with the Florentine palace. The first floor of the
Luxembourg entrance is immensely dramatic and powerful, and this feeling
of rough strength is heightened by the bold broken lines of the cornice seen
from below and outlined against the sky. In this, more than in any other part
of the palace, de Brosse, while creating something highly personal to himself,
has succeeded in fulfilling Marie de Médicis' wish, '. . . en quelque chose me
regler sur la forme et modelle du Palais de Pitti'.

Above the first floor, set upon a paved balustraded platform, rises the drum
of the dome, which has arched openings between the pilasters (Pl. 152).
Round it are placed eight statues, but they are replacements of the originals by
Guillaume Berthelot commissioned in 1662, about which Rubens and Peiresc
had an interesting exchange of views.[23]

22. The arched openings of the first floor are glazed; a clock has been introduced into the centre
of the drum of the dome on the south side. In 1649 Symonds wrote of the main entrance:
'Hostel de Luxembourg Over ye first Gate which has many heads of fooles gaping with hornes
on their eyebrows of brasse inlaid black marble and guilt letters cutt in Palais d'Orléans'. The 'heads
of fooles' etc. refers to the actual entrance-doors, of which a drawing survives in the Ecole des
Beaux Arts in Paris. The drawing is inscribed in a later hand with a description which tallies with
Symonds'. (Cf. below n. 39 and Cat. p. 260).
23. Cf. Cat. p. 263.

The balustrade at the spring of the dome is possibly modelled on one used by Jacques I du Cerceau in a different context;[24] it may be a restoration but its pattern probably follows the original design by de Brosse. The dome itself is ribbed, and this contributes further to the dynamic character which this pavilion shows in comparison with the one designed for Coulommiers (Pl. 121).[25]

The effect of the Luxembourg front and of the entrance pavilion in particular is grand and satisfying. It has immense visual impact, and this impact was obviously what de Brosse chiefly sought in his design. Academic criticism, such as Blondel's,[26] of disproportion in the orders is not altogether to the point. Although de Brosse used the orders far more correctly than any architect since Bullant and de l'Orme, he certainly conceived of his buildings primarily as three-dimensional compositions in mass, and then fitted the orders to the composition.

In this pavilion, as throughout the building, the pedestals and entablatures are returned not only round the columns but round every pair of pilasters as well. The consequent breaking-up of the cornice-line of the first floor achieves precisely the feature which de Brosse particularly sought – a dramatic sky-line. However, his desire to carry these breaks on over the pilasters has caused confusion, for the pilasters on the sides of the pavilion, at right-angles to one another, have to share a pedestal and an entablature. (Pls 148, 151). This seems to be an instance of the general fact that de Brosse broke rules not out of bold originality but because he got muddled. On the other hand, it must be emphasized again that to apply academic criteria of this kind too severely to his buildings is to misunderstand his intention and to miss the true quality of his work.

THE EAST AND WEST FAÇADES

The east and west façades of the Luxembourg, after having been inordinately lengthened by the addition of the extra pavilions, now present a somewhat heavy and monotonous appearance, and it is necessary to remove these addenda from the mind's eye before passing judgment on them. Yet

24. Second Book, *Tombs*, No. 6 of the set of ten.

25. In the *Petit Marot* engraving the dome is shown without ribs. This makes it closer in design to the dome projected by de Brosse for the Coulommiers entrance-pavilion, a much more static composition, and also, of course, to the dome of the Valois Mausoleum. (Pls. 6, 121). This is interesting in view of Blondel's opinion (Cf. Cat. p. 261) that Marot used de Brosse's drawings as a basis for his engravings. The *Procès Verbal* of 1623 throws no light on the form of the dome but Silvestre's engraving of 1649 (F. 117-1) shows it with ribs as Blondel does.

26. 'The Tuscan order is too fat, the Doric too short, the attic too low . . .', (Blondel, *Architecture François*, 1752, Vol. II, Book III, p. 51).

even in their original state, they must have been the least satisfactory elevations of the palace. The repetition of identical elements both in the doubled pavilions and in the wings, unbroken by any central feature, produces and must always have produced an effect of monotony (Pl. 156).[27]

The isolation of the angle-pavilions of the entrance-façade from those at the other end, not only by distance but by their differing proportions and wall-treatment, is highly effective from the frontal view, but less so when seen from the side. From this position we perceive that the entrance-front and the *corps-de-logis* with its flanking pavilions are not so much linked as separated by the two-storey wings.

The junction of the wings with the pavilions flanking the *corps-de-logis* is not altogether a happy one (Pl. 159). The upper windows of the wings are of the same type as those on the first floor of the pavilions, but lack the rusticated frame round the panels into which they are set. Below them, the meeting of arched and segmental openings, is also a little awkward. At the other end, where the wing meets the angle-pavilions of the entrance-façade, the junction has been arranged in a different, but still inharmonious way, by leaving the return window-bay of the pavilion without rustication (Pl. 158). A similarly dissonant arrangement occurs in the meeting of the doubled pavilions with the short wing which separates them (Pl. 157). Yet all the elements whose awkward juxtaposition has been mentioned are in themselves beautifully designed and some of them are, as well, evocations of the details of the lost façades of Blérancourt.

THE DOUBLE PAVILIONS, OUTER FAÇADES

The doubled pavilions of the southern end of the palace (Pl. 160) are massive (each sixty feet square) and extremely impressive. Their solidity and their strong horizontal lines are enhanced by the squared-off line of their pitched roofs. (The present dormers are a modern intrusion). Their greater size apart, these pavilions differ mainly from those at the entrance end in having, instead of an attic, a full third storey with an Ionic order; the central bay of this third floor on each of the principal façades is surmounted by an unbroken triangular pediment. The third-floor windows are of the same Vignolesque type used on the first floor of the court-frontispiece at Blérancourt (Pl. 98).

The introduction of the pediments in this particular way is one of de Brosse's most original inventions at the Luxembourg, and their satisfactory proportion to the pavilions is in contrast with the meagre appearance of the segmental pediment of the *corps-de-logis* on the court-side. The pavilion

27. Cf. Blomfield, II, p. 54.

pediments were originally surmounted by reclining figures, as is indicated
in the Louvre drawing and shown in the engravings (Pls. 143, 149).
Sculptors were apparently brought specially from Italy to execute these
figures – an enterprise later thought to have been a great waste of time and
money since the results were entirely pedestrian.[28] These pediments provide
a dignified, classical central feature for the top storey, and we find a later
and important recollection of it in François Mansart's remodelling of the
entrance of the Hôtel Carnavalet.

THE SOUTH FAÇADE

The southern (garden) façade of the Luxembourg, as we see it today
(Pls 161, 162), was built by Alphonse de Gisors between 1836 and 1841 to
link the extra pavilions which he had placed to east and west of it.[29] The only
fragment of de Brosse's original front surviving is a part of the attic of the
corps-de-logis and the chapel, hidden by the later building (Pl. 154).[30]
When Gisors rebuilt the south façade further forward, he took pains
to reproduce most aspects of de Brosse's original composition, as can be
seen by a comparison of the existing structure with the engraving (Pl. 143).
Thus, although no stone of the visible structure of this façade dates from the
seventeenth century, it can to some extent be used to judge de Brosse's design.
One traditional criticism of the seventeenth-century garden-front was that
the projection of the vestibule and the chapel above it and the even greater
projection of the lateral pavilions blocked off too much light from the rooms
of the corps-de-logis. In the modern version of the front the arcades have been
brought forward. Instead of both the first floor and the attic storey being
recessed above the arcades the first floor is now built directly above them;
only the attic storey is recessed. At first-floor level, therefore, in comparison
with the original structure, the projection of the lateral pavilions is somewhat
reduced and that of the central element of the corps-de-logis very much so.
Gisors used for his arcades and windows, as for his pavilions, the same
articulation and detail as de Brosse. In the central element, within the
limitations of the space left by the introduction of a storey directly over the
arcades, he has attempted to reproduce the old central pavilion in which de
Brosse had placed his vestibule and chapel, and the disposition of this tallies
with the original plans. The arrangement of columns and pilasters in de
Brosse's chapel-pavilion, and in Gisor's replacement, is the same as in the

28. G. Brice, *Description de la Ville de Paris*, 1706, p. 58.
29. A. Hustin, *Le Palais du Luxembourg*, 1904, p. 22 *et seq.*
30. Cf. above, n. 18.

K

entrance-pavilion, and Gisors has repeated de Brosse's unorthodox treatment of the pedestals and cornices of the pilasters on the return faces which
was mentioned earlier in connection with the entrance pavilion.[31]

Almost the whole of the east and west faces of Gisors' central element are
blocked, of course, by the new *corps-de-logis*, but what remains of the side
elevation of the attic resembles the engravings of the original building.
Malingre[32] described the exterior of de Brosse's chapel-dome as decorated
'de fort belles colonnes de marbre et de bronze et de très excellentes statues'.
The bronze and marble may be doubted.

On the ground and first floors the main façade of this pavilion is a faithful
copy of de Brosse (Pl. 161). In the attic the composition is the same as we see
in the engraving; there are figures in the same place above the Doric cornice,
and the pediment is of the same type, though the reclining figures are omitted.
Only the decoration of the space below the pediment, round the clock,
differs wildly from anything the seventeenth century could have produced.
The dome and lantern, too, are not related to the originals. Alphonse de
Gisors, called upon to make extensions to the Palace which would inevitably
cause drastic alterations to the original composition, approached his task
with great respect for the style of the first architect; today, the south front
of the Luxembourg, especially when seen from across the gardens, can in
almost every way be taken for the work of de Brosse.

THE COURT ELEVATIONS

The elevations of the courtyard retain their original proportions (Pls 142,
163, 166) not having been disturbed by the nineteenth-century adaptations,
only the roof of the *corps-de-logis* has been lowered and skylights inserted
into it. Of course, all the roofs of the Palace have been restored or replaced;
all have lost their ornamental coping, and the small dormers high in the roofs
of the wings, shown in the engravings, have disappeared. But only in the
corps-de-logis has the result been really horrible.

The other major alteration to the court itself has been the removal of the
terrace in front of the *corps-de-logis*, the semi-circular steps which led to it,
and the marble balustrade shown in the Louvre drawing (Pl. 149). The marble
for this balustrade, for the statues which once ornamented it, and for the
original paving of the courtyard, were brought at the Queen's insistence, and
much against the wishes of the religious authorities, from the workshop of
the Valois chapel at Saint Denis. It was marble which had been specially

31. Cf. above p. 119.
32. *Antiquités de Paris*, 1640, II, p. 401.

imported by Catherine de Médicis.[33] This terrace added dignity to the court-yard and point to the composition, so that its removal on the grounds of more convenient access to the *corps-de-logis* is aesthetically regrettable.[34]

In the courtyard of the Luxembourg the architect was faced with a problem which did not arise for Ammanati at the Pitti, for in the Italian courtyard the horizontal symmetry and unity are not broken by lower wings nor by the introduction of the re-entrant angles of flanking pavilions.

The entrance-screen is arcaded on the court-side, as it always was; the wings are rusticated throughout, and their window-surrounds are not left plain as on the exterior. The horizontal unity and the links between the buildings of the three sides of the courtyard beyond the screen is admirably maintained up to the level of the first-floor cornice (Pls 163, 166). Nor is there any problem of differing types of window-bays being juxtaposed as on the exterior lateral façades. Above this level, however, de Brosse has lost his way, and the Louvre drawing and the engravings show that this is not the result of later alterations (Pls 142, 149).

The unity is broken by the roof-lines in any case, each separate block of buildings being, as it were, cut off from the other, an effect already seen in the exterior elevations. But it is at the *corps-de-logis* end of the court that de Brosse's handling is least happy. The angle-pavilions are three full storeys high, but the *corps-de-logis* itself has, like the pavilions of the entrance-front, only an attic storey above the first floor. Thus the first floor, the cornice and the pediments of each great pavilion rise up to dwarf the *corps-de-logis* and to form a clumsy junction with it. Moreover, the frontispiece of the *corps-de-logis*, which should be the culminating point of the composition, does not make the impact that it should.

De Brosse evidently conceived the southern end of the Luxembourg as a similar composition to Blérancourt; yet at Blérancourt, if Tavernier de Junquière's drawing and Silvestre's engravings are to be trusted (Pls 91, 92, 94), he did not make the mistakes which he made at the Luxembourg, because he designed the attic-storey of his pavilions and his frontispiece to be of the same height. Also, as far as we can judge from engravings and the drawing of Blérancourt, the architect appears there to have used the *corps-de-logis* dormers to continue the horizontal line of the attic storeys.

It is hard for us to understand why de Brosse wilfully chose not to make the same kind of unifying arrangement at the Luxembourg, and not to wonder sadly why he did not make the pavilions and *corps-de-logis* the same height and

33. Cf. Ch. II, p. 19.
34. See note 5 above.

then raise the central frontispiece above all. That he later learned from his mistakes can be seen at Rennes (Pl. 201); what he might have done at the Luxembourg, François Mansart did later on the court-side of his block at Blois (Pl. 164).

The central element of the *corps-de-logis*, taken alone, is the penultimate variation in de Brosse's work of the theme of the three-storey frontispiece as it had been developed from Anet onwards. The ground-floor section has unusual rectangular openings containing busts above the windows flanking the central arch (Pl. 149). This arrangement was undoubtedly influenced by certain of Serlio's drawings and engravings. It is common in sixteenth-century northern Italian architecture, notably in Giulio Romano's Palazzo del Tè, but it is very unusual in France.[35]

The figures of the attic storey are arranged in the same manner as were those on the chapel-pavilion on the other side of the *corps-de-logis*; that is to say, they stand forward and do not support the entablature (Pl. 165). This again raises the question whether de Brosse is here repeating the frontispiece of Coulommiers (Pl. 126), or whether the figures in the latter were caryatids supporting the entablature of the pediments. The sculpture of the pediment is of a later date; originally it contained a coat-of-arms and swags, and the usual seated figures, now gone, surmounted it.

At the end of this examination of the plan and elevations of the Luxembourg it is important to consider Blondel's views on the palace in his *Architecture Françoise*.[36] First he praises: '. . . Les beautés reconnues telles dans la décoration de ce Palais, consistent dans le caractère de virilité qu'on remarque dans toute son ordonnance, dans la sévérité des formes, la pureté des profils, la proportion particulière de certaines parties, et, en général, dans un certain gout antique, également soutenu dans la totalité ainsi que dans les détails de l'architecture et les ornements qui le composent . . .'. Then, while recognizing the stature of the architect and of the building, he makes his criticisms, of which the most telling is that the variations in height of the different parts of the building were not consonant with its total scale. Such diversity, he says, is only tolerable in a building of great extent, where the object is to produce a pyramidal composition, by supporting the main block with the lower buildings.[37]

The engraved section (Pl. 142)[38] supports Blondel's contention. There is

35. It appears later at Wideville (*c.* 1630), a château considerably influenced by de Brosse's style.
36. Blondel, op. cit., Vol. II, Book III, p. 51 ff. quoted by Blomfield, p. 54 ff.
37. Blomfield's translation.
38. The sections through the entrance front and the *corps-de-logis* in Blondel's plate are made at a different point from those in Marot's corresponding engraving, thus enabling the entrance-pavilion and chapel-tribune to be included.

an inherent conflict at the Luxembourg, irrespective of scale, between the composition as a whole and the treatment of the various parts. The design is, in essence, an amalgamation of a block-château with one containing a court-yard and screen. Within this framework de Brosse certainly meant to make his buildings lead up to the central *corps-de-logis* with its flanking pavilions; and he would have succeeded better but for his strange mistake of making the *corps-de-logis* too low and too narrow.

There is, however, an interesting and positive side to Blondel's fault-finding in the implicit admission that here was a serious composition worthy of serious criticism. De Brosse was the first French architect since Philibert de l'Orme to exhibit a true sense of mass in architecture. To a greater extent than de l'Orme, and with a clarity far beyond the range of his other sixteenth-century predecessors, he realized that a whole building might be seen as a series of blocks which could be composed three-dimensionally, and demon-strate a progression dictated by considerations other than those of mere function, utility or decoration.

This is what de Brosse attempted in the elevations of the Luxembourg, and we must be thankful that the building still stands as a witness to his success. The massive grandeur of the whole palace far outweighs its faults of architectural detail and makes a profound impression of simplicity and strength. The sculptural quality of the building is enhanced by de Brosse's understanding of the importance of light and shadow, playing upon the voids and solids of the wall-surfaces. To see the Luxembourg on a day of cloud and sunshine is to see it at its best, to accept it as a notable achievement and to recognize the first of the great classical buildings which survive from seventeenth-century France.

THE INTERIOR

In 1649 Richard Symonds, an English royalist exiled in France, visited Paris, and at the Luxembourg Palace noted that 'The One side next ye nunnery of Mount Calvarie is finisht and fairely guilded withn. The One side is a gallery, flat roof but fairely guilded and on ye sides of ye story of the life of Marie de Medicis . . . Many old little and very wel painted pieces in a little Chappel neare ye Gallery. The Antichambre is square large and the roof guilded. The Cabinet of Madame is flord with wood wrought in little workes all severall forms pitcht in with Silver. The Sides wanscott wth boxes of Velvet Guilt above Italian pictures less than life of ye marriage of this Queene's Grandfather and Father. The Roofe is fairely guilt A little Roome wthin that where ye paintings of the king's best howses are as Louvre Fontaynebleau

St Germains . . .'. Nine years before, Malingre had described the same
interiors and praised their richness, adding 'ce département est dans le pavillon
d'en haut (au premier) à main droicte entrant au dict hostel'.[39]

Marie de Médicis had left the Luxembourg and France for ever when she
went into final exile in 1631, so that Symonds and Malingre are describing the
royal apartments as they were during their occupation by Madame, second
wife of Gaston d'Orléans, the King's brother.[40] But, as no major works had
been undertaken at the palace between 1631 and 1646, the year in which
the King officially handed over the building to Gaston, it is unlikely
that much had been done to alter the Queen's apartments since the
1620s.

'The One side' described by Symonds was the west wing in which was the
long gallery on the first floor containing the Rubens paintings of the life of
the Queen, hung in 1625, and to this he adds the first south-west pavilion
containing the royal apartments. He no doubt particularly describes this
part of the palace as 'finisht' because a great deal of the interior was
still incomplete, and some of it, notably the east gallery, was never
finished.[41]

Neither the Rubens gallery nor the Queen's rooms survive in their original
form, but some of the decoration of her cabinet (the Cabinet Doré) was later
transferred to and can be seen today in the room known as the Salle du Livre
d'Or. The gallery has been all but obliterated; Ruben's paintings hang in the
Louvre. Symonds's description has been quoted in full because it gives a vivid
picture of the interior decoration of the early seventeenth century, and helps
to bring alive for us a small part of Marie de Médicis' palace as it was in her
own day, and before the building suffered the first of the many alterations
which it has since undergone.[42]

39. Malingre, *Antiquités de Paris*, 1640, II, p. 401. Symonds modelled his itinerary in Paris on
Malingre's book. Cf. O. Millar, 'The Notebooks of Richard Symonds', *Studies in Renaissance
and Baroque Art*, Phaidon, 1967, p. 162, n. 22.

40. Cf. Cat. p. 264.

41. Alphonse de Gisors, *Palais du Luxembourg*, 1847, p. 38, remarked that at the end of the
eighteenth century the gallery of the east wing was still unfinished.

42. Malingre's description is as follows: 'Avant d'entrer dans cette galerie est la chapelle de la
Reine, avec ses lambris dorez et l'autel de mesme, de Très belles menuiseries en feuillage dorez,
et au fond un fort riche tableau . . . De ce même costé et département est la chambre de la Royne,
belle, grande et carrée, enrichie d'une cheminée admirable pour son ouvrage et dorure, garnie
de deux gros chenets d'argent. En cette chambre se voit la place du lict enfermée de balustres dont
les piliers sont d'argent. De cette chambre on entre au cabinet, le plus riche qu'on puisse voir.
Le plancher est faict de marquetterie de bois, la cheminée d'un ouvrage très rare et tout doré, le
lambris faict de pièces de menuiserie de rapport doré, les vitres de fin cristal, et au lieu de plomb
pour les lier, la liason est toute d'argent'. (*Antiquités de Paris*, II, p. 401 ff.)

The decoration of the Queen's rooms[43] dated from the 1620s, but we cannot tell with how much of it de Brosse may have been directly concerned. The *Procès Verbal* of 1623 assesses only the masonry work. A ceiling-design which may well be connected with this part of the palace survives and shows the type of decoration also called for in Tremblay's contract at Blérancourt.[44]

It is a pity that the many visitors to the Rubens gallery, who recorded their impressions of the paintings hung there, made few observations on the architectural decoration. We know that, in 1622, de Brosse furnished Rubens with drawings of some details for the gallery, for on 7–8 April Peiresc wrote to the painter: '. . . nous nous sommes rendus chez M. Brosse avec lequel nous avons pris les mesures exactes des espaces reservés dans la galerie pour les tableaux . . . M. Brosse me promet d'en faire faire le dessin la semaine prochaine avec les mesures des portes qui doivent y venir . . . Il fera de même pour les quatres petits champs à l'entrée mais . . . il doit d'abord faire le dessin de la cheminée'. There is a further reference in one of Peiresc's letters to 'M. Brosse's' fireplace for the gallery, and then, on 9 June, Rubens is informed: '. . . Il m'a été impossible d'obtenir les mesures de M. Brosse, celui ci se rejette sur les difficultés du lambris qu'il voudrait placer dans les panneaux, il cherche à lui trouver l'ornementation indispensable qui s'adapte le mieux autour des portes mais je ne le laisserai en repos qu'il n'ait terminé cette affaire.'[45] This last letter proves that de Brosse took an active part in the interior decoration of the gallery and its preparation for receiving Rubens's paintings, which hung between the nine long windows on either side and over the fireplace and doors.

Thus, as late as 1622, the gallery was merely a shell, lacking its principal architectural feature, the monumental fireplace at the south end flanked by the two doors leading from the Queen's apartments. Malingre praised the fireplace(s) (he wrongly mentions two, one at each end) as 'fort belles pour l'invention, façons et dorures'. Some reminiscence of the arrangement of the gallery may be found in the Grand'Salle in the Palais du Parlement in Rennes, whose general disposition was planned by de Brosse in 1618 (Pl. 208).

43. Cf. A. F. Blunt, 'A Series of Paintings Illustrating the History of the Medici Family Executed For Marie de Médicis', *Burl. Mag.*, CIX, November 1967, p. 565. Also cf. Hustin *Le Luxembourg*, p. 41 ff. One of the ceiling-paintings, which Marie de Médicis commissioned from Jean Mosnier after her return from exile in Blois, is now in the Salle du Livre d'Or. Hustin gives details of the artists who signed a contract with Marie for the decoration of the palace on 15 April 1621.

44. Cf. above, Chap. V, p. 80. A. F. Blunt (cf. n. 43) discusses and reproduces this drawing.

45. Ruelans and Rooses, *Correspondance de Rubens*, 1887–1909, II, pp. 372–437.

In 1623 the interior of the *corps-de-logis* of the Luxembourg was unfinished, but the principal staircase in the centre was already under construction; an important point because, on the authority of Sauval, it has always been attributed to Marin de la Vallée, who officially succeeded de Brosse as architect in charge at the Luxembourg in 1624.[46] This attribution may be right if Marin de la Vallée was in charge of this part of the work before de Brosse retired, and was left to his own devices, but this seems unlikely. So, on the evidence of the 1623 *Procès Verbal*, de Brosse must be held responsible for the staircase and for the faults in it pointed out by several writers. Darkness was the worst of these; Dézallier d'Argenville commenting that, 'On prétend que le grand escalier, si massif et si sombre, est du dessin de Marin de la Vallée. Il est indigne d'une maison royale'.[47] Blondel had similar criticisms to make, not just of the staircase, but of the whole entrance to the *corps-de-logis*: '. . . Le porche (est) une des parties les plus intéressante de cet édifice pour ce qui regarde la décoration extérieure; mais son peu de largeur annonce assez médiocrement l'entrée principale de ce Palais. Celle de la cour au jardin est encore moins digne de la magnificence d'une Maison Royale, l'escalier en occupant la plus grande partie, contre toute idée de vraisemblance: d'ailleurs cet escalier . . . est si massif, si sombre, et son échappée si basse, que le passage F (see Pl. 136) laisse à peine un accès convenable au concours de personnes qui viennent profiter de la promenade de ce Palais . . .'[48] In another passage he criticizes the stairs themselves: 'Les rampes des escaliers ajoutent beaucoup à leur décoration; mais pour qu'elles fassent un bel effet il faut qu'il ne s'y trouve pas les ressauts qu'on remarque à ceux du Palais Royal et du Luxembourg; . . .'[49]

As at Coulommiers, there was access at ground-level through the stair-chamber to the terrace beyond, though here the vestibule beneath the chapel intervened. The flights rose through two storeys and were vaulted over, but whether in the same old-fashioned Gothic manner, or with barrel-vaults,

46. Sauval, III, p. 8: 'Grand escalier ordonné par Marin de la Vallée et conduit par Guillaume de Toulouse'. However, a passage from the *Procès Verbal* makes it clear that the basic elements of the design were fixed before 1624: 'Les murs en quatre sens servant de noyaux audict escallier faicts en partie . . . aududevant desquels y a des balustres en appuye . . . La voulte de pierre de taille audessus des marches et palliers dudict escallier. Les costez de ladicte voulte aux dessoubz des marches dudict escallier au rez-de-chaussée le petit mur de pierre de taille audessoubz les marches audict endroict. Les deux petits murs de pierre de taille au dessoubz dudict escallier aux costez du passage pour aller au jardin. Les marches et palliers dudict escallier faict de liaiz'.

47. Dézallier d'Argenville, *Voyage Pittoresque de Paris*, Paris, 1787, p. 329. (First ed. 1749).

48. Blondel, op. cit., Vol. II, Book III, p. 49.

49. Ibid., Vol. I, Book I, p. 42. Sauval (III, p. 8) wrote: 'Les moulures de cet escalier ne se suivent et ne se continuent pas', indicating a change of architect, perhaps.

we do not know. But, whereas at Coulommiers the mezzanine-landings ran straight across the width of the stair-well, at the Luxembourg they were placed at each side of a short flight. Malingre, therefore, described the staircase as being '. . . un magnifique escalier en forme ronde et en coquille', and, he goes on, 'couvert de tous costez, et peut-on voir la cime d'icelluy qui abboutit à une forme de Dôme à l'Italienne, ainsi que celuy des Tuileries . . .'.[50]

Since it must be supposed that Malingre is not referring to the dome which lay over the chapel (although he is not always accurate), some kind of internal dome is presumably meant, and it is unfortunate, especially in view of Mansart's later staircase designs, that we have so little information about it. The comparison with the Tuileries is interesting; the dome over de l'Orme's staircase was not built by him but later, during the reign of Henri IV, and possibly by Jacques II Androuet du Cerceau,[51] and was of course visible from the outside.

The Luxembourg staircase, apart from the possible internal dome, was evidently neither novel in design nor graceful in execution. It is mainly interesting because it is one of the few parts of the original interior of the palace of which we have fairly adequate particulars, and because it has the negative function, like the Coulommiers staircase, of illustrating de Brosse's failure to learn much from de l'Orme's example at the Tuileries.

The plan of the chapel behind the staircase has been described in the preceding section.[52] Here, and in the vestibule below, de Brosse had to articulate his favourite form, a curving surface. As the chapel rose through two storeys, we can infer from the proportions of the bases on the plan (Pls 137, 138), that a Colossal order of pilasters ran up the whole height, and this arrangement may reflect de l'Orme's treatment of the chapel at Anet. The chapel also had a shallow semi-dome over the sanctuary. Blondel describes the interior thus: 'La chapelle placée du coté du jardin est estimée particulièrement parce qu'elle est terminée par une voute en cul-de-four d'un trait assez hardi pour le temps où elle fut bâtie et dont l'exécution est de Dominique de la Font. On remarque dans cette chapelle des peintures sur bois que l'on croit d'être d'Albert Durer – d'ailleurs tous les appartemens de ce palais ont de la grandeur et sont décorés avec magnificence dans le gout ancien'.[53] Of the rest of the interior we know almost nothing, although there exists at Waddesdon a ceiling-design that

50. Malingre, op. cit., II, p. 401.
51. Cf. Blunt, *Philibert de l'Orme*, p. 106; and Hautecoeur, III, pp. 347 and 517.
52. Cf. above, p. 112.
53. Blondel, op. cit., Vol. II, Book III, p. 50; and Sauval (II, p. 8) also give the semi-dome of the vestibule to Dominique de Lafonds who was one of de Brosse's kinsmen. In none of these references does the wording necessarily imply that Lafonds was responsible for the *design*.

may possibly be connected with the ceiling of the rectangular part of the chapel (Pl. 167).[54]

One of the most interesting parts of the Luxembourg, and one which still survives to a large extent unaltered, is the interior of the entrance-pavilion. This we can see in its original form in a drawing made in the late eighteenth century, probably by Soufflot (Pl. 169).[55]

On the ground floor the circular space contains four large arched entrances, leading from the street and through to the courtyard and giving on to the vaulted arcades beneath the first-floor terrace. The arches are divided by coupled Doric columns with niches between them, and, save that the entrances to the arcades are no longer open, the whole of this remains today as de Brosse left it and Soufflot drew it, a fine and monumental entrance (Pls 170–172). The first floor consisted of a *salon*, also open on four sides, with arched entrances to the first-floor terrace and great arched openings looking out to north and south (Pl. 168).

The earliest record we have of the inside of the entrance-pavilion is the 1623 *Procès Verbal*, where it is stated that on the first floor 'la Tribune' was destined to contain a Corinthian order, the various parts of which had not yet been put into place ('Les corps des quatres corniches et piedestaulz, non à présent coupés, audedans de la rotonde pour poser les coulommes de marbre d'ordre corinthin').[56]

In 1706 Germain Brice wrote, 'La principale entrée du palais se trouve sous le pavillon du milieu, dont l'intérieur où est le passage est décoré de colonnes doriques avec des niches entre deux. L'étage supérieur ouvert des quatre cotez par autant de grands arcs accompagnez chacun de quatre colonnes et orné en dedans d'un ordre corinthien en colonnes de marbre disposées comme celles du grand passage de dessous'.[57]

The *Procès Verbal* and Brice's description confirm the Soufflot drawing,

54. The design appears to be intended for an area of this shape having two entrances of which one is more important than the other, (as it might be, the one leading in from the Queen's apartments in the S.W. pavilion). At this end of the design are added two figures bearing the linked M's of the monogram of Marie de Médicis' widowhood. Like the Stockholm ceiling-design, this one is close to the type of work done by Fréminet and Tremblay at Fontainebleau and Blérancourt, and in both period and arrangement it supports a hypothetical connection with the Luxembourg, even if not precisely with the chapel, although the iconography does appear to be religious. Unfortunately we have no indication of the scale of the drawing. I am indebted to Professor Blunt for bringing this drawing to my notice.

55. Cf. Cat. p. 259.

56. *Procès Verbal*, fol. 255 verso; second estimate, by de Brosse's experts.

57. G. Brice, op. cit., ed. Le Gras, 1706, and also ed. of 1725. The ed. of 1685 omit the description of the Corinthian order. The reference in the 1706 ed. is III, p. 57.

which shows the entrance-pavilion prior to the alteration of the entablature and the roof by Chalgrin in the first years of the nineteenth century.[58] The analogy, drawn earlier,[59] between the entrance-pavilion chapel at Mont- ceaux and the Valois Mausoleum, is even more pertinent here at the Luxembourg, where the order used is the same as the one in the proto- type.

The *salon* is shabby and dirty now, cluttered with rubbish and with ugly nineteenth-century statues which are out of proportion to the niches. But despite all this, with its high openings, marble columns, niches and play of curves, it is a fine example of an impressive interior on a small scale; the kind of thing at which de Brosse excelled. The ceiling, before Chalgrin's intervention, was flat but rose in the centre into a shallow cylindrical drum which was surrounded by a cornice and covered with a flat ceiling. This, in embryonic form, is a feature later used by Mansart, particularly at Maisons-Lafitte.

The third floor of the pavilion contained a chamber within the drum of the dome called the 'Belvedere', where de Brosse returns to the Doric order for his sixteen pilasters set in pairs around the eight openings which decorate the exterior of the drum (Pl. 169). The pilasters stood on high pedestals, which have now been reduced by the higher rise of Chalgrin's shallow dome beneath, and had a Doric frieze which still survives. Above rose the dome, undecorated inside, with an open centre through which could be seen the interior of the lantern high above.

The original interior of the entrance-pavilion at the Luxembourg is a highly advanced composition for its date; it has a true feeling of *gravitas*, and is far more accomplished in its management of the classical idiom than any- thing by de Brosse which we have yet seen.[60]

It cannot so far be established whether or not de Brosse designed the gardens of the Luxembourg, as some authors have claimed,[61] but it is at

58. Chalgrin introduced a new and more elaborate entablature and a very low dome with simulated coffering.

59. Cf. above, Chap. III, p. 55.

60. Before leaving the interior of the palace, it is worth recalling that Hirschfeld, a very reliable although not much noticed writer on the Luxembourg, quotes Tallement des Réaux's story that Marie de Médicis told de Brosse to look at the interior of the Hôtel de Rambouillet before decorat- ing her palace. Hirschfeld, however, added that he did not do so, but modelled himself on Am- manati (*Le Palais du Luxembourg*, Monographies Laurens, Paris, 1931, p. 19). For the Hôtel de Rambouillet and the problem of its dating, cf. A. Blunt, 'The Précieux and French Art', *Fritz Saxl, 1890–1948, Memorial Essays*, Nelson, 1957.

61. Cf. above, note 4. Blomfield cites no evidence for his attribution, but Pannier's argument against Lasteyrie's similar attribution is by no means conclusive, merely that Boiceau, a Protestant,

least possible that the plan of the main *parterre*, so reminiscent on paper[62] of the plan of the Pitti courtyard (Pl. 135), and the series of steps leading to it, may have been suggested by him. The influence of de l'Orme at Anet is certainly suggested by the various flights of concave/convex steps on an oval plan. Blondel used these, among others, to illustrate the 'perron cintré . . . comme on voit dans les jardins du Belvedère à Rome; quelques uns ont des palliers ovales, comme au jardin du Luxembourg à Paris.[63]

The most celebrated feature of the Luxembourg gardens was the Fontaine Médicis, which has always been attributed to de Brosse (Pls 173, 174). Originally this was situated at the extreme eastern end of the walk which ran along the south side of the palace, known later as L'allée des Platanes. The fountain was approached along a raised part of this walk to which a convex/concave oval flight of steps led up (Pl. 135), and is inscribed in some editions of Marot's engraving[64] as 'La Graute du Lusanbourg au bout dune grande aller proche l'orangerie'.[65] Between 1801 and 1813, when embankment works were being carried out in that part of the garden, the fountain was moved to its present position further to the south-west, and the oval steps which approached it were demolished, together with the wall which originally flanked it. A good deal of re-cutting and restoration was done, and the niches furnished with modern statues.[66]

Though there were precedents for the style, with its 'rustic' decoration, in the elder du Cerceau's engravings, the inspiration for de Brosse's fountain was probably Buontalenti's grotto in the Boboli Gardens at the Pitti (Pl. 175). The water for this fountain, for the Palace and for some houses in the district, was supplied by the great Aqueduc d'Arcueil, built by order of the Queen Mother and very probably designed by de Brosse himself.[67]

De Brosse has skilfully combined the fantastic decoration conventionally associated with grottoes and fountains with a basically severe form; his

---

included some of the *parterres* of the Luxembourg in his book of garden-design. A de Gisors, op. cit., p. 41, says that the gardens were begun in 1613 by de Brosse.

62. In reality, of course, the Pitti plan has dramatic changes of level.

63. Blondel, op. cit., Vol. I, Book I, p. 44.

64. The print with this title is rare, an example is in Bib. Nat. Est. H^a 7c, fol. 93.

65. Cf. Mauban, p. 215, no. 210 and Pannier p. 242.

66. Blondel's plate of the fountain (Cf. Cat. p. 261) shows certain differences from Marot's, notably in the style of the cornice which is devoid of rustication and is, in general, nearer to the existing structure. Marot's engraving is used here (pl. 173) in preference to Blondel's, because it may possibly be based on an original drawing by de Brosse, known to Marot. Gisors, op. cit., p. 11, describes the moving of the fountain to its present site.

67. Cf. Cat. Appendix, p. 278.

conception is vastly more austere than Buontalenti's, and he obviously would not have been at home in a more 'naturalistic' style. The influence of de Brosse's adaptation of the Italian type of design, was considerable in France, and one of the earliest examples of it is the famous grotto at the Château of Wideville, dating from the 1630s.[68]

We must now return to the final phase of de Brosse's employment at the Luxembourg. On 3 February 1623 Peiresc wrote to Rubens: 'La Reine Mère va s'établir demain pour quinze ou vingt jours dans son Palais du Luxembourg, pendant la durée de la foire; c'est pour ce motif et pour se purger qu'elle a fait tapisser les apartemens du Palais Neuf, mais elle n'y veut pas coucher encore, et habitera le vieux palais du Luxembourg; celui-ci est contigu au Palais neuf et elle se rendra dans celui-ci par la galerie où doivent venir vos tableaux'.[69] The Queen evidently did not consider the palace comfortable enough to sleep in, and it was almost certainly during this visit that she began to have the serious misgivings which prompted the *Procès Verbal* to be undertaken a few months later.

In 1623 de Brosse was in receipt of 2,000 livres a week for the work at the Luxembourg. During the previous year Richelieu was, as we have seen, pressing d'Argouges, Marie de Médicis' treasurer, for particulars both as to the expenditure of the funds provided and the progress of the building. D'Argouges could assure the Cardinal both that the architect was honest,[70] and that the pavilion at present under construction would soon be ready for roofing. This was the north-east pavilion on the Rue de Vaugirard.[71] Nevertheless, the Queen was not satisfied; there had been trouble over the sinking of the foundations in various parts of the building,[72] which must, among other unforeseen items, have caused a good deal of extra expenditure. Things were, in her opinion – or the Cardinal's – getting out of hand financially.

De Brosse was not only the architect of the building, but contractor for all the stonework. He and his nephew, Jean du Cerceau, also owned the quarries

68. Cf. Ernest de Ganay's *Châteaux et manoirs de France, Ile de France*, 1938, IV, pls 71–73.

69. *Correspondance de Rubens*, III, p. 126.

70. Cf. above, Chap. I, p. 15.

71. The location of the pavilion is fixed by the *Procès Verbal*, fol. 46 recto. The original letters between d'Argouges and Richelieu are in the Archives du Ministère des Affaires Etrangères, Fonds de France 776, fols. 64 and 245, letters of March 1622, Richelieu to d'Argouges, and 26 July, d'Argouges to Richelieu.

72. Blomfield, II, p. 55 and n. 1, quoting Hustin.

from which the stone used was provided.[73] This combination of rôles was a
dangerous one, and had been strongly discouraged by de l'Orme in his
writings. We already know the outcome of the *Procès Verbal*, which resulted
in de Brosse's resignation as architect of the Luxembourg, and the financial
troubles which followed.[74]

De Brosse, however, did not sever all connection with the building, for
as late as June 1626, the year of his death, he and Alessandro Francini were
giving advice to Marin de la Vallée about the construction of the terrace and
steps in front of the *corps-de-logis* in the courtyard (presumably to de Brosse's
original design).[75]

By 1646, when the Luxembourg, still incomplete within, was handed over
to Gaston d'Orléans, it was already considered to be old-fashioned and
inconvenient, however much its architecture or decoration might be admired.
Marie de Médicis had, in fact, scarcely lived in it, for it was not really habitable
before 1625,[76] and in 1631 she had to leave it for ever.

The Florentine Queen had undertaken an ambitious project: a new Royal
Palace in Paris, a monument to her enlightened taste in architecture and the
arts. To help her realize her ambition she had the best French architect of
her time and the greatest painter in contemporary Europe. But, because of her
everlasting financial troubles, her stormy political career and ignominious
exile, she only enjoyed for the briefest time the building she had created. A
fitting epitaph for her great enterprise can be made from the words of
the English visitor of 1649; '. . . At each end of ye first building under an
arch stand the statues in white marble of Hen. 4 & his Queene, sister to ye
Duke of Florence. Behind each of them is a Peacock. She, in her pride, built
this'.[77]

---

73. Cf. E.-J. Ciprut, 'Notes sur un grand architecte parisien, Jean Androuet du Cerceau', *Bull.
Soc. Hist. Prot. Fr.*, CXIII, Avril–Juin 1967, p. 164.
74. Cf. above Chap. I, p. 6.
75. Cf. Cat. p. 258.
76. Hirschfeld, op. cit., p. 25.
77. Cf. O. Millar, op. cit., p. 162.

CHAPTER VIII

Saint Gervais and the Palais de Justice in Paris

THE CHURCH OF SAINT GERVAIS

D E BROSSE'S other major commissions in Paris during the period 1615 to 1619 were both concerned with the completion or replacement of older buildings; these were the west front of the Church of Saint Gervais and the Salle des Pas Perdus in the Palais de Justice (Pls 176, 195).

On Easter Day 1615, at the annual meeting held to elect the churchwardens of Saint Gervais, the decision was taken to complete the church as soon as possible by the erection of a façade (*portail*) on the west front.[1] Consultations were held throughout the year, the most important parishioners were canvassed, several drawings and at least one model were submitted: '. . . Ils auroient faict dresser plusieurs desseings et modelle desdict ouvrages'.[2] Among the churchwardens who took part in these deliberations was Jean de Donon, Contrôleur Général des Bâtiments du Roi.[3]

One of these designs having been chosen, a wooden model, some fourteen feet high was ordered to be made from it: '. . . Sur lequel desseing pour plus grande sureté et plus facilement exécuter lesdicts ouvrages lesquelz sieurs marguilliers auroient faict faire ung modelle de treize ou quatorze pieds'. This model now forms the retable of the Baptistery chapel and differs from the executed work only in minor details.[4] All the preparations having thus

1. Cf. L. Brochard, *Saint-Gervais*, Paris, 1938. These details come from the preamble to the 1616 contract which Brochard discovered and published. Cf. for Saint Gervais, Cat. p. 266.

2. Ibid.

3. Cf. Brochard, *Saint-Gervais*; *Histoire de la paroisse*, 1950, 'Liste des marguilliers', p. 404.

4. It is very curious that the principal writers on the church, Brochard, Dumolin and Boinet (cf. Cat. p. 266), although they knew the contract and mention the wooden retable, do not connect it with the model made for the façade in 1615, for Sauval (I, p. 453) distinctly states that the wooden model for the façade served as the retable in the Lady Chapel and was the work of de Hancy. Boinet, *Les églises parisiennes*, 1962, I, p. 380, rejects Dumolin's attribution of the model to Claude Molleur (Dumolin and Outardel, *Les églises de France: Paris et la Seine*, 1936, p. 100) in favour of Sauval's attribution to Antoine de Hancy, so also does Pierre du Colombier, 'Autour

been completed, the work for the west front was put out to tender, and was awarded to Claude Monnard, master-mason of Paris.

At the next churchwardens' election, on Easter Day 1616, Jean de Donon was joined in office by another influential figure in the architectural world, Jean de Fourcy, 'Surintendant des Bâtiments du Roi',[5] and on 2 April of that year the four churchwardens signed a contract for the west front with Claude Monnard, Claude Molleur, master-carpenter, and Clément Métezeau, 'architecte du roi'. Work was to begin without further delay on 25 April, although the first stone was not officially laid by Louis XIII until 24 July.

In view of the controversy which arose after the discovery and publication by Brochard (in 1938) of the 1616 contract for the west front,[6] it is worth quoting here part of the final section of the document, where the executants pledge themselves in the usual formula to carry out the work in accordance with the terms laid down: '... A ce faire vinrent et furent presens Clément Métezeau, architecte des bastimens du Roy ... et Claude Molleur, maistre charpentier à Paris ... lesquelz après avoir eu communication dudict devis et marché cy-dessus et iceluy à eux par nous notaires leu et fait entendre . . . . et promettant, obligent, chacun en droit soy lesdicts sieurs marguillers audict nom et ledsicts Métezeau et Mouleur avec ledict Monnard l'un pour l'autre corps et biens comme dict est ... ont signé.

Fourcy	Donon	
Sainct Genys	Nicolas	
Claude Monnard	Métezeau	Claude Molleur
Le Normant	de Monhenault'[7]	

The presence of Métezeau's name and signature in the contract has been taken to mean that he, and not de Brosse, was the architect of the west front of Saint Gervais. Although this contention is now by no means generally accepted, it has been persistent enough to need examination and refutation here.[8] For it throws doubt upon an attribution to de Brosse which goes back

des Métezeau', *Bibliothèque d'Humanisme et Renaissance*, III, 1943, pp. 168–189, who pointed out that Claude Molleur was only a carpenter, not a joiner or cabinet-maker.

5. The other two churchwardens of 1616, whose signatures appear on the contract, were Denis de Saint-Genis, 'bourgeois de Paris', and Jean Nicolas, 'procurateur au Châtelet'. Cf. Brochard, *Histoire de la paroisse*, p. 404.

6. Cf. below, n. 8.

7. The last two are the notaries.

8. Professor Blunt, *Art and Architecture*, p. 264, n. 26, sees no reason to doubt the traditional attribution to de Brosse. Dumolin, op. cit., and *B.S.H.A.F.*, 1933, p. 454, attributed the façade to

to the seventeenth century and is supported by all the old guide-books, by Marot's engraving and in the correspondence of de Brosse's descendants.[9]

The fact that Métezeau's name appears in the 1616 contract, even when described as 'architecte . . . du Roy', and his signature upon it, certainly should not be taken as proof that he was the designer of the façade; in fact, the reverse is true, as we can deduce from contemporary practice in the drawing up of contracts. Unless the architect was also the contractor for the building concerned his name did not appear in contracts for the construction, and he never signed them. Just occasionally the architect's name may be mentioned in the body of the document in connection with plans, drawings or models which he has provided or is to provide. This practice can be illustrated by examples from de Brosse's own career: at the Hôtels de Bouillon, de Bullion and Bénigne Bernard, for instance, de Brosse was both contractor and architect, but it was in the former capacity that he signed all the extant masonry contracts.[10] At the Hôtels de Fresne and du Lude, Claude Pouillet and Anthoine Petit respectively signed the contracts,

---

Métezeau alone, citing the 1616 contract as evidence, but his thesis is successfully contested by Pierre du Colombier, op. cit., n. 4 above. Hautecoeur, I, p. 505 and n. 7, admits that the appearance of Métezeau's name in the contract is not conclusive, and remains somewhat ambiguous about the attribution of the work. He also dates the contract wrongly: 'le 13 Avril 1616 . . . il (Métezeau) aurait été chargé par les marguilliers . . . de bâtir le portail de cette église, qui a été fréquemment attribué à Salomon de Brosse'. Boinet, *Les églises parisiennes*, I, p. 368–369, gives both points of view, and quotes Pierre du Colombier's theory about the nature of Métezeau's intervention (cf. below, p. 138 and n. 13). It should be noted here that a further masonry contract for Saint Gervais dated March 1622 was signed by Monnard alone (cf. Cat. p. 266).

9. Boinet, op. cit., p. 368 ff., and Colombier, op. cit., p. 168 ff., give a useful summary of old attributions to de Brosse: Sauval, Germain Brice, Blondel, Marot, Mariette, Le Maire, Piganiol de la Force, Dézalier d'Argenville and d'Aviler all attribute it to de Brosse. (For Marot, Mariette and Blondel, cf. Cat. p. 267). Brice, in his first edition (1684) gave the west front to Métezeau and de Brosse, but in subsequent editions there is no mention of Métezeau. This double attribution was followed by Nicolas Catherinot, *Traité d'Architecture*, 1688, and various writers of Dreux (Métezeau's home-town) attribute it to Métezeau alone. Pierre du Colombier (op. cit., above, n. 4) cites a letter written by Simon-Louis du Ry, 'architecte de la cour de Cassel', to his sister, c. 1740, saying that he has been to see the 'portail' of their ancestor, Salomon de Brosse. Pannier, p. 226, quotes a letter of Simon-Louis' sister, Jeannette-Philippine Leclerc, of 9 August 1733 (published in *Bull. Hist. Soc. Prot., Fr.*, 1902, p. 556): 'J'ai considéré avec attention le portail Saint-Gervais malgré le peu d'espace qu'il y a devant; j'ai vu avec plaisir de connaisseur ce monument du sçavoir de notre parent'. (For the sense in which de Brosse was the 'parent' of du Ry's descendants, cf. Chap. I, n. 25). Dumolin, while supporting the attribution to Métezeau, quoted a *Procès Verbal* of 1678 ordered by Colbert for the examination of stone used in all the principal buildings of Paris, wherein 'Le Portail Saint-Gervais' is listed as built by Salomon de Brosse in 1616. The question of the attribution is gone into at length by Pierre du Colombier in his article cited, and he also discusses contractual procedure. I have repeated his arguments (and in part added to them) because the article is not easily available.

10. Cf. Cat. pp. 238–247.

but in each case there happens to be a mention in the document of the architect, de Brosse, whose drawings were to be adhered to. In the same way, at Coulommiers in 1613, the carpenter promises to do all his work 'suivant les desseins qui ont ésté faictz pr intention du Sieur Brosse'. Again, in 1631, also at Coulommiers, du Ry undertakes to build in accordance with 'les desseins qui sont demeurez ès mains du Sieur Mansart'. In connection with Saint Gervais itself, we may note that in 1618 Clément Métezeau made designs for two wooden screens for the church, and this is mentioned in the contract for them signed by Guillaume Noyer, master-joiner.

It must be stressed, however, that the architect's name is usually omitted altogether from the contracts for buildings which he designed but which he did not undertake actually to build. In the light of contemporary contractual procedures, therefore, Métezeau's appearance in the 1616 Saint Gervais contract is a puzzle. He is designated as *an* architect, but that merely gives him his official title; he is certainly not referred to thereby as *the* architect. The preamble to the document[11] makes it clear that Monnard was the building-contractor, the 'entrepreneur' or 'conducteur des bâtiments', and it is obvious that Molleur was the sub-contractor for the carpentry. Why therefore was Métezeau present at all at the reading of the contract, why was he named in it, and why did he sign it?

One suggestion is that he stood surety financially for the enterprise ('se porter caution').[12] We know that he engaged himself in this way for a reservoir and other water-works carried out in the Place Saint-Germain-l'Auxerrois,[13] so he may have done so for Saint Gervais. Another possible explanation is that Métezeau, who knew de Brosse, having been associated with him at the Luxembourg since the previous year, undertook to supervise the building operations on de Brosse's behalf while the latter was fully occupied with his work at the Luxembourg.[14]

The churchwardens of Saint Gervais had a well-developed sense of the importance of their church: '. . . (d')un tel et sy magnifique bastiment qui est celuy d'icelle église de Saint-Gervais l'une des plus célèbres de cette ville de Paris . . .'.[15] De Fourcy and de Donon were men in a position to appreciate

11. Min. Cent XXVI—33, April 1616, cf. Cat. p. 266.

12. This explanation was put forward by P. du Colombier, op. cit., above, n. 4, and is quoted by Boinet, op. cit., p. 369.

13. Ibid.

14. Pierre du Colombier, op. cit., p. 172, disagrees with this supposition, but his reasons for doing so are perhaps not absolutely conclusive. For Métezeau at the Luxembourg, cf. Thieme-Becker, *Kunstlerlexikon*.

15. Preamble to the 1616 contract.

and engage the best talent of the day. There is no documentary evidence that they chose de Brosse to design the façade of their west front, but the whole conception and style of the work is sufficient indication that they did. Clément Métezeau was a very competent architect of the second rank, but nothing we know about him suggests that he was capable of producing anything of this calibre,[16] nor do his surviving works have much in common stylistically with the façade of Saint Gervais.

The façade is advanced for its period, not only in its classicism, but also in its inventive and highly individual solution to a particular architectural problem: that of the conjunction of a classical façade with a tall late-Gothic nave. At this distance in time, and because of our familiarity with classical church-fronts, it is perhaps difficult to appreciate how original de Brosse was in his approach to this problem, or to comprehend the impact which his façade made upon his contemporaries and immediate successors. It is only by considering previous essays in this style that de Brosse's achievement can be understood.

Since the mid-sixteenth century the naves or transepts of many Gothic churches in France had received façades which incorporated Serliesque or other classical features, and which displayed varying degrees of competence in the handling of the new idiom. De Brosse's grandfather du Cerceau, for example, had designed an exuberant west front for the lofty church of Saint Eustache, in Paris.[17] Of these façades in the new style, affixed to Gothic churches, two are particularly important in relation to what de Brosse did at Saint Gervais. The first, which dates from 1582, is at the church in Le

16. Clément Métezeau (Jacques Clément II) became 'architecte du roi' when he inherited the pension on the royal payroll of his brother Louis in 1615. In 1610 he had begun the town of Charleville, near Mézières, for Charles de Gonzague, Duc de Nevers (cf. above, Ch. III, p. 44). The architecture of this town is admittedly more sophisticated in detail than its contemporary, de Brosse's Henrichemont, but lacks any of the latter's imaginative monumentality. Métezeau was associated with the Church of the Oratoire in the Rue Saint Honoré, and he built the new fortifications at La Rochelle in 1627. In Paris he built the Hôtel de Longueville in the Rue Saint-Thomas-du-Louvre, engraved by Marot and Abraham Bosse. Hautecoeur, I, p. 505–506, attributes other hôtels to him, but his topography is confusing. Métezeau is also believed to have built the Château of La Meilleraye (ibid.). The Château of Chilly-Mazarin may be by him, but has also been attributed to Lemercier; cf. Blunt, *Art and Architecture*, p. 266, n. 7., who believes it to be slightly closer to the style of Métezeau. Charleville, where the Grande Place survives in good preservation, is the best indication of this architect's capabilities. Métezeau also designed church-furniture (see above, p. 138, for the screens he designed for Saint Gervais; Boinet, op. cit., p. 369, n. 3; Min. Cent. XIX, 385). He is mentioned in another contract as the designer (Noyer again being the executant) of joinery for the church of the Jacobins in Paris (Min. Cent. XXIV–306, 29 October 1619; cf. E.-J. Ciprut, *B.S.H.A.F.*, 1934).

17. Cf. Geymüller, p. 77 and fig. 37; also Hautecoeur, I, pp. 374–379 and pp. 640–667, for a résumé of the development of the classical church-front.

Mesnil-Aubry, between Paris and Chantilly, and the second, begun in 1610, is at Saint Etienne-du-Mont in Paris.

At Le Mesnil-Aubry the nave was begun in 1564 and was built with a high Gothic roof.[18] The belfry-tower and façade are in the classical manner, but as the tower is attached to the west end of the north aisle, the west front is asymmetrical (Pl. 177). Within this limitation, however, the Serliesque orders and other motifs of its three-storey façade are arranged with a clarity more characteristic of the first half of the sixteenth century than of the 1580s. The façade is obviously influenced by a design, 'un tempio Sacro', in Serlio's Fourth Book,[19] and by Vignola's original design for the façade of the Gesù.[20]

The strong verticality imposed by the high nave at Le Mesnil-Aubry has been successfully counteracted in the façade by treating each storey with as much horizontal emphasis as possible, and by dividing each from the other with strong unbroken entablatures. The bold segmental pediment at the summit also contributes to this minimization of the vertical stress. The two upper storeys are connected to each other and to the lower one by one of the curved elements typical of the Vignolesque façade. The great interest of Le Mesnil-Aubry lies in the way in which the Italian prototype, an essentially two-storey construction, has been adapted for a three-storey façade by a French architect.[21]

The west front of Saint Etienne-du-Mont is less explicit in its derivation than Le Mesnil-Aubry (Pl. 178). The separate elements are mostly old-fashioned, and except for the two lower storeys of the central part, not very coherently organized. Nor does the façade as a whole marry well with the pre-existing structure or disguise its Gothic character; it certainly does not mask it. In all these ways it is less advanced than Le Mesnil-Aubry, but two of its features, which are far more three-dimensional in handling than anything in the earlier façade, are very important: the heavily-pedimented frontispiece, and the equally weighty curved pediment of the second storey, deeply broken to accommodate the rose window.

---

18. See below, n. 21, and cf. Hautecoeur, I, p. 389 and fig. 271.

19. IV, 175 verso.

20. In the sixteenth century in France a complete Roman church-façade on a miniature scale had been introduced into the top of the tower at the east end of Rodez cathedral. Cf. Blunt, *Art and Architecture*, p. 57 and pl. 36(A); and Hautecoeur, I, p. 388 and fig. 270.

21. Hautecoeur, does not mention the name of the architect. The Guide Bleu, *Environs de Paris*, 1948, p. 342, gives the following: '. . . église de la Renaissance construite de 1531 à 1582 sur les plans de Nicolas de Saint-Michel'. According to Hautecoeur, the north aisle was begun in 1531 and the nave in 1564 when the Connétable de Montmorency acquired the Seigneurie du Mesnil-Aubry. The date 1582 is inscribed on the façade, over the west door.

At Saint Gervais de Brosse was faced with an extremely high Gothic gable on to which he had to build his façade (Pl. 179). The height of the new front, from the ground to the top of the Corinthian order, is just over one hundred and thirty feet;[22] even with this height, only the great curved pediment rising above that actually clears the old gable. De Brosse's solution to this difficult vertical stress was to produce a design for the façade which combined two prototypes: the Roman church-front, and the version of the three-storey frontispiece of the French château which de l'Orme had created at Anet (Pl. 1). For the central part of his façade at Saint Gervais, de Brosse has simply taken de l'Orme's composition and added to it a triangular pediment over the entrance and a curved pediment at the summit;[23] the relationship of both these features with Saint Etienne-du-Mont, begun only six years previously, cannot be ignored.

This central part of de Brosse's façade follows the verticality of the structure which it masks, even underlining it by the deep forward break of the orders and by the superimposed openings in the bays which they enclose. Only the large triangular pediment over the portico breaks the upward thrust which is finally arrested by the bold lines of the curved pediment at the summit; a device reminiscent of Le Mesnil-Aubry. The horizontal balance of the composition is restored by the bays added on either side of the frontispiece on the first and second storeys, and by the fact that both these storeys are of the same width. A horizontal accent is further maintained by the pedestals of the Ionic and Corinthian orders, and by the pedestals at the outer edges of the top storey which bear statues instead of Corinthian columns. The shallow swags of drapery between the top row of pedestals serve the same purpose. The second and third storeys of the façade play a dual role; they are part of the whole three-storey composition, but, taken alone and linked together by the Vignolesque curved elements each side of the Corinthian order, they form de Brosse's version of the two-storey Roman church-front.

De Brosse almost certainly knew Vignola's original design for the west front of the Gesù from Villamena's engraving of 1570, and it is also likely that he knew, by report or from drawings, of other Roman church-façades such as Giacomo della Porta's Santa Maria dei Monti, the façade which the same architect executed for the Gesù, and even possibly Carlo Maderno's Santa

22. Blomfield, II, p. 56.
23. Another example of the adaptation of the château-frontispiece to church architecture is the façade of the south transept of Saint Germain at Rennes. This was built by Germain Gaultier between 1606 and 1623. It has the added interest of incorporating features which influenced Gaultier's brother-in-law, François Mansart. Cf. Hautecoeur, I, p. 644. The influence on Mansart was pointed out to me by Dr Peter Smith.

Susanna, dating from the turn of the century. Awareness of such buildings is unusual for this date, for even as late as the second decade of the seventeenth century, the two-storey church-façade, chiefly deriving from Vignola's Gesù design and current in Rome since the latter part of the sixteenth century, had had a negligible influence in France. The church at Le Mesnil-Aubry is a curious and isolated example of the adaptation of Roman ideas.

One new Italianate church had been built in Paris before de Brosse began Saint Gervais; this was Saint Joseph-des-Carmes, near the Luxembourg in the Rue de Vaugirard. It was begun in 1613 when Marguerite de Valois laid the first stone. The front is a rather naïve attempt at the Roman façade, but it is important because of its novelty in Paris and because, like most of the Roman façades mentioned, the west front of Saint Joseph is not all built on one plane; the outer bays are recessed so as to lead up to and enhance the central feature.[24]

At Saint Gervais in the lowest stage the inner Doric columns flanking the central door are almost free-standing, attached to the wall only by their bases; the pairs flanking the outer bays are engaged to about a quarter of their diameter. On the second storey, where the order is Ionic, the outer columns are engaged at the base, and the central ones are completely free-standing (Pls 182, 183). The four Corinthian columns of the top storey are all completely free-standing, supporting the boldly-projecting cornice which forms the base of the segmental pediment. In this way the outer part of the façade is set back, and the central part projects a much more dramatic interpretation of the variation of planes attempted at Saint Joseph.

Because of the way in which he used the Doric order at Saint Gervais, de Brosse has led himself into certain complications which have resulted in some clumsy detail. By using coupled Doric columns, he is faced with problems of classical usage related to those which he had encountered in the entrance-pavilion of the Luxembourg.[25] At Saint Gervais, the spacing of the metopes and triglyphs is upset by coupled columns; the metopes should all be square, but between two columns they cannot be, so de Brosse fills in the

24. Cf. Dumolin and Outardel, op. cit., p. 128–131; Boinet, op. cit., II, pp. 42–66; and Jacques Vanuxem, *Saint-Joseph-des-Carmes*, Editions du Cerf, 1948, Série 'Nefs et Clochers'. One should mention here the church façade painted by Fréminet in the background of the large square panel nearest the altar of the Trinity Chapel at Fontainebleau. (Pl. 88). This is an astonishing piece of painted architecture for its period (the more so since the barrel vault on which it is depicted gives it a high-baroque curve). The upper part of this building invented by Fréminet in c. 1613 makes an interesting parallel with the topmost element of Saint Gervais designed by de Brosse about two years later.

25. Cf. above, Chap. VII, p. 119. Dézallier d'Argenville in his *Vies des fameux architectes*, (ed. quoted 1788), pp. 329–330, analyses the use of the orders and makes some useful criticisms of the west front as a whole.

added space with other decoration (Pl. 181). The spacing of the mutules over the triglyphs in the cornice above the coupled Doric columns is irregular; the disadvantage of this can be seen under and within the pediment (Pls 180, 181). When it comes to handling the mutules in the returns of the Doric cornice, things become even more difficult, for the greater projection of the entablature over the central pairs of columns and the lesser projection over the outer pairs, lead to complications in the angles. The triglyph on the returned frieze of the portico is necessarily placed further forward than its opposite number on the returned frieze of the half-column. So the mutules, having been 'run together' in the angles (as in the Luxembourg entrance-pavilion), those next to the portico have had to be further manoeuvred and a piece 'cut out' in the most curious way (Pl. 180). In fact, the problem of symmetry in this part of the entablature has defeated the architect.

The huge Doric columns of the portico are, it must be admitted, somewhat clumsy; they do not, because of their pronounced entasis, marry very happily with the extremely shallow pilasters behind them, which appear crushed. Also, because of the steps, the pedestals of all but the outer half-columns are greatly reduced; this gives to the whole order an appearance of sinking into the ground. Indeed, Blondel's criticism to this effect, and his suggestion that it would be a good idea to take the pedestals away from the Ionic and put them under the Doric order, is not unjustified. Nevertheless, the clumsiness of detail in this Doric order is very largely made up for by the sober monumentaility of its treatment. Unfortunately, the smallness of the *place* in front of the church, even though it was enlarged in the nineteenth century, prevents the large-scale façade from being seen to advantage.[26]

A criticism which might be made of the façade as a whole is that it is too 'open-ended'. This is not so apparent in the lower storey, where attention is more definitely drawn to the centre to the portico and pediment, but it is a pronounced feature of the second storey, where there is no similar element to arrest the march of the Ionic columns across the façade. There is nothing to bring the eye to a stop because, as usual, de Brosse has left the corners of his structure without emphasis. This makes it possible to think of the church-front, at this level, not as a self-contained unit, but as the central part of a composition which could be prolonged by an indefinite number of bays on either side.

The frieze of the second storey is a torus moulding, a motif repeatedly found in this position in the later drawings of Jacques I du Cerceau (Pl. 138).

26. Cf. Blondel op. cit. Vol. II, Book VI, p. 118. Voltaire commented: '. . . un chef-d'oeuvre qui ne manque qu'une place pour contenir ces admirateurs'. Cf. Pannier, p. 225.

The broken segmental pediment above the Corinthian order of the third storey, like the triangular one over the portico, owes something to Saint-Etienne-du-Mont.[27] The windows of the two upper storeys are of a classical form used again by de Brosse in the Salle des Pas Perdus of the Palais de Justice in Paris, though the tracery of the one in the second storey seems so ill-suited to its classical surroundings as to suggest its retention as part of the older structure. It is, however, close in type to tracery considered suitable by du Cerceau for his imaginary and 'reconstructed' antique classical buildings, and also for his design for the façade of Saint Eustache.

Decoration on the façade is kept to a minimum. Originally there were two statues on the top pediment – an arrangement frequently used by de Brosse – but to judge from the engravings they must have been somewhat top-heavy. The statues of St Matthew and St John the Evangelist on the outer pedestals of the top storey, and those of St Gervais and St Protais, the patrons of the church, which stand in the niches of the second storey,[28] are nineteenth-century replacements for those destroyed in the Revolution. Apart from these figures, the austerity of the architecture is unrelieved by more than the simple swags between the outer pedestals of the top storey and balcony in front of the window, the reliefs in the extended metopes over the coupled Doric columns, and tablets over the doors. For the appeal to the eye in this façade is made through its architectural and three-dimensional, not its decorative qualities.

The surface interest lies in the innumerable projections and recessions, great and small, within the almost cliff-like structure, and in the opportunities which these provide for sharp contrasts of light and shade (Pl. 186). The mouldings are strong and simple, and all are kept as plain as possible. The unbroken segmental door-pediments, the tablets over the lateral doors, with only a mask-scroll at the bottom and a sharp straight moulding above, the spring and mouldings of the central arch: all these are serene and monumental. So also are the niches of the second storey, above which the wall-surface is cut back into two sharp layers, still further to enhance the play of light and shade. In all these ways de Brosse has made his architecture sculptural, so that it needs no sculpture to adorn it (Pls 180, 184, 187). The façade makes the same three-dimensional impact as the Luxembourg, and as at the Luxembourg

27. There may also have been an influence of Montanus in the pedimented portico; his drawings seem to have been known to some in France, though they were not engraved until later. Cf. Chap. II, n. 12.

28. According to Boinet, op. cit., II, p. 369, Michel Boudin made the statues of St Gervais and St Protais and Gilles Guérin those of the Evangelists. But cf. Sauval (I, p. 453): 'Le portail est du dessin de Brosse, fait par Monnart, les figures hautes de Guilain et les basses de Boudin'.

the effectiveness of the whole overcomes any lack of assurance over details, and mistakes in handling them. Despite its borrowings, it is a truly original composition, which rises above its models in a way that Le Mesnil-Aubry and Saint Etienne do not.

The importance of the Saint Gervais façade lies not so much in its direct influence on a great number of other façades as in the admiration which was felt for its originality and its classicism. Sauval wrote: 'Le portail de St Gervais . . . est si plein de savoir, de majesté, de grandeur, que ceux du métier le tiennent pour le plus excellent de l'Europe'.[29] This praise of Saint Gervais in a European context may be exaggerated, but it was obviously a work which commanded much esteem. Later, Voltaire was to write that it 'devrait immortaliser le nom de Brosse encore plus que le palais du Luxembourg'.[30] These writers and others have recognized in de Brosse's façade qualities which Blondel, so concerned with academic correctness, failed to appreciate.

The classical feeling expressed by de Brosse at Saint Gervais, is close in spirit to certain works by Philibert de l'Orme, to whom de Brosse looked for far more than just the form of the Anet frontispiece. Though the link between these two architects is one of the most important factors in the development of French classicism, it is by no means always easy to define. A sufficient and eloquent indication of it in this case can be seen by a comparison of details from Saint Gervais with one from de l'Orme's architecture at Anet (Pl. 185).

The work most directly influenced by Saint Gervais was François Mansart's façade for the church of the Feuillants, begun in 1623.[31] Mansart, for his two-storey front, virtually copied the two upper storeys of Saint Gervais, adding to them only some Vignolesque and mannerist ornament. In 1624 Charles du Ry, Jean Androuet du Cerceau and Paul de Brosse submitted a design for the façade of the new transept at Orléans Cathedral.[32] This was a three-storey classical façade, clearly derived in almost all its elements from Saint Gervais. It had, however, an extra recessed bay at each side articulated with a single pilaster in the first and second storeys. The top storey had a plain segmental pediment and a round window, closer to Serlio and Rome than to de Brosse. It was a weak design, was disapproved of by de Brosse himself in 1626 and was never carried out. Another drawing, presumably submitted at

29. Sauval, III, p. 48.
30. In the *Temple du Gout*; cf. Pannier, p. 225.
31. The body of the church was built by Rémy Collin (1600). Cf. below, p. 151 and n. 51.
32. For Orleans, Cathedral of Sainte Croix and drawings for it, cf. Cat. p. 235.

the same time, shows a plan for the transept façade which is almost exactly copied from Saint Gervais.[33]

The three-storey classical façade was of its nature a short-lived innovation. Later architects were not concerned with classical façades for Gothic churches, and classical churches only need two-storey façades. For these the architects looked principally to Italy for inspiration, and this was particularly true in the case of the Jesuits who, in the years immediately succeeding the building of the Saint Gervais façade, erected many new churches in France. Their outstanding architect, Martellange, was however more original than most, and seems to have felt the influence of de Brosse, particularly in the façade which he designed for the church of Saint Paul-Saint Louis in Paris in 1627. He intended for this a façade in two storeys, of which the boldly-projecting coupled columns are an obvious reference to Saint Gervais. Unfortunately, in 1629, Martellange was superseded at Saint Paul-Saint Louis by Derand, and his façade, just begun, was completely altered.[34]

Derand began his façade at Saint Paul-Saint Louis in 1630, so that by using de Brosse's three-storey composition he was already being old-fashioned. But the church, though classical in style, had a Gothic height in the nave. Derand followed the Roman method of recessing the outer bays of the façade and bringing the central element forward, but despite these variations of plane, his whole design is far less three-dimensional than Saint Gervais, and is the exact opposite to de Brosse's composition, in that it is the decoration of the surface, not the architecture, which makes the impact.

PALAIS DE JUSTICE – SALLE DES PAS PERDUS

Saint Gervais and the Luxembourg mark the high point of de Brosse's middle period which had started with Blérancourt and Coulommiers. The other important commission which he received in Paris during the period 1616 to 1619 was for the public hall of the Palais de Justice on the Ile de la Cité. One of de Brosse's lesser-known works, this is interesting both for its style and for its history (Pls 188–195).

33. It differs only in having a double central portal and half-columns on the return faces of the façade. The elevation was published in 1921 by A. Chénesseau in his *Sainte Croix d'Orléans*, I, fig. 61. Fig. 62, placed beneath the elevation, is the plan referred to in the text, and is entitled by Chénesseau, 'Les "Portaux" de la croisée', although quite plainly plan and elevation do not correspond.

34. Cf. Pierre Moisy, *Les églises des jésuites de l'ancienne assistance de France*, Bibliotheca Instituti S.I., XII, 2 vols., I, p. 123; II, pls. XIVB and XXIA. Professor Blunt, in a review of this book (*Burl. Mag.*, CI, 1959, p. 112) points out that another feature of Martellange's façade, the concave

The medieval Salle des Pas Perdus was almost completely gutted by fire on 7 March 1618. It had been an imposing place, 122 feet long by 84 feet wide, double-aisled, divided down the centre by a slender arcade, and with a high wooden vault over each aisle. All along the side-walls and down the arcade stood statues of the Kings of France on slender colonnettes under carved canopies. A lively impression of this hall on a busy day is preserved in an engraving by Jacques I du Cerceau.[35]

After the fire only part of the outer walls, a fragment of the arcade and a few statues remained. It was decided to rebuilt the hall in a new style, while preserving the original interior arrangement of double aisles and double vaults. A commission of magistrates from the Parlement was formed at the King's command to deal with the project, and architects were invited to submit designs in competition. There is no direct evidence that de Brosse was chosen as architect as well as contractor, but the attribution is traditional, well-established and has never been disputed.

The deliberations of the commission cannot have been far advanced when four Parisian master-masons formed a partnership with the intention of bidding for the contract when it was put out to tender.[36] Their deed of partnership was drawn up on 30 March 1618, twelve days after the fire, and the senior partner and moving spirit was Jean Gobelin, who as a member of de Brosse's team of masons had taken part in the work at Coulommiers under Charles du Ry.

The official decree for the rebuilding was promulgated on 18 April and between then and 3 August de Brosse had been awarded the building contract (and presumably had also won the competition for the design itself): '... (Que)icelluy Gobelin face (fasse) lesdictz ouvraiges et refection de ladicte Salle du pallais, circonstances et deppendances, conformément et ainsy que l'adjudication luy en a esté faicte et à Me Salomon de Brosse

---

central bay approached by convex semi-circular steps, was exceedingly advanced, even for Italy, let alone France, in 1627. Nevertheless a design for a two-storey building, possibly a church, with a concave central bay in a façade articulated by coupled pilasters, occurs on fol. 7 recto of the 'de Brosse' album in the Louvre. That this design had some connection with Coulommiers is suggested by a church with a concave entrance appearing next to the château in Silvestre's engraving (cf. Cat. p. 221). Charles du Ry's Capuchin church at Coulommiers (cf. above, Chap. VI, p. 96, n. 19) begun in 1618, was nothing like this engraving, and the façade was in any case never built. We know however that there was in the de Brosse/du Ry circle an interest in the concave façade which (itself influenced by the elder du Cerceau, cf. Chap. II) may have influenced Martellange's design for Saint Paul-Saint Louis. Derand's façade is illustrated in Blunt, *Art and Architecture*, pl. 80A.

35. Cf. Cat. p. 255.
36. Ibid.

architeycte du Roy par Messieurs les commissaires et deputez du Roy . . .'.[37]

On 3 August Jean Gobelin and Paul de Brosse signed an agreement with a bargee ('voicturier en eau'), named Chabanne to the effect that the latter would be responsible for the removal of the debris from the old 'Grande Salle du Palais'. One of the other masons of the original partnership also signed, but the other two had opted out, though not yet officially, because of disagreements.[38]

Paul de Brosse signed for his father ('stippulant pour son père'), because Salomon was absent from Paris on his way to Rennes to make plans for the Palais du Parlement. However, even after his return, de Brosse seems to have left the responsibility for overseeing and sub-contracting to his son and Jean Gobelin, for, on 28 September Paul signed again on his father's behalf an agreement about the provision of stone for the new building. De Brosse may, however, have been away in Orléans at this time.

On 5 May 1619 the partnership of four formed by Gobelin in the previous year was formally broken up. Reading between the lines of the Deed of Annulment,[39] it looks as if the two departing members, Benoist and Girard, had had their noses put out of joint by the arrival upon the scene of Salomon and Paul de Brosse. They seem to have hoped that the partnership would be asked not only to build but also to design the hall, and to have felt aggrieved that their efforts in the latter direction had been passed over. Gobelin promised to recompense and reimburse Benoist and Girard 'de leurs frais, paines, sallaires et vacations par eulx faictes et employés tant pour parvenir à l'adjudication dudict contract desdictz bastiments soubz le nom dudict Gobelin que pour avoir par eux dressé divers desseings et employé partye de leur temps à la direction, conduicte et élévations des ouvraiges dudict pallais jusques à huy'. It may be, however, that these designs were not theirs, or even Gobelin's, but de Brosse's passed on by Gobelin.

By the spring of 1619 the work was well enough under way for the *Mercure Français* to report that the new Salle des Pas Perdus was 'plus belle encore qu'elle n'estoit', but there were to be delays, and shortage of funds necessitated grants by the King of further money. In November 1623, the annual 'Messe du Saint-Esprit' was celebrated in the hall: '. . . Sambedy 12e jour de novembre, Messieurs, assemblés . . . en robes rouges et chapperons, sont allés en la grand' salle du palais où a esté dite et cellebrée la messe par

37. From the Annulment of the 1618 partnership; cf. Cat., p. 255.
38. Cf. Ibid. and E.-J. Ciprut, *Bull. Soc. Hist. Prot. Fr.*, CX, October–December 1964, pp. 260 ff.
39. Ibid. and Cat., p. 253.

l'evesque de Soissons'.[40] Next year, however, Messieurs, in full regalia, had to take themselves elsewhere for the Mass, 'à cause que la grande salle estoit occupée des massons'. The work appears finally to have been completed in 1624.

There was a minor outbreak of fire in 1676 which did no serious damage, but in 1776, not only the Salle des Pas Perdus, but the buildings adjacent to it in the courtyard (the Cour du Mai) were gutted by a disastrous conflagration. From 1777 to 1787 the rebuilding in the Cour du Mai was in charge of four successive architects, the last of whom, Jacques-Denis Antoine, was responsible for restoring the Salle des Pas Perdus. Antoine began this work about 1785; the main fabric of de Brosse's building, apart from the roof, had withstood the fire well, but Antoine had to rebuild the vaults completely. This provided an opportunity to introduce, above the Salle and within the roof-pitch, galleries to store archives, space for which was by that time badly needed. Antoine made a wooden model[41] showing this ingenious piece of construction, and this survives today in the Musée Carnavalet in Paris, providing some invaluable evidence as to the original appearance of de Brosse's interior (Pl. 194).

During the rebuilding of the Palais after the 1777 fire, the east façade of the Salle was re-faced in the classical style, and the medieval windows finally disappeared.

In 1812 part of the floor of the Salle collapsed; the vaults of the medieval undercroft had given way because de Brosse had failed to site the eight piers of his arcade directly over the columns of the arcade in the Salle des Gardes beneath, of which, in any case, there are only seven. Strengthening and repairs were carried out and engravings made at this period show the interior of the building as Antoine had left it (Pl. 193).[42] Further alterations were made to the east end in 1852, but in 1871 another fire attacked the Salle. Further repairs and some rebuilding were necessary, although once more the walls and arcade withstood the flames.

The building, therefore, has undergone considerable vicissitudes since de Brosse designed it; even so, as we see it today (Pl. 195), it is possible to recapture much of its original impact, and its interior still conforms essentially to de Brosse's conception. Major exceptions to his design are the blocking of the south windows; the interior access-staircase and windows introduced at

40. *Registres du Parlement*, quoted by Pannier, p. 74.
41. Cf. M. Gallet, 'Modèle de Jacques-Denis Antoine pour la Grand'Salle du Palais de Justice', *Bull. du Musée Carnavalet*, 'Collections historiques de la ville de Paris', June 1963, pp. 2–4.
42. Cf. Sauvan and Schmit, *Histoire et description du Palais de Justice de la Conciergerie*, Paris, 1812.

the east end in 1852; and the second remodelling of the doors of the west wall which, with the heavy painted coffering of the vault, date from the 1871 restoration.

The Salle des Pas Perdus stands along the north side of the main courtyard of the Palais, the Cour du Mai, opposite the Sainte Chapelle (Pls 188, 190, 191). A plan of de Brosse's building, forming part of a plan of the Ile de la Cité made before 1777,[43] shows the original south windows on to the Cour du Mai and the outside staircase leading up to the medieval door of the old hall (Pl. 189). (It also shows some interesting internal staircases with semi-circular projecting steps at the base, but these must be later additions, for such a form would be too advanced for so early a date).[44]

The exterior of the Salle as it now stands bears almost no resemblance to the original, known through drawings and engravings. The south windows have disappeared completely, blocked by the building containing Antoine's late eighteenth-century staircase, built on the site of the Salle Dauphine, which had been added to de Brosse's south front in about 1640.[45] The strange features now capping the entablatures of the Doric pilasters are nineteenth-century embellishments, and whole of the east front dates from 1852 onwards (Pl. 190).[46] The west front, once partially free-standing, is now entirely blocked by later buildings.

A drawing made by Thomas Froideau just after the fire of 1777[47] is the most reliable representation of the south façade of the Salle and the source of most of the engravings of it (Pl. 191). It shows how much of the medieval work surviving at the south-east corner of the building had to be incorporated in de Brosse's design.[48] On this façade de Brosse has reverted to the use of a Colossal order of Doric pilasters, not seen in his work since the courtyard chapel at Montceaux. He uses them here of necessity, not as decoration, but together with the heavy entablatures as vertical buttresses and counter-thrusts for the two barrel-vaults of the interior.

Despite the proximity of the medieval survivals, which prevented de Brosse from producing a completely harmonious and classical south façade, the drawing shows that his new work, though possibly a little clumsy, was

43. In the Bibliothèque Nationale. Cf. Cat., p. 254.
44. The earliest example of this 'spreading' of the lower steps in a French staircase seems to be Mansart's staircase at Coulommiers, c. 1631.
45. Cf. Cat., p. 256 (1630 and 1640).
46. Ibid. (1852-1875).
47. In the Musée Carnavalet; cf. Cat., p. 254.
48. The tower is shown in the plans in the Bibliothèque Nationale made by Couture in 1777; cf. Cat., p. 254.

grand and impressive. The arrangement of the windows, with decorative *tablettes* above them, is interesting as it derives directly from the principal façade of Vignola's Caprarola.

The exterior of the east end of the Salle, as it was before 1777, is recorded in a seventeenth-century engraving by Boisseau (Pl. 188).[49] This shows fully what Froideau's drawing merely indicates, namely that de Brosse retained the medieval arrangement of twin pointed roofs over the two vaults of the interior. He also retained the medieval exterior of the east end in its entirety. Boisseau indicates, and other evidence confirms, the presence of two pairs of tall pointed windows beneath each gable, and small rose windows above each pair.[50] It is possible that the medieval west end and its fenestration also survived and was retained, but Gomboust's plan of 1652, the only representation we have of this façade, is too small in scale to indicate whether the four tall windows in the two gable-ends are the original Gothic ones. This plan does, however, indicate that these windows gave on to what was then a quite large open space in the court of the Conciergerie.

The interior design of the Salle des Pas Perdus was very advanced for its date. De Brosse's achievement here was to combine Roman *gravitas* with the medieval inventiveness of the double-aisled hall. The interior has a monumental spaciousness, unknown in French sixteenth-century architecture, which reveals a deliberate attempt on de Brosse's part to emulate the grandeur of the ancient Roman basilicas, a conception he saw to some extent through the eyes of Vignola and of Jacques I du Cerceau. Some of his grandfather's 'reconstructions' of ancient temples have features in common with the Salle (Pl. 192).

De Brosse would have known, or known of, the interiors of certain French churches of very recent date which were influenced by Roman models themselves deriving from Vignola's Gesù. These were the nave and choir of the Church of the Feuillants[51] in Paris, begun in 1600, Saint Joseph-des-Carmes,[52] the façade of which was mentioned earlier in connection with Saint Gervais, and some Jesuit churches, notably those at Le Puy, Avignon and Roannes, the interiors of which were under construction in the years immediately preceding the building of the Salle des Pas Perdus. Martellange, on his travels

49. Cf. Cat., p. 255.
50. Ninteteenth-century prints based on Boisseau show these windows more clearly than does the reproduction of his engraving. They also feature in reliable reconstruction-models of the Cité made in the nineteenth century, now in the Musée Carnavalet in Paris.
51. By Rémy Collin; cf. E.-J. Ciprut, 'L'église du couvent des Feuillants, rue Saint-Honoré', *G.d.B.A.*, L, 1957, pp. 37–52.
52. Cf. Vanuxem, op. cit., plan opposite p. 7.

round France, made drawings of the churches of his Order while they were being built, and these he would have brought back with him to Paris.[53]

All these new churches had one thing in common, a wide nave articulated by an order of pilasters, the cornice of which, whether returned or not over the order, maintained an unbroken line round the whole church.[54] There are no aisles, and the side-chapels, which may or may not lead into one another, are shallow and divided from the nave by an arcade. Although in the Salle des Pas Perdus spaces corresponding to the side-chapels are not part of the design, the blind-arcades in the side-walls relate to the ecclesiastical arrangement. The continuation of the blind-arcades at the end of the Salle echoes the 'screen' of du Cerceau's prototype temple (Pls 192, 194, 195).[55]

Antoine's model shows the wall at the west end of the Salle (Pl. 194). In it the four doors, surmounted by roundels framed in decorative plasterwork, are Antoine's own creation, replacing some rather haphazardly-situated doors dating from after de Brosse's time.[56] Antoine's doors led to the new rooms beyond the Salle which were built after the fire of 1777. The blind-arcade in which they are pierced, however, apparently represents de Brosse's original design – with one significant exception.

Writing in the 1820s, J.-B. de Saint-Victor criticized one element of de Brosse's interior as follows: '. . . La décoration est en ordre Dorique, et cette sévérité d'ornement convient à son caractère. Debrosses s'y est permis, tant dans l'ajustement de l'ordre lui-même que dans sa frise, des disparités qu'on n'aime pas à rencontrer dans un genre d'architecture dont la régularité fait la principale condition; les deux arcades du bout de la salle présentent aussi quelque chose d'irrégulier et l'on remarque qu'il y a un demi-pilastre de moins du coté de la plus petite'. Dézallier d'Argenville, writing some thirty years earlier, had also remarked on the latter irregularity.[57]

53. Cf. Pierre Moisy, op. cit., II, pls. XLIV, XLVa, XLVb and LLb.

54. The arrangement of the order in the choir of the Feuillants may have been different from that in the nave; engravings suggest this (the church was pulled down). The nave and side-chapels, however, conform to the Jesuit pattern.

55. In the absence of certain evidence to the contrary, we may presume that the arrangement of the east end of the interior corresponded to that of the west end. It does so in the B.N. plan, but (cf. below) Saint Victor speaks of 'les deux arcades au bout de la Salle', possibly implying that they existed at one end only.

56. When de Brosse designed the Salle there was no building directly beyond its west end and therefore no doors at all were needed here. Cf. the B.N. plan; but doors are present in the large Terrier du Roy plan of c. 1700-5 (cf. Cat., p. 254).

57. Tableau historique et pittoresque de Paris, 2nd ed. 1822–1827 (the 1st edition appeared in 1808–1811). In his Vies des fameux architectes (Paris 1788), p. 331: 'Les deux arcades du fond sont inégales . . .' and the rest of his criticism of them obviously forms the basis for Saint Victor's description.

In the model Antoine corrected these errors; the blind-arcades are all the same width and all the profiles are complete. But, in the actual building, as Saint-Victor says, the blind-arcades next to the central arcade dividing the Salle are smaller than those next to the outer walls, and on the side nearest the central arcade each has a half-pilaster missing. The reason for this asymmetry is presumably that the width of the old Salle, to which the new one had to conform, was insufficient for the classical design to be properly carried out.[58]

It would seem, therefore, since the irregularities which were corrected in the model of 1777 still exist in the building today, that Antoine did not in the event rebuild de Brosse's west end but simply restored it. He would appear to have confined his innovations to the four doors and possibly the two large semi-circular windows above them. The disposition of the blind-arcades and half-pilasters is as Saint-Victor described it, though the doors and the tracery of the windows above date from after 1871.

One difficulty arises from the assumption that it was de Brosse and not Antoine who designed and built the blind-arcade at the west end of the Salle, of which a counterpart probably existed at the east end. At the east end certainly, and at the west end possibly, this arcade would have blocked a large part of the surviving medieval windows which, with the rose-windows over them, would have looked very odd rising above the classical 'screen' below. At the west end, however, where they may not have survived, de Brosse himself could have introduced semi-circular lights like those seen in Antoine's model and the later engravings.[59]

The central arcade is somewhat thin in proportion to the space which it divides, but its dimensions were circumscribed by the weight-bearing capabilities of the columns beneath. It is composed of Doric pilasters, supporting the vault and set against narrow piers which carry the plain round arches. Both in the arcade and in the order decorating the walls de Brosse follows his usual practice of returning the entablature round each member, but he uses dentils instead of mutules in the cornice, thus avoiding the complications which he encountered at the Luxembourg and Saint Gervais.[60]

58. This asymmetry also exists in the present east end of the building in the pilasters of the arcades opening on to the interior staircase. (Pl. 195).

59. After the blocking of the south windows, the Salle was very dark. (There had been at least one window on the north side, now visible but blocked from a small courtyard of the Conciergerie). *Oeils-de-boeuf* were pierced in the vault and are seen in the early-nineteenth-century engravings. After 1871 these were suppressed as sufficient light came from the staircase windows.

60. At this date the use of dentils proper to the Ionic and Corinthian orders was sanctioned for the Doric order by Vignola and by Philibert de l'Orme who uses the Theatre of Marcellus in Rome as an example.

M

The ribs of the vault were presumably stone and the vault itself probably of brick in-filling plastered over, as it is today, although it is just possible that the in-filling was originally of wood and plaster.[61]

The first vault may have been intended by de Brosse to receive some sort of decoration, but Antoine's was left plain and looks very austere in the 1812 engravings. If the austerity of Antoine's vault repeated de Brosse's design, however, it is in keeping the precise and severe treatment of the walls and arcade.

It is unsatisfactory to have to judge the Salle des Pas Perdus from a model, pictorial records and a nineteenth-century reconstruction of an eighteenth-century restoration. But these provide sufficient evidence to show that the Salle des Pas Perdus is yet another striking example of de Brosse's ability to assimilate and transmute his sources of inspiration.

A passage from Sauval,[62] where he is discussing aspects of modern French architecture and town-planning, is worth quoting in connection with de Brosse's building. It indicates the estimation in which the Salle des Pas Perdus was held by connoisseurs thirty years or so after it was built. 'Quant aux Places, et aux Basiliques des Grecs et des Romains, quoiqu'il ne nous en reste que des descriptions, je ne crois pas néanmoins que les nôtres leur puissent être comparées en aucune façon; mais je puis dire qu'à l'exception des dehors de la Basilique de Vicence, qui égale l'Antique, la Grande Salle du Palais, pour les dedans l'emporte, et sur elle, et sur la Basilique de Padoue; et de plus, que jusqu'à ce qu'on ait fait la Place de devant Saint-Pierre de Rome, la Place Daufine et la Place Royale seront les plus belles du monde et qu'il n'y en aura point qui leur puissent être comparées, que la Place St. Marc de Venise'.

'La Grande Salle du Palais est double, longue de (lacuna) sur (lacuna) de large, pavée en eschiquier de quartiers de pierre blancs et noirs, entourée de riches boutiques, d'arcades fort larges et fort hautes, ornée d'une ordonnace de pilastres Doriques qui regne de haut en bas; et couverte d'une voute fort élevée'.

The Salle du Palais here keeps illustrious company, and the mention of Greek and Roman architecture in the same context is important. It is a measure of what Sauval and his contemporaries felt that de Brosse had achieved for French classicism in the interior of the Salle des Pas Perdus.

61. An example of wood-and-plaster construction in the early seventeenth century is seen in the vaults of the arcades of the Place des Vosges in Paris. For the construction of vaults in the seventeenth century, cf. Hautecoeur, I, pp. 674–679. The decoration of the modern vaults in the Salle des Pas Perdus is not unlike that in du Cerceau's temple design reproduced in pl. 192, and that which occurs in other similar drawings by him.

62. Sauval, III, p. 47 ff.

CHAPTER IX

The Palais du Parlement at Rennes

DE BROSSE was called to Rennes in August 1618 to advise upon and submit plans for a new Palais du Parlement for the province ('Pays d'Etat') of Brittany. This building had been under consideration and constant discussion since 1609, but when de Brosse arrived the work had got no further than the preparation of plans and the choice, clearance and measuring of the site.[1] During these nine years the project for the Palais had been in the hands of Germain Gaultier, described as architect and sculptor, who had been appointed 'conducteur des oeuvres de la ville' at Rennes in 1609.[2]

Gaultier and a colleague, Thomas Poussin, had prepared a plan in October 1614, but this was not approved. Later Gaultier submitted two further plans, known as 'le grand dessin' and 'le petit dessin', and in September 1617 the 'petit dessin' was officially approved by the Parlement. In the meantime, probably during 1615, Gaultier had written out a long description of his proposed building entitled *Devis et état général de touttes choses utiles et nécessaires pour la construction du Bastiment du Pallays*.[3] Gaultier's plans are now lost so that, apart from some notes and a sketch for the roof-timbers of two of the pavilions, this document is the only remaining evidence we have of his proposals.

In September 1617 measurements were taken on the site, materials bought and transported there, owners of adjacent property which had to be demolished were compensated, and a well dug in what was to be the courtyard. Looking ahead, the commissioners recommended the purchase of stone for the columns destined for the principal façade and for the exterior staircase in front of it; all in all, 48,626 livres were spent before de Brosse arrived upon the scene. But still the building was not begun.

So far there had been no indication that the commissioners were dissatisfied with Gaultier, but now they began to have second thoughts. On 4 March

1. Cf. Cat. pp. 268–273.
2. Bourde de la Rogerie, *Germain Gaultier et les premiers projets du Parlement de Bretagne*, Rennes, 1930. This rare book is indispensable for the early history of the Rennes project.
3. Publ. by Bourde de la Rogerie, op. cit., *Annexe*, pp. 51–58.

Président de Haultaye proposed that, since the project was so large and important, it should be confided to architects 'bien experimentez aux bastimens royaux', and to equally experienced masons.

This suggestion made, Haultaye at once produced the solution. One of their number, Président de Cucé, was in Paris and had advised him that he had been in touch with 'un architecte du Roy appelé de Brosse et ung maistre maçon'. Obviously Haultaye and Cucé had already made up their minds. In the end the services of another master-mason were dispensed with, and the King, by *lettre-de-cachet*, commanded de Brosse to go to Rennes and treat with the commissioners.[4]

On 8 August de Brosse arrived, and six days later (having examined Gaultier's previous plans 'tant du grand que du petit desseign'), he had prepared one of his own which he submitted to the commissioners and the City Representatives sitting in council jointly, on 14 August. His plan was then compared with the two by Gaultier and the council, having discussed the matter thoroughly, requested de Brosse to make a further plan 'en la forme qui luy a été prescripte'. This he did, and presented it on 16 August, when he was nominated by official decreee 'Architecte du Palais du Parlement'.[5] De Brosse was instructed to prepare a detailed *devis descriptif* and to assess the relative cost of his proposals and those of Gaultier. Finally, his definitive plans were signed by the commissioners and copies were ordered to be made for the Procureur Syndic, after which the originals were to be lodged in the commissioners' files.

De Brosse did not stay long enough to write the *devis descriptif* in Rennes. He soon notified the commissioners that the King wanted him back, and he left Rennes for Paris on 23 August. On 24 August the commissioners showed the copy-plans to the City Representatives, and at last on 15 September 1618 the first stone was laid and medals 'already struck' (a long time ago, apparently) were put in the foundations. Gaultier and his men set to work.

De Brosse never returned to Rennes; in January 1619 Gaultier went to Paris to fetch further plans and elevations, also the promised *devis descriptif.* De Brosse was away at Orléans when Gaultier arrived, and seems not to have hurried himself on return to produce what was required, for Gaultier did not get back to Rennes until March, when he handed over the drawings and the *devis* to the commission. In June 1620 he set off again for Paris to see de Brosse, from whom he obtained a *Mémoire fait pour le Pallais de Rennes,* dealing

4. Cf. Cat., p. 266 and Chron., p. 270.

5. Cf. Cat., p. 270 and Pannier, p. 259, gives the full text of the decree. For de Brosse's dealings with the commissioners, cf. Cat., pp. 270–271.

with such matters as materials for the vaults, the maintenance of horizontality in the lateral façades despite the slope of the site, and the disposal of rainwater. It seems odd that Gaultier, who was an experienced builder, had to go to de Brosse for such information. The commissioners obviously thought so too, and suspected that this time he had simply found a pretext for a free trip to Paris. He had an interesting time there, for de Brosse, recommending the Luxembourg as an example in certain technical matters, took him round the buildings of the Palace himself.[6]

All the drawings, the *Mémoire* and the *devis descriptif*, given to Gaultier by de Brosse in Paris, are now lost. His plans, made in Rennes, on three separate sheets for the three storeys, survived into this century and are recorded in photographs (Pls 196–198). Their loss[7] is particularly tragic as documents prove that they were by his own hand, and the inscriptions correspond with the only other known specimen of his handwriting which survives apart from formal signatures.[8]

It speaks well for Gaultier that he never made any objection when de Brosse was suddenly called in over his head in 1618, and he made no difficulties later. The collaboration was a friendly one, but unfortunately the rapport between de Brosse in Paris and the man-in-charge at Rennes ended abruptly. In January 1624 Gaultier was hit by masonry falling from the vault of one of the ground-floor rooms and died of his injuries in March.

As we have seen, de Brosse was only in Rennes for six days before he presented his first draft-plan to the commissioners. The proposed building was large and quite complex, and he had had no previous experience of building a Palais du Parlement, which required very special interior arrange-ments, laid down by precedent. It would have been impossible for de Brosse to have designed the whole building in so short a time, and a comparison of his plans with the text of Gaultier's *Etat et Devis* shows that he incorporated most of Gaultier's lay-out into his plan. He himself concentrated mainly on the south front, which was the principal façade, and on the Grand'Salle des Procureurs and adjacent rooms which lay behind it. Even here the actual arrangement is close to Gaultier's as far as the rooms are concerned. It was Gaultier's idea too, and not de Brosse's, to have a central courtyard completely surrounded by open arcades with a gallery above. His *devis* speaks of 'les

6. Bourde de la Rogerie, op. cit., p. 28.

7. Just before or during the Second World War, in unknown circumstances.

8. *Min. Cent. VI–472*, 6 May 1615. A signed note, acknowledging receipt of money owed to him. The document, of no intrinsic interest, is not listed in the Cat. (Cf. Chap. I, p. 11 for remarks concerning de Brosse's handwriting, based on this specimen).

pilliers des arcades qui porteront la gallerye qui circuit diametrallement de la court ladicte conciergerie'.

Gaultier's plan had been for a rectangular building, 160 x 210 feet, having pavilions at each angle, surrounding the courtyard already mentioned. It is possible that Gaultier based this plan to some extent on Serlio's project for the mysterious château 'Rosmarino'. Rosmarino[9] follows a traditionally French arrangement of four blocks with pavilions at the angles, surrounding a court, but like Rennes it breaks with French tradition by having an arcade round all four sides of the court. This very Italianate feature is most unusual in French secular architecture of the sixteenth and early seventeenth centuries. The only precedents for it in France, outside Serlio's work, seem to have been the plan for Charleval by Jacques I du Cerceau (Pl. 28), various other plans

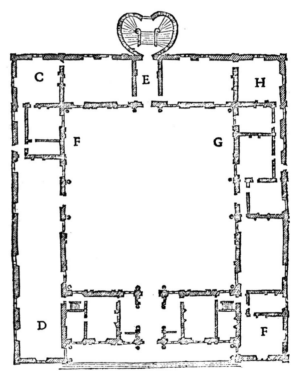

Fig. 4.   Philibert de l'Orme. Saint Maur-lès-Fossés. Original Plan. (*Architecture*. Fol. 17 *verso*)

9. Rosmarino, Serlio, VII, Cap. 2, pp. 208 ff. Cf. Rosci and Brizio, *Il trattato di Architettura di Sebastiano Serlio*, Milan, 1967, pp. 34, 49 and 68–70. Rosmarino has some features in common with Ancy-le-Franc, which Serlio did not engrave, but of which a version was presented by Jacques I du Cerceau in his *First Book*, 1549, p. X.

engraved by him and based on Serlio, and de l'Orme's project for the Hôtel-
Dieu de Saint-Jacques.[10] Gaultier, in choosing this arrangement, may have
wished to incorporate into the new building a reminiscence of the cloister in
the Convent of Saint François at Rennes, where the Parlement sat until the
new Palais was ready.

It is certain that Gaultier intended his building to have a pavilion at each
angle, but it appears from the wording of his *devis* that these were not to
project on plan but to rise one storey above the roof-line, as the north pavilions
do today: 'La charpente dudict bastiment est composée au dessus de l'arraz
et entablement d'icelluy de quatre groupes de chappes rabattues qui sont les
combles . . . lesquelles chappes rabattues seront accompagnées de quatre
pavillons au dessous desquels seront les logements des chambres des requêtes,

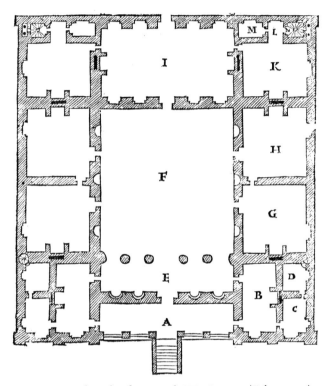

Fig. 5.   Serlio. Plan from Book VII. Cap. 15. (Fol. 35 *recto*)

10. Cf. Serlio, I, pls XLI, XLII, XLIII, and XLIX; and Philibert de l'Orme, *Architecture*, Book
VIII, 1648, fol. 259. The continuous loggia of the original Cour de l'Ovale at Fontainebleau may also
be cited as a possible precedent.

la chancellerye . . . (etc.) . . . lesquels quatre pavillons porteront double estaige, pour servir aux urgentes nécessités et accomodations requises pour ledit Pallays . . .'.[11] This is quite explicit as far as the roof-line is concerned; Gaultier says nothing to suggest any projection of the pavilions below, and the constriction of the site would in any case have made this extremely unlikely on the east, west and north sides.

In his project de Brosse changed Gaultier's rectangular building to a square, 200 x 200 feet, a much more unusual conception for its date. In its general outline his plan is probably derived from Philibert de l'Orme's revolutionary design for Saint Maur-lès-Fossés, but the idea of the square is closer to a scheme in Serlio's Seventh Book (Figs 4–5).[12] Another remarkable feature of the plan is its 'contained' character; nothing breaks the square at ground-level save the outside staircase or *perron* (Pl. 196).[13]

On his plan of the Palais and the surrounding site (Pl. 198) we see that, at each side of the principal façade and slightly set back from it, de Brosse has introduced some kind of formal entrance to the spaces flanking the building. This attempt to link the Palais to the neighbouring houses is interesting; it may owe something to the entrances to the Place des Vosges in Paris or to ideas in Serlio's Second Book.[14] On the east (right) side of the plan de Brosse has written 'Entrée pō la basse-cour des Cordeliers' (Convent of Saint François), and on the other side 'il sera à propos de laisser ceste espace le long du Palais entre les Jardins et ledit Palais qui est de pareille distance que celle du costé des Cordeliers'; indications perhaps that he was trying to create a townscape.

The ground floor of the Palais (Pl. 196) was taken up by the various prisons, accommodation for the concierge and general offices. The large space, open to the court, which lay under the Grand'Salle was 'un lieu publique pō tous les prisonniers et pour autres qui les viendront voir'. At the north end of the

11. Bourde de la Rogerie, op. cit., pp. 57 and 58.

12. Serlio, VII, Cap. 15, p. 35 recto. De l'Orme, *Architecture*, fol. 17 *verso*. The courtyard only at Saint Maur is square, the complete ground-plan, including the projecting pavilions of the entrance-front, is of course, rectangular. The conception of the south front of the Rennes plan, is, however, obviously close to de l'Orme's design. The Serlio plan, like de Brosse's, contains the projecting pavilions and linking terrace within the square.

13. From Gaultier's *devis* it is not clear whether or not he intended such a terrace. Serlio's *Seventh Book* has several 'contained' plans, but only the one mentioned in n. 12 above and reproduced in Fig. 5 is square.

14. Also, perhaps, from the 'Scena Tragica', Serlio, II, p. 46 verso. It is also possible to suggest a link with the idea of the terminal arches of the Innocenti loggia in Florence, especially that to the left when one faces the building.

building de Brosse makes the disagreeable if practical suggestion 'au dessous
. . . se pourront faire les chachots noirs'.

The outside staircase or *perron* was approached by three steps and had three
flights on either side. Beneath it a door led to the 'lieu publique' and thence
to the courtyard. The exterior staircase was not a new feature in French
architecture, but this one was more complicated in form than some.[15] At
Saint Maur de l'Orme had designed a three-flight stair with curving sides
leading to the garden, and at Fontainebleau he had built a curved *perron* in
the Cour du Cheval Blanc, known now only through du Cerceau's engraving
in *Les Plus Excellents Bastiments*.[16] De Brosse's *perron* at Rennes, unlike de
l'Orme's two designs, is sharply rectangular with no curving elements at all.

The *perron* led up to the terrace, 24 feet deep and running across the whole
width of the Grand'Salle on the first floor. The east and west wings, projecting
beyond the Grand'Salle by one bay and forming pavilions, enclosed this
terrace, just as in the courtyard of de l'Orme's Saint Maur the projecting wings
enclosed flights of steps leading to a terrace which occupied the entire width
of the *corps-de-logis*.

The long Salle des Procureurs (Pl. 198) behind the terrace is close to Serlio's
Rosmarino plan and to Gaultier's proposals. To the left of this Grand'Salle de
Brosse placed the Chancellery and the chapel, to the right the Chambre des
Requêtes and the Parquet des Gens du Roi. This was almost the same as
Gaultier's lay-out but on a larger scale. The disposition of the principal rooms
on this floor also follows Gaultier's *devis*.

On this floor, over the arcades below, a gallery ran round three sides of the
court, giving access to some of the principal rooms and to the staircases of the
north wing. It was this first floor which was known technically as 'Le Palais'
and is referred to in the documents as 'Le Palais de Messeigneurs du Parlement'.

The second floor (Pl. 197) was an attic-storey covering all but the south
wing where the Salle des Procureurs rose through two floors. This attic was
lit by large dormer-windows in the exterior walls and by lucarnes in the roof
on the court side.

The history of the actual building-operation is a complicated one, difficult
to piece together because it took a very long time to build the Palais, and
because so many of the relevant drawings and documents are lost. The main
structure was not finished until 1655, and even then much still remained to be
done in the interior. The Parlement took possession of the building in January

15. Cf. Blunt, *Philibert de l'Orme*, p. 25.
16. Ibid., and pl. 37 reproducing du Cerceau's engraving which may not be exact but which
gives a generally satisfactory impression.

1655, but the decoration of the rooms was scarcely begun when they moved in.[17]

After Gaultier's death in 1624, an architect named Jacques Corbineau was appointed to take charge of the work and was made to promise to follow de Brosse's intention exactly. Corbineau wrote out a *devis* (in a *Procès Verbal de l'Etat des travaux*), a long report outlining the state of the building when he took it over, what had been done and what still remained to do.[18] This document is extremely important, for it consistently refers back to the lost *devis* made by de Brosse for Gaultier in Paris in 1619, and to his plans and elevations. From Corbineau we learn that when he took over from Gaultier, the north, east and west wings were built up to within a few inches of the first-floor level, the principal façade had also reached this stage as far as the pavilions were concerned, but the rest was not begun.

From 1624 to 1627 work went on, but slowly. Money was not easily forthcoming, for Rennes was not a wealthy city and most of the charge fell upon the citizens.[19] In 1627 plague broke out; work on the Palais was suspended and money hastily diverted to build a hospital. Corbineau went off with his brothers Pierre and Etienne, masons who were 'conducteurs du bâtiment' under him, to find work elsewhere. Nine years later the commissioners called in a company of contractors for public works from Paris, directed by Guillaume Mathurin, Jean Duris, or Dury and Pierre Hardy but things did not go well. From 1640–1646 an architect called Tugal Caris took over; and finally Jacques Corbineau's brother Pierre returned to Rennes and was appointed to succeed Caris; he was still in charge when the Parlement moved in in 1655. By this date, as far as the exterior and courtyard were concerned, de Brosse's building was complete, but its chequered history was by no means ended.

On the evidence of Corbineau's *devis* it appears that at some date after 1627 a radical alteration was made to the design of the north end of the building; the roof was raised at the north-west and north-east angles to accommodate an extra storey below. This change will be discussed in detail later.

17. Cf. Cat., p. 273, (1655).
18. Ibid., p. 268 and p. 271.
19. A. Mussat, *Quelques précisions sur la décoration intérieure du Palais du Parlement de Bretagne* (I have unfortunately been unable to obtain from M. Mussat the publication-reference for this article of which he kindly sent me a typescript some years ago): 'La construction du gros oeuvre du Palais nouvel s'inscrit entre le 15 Septembre 1618 . . . et le 11 Janvier 1655, jour de la prise de possession de l'édifice par ces Messieurs du Parlement. Les travaux furent donc longs; ils représentaient une lourde charge pour la ville, dont, en 1636, Dubuisson-Aubeney écrivait: "il y a peu de bonne bourgeoisie, le trafic y estant triste comme en une ville de terre et de peu d'abord"'.

By 1726 so many complaints had been received about the inconvenience, especially in cold or wet weather, of an outside staircase to the principal entrance that the architect Jacques V. Gabriel was called in to remodel this part of the building. He demolished the *perron*, removed the terrace, and transferred the principal entrance from the first to the ground floor. This new entrance led to a covered ceremonial staircase which blocked most of the arcade on the south side of the courtyard and considerably reduced the size of the courtyard itself. In 1838 extra windows were pierced on the ground floor of the north, east and west wings, and in the north wing the roof-line was raised so that the dormers no longer stood free of it. On the principal façade, small windows were substituted for the doors on the ground floor of the projecting pavilions. Since the Second World War restoration has been carried out on worn or damaged parts of the fabric, but nothing has been radically altered.

After the commencement of building-operations Gaultier evidently collaborated very closely with de Brosse, but his activity after 1618 was, as we have seen, to result only in the raising of three sides of the building to just below first-floor level. Jacques Corbineau, when he took over from Gaultier in 1624, and wrote his *devis*, followed closely and constantly referred to de Brosse's original plans, elevations and *devis descriptif*. But he carefully inserted the following clause in the final section: 'Seront tenuz les preneurs qui prendront taille et massonerye de prandre alignemens et panneaux de toutes sortez et mesures et eglissemans du conducteur de l'oeuvre sellon et au désir des plans et eslevations qu'en a fait le sieur de Brosses arquitecte du Roy, lesquelz plans et eslevations sont entre les mains dudit conducteur. Aussy lesdits preneurs ne seront point tenuz de faire aucune des figures portées au plan et eslevations si messieurs ne les y oblige cy apprès . . .'.[20] This left freedom, not for him, nor for successive 'conducteurs', but for the commissioners to decide upon modifications.

Corbineau's *devis* and his slightly later *mémoire* have not hitherto been completely transcribed or thoroughly studied; now that this has been done[21] we know a great deal more about the modifications which were made to the original design, and also about when they were made. The architectural history of the building is thus much clearer.

20. Corbineau, *devis*, fol. 47 verso. Pannier made an inaccurate transcription of a very small section of Corbineau's *devis*. He defines this passage quoted as referring to decoration only, but the sense of the original document does not imply this limitation (cf. below, n. 68).

21. I am obliged to the Archivist of Ille-et-Vilaine for allowing the 174 pages of Corbineau's writings to be photo-copied for me, and to Mme Françoise Hamon of Rennes for her assistance in arranging this.

De Brosse's plan for a perfect square of 200 x 200 feet was evidently abandoned from the start, for Corbineau gives the dimensions of the building as 193 feet for each side and just over 190 feet at the north end. This meant that the dimensions, given in Corbineau's report, of certain rooms and for the gallery differ from those written on de Brosse's plan.[22]

When we turn to the elevations of the Palais (Pls 201–204), even a quick glance shows the difference in style and feeling between the principal façade and the three others. Where the principal façade is strictly classical, with an applied order and with an unbroken cornice which stresses the horizontal, the other elevations are astylar, having nothing particularly classical in feeling, despite the details of cornice or window-pediments. They have been given, too, through the breaking of the cornice by the dormers, a strong vertical accent.

It might be assumed that de Brosse did not intend this difference in the treatment of the principal and subordinate façades, and that he would not have planned such old-fashioned features as the existing large dormer windows breaking through the cornice. Corbineau's *devis*, however, makes it clear that, apart from certain subsequent modifications, the design in its essentials is that accepted by the Parlement in 1618.

We have seen that the speed at which de Brosse worked on the project at Rennes in 1618 led him to incorporate most of Gaultier's dispositions for the interior into his own plan. For the same reason his contribution to the elevations was probably mainly confined to the remodelling of Gaultier's design for the principal façade, while leaving the subordinate ones much as Gaultier originally intended. It is conceivable, therefore, that de Brosse introduced the gateways to the streets on either side of the main front partially to mask, and to distract the eye from, the abrupt change of style between the front and the sides of the building.

Since the principal façade was the last to be built, and can be considered quite separately from the others, the east, west and north wings will be discussed first.

The vertical feeling of these façades, already noticed, has been increased by abandoning the original spacing and grouping of the dormers which can be seen in de Brosse's plan of the attic storey (Pl. 197). The rhythm of 3–4–3 on the lateral façades, and 1–2–1–2–1 on the northern one,[23] has given place

22. Corbineau gives the dimensions of every room in the building and of every pier, pilaster, window-embrasure, etc.

23. The small aperture lighting a *cabinet* which breaks the grouping on the N. façade was obviously to be made as inconspicuous as possible.

to a continuous row of dormers, one above each first-floor window on all three façades. This alteration was made at least as early as 1624–1625, for Corbineau describes the system of fenestration as it is now,[24] with the exception of certain further alterations at the north end due to the changes of height at the north-west and north-east angles already referred to. Incidentally, the number of bays on the lateral façades was reduced from the twelve shown by de Brosse to eleven, by the suppression of one of the windows, on the east and west sides respectively, in the rooms at the north end of each side wing. This modification, due presumably to the reduction in length of the building, already mentioned, is explicitly referred to by Corbineau.[25] On de Brosse's plan all the windows and dormers except the windows of the Salle des Procureurs have mullions, and Corbineau specifies them: 'lesquelles croisées sont ramplyes de maineaux et de croissons dont il y a deux travées et deux maineaux'. As executed, however, none of the windows or dormers have mullions or transoms.

The upper storeys of the subordinate façades originally stood upon a solid base, like a plinth, for the ground floor until 1838 was almost windowless (Pl. 196).[26] This nearly unbroken horizontal area would have served to counteract the strong vertical lines of the rows of windows and dormers above it, and would have been a far happier arrangement than the existing one. Security of the prison which it enclosed dictated the outward appearance of the ground floor at Rennes; both the need for security and its architectural solution are reminiscent of, and may have been influenced by, fifteenth-century Florentine *palazzi*, though the latter were designed rather to prevent assault from without than escape from within. At Rennes the ground floor of the three subordinate wings was not rusticated, which further stressed the difference between them and the principal façade.[27]

Despite a certain amount of re-facing and other restoration, most of the original details of the east, west and north façades are preserved and correspond

24. Corbineau, *devis*, fols. 22 recto and verso. At one point Corbineau specifies twelve dormers to eleven windows, but this is clearly an error.

25. Ibid., fols 26 verso and 27 recto and verso; also fol. 30 verso and 31 recto; 'Et est a notter que le plain du second estaige porte douze croisées au costé doriant et le plain de la muraille en la forme que elle est et n'en porte que unze'.

26. On de Brosse's ground-floor plan only seven openings are shown; four in the W. wing (where the concierge's quarters were situated), two in the N. wing and one only (the window of the prisoners' chapel) in the E. wing. The N. window of the W. wing is indicated as an afterthought by the architect, with inked-over lines and an inscrption.

27. Corbineau writes frequently of 'le rustique' in the context of the principal façade, but never for the others, so that certainly this difference was intended from the start.

exactly with Corbineau's description;[28] string-courses, window-mouldings, raised tablets beneath and rustication round the first-floor windows, the pediments of the dormers and the form of the cornice and frieze; the latter being '... de mesme architecture que de quoy nous avons parlé du costé du préau de ladicte grande salle et est composée de l'ordre dorique et aussy tous ces mambres d'architecture et modellons'.[29]

Corbineau's description of the courtyard[30] corresponds with what we see today (Pl. 207), with the exception of the south end, blocked by Gabriel's staircase, and the pavilion roofs which rise from the angles of the north wing.[31] The lower arcade, now glazed, was open; about the upper gallery Corbineau is not specific, and it remains uncertain whether this was originally open or not.[32] The entablature and the circular lucarnes, 'qui sont faictes en O's', are described in detail, and were executed accordingly, save that the vases on pedestals which should have surmounted the lucarnes have disappeared or were never carried out.[33] It is the disappearance of these vases which makes the severe style of the lucarnes seem later in date than it actually is. The court-yard is the only part of the Palais, except for the chimneys, where brick and stone are used together.

At the end of the passage in which Corbineau describes the upper part of the courtyard, he gives one of his very infrequent indications of de Brosse's original intentions for interior detail at Rennes: 'Aussy faut notter que les portes qui sont à entrer de la grande salle et autres chambres, chappelle et cabinetz sont des portes à pillastres unne frize et unne corniche...sur laquelle y aura fronton brizé des tables ou mettre armes ou escriptures aussy aux

28. *Devis*, fol. 13 verso and fols. 22 recto and verso; the latter deal with the fenestration, and also contain a full description of the wall-surface and entablature of the W. façade. On fol. 23 verso it is stated, 'Ces articles seront à faire mesme ordre, pour ledict costé de devers loriant la costière pan de muraille de Septentrion et le pan et costière de l'Occidant seront tous de mesme ordre'.

29. Ibid., fol. 22 verso. 'Le préau' is the courtyard, and in fact the entablature of the three wings and of the courtyard is the same.

30. Ibid., fols. 18 recto and 19 verso, fol. 33 verso and fols. 32 verso to 35 verso.

31. Cf. below, p. 169.

32. Tradition claims that they were. M. Raymond Cornon, until recently architect in-charge of the fabric believes the glazing to be a later addition, as in the arcades below.

33. *Devis*, fol. 19 verso: 'Ladicte corniche est une corniche d'ordre dorique a modellons et toutte ces mambres darquitecture. Ladicte corniche, frize et arc qui trave seront faictz de bonne pierre blanche comme tuffeau ... ladicte corniche sert dentablement. Sur chascune desdictes arcades il y a unne Lucarne qui sont cinq Lucarnes qui sont faictes en O's et ont de face aussy grandz que le dedans desdictes arcades ... et sur le millieu dud. O, il y a ung carré pour des voises ou autre choose qui plaira a Mssrs ...'.

portes qui entreront des galleryes et escalliers et aux deux salles. Le tout faict sellon l'ordre de Monsieur de Brosse, architecte du Roy'.[34]

We must now turn to the arrangement of the northern part of the Palais, for there is at this point a great and hitherto unsuspected difference between the original design as specified by Corbineau and the executed building. The evidence for this difference is chiefly to be found in the later pages of the *devis*, which deal with the roofing.[35]

It can be assumed that the north wing was the first to be completed – as far as the outer walls were concerned – up to cornice level, for in 1627 Corbineau wrote a *mémoire*, additional to his long *devis*, dealing with what remained to be done in this wing. This was the completion of the dormers and lucarnes, and the cleaning-up and perfecting of the stonework generally.[36] Nothing was said about the roof, for the instructions about that were, as has been mentioned, contained in the main *devis*.

In the earlier section of the *devis*, dealing with the lateral façades,[37] Corbineau says nothing whatsoever about any change of level at their northern ends, nor does he do so with reference to the east and west ends of the north façade. Neither is there any mention of extra windows in any part of the three subordinate façades.

When we come to the long and complicated section of the *devis* dealing with the timbering and slating of the roof of the Palais, the intention to keep the whole roof-line at one level is several times declared: 'Et que pour couvrir le corps de logis de Loriant faut y joindre le pavillon qui est audict costé doriant Mesme et du costé qui Regarde loccident devers le préau La couverture couvre la Gallerie Et le corps de logis tant soubz un mesme chevron qui Portera depuis Le Saut du feste Jusques à l'entablement ...', and later: '... et au boutz des Corps de logis du coté de loriant et de septentrion et loccident Il y aura aussy des Chevrons d'arreste qui seront Portez de mesme chosse et mesme liason qu'aux pavillons susdicts toutes lequelles charpentes seront de mesme haulteur que celles de la Grande Salle des procureurs'.[38]

According to Corbineau's *devis* the central rooms on the first floor of the east and west wings (the Salle de l'Audience and the Salle de la Tournelle) rose six feet higher than the remaining rooms of the three wings, reaching the

34. Ibid., fols. 35 verso and recto.
35. Ibid., fols. 80 recto *et seq*.
36. Cf. Cat., p. 268.
37. *Devis*, fols 22 recto to 24 recto.
38. Ibid., fols. 82 recto and 87 recto. The pavilions referred to are, as we shall see later, those of the South front.

height of the Salle des Procureurs.[39] The upper galleries also were higher than the ordinary rooms and the same height as the two Salles. He deals with the problems raised by these variations as regards the arrangement of the roof-timbers, again stressing that the roof-line should be unbroken throughout the three wings, the galleries and pavilions.[40]

At the end of this section concerning the roof-carpentry, Corbineau, having given all the details for the east wing, writes, 'Il est a notter que tous les trois corps de logis seront faictz de la mesme construction que celluy qui est declaré cy dessus de toutes sortes de pièces . . . scavoir le costé de Septentrion et celluy d'occidant et les galleries comme elles sont déclarées'.[41] No mention is made throughout the section of any break in the roof at coping-level. It is also significant that, though the beginning of the section is entitled somewhat ambiguously 'Mémoire et devis pour parler de ce qui est necessaire pour la housse de la Charpente quil faut pour couvrir tous les quattre corps de logis et Pavillons qui sont au pallais', at the end it is explicitly stated that there are two pavilions only. '. . . Il est aussy a notter pour faire entendre aux charpentiers la Longueur et largeur que ont ces trois corps de logis et Les Pavillons Scavoir Les deux pavillons ont en leur face du costé de midy quarante piedz et chaincun pavillon faict le bout de chaincun corps de logis . . .'.[42] At the beginning of the next section, dealing with the slate covering of the roof,[43] this continuity of wing and one pavilion is indicated once more and with no ambiguity.

When he is dealing with the junction of the east and west wings with the north wing, Corbineau instructs the slate-layer thus: '. . . Et le corps de logis de septentrion . . . lequel corps de logis et les deux aultres . . . s'accompagneront ensemble les ungs contre les aultres en telle sorte que les deux se puissent bien et deubment tirer du costé de dedans seront faictz en long et le costé de dehors sera faict en arrest . . .'.

39. Because of this internal change of level, the lower part of the dormers over the windows of the higher rooms are blocked; only the upper half is a true window, lighting the low attic above these rooms.

40. *Devis,* fol. 83 verso *et seq.*: 'et pour venir à la haulteur du galletas des Salles et galleries il y aura encore sur touttes lesdictes chambres un autre galletas qui aura neuf piedz de haulteur de sorte que de ceste mesme haulteur seront tous les tirans de tous les corps de logis et pavilons de ceste mesme haulteur qui sont ceux des Salles'. It is to be noted that the 'second attic' was not a true extra storey; its floor was simply formed by tie-beams and open joists. The slope of the roof on the court side of all three wings was longer than on the outer side, since it had also to cover the upper gallery.

41. Ibid., fol. 87 recto.

42. Ibid., the beginning of the section fol. 80 recto; the quotation from the end fol. 88 verso.

43. Ibid., fol. 89 verso: *Mémoire et devis pour le couvreur en ardoise pour couvrir les bastiments qui sont au Palais de Rennes . . .*

This is the evidence which leads to the conclusion that at some time after about 1627, the original design of the north-east and north-west angles of the façade, was modified. Here we now see the cornice broken upwards by the insertion of a mezzanine floor and a pavilion rising up through the roof (Pls 205, 206). This is in fact a reversion to Gaultier's intention to provide extra accommodation in four pavilions,[45] and to a much more conventional form of roof-stystem than that which de Brosse evidently proposed for the Palais.

The alteration was possibly decided upon when work was resumed after the plague of 1627,[46] but the first indication of it does not occur until 1643. From 1627 until 1651, the Palais remained roofless, but in the 1640s some attempt was being made to remedy this state of affairs, and a contract was signed in 1642.[47] In April 1643 the Parlement was informed that there was trouble over part of the roofing, and representatives went to see what was wrong. 'Après avoir visité le bâtiment du Palais et reconnu oculairement la diformité qui serait en la cour d'iceluy si'il n'y était remédié par l'exhaussement des murailles d'une partie du logis et couverture en forme de pavillon . . . '.[48] It is reasonable to suppose that the need to raise the walls and roof 'en forme de pavillon' was caused by the insertion of the north-eastern and north-western mezzanines.

By means of an aerial view of the Palais we can discern the original conception of a continuous roof-line, still remaining over the wings and pavilions to the south, and can see better the clumsiness of the junction of roofs and higher pavilions to the north. This clumsiness is also apparent in the view from the courtyard (Pls 204, 207).

There is no reason to suppose that Corbineau's specification for the roof line of the Palais departed in any way from de Brosse's original instructions.[49] We can therefore assume that, although de Brosse may have left Gaultier's subordinate wings much as they were as regards their façades and their in-

44. Ibid.: 'Aussy faut que ledict couvreur entend que ledict corps-de-logis de loriant y comprins le pavillon a de longeur trante et ung pied'. The 'trante et ung pied' refers not to the horizontal length of the roof but to the height of the pitch. On the court side it was 46 feet to cover the galleries.

45. Cf. above, pp. 159–160.

46. Cf. Cat., p. 271–272.

47. Ibid., p. 272.

48. Ibid.

49. Even to the minutest detail of the interior arrangements, Corbineau's *devis* corresponds with what we know from de Brosse's plan, and, if he made any alteration he always says so, as he did concerning the number of windows in the east and west façades.

terior dispositions, he discarded the idea of an extra storey in any pavilion, and eliminated the northern pavilions altogether. This conception of an unbroken roof-line, which moreover repeated exactly the dispositions of the 'contained' ground-plan beneath, was entirely revolutionary for its date,[50] and foreshadows ideas embodied in Mansart's roof at Blois begun nearly twenty years later.

The principal façade of the Palais is formed by the two pavilions, which are in fact the southern projections of the east and west wings, and by the south face of the Salle des Procureurs and its terrace lying between them (Pl. 201). The ground floor provided a powerfully rusticated base pierced by doors and windows; the outside staircase which de Brosse designed was rusticated also and contained beneath its central element the entrance to the courtyard and prison-area. The original appearance of this façade can be seen in two early representations; a drawing by Gabriel in about 1726, before he made his alterations and an engraving made in 1690 which, however, does not show the ground floor (Pls 199, 200).[51]

As we have already mentioned,[52] this façade was considerably less advanced than the other three when Corbineau took over in 1624.[53] When dealing with the main front, Corbineau wanders erratically between the present and future tenses, but generally an implication of the future is clear.

The main front and the Salle des Procureurs were also by many years the last parts of the building to be completed. This is shown by a report of the Parlement, dated 1647, which stipulates that the original drawings for the principal façade should be adhered to: '. . . ayant conféré les dessins qui ont été cy-devants faits, le premier se trouvoit sans comparaison plus beau, que ce qu'il y avoit de plus magnifique à la structure, face et frontispièce

50. It was of course facilitated by the fact that the Palais, not being a dwelling, did not need the usual system of *appartements* contained in pavilions and common to French châteaux and hôtels. It should be mentioned here that in Corbineau's *devis* and in the executed building the S. pavilions do project a fraction where they meet the E. and W. façades – i.e. where 'le rustique' meets the plain surface – but this is a negligible break in the line of the building. Equally undistracting is the slight diagonal break in the pitch of roofs of the S. pavilions above the second bay of the lateral façades.

51. Cf. Cat. pp. 269–270.

52. Cf. above, p. 164.

53. '. . . Les costières de dehors vers loriant, occidant et septentrion sont eslevées prestes à receptvoir le cordon . . . Le devant dudit bastiment sera basty en forme de rustique comme il est planté aux deux costières jusques au premier estaige preste à recepvoir les embasses, lequelles embasses auront ung pied et demy de haulteur pour venir à la haulteur du cordon ainsin que porte le dessin . . . Ledict perron . . . auquel n'a esté encore travaillé et n'y a que les attentes dans les fondements de ladicte terrasse'; *devis*, fols. 1 verso and 2 recto.

avoit été changé, et arrête que le premier dessein qui a été fait sera executé . . .'.[54]

If however, we compare de Brosse's plan of this front, the 1690 engraving and Gabriel's drawing (Pls 198–200) with Corbineau's specifications, we find that there were several departures from the architect's original intentions. The rusticated ground floor, the *perron* and the terrace correspond to the plan and to Corbineau's description of how they were to be built;[55] on the first floor discrepancies arise. Corbineau's description of this floor,[56] the Gabriel drawing and the 1690 engraving – allowing of course for the simplification of the latter – correspond with the executed building, but not in one important particular with de Brosse's plan. For de Brosse shows us no columns framing the entrance to the Salle des Procureurs.

Gaultier had intended the whole façade to be articulated by Corinthian columns.[57] This idea de Brosse rejected, and his plan shows the coupled pilasters for the exterior of the Salle des Procureurs and coupled pilasters for the pavilions, with a single pilaster between the south windows of the latter. Characteristically, he has chosen the Doric order, but uncharacteristically he has left the central entrance-bay of the façade quite unaccentuated except by two steps leading up to it.[58] Yet Corbineau continually refers to the coupled columns framing the entrance.[59] It looks, therefore, as if in haste de Brosse omitted the columns from his plan, but introduced them into the elevations and *devis descriptif*. The phrase which occurs in Corbineau's description 'et toutes ces pierres retournent sur les coulommes et pillastres', reveals the hallmark of the architect of the Luxembourg.

54. Cf. Cat., p. 272, entry for Nov. 26. It is not stated that the 'premier dessin' means de Brosse's, but it is scarcely conceivable that it refers to Gaultier's.

55. *Devis*, fols. 2 verso to 4 verso, and fol. 15 recto.

56. Commencing fol. 15 recto, 'Costé du Midy'.

57. Gaultier, *devis* of 1614–1615, quoted by Bourde de la Rogerie, op. cit., p. 58: 'Et particulièrement de la principale face qui représente un ordre corinthe suivant l'anticque comme estant approuvé et recogneu par les excellens autheurs estre ordre le plus grave et magnifique convenable et propre pour décorer et adobter aux Pallays et bastimente d'importance'.

58. Contrast this flat treatment with Saint Gervais, Blérancourt (the main door of the *corps-de-logis*) and the massive composition of the columns of the entrance-pavilions at Coulommiers and the Luxembourg.

59. *Devis*, fols. 15 verso and 16 verso to 17 recto: 'Et au droict du perron Il y a quattre Coulommes avec leurs piedestaux sortant du costé de la muraille'; '. . . . les piedz dessau, basses, Coulommes, frize et corniche sont faictz de l'ordre dorique aussy tous les ornements darquitecture et toutes cesdictes pierres retournent sur les coulommes et pillastres sellon l'ordonnance qu'en a donné le Sieur de Brosse, arquitecte du Roy . . .'. Concerning the columns, Corbineau adds: 'Toutes les coullomes seront faictes de marbre ou dautre pierre blanche ou de grain et les pillastres leurs piedestau basses arc qui trave frize corniche seront faictz de bon tuffeau en vallable sellon le plaisir de Messieurs': ibid., fol. 17 recto.

Corbineau described the decoration of the frieze above the first floor in detail: ('. . . des carcasses (viz. cuirasses) avec des troffées d'armes et sur les arcades des fleurs de lys et ermines . . .'),[60] but not, alas, that of the pavilion-windows. Of these he says '. . . la haulteur desdictes croisées est de treze piedz, alentour dicelles croisées Il y a ung pilastre[61] qui regne tout a lentour ladicte croisée dans lequel il y a trois mambres d'arquitecture . . . unne consolle carrée qui porte de timpan et la corniche du fronton . . .'. Nowwhere in the *devis* or elsewhere is there positive evidence that these beautiful windows were designed by de Brosse (Pl. 209). Yet negative evidence points to his authorship, in that in no other particular did the original façade depart from his design, and we have the instruction of 1647 that the 'first drawing' be adhered to.

The balustrade which runs along the whole façade above the entablature is as originally designed, but lacks the statues which de Brosse intended for the pedestals provided: 'Sur chacun desdictz pillastres et aux plan d'iceulx est planté des corps carrez sur (lequelz) corps sont portez chancun deux figures'.[62] These figures, as Corbineau points out, surmounted not only the central part of the façade, but also the pavilions.[63] Whether they were ever executed is not known, but it seems unlikely in view of the following facts.

The central element above the cornice, the frontispiece over the entrance-bay, is the only part of this façade where de Brosse's original design seems to have been deliberately altered. It was probably considered too elaborate when time and money were running short in the 1640s. The 1690 engraving and Gabriel's drawing show the same sundial flanked by pilasters and surmounted by a curved pediment (Pls 199–200). Probably in the nineteenth century, a shield and swags breaking the pediment were added – these in fact were nearer in spirit to de Brosse's original design. Unfortunately the most recent restoration has returned to the design of the 1640s. Here is Corbineau's description, probably based directly on de Brosse's drawing for this element:

'Sur lesdictes coullommes par dehors Il y a unne lucarne, plantée sur le plan desdictes coullommes et a plaine desdictes coullommes de chaincun costé deux pillastres entre lesquelz Il faut la place de deux figures. Les quattre pillastres en basse de l'ordre ionique. A lentour desditz pillastres deux mambres d'arquitecture, larc qui trave la frize qui se retourne au droict des pillastres et aussy quelques ornements qui sont en des modellons au droict des pillastres. Au millieu de ladicte frise quelque petit feuillant. La corniche est unne

---

60. Ibid., fols. 17 recto and 21 recto.
61. Used here in the sense of a plane surface.
62. *Devis*, fols. 17 verso and 18 recto.
63. Ibid., fol. 21 recto.

corniche enrichie de modellons couvertz de feuillants et entre les modellons y a des rozes. Sur ladicte corniche est planté un cuir (viz. écusson) duquel sort deux festons et dedans ledict cuir se sont les armes du Roy avecq les ordres et unne Imperialle. Entre les pillastres la basse larc qui trave,[64] Il y a ung cadre qui est enrichie dornemantz qui est pour mettre les devises . . . '.[65]

The frontispiece described by Corbineau, with its lucarne, pilasters, sculptured figures, cornice, arms and swags, is far more in keeping with the solidity of the central part of the façade beneath than is the pawky design carried out. It is also comparable in feeling with works such as the door of the Hôtel de Soissons and the Porte d'Honneur at Blérancourt, and with many early seventeenth-century door-designs obviously influenced by de Brosse.[66] The use of the Ionic order above the Doric of the façade beneath is more correct too than the 'Corinthian' foliage-capital substituted for it, although the latter is of the type used above the Doric by de Brosse at Blérancourt, Coulommiers and the Luxembourg.

The Palais has recently been re-roofed, and the decoration on the ridge replaced. This corresponds well enough with Corbineau's *devis*, except that lead figures replace the vases originally intended.[67] Corbineau's description of the roof gives a vivid picture of how it was meant to look, with its mixture of blue-grey slates and gilded metal-work: 'Et pour le regard de la grande salle et pavillons qui regardent le midi, faut que ce soit du plomb qui soit tout doré avecq rozes et feuillages et bouttons pandans; des plomberies aux quattres coings du pallais avecq voises corps carrez, et ausdicts voises six muffles de Lyon et linge sortans de la gueule dudict lyon et que ledict linge soit pendant et au bas dudict vaze gaudronné de rellief, et sur le sault dudict vaze il y a ung ballustre fort eslevé de quoy il sort des fourreaulx forme feuillage tout dorez et faut ces faire en telle façon qu'ils soient faictz sellon le desseing qu'en a donné Monsieur de Brosse arquitecte du Roy qui est entre les mains du conducteur'.

Corbineau's *devis* gives us very adequate information regarding the interior

64. This is very confusing, but what he means is 'between the pilasters, resting on the lower architrave', viz. the base.

65. *Devis*, fol. 17 verso. In the present rendering the punctuation has been altered to make the meaning clearer.

66. Paricularly those in the 'de Brosse' album in the Louvre.

67. They had already done so by 1690, cf. the engravings of that date. Also, for the roof-ridge, cf. Gabriel's drawing, and cf. these drawings and description with the drawings of the roof at Blérancourt (Pls 99, 101). Corbineau's description is in the *devis*, fols. 92 recto and verso. The rows of gargoyles beneath the roof, strangely medieval features of the three subordinate façades, are part of the original design.

of the Salle des Procureurs.[68] The measurements correspond with those on de Brosse's plan: 'Et pour lornement de cedict pan de Muraille du costé de la Salle, il y aura aussy piedestaux, basses, arc qui trave, frize et corniche comme celle-cy devant dite (viz. as the outer wall, the south façade). Et larc qui trave regnera à travers les pilliers jusques aux (-?-) des arcades. Laquelle besoin que sera aussy faicte de bon tuffeau, tant les parements que les pillastre, piedz destaux, basses, arc qui trave, Frise et corniche; de mesme ordre dorique que celle du devant; sur laquelle corniche sera posé le lambris de ladicte salle . . .'. There are seven 'arcades' or bays on each side (Pl. 198).[69]

There was to be a door leading from the Salle to the chapel, and doors to either side of this leading to the Chancellery and the 'Consultations de la Tournelle'.[70] The central door 'doibt estre ronde'. For the covering of the Salle, 'il y faut une bonne housse de charpente . . . en telle sorte que lad. charpente soict faicte en vouste pour lambriser ladicte salle de boys. . . . Laquelle charpente sera faicte a point rond affin que les lambris sen monstrent plus beaux et agréable . . .'.[71]

The Salle des Procureurs, as we see it today, lacks the pilasters between the windows shown on de Brosse's plan and described by Corbineau (Pl. 208). The entablature is of a later date, and so is the wooden barrel-vault and its decoration, though the type of vaulting is as intended by the architect. The round-headed central doors at each end of the room exist, albeit in much later frames. The doors to either side probably date from the 1640s. The door in a wooden casing, which now blocks the central bay, on the north side, is the entrance from Gabriel's courtyard staircase, and de Brosse's door to the outside staircase of the south side was made into a window by Gabriel.

Despite its unfinished state and later accretions, it is easy enough in the mind's eye to restore to this still most impressive room the internal appearance intended by de Brosse, comparing it for this purpose with his exactly con-

68. Pannier, pp. 218–219, quotes a section of Corbineau's *devis* as a description of the interior of the Salle des Procureurs. What in fact he is quoting is the description of the central part of S. façade contained on fols. 16 verso and 17 recto, which has been given in the present text. The actual details of the interior are further down on fol. 17 recto and continue on fol. 17 verso.

69. Punctuation inserted for easier reading.

70. *Devis*, fols. 33 verso and 34 recto. The number and disposition of the doors at the other end of the Salle correspond, but the shape of the central one is not specified. (The disposition is not given here but can be deduced from the description of the rooms concerned at the E. end of the Salle). De Brosse in his plan shows all the seven bays as containing windows, so it is to be supposed that, in doing this, he made a mistake as regards the two giving on to the gallery, which must surely have been doors, otherwise communication between the Salle and the rest of the first floor would have been extraordinarily restricted.

71. *Devis*, fols. 81 recto to 82 recto.

temporary design for the Salle des Pas Perdus of the Palais de Justice in Paris (Pl. 195). We can then see how greatly its dignity and classicism would be enhanced had the vault been carried on de Brosse's order of Doric pilasters.

The only other room by de Brosse in the Palais[72] of which Corbineau gives any extra details is the chapel. The large round-headed door was to be of stone, and over the altar, which stood on two steps, the window was to have no tracery and to contain clear glass, 'non pas ung vitral, pour garder la symetrye de cedict costé doccidant . . .'.

Corbineau's *devis* makes it possible to assess far more accurately than formerly de Brosse's exact contribution to the Palais at Rennes. It also provides evidence that this building in its original form represented the peak of de Brosse's architectural career, both in his understanding of the classical spirit and in his handling of the classical idiom.

The principal façade was evidently intended to convey the impression, when viewed frontally, that the building behind is continued in the same style of architecture, and, as we have seen, the 'screening' gates at the entrance to the streets on either side, had they been built, would have strengthened this illusion. This sense of continuity in the building, implied by the south front, would despite the change of style on the other façades, have been greatly helped by the unbroken roof-line which de Brosse originally intended.[73]

As we have seen, the principal façade was not executed exactly as de Brosse designed it; the statues of the roof-balustrade were missing, and the central element above the cornice over the entrance was modified. The loss of the statues is perhaps the gravest of these two differences, for they were an essential part of the classical conception of the façade, and a development of an idea introduced at Verneuil by Jacques I du Cerceau and at Coulommiers by de Brosse himself.[74] Nevertheless, by far the greater part of de Brosse's design was faithfully carried out.

72. Assuming that the main features of the principal rooms directly behind the S. façade on the first floor and communicating the Salle des Procureurs were designed by him.

73. It might be argued that the long unrelieved roof-line, extending round three sides of the large building, would have been monotonous; this is, however, to ignore the relation of the Palais to its site. To the north the ground continues to rise steeply, and it was probably only from the north that it was possible to see the N.E. and N.W. angles and the N. façade properly. Maybe they were always, as now, obscured by buildings. The introduction of higher walls and pavilion-type roofs at these angles may provide a more picturesque outline, but appreciation of this from the exterior of the building is extremely limited by the site. De Brosse therefore was not only developing ideas of continuity and unity in relation of roof-line to building, but was also providing the most suitable solution to the roofing of a building on a hemmed-in and steeply-sloping site.

74. Du Cerceau mounted classical trophies on the 'corps carrés' of his balustrades above the cornice in the courtyard at Verneuil. De Brosse placed statues of women between the *lucarnes*

Unfortunately Gabriel's eighteenth-century alterations have modified de Brosse's original intentions and upset the proportions and balance of his façade. Because Gabriel removed the *perron* and the terrace, the whole outline of the ground-plan has been spoiled and the wings are left starkly projecting right up from ground-floor level. The façade, especially the central part, now looks as if it had been lifted up on stilts. Above the heightened basement-door, the old door into the Salle has been given a balcony and made into a french window; all this adds to the vertical distortion. Thus, on the ground floor, Gabriel completely reversed de Brosse's strong horizontal stress, with unfortunate results. At first-floor level the original design is less altered, and here, despite the modification of the central part, the horizontal feeling of the façade is still dominant.

The Italian influence embodied in the statues designed for the balustrade is again evident in the treatment of the details of the first floor. Here de Brosse has borrowed from Vignola's Caprarola the same windows which he used on the south face of the Salle des Pas Perdus in Paris, omitting the *tablettes*. The arches and panels behind the windows are copied from Vignola's engraving, 'portici ovvèro loggie d'ordine Dorico'.[75] The use of a row of round-headed windows across a façade was not at all common in France at this date,[76] so that the windows of the Salle des Procureurs at Rennes must have made a considerable impression, particularly in view of the sophisticated handling of their detail. The shallow, crisp 'cutting-back' of the wall-surface behind the arches, again Vignolesque in origin, is comparable with the 'panelling' of the pavilions at Blérancourt, and we see the same kind of manipulation of surface in the brick-and-stonework of the courtyard at Rennes (Pl. 207). All this is a considerable change in feeling from the grave, sculptured solidity of the Saint Gervais façade, though some of the details of the church front and of the Luxembourg façades anticipate this more fine-drawn approach. Always nearest to Rennes, stylistically, however, is the Salle des Pas Perdus in Paris.

The windows of the pavilions are exceptionally beautiful and closely linked

---

in the court at Coulommiers. The inspiration was, of course, and especially at Rennes, Palladio in Vicenza, in the Basilica, and in his Libro Secondo. De Brosse was probably also influenced by Sansovino's Library in the Piazzetta in Venice.

75. *Architettura*, XI. It should be noted that Caprarola was engraved by an unknown Frenchman in the 16th century, cf. Walcher Casotti, *Il Vignola*, 1960, II, fig. 45, who dates the engraving before 1565. Villamena also engraved Caprarola, as he had the Gesù. However, de Brosse's knowledge of Vignola's building, through his contact with the Potiers of Blérancourt, should not be forgotten here.

76. It made a rare appearance at the château of Grosbois at the turn of the century.

in style with some of those designed for Blérancourt. The details are sharply-cut and, except for the mask and the foliage, have an incised quality. The design of drapery 'pulled through' the consoles is something which had become almost a trade-mark of decoration inspired by de Brosse,[77] such as we find in the drawings of du Ry and in the early decorative sculpture of François Mansart.

The main front of the Palais du Parlement at Rennes is the most sophisticated, and was probably the most influential, of all de Brosse's works. Nothing like this self-contained, Italian-inspired, yet wholly French façade had been seen before in France. Mansart worked at Rennes in his youth, with his brother-in-law, Germain Gaultier.[78] At that time, of course, the Palais was scarcely raised above its foundations, but Mansart must have known all de Brosse's directions for its building, plans, *devis descriptif* and elevation drawings. There is no doubt that later these influenced his own work, most particularly and impressively in the wing which he built for Gaston d'Orléans at Blois.

77. Cf. the Louvre 'de Brosse' album and also the Louvre 'Derand' album, already referred to in this connection. The *devis* for Tugal Caris (cf. Cat., pp. 268–269) dated 1640, shows that the windows of the first floor were still unfinished, those of the S. front probably not begun. The *devis* however continually stipulates that the 'first drawings' will be followed.

The *devis* and the *marché* made with Tugal Caris, together with the memorandum (*Estat des Travaux*) of Pierre Hardy dated 1636 (cf. Cat., p. 268), were communicated to me from Rennes after his chapter was completed. They do not, however, alter the conclusions reached, nor do they add anything unexpected to the history of the building. I am again indebted to Mme F. Hamon for providing me with photocopies.

78. Cf. P. Smith and A. Braham's forthcoming work on Mansart.

CHAPTER X

The Last Years, 1619 to 1626

THE commissions for the Salle des Pas Perdus in Paris and the Palais du Parlement at Rennes mark the end of de Brosse's really active career. The building of the Luxembourg continued under his direction until Marin de la Vallée took over in 1624, but by this time the work had outgrown the creative stage and required only technical attention and general surveillance. From 1618 onwards, he was involved in the discussions and projects concerning Orléans Cathedral,[1] but these, through his own dilatoriness, came to very little as far as he was concerned. After that date de Brosse's failing powers of concentration and increasing ill-health seem to have precluded him from receiving any important commissions. At this time he was only in his late forties but, though he was respected, consulted and deferred to, he did very little building.

Peiresc records the fact that he worked at the château of Limours for Cardinal Richelieu,[2] but we know nothing of what he actually did there. Philibert de l'Orme had preceded him at Limours, and François Mansart was to succeed him, but the château has disappeared and is ill-documented.[3]

In 1619 and 1620 de Brosse made designs for the château of Bois-le-Vicomte, which was being altered and extended by Antoine Feydeau, Intendant of Marie de Médicis' household, who had recently purchased the estate. Bois-le-Vicomte lay on the eastern outskirts of Paris, not far from Montceaux. The château and all its dependencies and gardens have disappeared, but, unlike Limours, it is well-documented, several contracts having recently come to light.[4]

As soon as he had bought the property, Feydeau proceeded to turn the manor-house which stood upon it into a château. The original house appears

1. Cf. above, Chap. I, p. 7, and Chap. VII p. 145 and Cat., p. 235.
2. Cf. Chronology and Notes, p. 201 (1623, May 4).
3. Cf. Cat., p. 225. I am grateful to Dr Peter Smith for all my information concerning the activities of de l'Orme and Mansart at Limours.
4. Cf. Cat., p. 209. The site of the château was just north of Villeparisis and south of Mitry-Mory (now both suburbs of Paris). The moat remains and it is still possible to trace, on the edge of a small housing-estate, the lay-out of the esplanade and courtyards.

to have been built, but possibly not completed, between 1585 and 1595 by Claude de l'Aubespine and her husband, Emery de Barbézières, to whom she had brought Bois-le-Vicomte as part of her dowry.[5]

The first contract for the new work, dated 6 March 1619, makes mention of plans and drawings to be produced, but not of their author's name. However, two subsequent contracts[6] strongly suggest that de Brosse was the architect of the new buildings of the château itself and leave no doubt that he was the original creator of the two courtyards and the garden lay-out. Bois-le-Vicomte became famous for the embellishment of its courtyards and the lay-out of its surroundings, but they may not have been completed under Feydeau's ownership, and were certainly altered in the eighteenth century. The contractor and mason-in-charge of the whole architectural project between 1619 and 1622 was Jean Thiriot, one of the most prominent master-masons of the early seventeenth century.[7]

The contracts for Feydeau's projects at Bois-le-Vicomte tally in nearly every particular with the description given by Dézallier d'Argenville in his *Voyage pittoresque des environs de Paris*.[8] With one particular exception, noted below, they also agree with the small engraving of the château and park made for the border of his Plan of Paris by Gomboust (*c*. 1649–1652). The contracts date at intervals from 1619 to 1621 and are supported by a *Mémoire* by Thiriot concerning the work still remaining to be done in October 1622. Feydeau only owned Bois-le-Vicomte for a further eight years, after which he sold it to Cardinal Richelieu.

Gomboust's vignette and Delagrive's plan of the château (1729) (Pls 211, 212) show that after Feydeau's day the main building at Bois-le-Vicomte consisted of a *corps-de-logis* flanked by large single pavilions. Dézallier d'Argenville says: '. . . Le château a onze croisées de face et deux pavillons qui saillent peu . . .', which agrees with Gomboust's rendering of the number of bays. The pavilions projected further, in fact, on the court-side than on the

5. Cat., pp. 209-210.

6. Cf. Cat., p. 209.

7. He died in 1647. He seems always to have been an executant, not a designer, but worked on many important buildings. His chief employer was Jacques Lemercier. Cf. R. A. Weigert, 'Jean Thiriot', *B.S.H.A.F.*, 1962, p. 189; Blunt, *Art and Architecture*, p. 263, n. 14; and J.-P. Babelon, *Demeures parisiennes*, p. 259.

8. First published Paris, 1749. The 1779 edition (the last, and the one quoted here) contains many additions and amplifications. Another source of information for the château is an article by T. Lhuiller, 'Etude historique sur l'ancien château, la seigneurie et les hôtes de Bois-leVicomte à Mitry-Mory', *Bull. Soc. d'Architecture de Seine-et-Marne*, IX, 1884, pp. 261–279. This, however, though accurate and valuable for the history of the ownership of the estate, is unreliable as regards its appearance and its architectural history.

garden-front, as Delagrive shows.[9] Gomboust shows a small, projecting entrance-pavilion in the centre of the *corps-de-logis* on the court side which is not present in Delagrive's plan.[10]

The château, which was built of brick and stone, was essentially a free-standing block like Blérancourt. (Delagrive's plan is deceptive on this point because, of course, it takes no account of the difference in height of the one-storey buildings of the *basse-cour*, which Gomboust clearly shows). Its plan is of the same type as Blérancourt too, though here there are single, not twin, pavilions at each end of the *corps-de-logis*, so that the nearest exact prototype is the plan of the Hôtel d'Angoulême (Pl. 30).[11] Whether the original late sixteenth-century house was intended to be free-standing, or whether de Brosse was responsible for making the château so, is not known.

The principal courtyard in front of the château was surrounded on three sides by an ornamental wall, pierced by gateways leading to the forecourt, the *basse-cour* and the *grande allée* in the park. At each end of the wall opposite the château was a small, domed pavilion. The forecourt was in reality an esplanade, and with the exception of one pavilion at its main entrance (not shown by Gomboust),[12] was apparently never intended to be built upon. It was approached by a magnificent avenue of elms leading to it from the village of Mitry.

The *basse-cour* lay to the side of the château and was entered from the esplanade by a large gateway set in a screen. This screen was flanked by one of the domed pavilions of the main court-screen and on the other side by the pavilion which terminated a range of service buildings or stables. The *basse-cour* had only two ranges of buildings, the one mentioned and another opposite the entrance, adjoining the château itself.

The three courts were surrounded by a moat, a branch of which separated the principal court and the *basse-cour* from the forecourt. Today all that remains of Bois-le-Vicomte, save a small pile of grass-grown rubble, is a part of the moat behind the château.

The work which Feydeau commissioned for the château itself is chiefly dealt with in a contract signed in March 1619. The façades of the *corps-de-logis*

9. The contract dated November 1620 speaks of 'four pavilions', possibly meaning four projections? Or it may have been intended to have twin pavilions at each end, as at Blérancourt, and the design was later modified.

10. The contracts are nowhere specific about this and none of the later eighteenth-century plans (cf. Cat., p. 210) show it. It may have been removed during a later alteration to the façade.

11. Cf. above, Chap. II, p. 33 and Chap. V, p. 84, n. 27.

12. It was contracted for and is mentioned in Thiriot's *Mémoire*. It was possibly never executed.

appear to have been re-built and a new entrance to it from the court was made.[13] Two doors from the *corps-de-logis* to the garden were pierced on the other side of the building. The entrance from the court, according to Dézallier d'Argenville, led to a vestibule decorated with Tuscan pilasters and columns, 'dont celles du milieu sont groupées . . .', a description which possibly indicates that the vestibule did not date from 1619–1622, but was a later addition. Such a disposition of the Order sounds unusually advanced for so early a date.

It is possible that the principal staircase of Feydeau's château never occupied a central position in the *corps-de-logis*. D'Argenville makes no mention of it rising from the vestibule, and he particularly commends the fine uninterrupted enfilade of rooms on the first floor, which implies that this vista was not interrupted by a stair-well or lobby. The removal of the staircase from the central position, if indeed it dates from Feydeau's time, is significant, and recalls de Brosse's innovations in the placing of staircases in his Paris hôtels.[14]

There were, in the château, two staircases which, according to the 1619 contract, were housed in two round towers, one of which already existed and one of which was to be built. It is not certain whether the existing tower was part of the old house or new work, for the wording is ambiguous, but presumably it was newly-built, if a staircase still had to be set into it.[15] It is odd to find such medieval features as staircase-towers at this date, and especially so if one recalls the tower which de Brosse had had pulled down at Bléran-court.[16] It is also odd that, although in his *Mémoire* of 1622 Thiriot states that the new tower is ready for flooring, no towers at all appear in Gomboust's engraving or Delagrive's plan, nor are they mentioned by Dézallier d'Argenville. Either they were pulled down between 1622 and 1649, or else

13. No details are given, so we cannot check Gomboust's representation of the main entrance.

14. But the wording of part of the 1620 contract for Bois-le-Vicomte suggests the possibility of a principal staircase apart from those in the towers and at that date this may have been intended for the centre of the *corps-de-logis*.

15. The passage concerning the staircases in the 1619 contract is as follows: '. . . Et seront faicts cinq portails de pierre de taille à servir aux deux escalliers quy seront appliquez dedans les deux tours et une aultre quy sera appliquée du millieu du grand corps d'hostel et deux du costé du jardin . . . Plus fault ediffier une tour qui est pour servir à l'escallier du costé de la basse cour de la mesme largeur et haulteur qu'est laultre faict au logis et les niveau avecq la mesme espoisseur qu'est (ladicte?) tour . . . Plus fault ediffier une chapelle qui est auprès de la tour ronde où sera lescallier du coste de la bassecour et les niveaux avecq les mesmes espoisseurs que les tours'. It is to be noted that the main *corps-de-logis*, where identifiable in the contracts, is referred to as 'le corps d'hostel' or 'le grand corps d'hostel', so that 'au logis' is not specific. The whereabouts of the chapel referred to is not certain; a chapel was later made in a detached pavilion; cf. below, p. 183.

16. Cf. above, Chap. V, p. 82.

they were never external to the building but were enclosed within it, possibly in the pavilions.

The most interesting buildings at Bois-le-Vicomte were, however, those surrounding the main château, and here de Brosse was indisputably the architect. Into the entrance-screen of the main court a new and elaborate gateway was set, which is mentioned in the 1619 contract; this, the 'principalle entrée du chasteau', was undertaken by Thiriot by special arrangement with Feydeau, and paid for separately from all other work. The ordinary rate was to be seven livres per *toise*, but the price of the entrance-gate was fixed at 1,000 livres for the whole. A drawing was to be provided, which is referred to in the 1620 contract as 'le plan et desseing de ce faict par ledict Sieur Brosse'.

Unfortunately the contracts and *Mémoire* provide us with hardly any clues about the appearance of this gate, save that at each side it was to have two 'culs-de-lampe' surmounted by 'dosmes'. These were presumably little *trompes* such as Philibert de l'Orme had used at Anet. The work seems to have been sufficiently advanced by 1622 for the gate to be omitted from Thiriot's *Mémoire* on work still outstanding. Gomboust shows the gate, but on so small a scale that no *culs-de-lampe* are visible. It is a great pity that no adequate visual record exists of this, the last of de Brosse's long series of designs for gates and *portes-cochères*.

The walls of the main court and the *basse-cour* were of stone, decorated with brick panels, and the one forming the entrance-screen was surmounted by stone urns.[17]

The pavilions at the ends of the entrance-screen of the main court are referred to in the *Mémoire* as 'les dosmes'. In August 1621, Claude Molleur, who had been master-carpenter at Saint Gervais, undertook to make the roof-timbers for the 'dosmes', '. . . suivant et conformément le desseing qui en a esté faict par le Sieur Brosse, architecte du Roy'.[18] We further learn from the *Mémoire* that one of these 'dosmes' (the one on the west side, to the left in Gomboust's engraving) contained a chapel. A hundred and fifty years later d'Argenville noted that one pavilion contained a chapel, and the other a billiard-room, and that both pavilions were 'surmontés d'une petite terrasse'. The 'terrasses' (i.e. flat roofs) may by that time have replaced the domes; or

17. The only mention of urns is in the 1622 *Mémoire*, which specifies seven, intended for the gate and walls of the *basse-cour*. But Gomboust shows what appear to be urns on the summit of each semi-circular element on the entrance-screen.

18. Published by J.-P. Babelon, *B.S.H.A.F.*, 1962, p. 144 (cf. Cat., p. 209). This author also gives a short history of the château which corrects several of Lhuiller's errors.

there may have been balustraded spaces round the domes, small-scale versions of the arrangement in the entrance-pavilion at the Luxembourg.

This position for a chapel, in a pavilion flanking the entrance, was a new departure in de Brosse's château-designs, and in French châteaux generally, and may have influenced Mansart's similar use of one of the single-storey pavilions flanking the approach to the main block at Maisons-Lafitte.

Thiriot's *Mémoire* ends: 'Plus fournira grandes figures de pierre de taille pour mestre dans le jardin aux lieux ou ledict Sieur de Bois-le-Vicomte ordonnera, et generallement parachever tous les avandits ouvrages j'a commancez'.

Cardinal Richelieu ceded the property in 1635 to Gaston d'Orléans in exchange for Champigny,[19] and it was used on and off for some time by his daughter, Mlle de Montpensier. In 1636 a carpentry contract passed by Gaston on her behalf speaks of work which had been going on for the past nine years, on the roofing of all the buildings, including 'pavillons qui sont dans l'enclos et au partour du parc'. The property passed in 1664 to the Duc de la Meilleraye, then to the rich financier Hervart, and finally to the Sénozan family. It was totally destroyed by the 'Bande Noire' in 1817–1818, except for one pavilion which disappeared later.

The importance of Bois-le-Vicomte undoubtedly lay in its character as a great ensemble of château, moat, ornamental entrances, avenues, esplanade, gardens and garden-pavilions. All are conceived as one integral composition, and this conception, which goes back to ideas expressed by the elder du Cerceau in his lay-out for the *First Design* at Verneuil, must have influenced later projects of this kind. There are elements in Mansart's design for Berny, for instance, which suggest that he was influenced by this attention to the whole *mise-en-scène*, and these were developed by him to a much higher degree at Maisons-Lafitte.[20] Another interesting possible offshoot of the Bois-le-Vicomte setting is at Brécy in Calvados (once attributed to Mansart), where a small plain manor-house is surrounded by an elaborate lay-out of ornamental walls and gateways (Pl. 213).

In 1621 the Protestant Temple at Charenton, just outside Paris to the south-east, which had been built by de Brosse's uncle, Jacques II du Cerceau, in 1607, was burned almost to the gound.[21] In June 1623 two contracts were

19. Lhuiller, op. cit.
20. To be discussed in P. Smith's and A. Braham's forthcoming book.
21. It used to be attributed to de Brosse, but E.-J. Ciprut, in 'Le Premier Grand Temple de Charenton Saint-Maurice', *Bull. Soc. Hist. Prot. Fr.*, January–March 1968, has published the documents proving that it was designed by du Cerceau.

passed for its rebuilding, one for the masonry and one (needing four master-carpenters) for the great wooden roof and the galleries.[22]

The new Temple, like the old, was rectangular, but larger and more sophisticated. Jacques du Cerceau's interior was a plain open space, the galleries supported on timber joists. Outside it had one row of windows to light the main hall and a row of *lucarnes* to light the galleries. The second building is known through Marot's engraved plan and sections, inscribed 'Plan et profil du Temple de Charenton du dessin du Sr. de Brosse' (Pls 214, 216). At this date de Brosse would have been the natural choice of the Parisian Protestant community, and, although his name is not mentioned in the contracts, the attribution has never been contested. The accuracy of Marot's plan is vouched for by a copy of the contract-plan, the original of which is lost, made by Salvé for his treatise on architecture published in 1662.

If the inferior representations which remain to us are to be relied upon, the outside of the new Temple was not particularly distinguished (Pl. 215). However, de Brosse, bolder than his uncle, broke the monotony of three superimposed sets of windows by inserting large vertical windows carried up through the cornice and cut across by the galleries. The extension of the windows through the cornice produced more light for the upper galleries, and this vertical treatment, which at Rennes seemed anachronistic, is at Charenton more successfully incorporated into this four-square building. Maybe, as Blomfield remarked,[23] the architect in this elevation lacked the genius which enabled Inigo Jones to make of Covent Garden Church 'the handsomest barn in England'; on the other hand the different religious practices of Anglican and continental Protestantism would naturally dictate a different architectural approach. The interior, however, though equally austere, is very much more interesting than the exterior in its approach to the problem posed by a French Protestant place of worship.

In the late sixteenth and early seventeenth centuries the Continental Protestants were evolving their own religious architecture, seeking a style which would be suitable to their services and would express in itself the break with traditional church-building. One type which they favoured was the centralized plan (though never the Greek-cross). Early examples of centrally-planned Temples in France were those at Petit-Quévilly, near Rouen, a

22. Cf. Cat., p. 212. Dézallier d'Argenville (*Vies des fameux architectes*, Paris 1788, pp. 331–332), gives a description of the Temple which he attributes to Salomon de Brosse. His description adds nothing, however, to the knowledge obtainable from Marot's plan and elevations, on which it was, in any case, probably based, as the building no longer existed at the time when d'Argenville was writing.

23. II, p. 57.

twelve-sided wooden structure built in 1599; at Dieppe, in wood and brick, built in 1606; and at Caen, built in wood, in 1612.[24] The centralized plan did not become the dominant form, but is the ancestor of such Protestant churches as the seventeenth-century Marenkerk at Leyden, in Holland.

Perret, in his book on Fortifications,[25] produced some rather grand rectangular designs for 'Temples', and it was a modest version of this type of building which Jacques II du Cerceau had erected at Charenton in 1607. It has been suggested that de Brosse's design is based on Vitruvius's description of the Basilica which he built at Fano,[26] and a comparison of the two designs confirms the probability.[27]

The Temple of Charenton was a much smaller building than the Basilica; 100 by 50 feet, instead of 160 by 100 feet; and de Brosse does not adhere to the same system of proportion within this scale; nevertheless the links are significant. At Charenton, as at Fano, the interior columns rise up through two storeys, an arrangement which was a great innovation in France, although it had been used by Palladio and engraved in his book. As at Fano, so at Charenton, there were eight columns down the length of the hall and four across the ends, including the corner ones; and the ambulatory runs right round the space between the columns and the walls. The columns at Fano supported a wall above the entablature, articulated by pilasters which carried the great wooden vault. De Brosse, however, needed this space for his upper gallery, and so it was left open. Piers, instead of a wall and pilasters, supported the vault.[28]

There were four staircases in the angles of the ambulatory at Charenton giving access to the double gallery; at Fano there were two leading to the single gallery, apparently on exactly the same plan.[29] Jacques II du Cerceau had placed only two entrance-doors in his rectangular Temple; de Brosse added another, a single side-entrance which broke the symmetry of the plan. This suggests that the side door may have been so placed, not merely for convenience, but out of a desire to imitate the prototype plan more closely. Vitruvius had a good reason to make an asymmetrical side-entrance, as his

24. Hautecoeur, I, p. 712.

25. Published in 1601; cf. Chap. III, n. 20.

26. Hautecoeur, I, p. 714.

27. De Brosse probably used the French translation of Vitruvius made by Martin in 1547.

28. A derivation of the arrangement above the entablature at Fano can be seen in Lord Burlington's Assembly Room at York, built in 1731–1732. This room, though based on Palladio's 'Egyptian Hall', ultimately derives, like its prototype, from Vitruvius. De Brosse would also have known Palladio's reconstruction of the 'Egyptian Hall' engraved in his Second Book, Chap. VII

29. Cf. J. Prestel, 'Des Marcus Vitruvius Pollio Basilika zu Fanum Fortunae', in *Zur Kunstgeschichte des Auslandes*, IV, Strasbourg, 1900.

description, quoted below, reveals. He needed an exit to the *pronaos* of the Temple of Augustus.

Finally, we may compare the Charenton plan and section with Vitruvius's own description:[30] '. . . At the Julian colony of Fano I let out for contract and superintended the building of a basilica. . . . There is a vaulted nave between the columns 120 feet long and 60 broad. The aisle between the columns of the nave and the outside wall is 20 feet wide. The columns are of unbroken height . . . above them are pilasters 18 feet high which carry the principals of the main roof and roofs of the aisles which are lower than the vaulting of the nave. . . . In the width of the nave cutting the angle columns right and left there are four columns at each end. On the side adjoining the Forum there are eight, including the angle-columns. On the other side there are six, including the angle-columns. The two columns in the middle are omitted so as not to obstruct the view of the pronaos of the Temple of Augustus . . .'.

De Brosse converted his Vitruvian basilica into a Protestant church by placing the pulpit in a central position in the 'nave' and a little belfry on the roof. It is a pity that Sauval did not write about the Temple, for here was a true attempt to reproduce aspects of the Roman basilicas which he mentioned in connection with the Salle des Pas Perdus, and it would be interesting to know how he would have reacted to it, and whether he would have recognized its source.

The Temple of Charenton was extremely influential. It was ideal for the European form of Protestant church-service, which above all required a good, unobstructed auditorium. It was built of stone throughout and it was simple and austere, but extremely dignified. Based on a secular Roman antique prototype, with early Christian connections that were acceptable, it completely avoided the Catholic Greek or Latin-cross plans. It became the inspiration for numerous later French temples, for Reformed churches in many other parts of northern Europe, and for early Non-Conformist English chapels. The interior of Wren's Church of St James, Piccadilly, is derived from de Brosse's design, though of course adapted for the different pattern of Anglican worship.[31]

Charenton also influenced synagogue architecture in north-west Europe, where the Jewish communities were likewise seeking an acceptable form of

---

30. The transcription is made from the English translation by F. Granger in the Loeb Classical Library, Heinemann, 1931–1934, vol. V, Chap. I, p. 259.

31. Cf. 'Saint Jacques de Londres et le Temple de Charenton', *Bull. Mon.*, 1956, CXIV, no. 4, p. 286; also M. D. Ozinga, *De Protestantsche Kerkenbouw in Nederland*, 1929, especially p. 116.

religious architecture.[32] The basilica-form with its centrally-placed pulpit and galleries (used for the women in a synagogue) was well adapted for their needs. The Sephardic Synagogue in Amsterdam, begun in 1671 by Elias Bouman, the Ashkenazic 'New' Synagogue in the same city, and the Sephardic Synagogue in the Hague designed by Daniel Marot, are all directly derived from de Brosse's Temple.[33]

After the Revocation of the Edict of Nantes in 1685 the Charenton Temple was pulled down by order of the King, and no trace remains, save part of the floor in a convent now on the site.

De Brosse's last known work, and his most curious creation, is the architectural setting which he designed (and signed) for an engraving by Michel Lasne in honour of Pope Gregory XV (Pl. 210). It is strange to find this respected member of the Paris Protestant community, and the designer of their new Temple engaging in so uncompromisingly Catholic and ultramontane an undertaking. Not that de Brosse, any more than his Protestant fellow-architects and artisans, objected to working for Catholic patrons, embellishing Catholic churches or building Catholic chapels, but, since this is the only surviving engraving from de Brosse's design, its theme seems slightly ironic.

The occasion for the engraving is not known; it may have been the election of Gregory to the Papacy in 1621, or his elevation of the See of Paris to an Archdiocese in 1623. Michel Lasne had arrived in Paris from Antwerp in 1620; in the following year his celebrated series of biblical engravings was first published.[34] It is arguable that Lasne would have been better known in Paris, and more likely to have received this commission, in 1623 than in 1621, but until more evidence is available no firm date within Gregory's short pontificate (1621–1623) can be assigned to this work in his honour. Michel Lasne was presumably responsible for the figure of the Pope, the other figures in the composition and the decorative treatment of the Ludovisi arms above the central feature.

32. In Eastern Europe the round hexagonal or octagonal form found more favour, which is closer in style to the earlier French temples.

33. Cf. Ozinga, *Daniel Marot*, 1938; and Helen Rosenau, 'The Architectural Development of the Synagogue', Thesis in the University of London, December 1939; and 'The Early Synagogue', *Archeological Journal*, XCIV, 1937, Part I, p. 64.

34. Michael Lasne was born in Caen before 1590 and died in Paris in 1667; he was trained by Léon Gaultier in Rouen. In 1617 he joined the Guild of Saint Luke in Antwerp. In 1628 he published a series of engraved portraits after Callot, and he became celebrated as an engraver of portraits and of biblical and historical subjects. Cf. J. Duportal, 'Etude sur les livres à figures édités en France de 1601 à 1660', *Revue des Bibliothèques*, Suppl. XIII.

This composition may represent, in more lasting form, one of those lath-and-plaster triumphal arches which, in Paris and other cities, it was the custom to erect in celebration of the Victories, Marriages and Joyous Entries of Kings, Queens and other personages. Its form may also be connected with the conventions of Italian stage-design and scenery.[35]

The architectural scheme of the engraving has links with de Brosse's buildings, notably with the columns and niches of the entrance-pavilion at Montceaux and the quadrant-arcades at Coulommiers (Pls 69, 130). The Corinthian order is basically Vignolesque; not a pure derivation, but a combination of one of his Corinthian columns with the base of one of his examples of the Composite order. Nevertheless, the use of the order and the whole arrangement is unusual in current French architectural practice.

The most remarkable part of the whole design is the central arch, with its coupled columns and heavy broken pediment. Though it is to some extent comparable with the topmost element of the Saint Gervais façade (Pl. 176), it is a startling invention to appear in France in the early 1620s. It is significant that its closest link with a French work is with Martin Fréminet's design for the altar of the Trinity Chapel at Fontainebleau which shows strong Italian influence (Pl. 87). The treatment of the pediment probably owes something to the sarcophagi of Michelangelo's Medici Chapel and to his Porta Pia in Rome, and it also reminds us of the outer gate at Blérancourt (Pl. 113).

If we compare the central element of the engraving with any of the drawings for doors or gateways attributable to du Ry in the 'de Brosse' album, or with those of the 'Derand' album, we see immediately that it is far more grave, serious and 'Roman' in feeling than anything which they could produce. It is, in fact, an extraordinary phenomenon in French architectural design of this period and, in the absence of any surviving buildings from the last years of his life, provides invaluable evidence of the way de Brosse's style was developing just before his death.

35. Cf. A. M. Nager, *Theatre Festivals of the Medici*, Yale University Press, 1964.

Conclusion

THE influence of Philibert de l'Orme, Jacques I Androuet du Cerceau, Serlio and Vignola upon de Brosse, both in general and in connection with particular buildings, has been traced, chapter by chapter, through this book. In the process of isolating and analysing these influences we have found that, as de Brosse's career progresses, some of them become more powerful factors in his work while others lose their hold on him. This progression coincides with de Brosse's growing awareness of the three-dimensional approach to architecture, and his increasing grasp of the fact that classicism should be a quality intrinsic to a building and not merely a decorative adjunct to it. Thus, he turns less and less often to du Cerceau, though he never ceased to be influenced by some of his grandfather's plans and drawings, and more frequently to Italy, and to Vignola in particular. Then at the end of his career we find him, at the Temple of Charenton, making a deliberate attempt to reconstruct the Antique according to Vitruvius.

While he found inspiration in Italian and Antique sources, however, de Brosse continually reveals in his work his debt to his sixteenth-century French predecessors, Philibert de l'Orme and Pierre Lescot. Lescot's influence upon him is easier to define than de l'Orme's, for it is more direct and factual. The borrowings, which de Brosse made from the Louvre façade for Bléran-court and Coulommiers, for instance, are immediately recognizable indications of the appeal which Lescot's approach to classicism had for de Brosse.

De Brosse also borrowed, but not so directly, from Philibert de l'Orme. The frontispiece at Anet was the prototype for the central part of the Saint Gervais façade; the plan of the Château-Neuf at Saint Germain influenced the plan of Blérancourt; the *cryptoporticus* and the chapel at Anet inspired the manipulation of space in the interior of the Queen's chapel at Montceaux. Nevertheless, de l'Orme's influence on de Brosse is at once less obvious and more fundamental than Lescot's.

Serlio and Primaticcio, working in France, Lescot at the Louvre and de l'Orme in his buildings and writings had provided a starting-point for the development of a classical style in French architecture. Bullant had moved away, pursuing a different, subtly anti-classical approach. De l'Orme's aims were disregarded entirely – they were probably not even understood – by the circle in which de Brosse grew up. Only the elder Jacques du Cerceau seems in later life to have been aware of some of them.

In the 1580s and 1590s, therefore, classical elements were more often than not employed merely decoratively, sometimes in a disorted and frivolous manner which had no true relationship to the building itself. Indeed, the building largely became a two-dimensional background for this 'classical' ornament.

As he outgrew the influence of this late sixteenth-century mannerist style, de Brosse returned to de l'Orme's conception of classicism in which all the separate elements of a building were considered as an integral part of the whole composition. He eliminated arbitrary and irrelevant details and concentrated on the essentially architectural character of his work, especially developing two aspects of it, the application of the Orders and composition in mass. In both he was helped by de l'Orme's example, and in the second he particularly excelled.

De Brosse's earlier building-projects, particularly Blérancourt and Coulommiers, gave impetus to a school of decorative sculptors who rejected the over-elaboration of the du Cerceau style and turned largely for inspiration to earlier sixteenth-century French models such as Lescot's Louvre, and to Italian, particularly Florentine, sources of the later sixteenth century. The character of their work can be seen in the fragments of Blérancourt which remain, and in the drawings of it, and in some of the drawings for Coulommiers in the 'de Brosse' album in the Louvre. Many other designs in that album reveal the same trends. The sculptors who decorated the Mansart pavilion at Coulommiers developed this style, and it influenced Marot in his *Vignole Français* of 1630. Later it was given a remarkable expression in the decorative scheme of the forecourt and gardens at Brécy. Above all it considerably influenced the decorative sculpture used in François Mansart's work.

De Brosse's influence on the next generation was crucial for French classicism, but it was by no means generally or directly felt. If we attempt to trace direct borrowings from him in the buildings of his successors, we do not find a great deal of evidence of them.

Certain later architects, notably Le Muet, and some members of the Gabriel dynasty make clear references to him in their designs, and we have already noted specific cases where his ideas were used by Mansart, as in the quadrant-arcades of Berny and Blois. But other major architects, like

Lemercier and Le Vau, appear to owe him little; these two certainly did not follow the advances he had made in the composition of buildings in mass.

Nevertheless, his work opened up a whole new approach to the conception of buildings as three-dimensional structures, to a serious and highly inventive use of the orders and to the further evolution of a wholly French type of classicism.

This approach and the spirit which informed it was to be embodied in the work of François Mansart and found its fullest expression in his buildings and drawings. So de Brosse deserves to be remembered not only for his own works, splendid examples of which survive at the Luxembourg, Saint Gervais and Rennes, among the fragments of Blérancourt and in the Salle des Pas Perdus in Paris, but also for his fundamental influence upon Mansart, his true heir in the next generation.

APPENDIX

THE table below shows the drawings of du Cerceau which I consider to date from after 1560, and their connection with the *Troisième Livre d'Architecture* of 1572.

P.M.L. = Pierpont Morgan Library Album
MS.B. = Vatican album (MS. Barberini Lat. 4398)
L.III = *Troisième Livre d'Architecture*
B.M. = British Museum drawings (Print Room, 99ᵃD)

P.M.L.	MS.B.	B.M.	L.III
fol. 50	28		
62			XXXIIII
72		119	I
78			XXIII
84a	17		XVIII
84b			XXI
86			XXXIIII
96	7		XXXVIII
98		119	XXXV
100b			XX
100c			
102	24		XX
108	7		XXXVIII
110		119	
112	49		
114a			
114b★			
116a★			
116b	49		

Apart from this evidence for the late date of the Morgan Library, the B.M. and the Vatican drawings, there remains the evidence of style, both of drawing and of architecture. To make a comparison between du Cerceau's earlier and later style

★ These drawings are of fountains at Anet and Verneuil engraved in the *Plus Excellents Bastiments*. 116a is in reverse from the engraving (no drawing for this fountain in the B.M.). 116b is adapted from the Diana fountain at Anet engraved in the *Plus Excellents Bastiments*, but in this drawing the figure is draped. Where the Morgan drawings correspond with the other late drawings or engravings, there are usually some variations.

Note: Three of the drawings correspond also with plates in du Cerceau's *Perspectives Positives* of 1576.

of drawing, we can compare the Morgan Library album and the Barberini
album with two others which have the characteristics of du Cerceau's earlier
style. These are an album belonging to Mr Philip Hofer, at present deposited
in the Houghton MS. Library at Harvard University, and a similar album in the
Petit Palais in Paris (Cat. No. 188, Cat. E. Rahir). These have bindings of a similar
style and date, and the drawings are on vellum, in pen-and-ink, with monochrome
wash and sometimes with colour-wash added. They are characterized by nervous
outline and spiky use of the pen, especially in the drawing of such ornaments as
swags of fruit and flowers. The wash is put on in a rather general and flat way.
The architectural and decorative elements themselves are close to the early engraved
books such as the *Arcs*, *Temples*, *Compositions d'Architecture*, and *Fragments Antiques*.
The drawings have inscriptions in the characteristic sixteenth-century hand
usually associated with du Cerceau.

In contrast to the Harvard and Paris drawings, the later ones are much more
rounded, the line is less nervous, and there is much less spikiness in the drawing of
detail. The wash is now used to define contours in order to give a more three-
dimensional and solid impression. The architecture and decoration are also much
weightier. One reason for dating the Morgan album to the late 60s or early 70s
is the closeness in type of some of the fireplace designs to the ones du Cerceau
published among his plates of Verneuil in the *Plus Excellents Bastiments*. The
writing in the Morgan album, the Barberini album and the British Museum
drawings are all in the same hand, which differs from the angular, formal
inscriptions of the earlier albums. The script on the later drawings suggests
preparation for engraving.

The dating of du Cerceau drawings by the costumes of the figures is not
reliable, as in late drawings more often than not costumes of twenty years earlier
are shown.

Catalogue

For the convenience of the reader, original documents listed in the Archives Nationales are divided into those found in the Minutier Central and those in the Main Archives. All drawings referred to as in the Archives Nationales are in the Main Archives.

Salomon de Brosse

CHRONOLOGY AND NOTES

1568 Jehan de Brosse 'maître architecteur', recorded as resident in Verneuil-sur-Oise and buying land there (*Acte du Terrier de Verneuil*, publ. by Pannier, p. 26).

1571 Birth of Salomon de Brosse, presumably at Verneuil. His father was Jehan de Brosse, his mother Julienne Androuet du Cerceau, daughter of Jacques I Androuet du Cerceau; *Tablettes Historiques et Chronologiques*, Amsterdam/Paris, 1779, in which de Brosse is listed as 'né à Paris'; cf. Pannier, p. 16. No other record of the date is known, but that of the *Tablettes* corresponds with what is known of his early life.

Before 1585 Death of Jehan de Brosse. In 1585 Julienne is recorded as a widow, legal guardian of her children who are all minors: *Acte du Terrier de Verneuil*, Pannier, p. 26. It is to be noted that in the sixteenth and seventeenth centuries the age of majority for commoners was twenty-five (Cf. Merlin *Répertoire de la jurisprudence*, Paris, 1827).

1588 *October 27* Salomon de Brosse appears in the Verneuil Parish Register as godfather to Camille Brai.

November 9 Godfather to Jeanne Escouville. The godmothers were Florence Métivier, future wife of de Brosse, and Perette de la Fonds, a relative.

1589 *November 20* Godfather to Salomon Massue.

1590 *January 13* Godfather to Salomon de la Fonds.

March 2 Godfather to Marguerite Dublain.

1592 *February 9* Godfather to ... (name illegible in Register).
(The relevant section of the Register is published in Pannier, p. 251).

1598 *May 21* Placin, treasurer to Gabrielle d'Estrées, Duchesse de Beaufort, pays 'le Sieur du Cerceau' and Salomon de Brosse for work, unspecified, at Montceaux (Chap. II and Cat. p. 232).

1600 *January 25* Marriage of Hugues de la Fonds and Elisabeth Coupel, niece of Jacques I du Cerceau. Salomon de Brosse witnesses the marriage and signs with the title 'ingénieur de la Reyne de France' (Min. Cent. XXIX–103, fol. LVII).

1602 *February 6* Marriage of Jacques II du Cerceau to Marie Malapert, witnessed by de Brosse who signs as 'architecte de la Reine' (Cf. Chap. I, p. 4, n. 6).

1600–1608 Working for Henri IV and, after 1601, for Marie de Médicis as well, at Montceaux (Chap. III and Cat. pp. 232-234). During this period also working for Henriette d'Entragues at Verneuil (Chap. III and Cat. p. 277).

1605 Marie de Médicis refers to 'le Sieur Salomon de Brosse architecte de nos bâtiments' in a letter of this year (L. Battifol, 'La vie intime d'une reine de France', 1931, Vol. II, Letters of Marie de Médicis).

1608 De Brosse makes drawings for Sully's town of Henrichemont (Cher) (Chap. III and Cat. p. 223).

March 29 Masonry contract between Claude Pouillet and Pierre Forget de Fresne for extensions to the Hôtel de Fresne, Paris, naming de Brosse as architect (Min. Cent, XLII–48, fol. 87).

1609 The forecourt at Montceaux already begun under de Brosse's direction, Marie de Médicis apparently having inaugurated her personal building-programme at the château in 1608 with de Brosse as her architect (Chap. III and Cat. p. 233).

1610 *August 7* De Brosse named in contract as designer of buildings at Henrichemont (Chap. III and Cat. p. 223).

September 28 De Brosse possibly involved in the project for the Collège de France. Louis XIII lays the foundation stone (Cat. Appendix p. 284).

1611 *February* Two contracts for Henriche-mont naming de Brosse (Chap. III and Cat. p. 223).

1611–1612 Charles de Bourbon, Comte de Soissons, building at the Hôtel de Soissons. Probable date of the *porte-cochère* by de Brosse (Chap. IV and Cat. pp. 251-252).

1612 *April 11* Contract between Charles du Ry and Charlotte de Vieuxpont, wife of Bernard Potier, for part of the building at the château of Blérancourt (Chap. V and Cat. p. 203).

September 1 Contract between Salomon de Brosse and Henri de la Tour, Duc de Bouillon and Prince de Sedan, for the enlargement of the Hôtel de Bouillon, Rue de Seine (Chap. IV and Cat. pp. 242-243). In this contract de Brosse is called 'architecte du Roy et de la Reyne', the earliest known record of his title as such. 'Demeurant à présent en ceste ville de Paris, rue Sainct Honoré, paroisse St. Germain l'Auxerrois'. Also the first record of de Brosse as resident in Paris. He possibly arrived there with Jacques II du Cerceau in the 1590's.

1613 *January 3* First masonry contract for Coulommiers for which de Brosse provides drawing (Chap. VI and Cat. p. 221).

March 20 'M. de Brosses, architecte, Jean Coingt and Jean Gobelin, son gendre et Charles du Ry, architecte, d'Argentan prirent l'alignement du château de Coulommiers'. (Fleigny, *Mémoire*; Chap. VI and Cat. p. 221).

February–April Payments for work on the Hôtel de Bouillon (Chap. IV and Cat. p. 243).

September 10 De Brosse signs a document as 'je soubsigné, Salomon de Brosse, architecte des bâtiments du Roy et de la Royne, sieur des fiefs de Royaumont et de Colombier sis à Verneuil-sur-Oyse' (publ. Pannier, p. 267).

December 7 Main contract for the roof-timbering at Coulommiers for which de Brosse provides designs (Chap. VI and Cat. p. 221).
De Brosse involved in design for the Aqueduct at Arceuil (Cat. Appendix p. 278).

1614 *January 30* Contract between Salomon de Brosse and Claude de Bullion for the enlargement of the Hôtel de Bullion, Rue Plastrière (Cat. p. 246). De Brosse is named 'Honorable homme Salomon de Brosse, architecte du Roy et de la Royne demeurant à Paris rue des Viels Augustins, paroisse St Eustache.

September Jacques II du Cerceau dies and de Brosse inherits his position and pension on the royal pay-roll (cf. E.-J. Ciprut, 'Notes sur un grand architecte parisien, Jean Androuet du Cerceau', *Bull. Soc. Hist. Prot. Fr.*, CXIII, April–June, p. 149 ff.).

1614–1616 Various payments for building at the Luxembourg (Arch.Nat. KK–193/4, Comptes de Marie de Médicis).

1615 De Brosse named in Marie de Médicis' accounts as 'conducteur des Bâtiments' at Montceaux (Chap. III and Cat. pp. 233-234).

February 25 Contract between Salomon de Brosse and 'Messire Bénigne Bernard,

Sieur de Baune' for the enlargement of the Hôtel Bénigne Bernard, rue Coquillière (Chap. IV and Cat. p. 239). De Brosse, is recorded here as 'demeurant à Sainct Germain des Prés lez Paris, rue de Vaugirard, paroisse St Sulpice'.

October 6 Obligation: Humphrey Bradley to 'noble homme Salomon de Brosse, architecte et controlleur générale des bâtiments du Roy et de la Royne, demeurant à Saint Germain des Prés (Min. Cent. VI–251). The sum involved is very small and the document curious, as Bradley was a very rich man to whom at one time the du Cerceau family owed 12,000 livres. Despite his description as 'Humphray Bradelay, Gentilhomme flamand de Bergues-sur-le-Son (Bergen-op-Zoom) he may have been an expatriate Englishman. In 1610–1611 he took part in an *expertise* at Henrichemont to correct an error in calculation made by Hugues Cosnier when planning the locks for the canal at Briare (Mallevoüe, *Les Actes de Sully* 1610–1611, 1911, p. xxxv. For Bradley, cf. also Pierre du Colombier, 'Autour des Métezeau', *Bibliothèque d'Humanisme et Renaissance*, III, 1943, pp. 179 and 180).

October 19 Receipt acknowledged by de Brosse of payment for work done on the 1614 contract for the Hôtel Bénigne Bernard (Chap. IV and Cat. p. 239).

1616 *March* Paul de Brosse is involved in a street-brawl and is bailed out by his father. Both are living in the 'hostel de Lucenbor, faubourg St German des Prés' (Pannier, p. 110).

March 7 Carpentry and masonry contracts passed for the façade of Saint Gervais (Chap. VIII and Cat. p. 266).

May 17 Marie de Médicis is exiled to Blois.

1617 *June 30* Marie de Médicis commissions de Brosse to make plans and drawings for a small pavilion at Blois (Cat. p. 208).

December 20 Acte de foi et d'hommage by de

Brosse for the Seigneurie of du Plessis Pommeraye near Verneuil, received on 23 June 1616 from Henriette d'Entragues, Marquise de Verneuil, in lieu of payment for work done by him at her château of Verneuil (Chap. III and Cat. p. 277, and Pannier, p. 252, *et seq*).

1618 In this year de Brosse's name comes at the head of the royal pay-roll for the 'Estat des Officiers'; '. . . tant pour ses gaiges antiens que d'augmentation par de decedz du feu Sr. du Cerceau son oncle, la somme de IIm. IIIIc, Is.' (Pannier, p. 50).

July 30 De Brosse first consulted by the Cathedral authorities at Orléans (Chap. I and Cat. p. 236; ibid; date note, col. 1).

May 19 Procès Verbal concerning the château of Lesigny (Seine-et-Marne), formerly the property of the Maréchal and Maréchalle d'Ancre (Concino Concini and Leonora Galigai, the favourites of Marie de Médicis, by then deceased) (Min. Cent. VI–6: receipt by Charles David for masonry work done for the above owners at the château: '. . . ledict payement faict suivant le procès verbal faict par Mr Salomon de Brosse Conseiller et architecte ordinaire de sa Majesté et Jehan Autissier juré de sadicte Majesté ès oeuvres de maçonnerie des 19, 20 et 21 fevrier dernier . . . des ouvrages de maçonnerie faict de neuf par ledict David'). The association with Autissier is interesting, he was to be one of de Brosse's experts for the *Procès Verbal* of the Luxembourg in 1623. (I am obliged to M. E.-J. Ciprut for this unpublished reference).

August 1 De Brosse further advises the Cathedral authorities at Orléans; his visit there a little later is noted in the Cathedral records and it probably took place after his return from Rennes (Chap. VIII and Cat. p. 236, *August 4*).

August 3 Paul de Brosse and Jean Gobelin sign an agreement for the removal of debris from the site of the Salle des Pas Perdus of the Palais de Justice in Paris, which had been burnt down on March 7. Paul de Brosse signs for his father, absent from Paris (Chap. VIII and Cat. p. 255).

August 8–22 De Brosse in Rennes, making the plans for the Palais du Parlement (Chap. IX and Cat. p. 270).

September 28 Contract for the furnishing of stone for the Salle des Pas Perdus signed by Paul de Brosse for his father, and by Jean Gobelin (ibid. p. 255).

September 30 Contract between Salomon de Brosse and François de Daillon, Comte du Lude, for alterations and enlargements to the Hôtel du Lude, Rue du Bouloi (Chap. IV and Cat. p. 249).

1619 De Brosse and others concerned with a project for a new bridge at Rouen, and meetings concerning this, held at de Brosse's house: E.-J. Ciprut, 'Oeuvres inconnues de François Mansart, *G.d.B.A.*, LXV, January 1965, p. 40.
Re-issue of Jean Bullant's *Reigle Générale d'Architecture*, purporting to be edited by de Brosse (Chap. I).

May 5 Document signed in which de Brosse is officially referred to as contractor, with Gobelin, for the Salle des Pas Perdus of the Palais de Justice (Chap. VIII and Cat. p. 255).

June The château of Blérancourt nearly completed (Chap. V and Cat. p. 206).

1620 *August 13* Return from exile to Paris of Marie de Médicis.

November 21 Contract between Jean Thiriot and Antoine Feydeau for alterations and enlargements to the château and gardens of Bois-le-Vicomte (Seine-et-Marne). De Brosse named as architect. A previous contract had been signed by Thiriot on 6 March 1619 and a further contract was signed by him on 13 March 1621 (Chap. X and Cat. p. 209).

1621–1623 At some time during this period de Brosse collaborated with Michel Lasne in an engraving in honour of Pope Gregory XV.

The Pope was elected in this year and died in 1623 (Chap. X and Pannier, p. 151).

May 23 Receipt signed by de Brosse for the sum of 15,000 livres lent to him by Jean de Fourcy, 'surintendant des bâtiments du Roi' (Min Cent. XIX–394, Inventory of Jean de Fourcy, fol. 159 *recto*, item 662).

August 2 Contract between Jean Thiriot and Antoine Feydeau for the construction of two domes at Bois-le-Vicomte, designed by de Brosse (Chap. X and Cat. p. 210).

1622 *March 31* Letter from Peiresc to Rubens about the measurements to be provided by de Brosse of the West Gallery of the Luxembourg (*Correspondance de Rubens*, ed. Ruelens and Rooses, Antwerp, 1887–1909, II, p. 357).

April 7–8 Peiresc reports de Brosse as absent in Verneuil (ibid., p. 370).

April 14 De Brosse engaged on drawings for Rubens of the fireplaces of the Luxembourg gallery and the spaces above and beside them (ibid., p. 384). These drawings are lost.

July 21 De Brosse, because of a sprained foot and gout, has still not provided the measurements and drawings required by Rubens (ibid., p. 471).

September 8 De Brosse again absent from Paris, at Verneuil. Rubens sends Peiresc copies of his *Palazzi di Genova* (1622), for de Brosse and Berthelot, but de Brosse is away at Verneuil (ibid., III, p. 34).

September 18 De Brosse still at Verneuil (ibid., p. 42).

September 21 De Brosse returns from Verneuil, but evades Peiresc (ibid., p. 34).

September 29 Peiresc gives de Brosse Rubens's book, but no measurements or drawings are yet forthcoming (ibid., p. 50).

November 4 Difficulties made by de Brosse over piercing an opening, at Rubens's request, over 'la porte de la terrasse de la galerie' (ibid., p. 65).

November 11 De Brosse leaves Paris; drawings and measurements for Rubens again delayed and discussions held up (ibid., p. 70).

November 18 Peiresc reports that he has, on Rubens's behalf, thanked de Brosse 'pour l'exactitude des mesures qu'il vous a envoyée', and that by the next morning the architect was to have provided a drawing for the disputed opening over the gallery-door on to the terrace (above the entrance-screen). The latter not made as de Brosse 'n'ayant pu dormir la nuit il lui a été impossible de terminer ce travail' (ibid., p. 75–76).

December 1 The final drawing required by Rubens 'a été fait dans la chambre de M. de Brosse' (ibid., p. 88).

1623 *February 3* Marie de Médicis visits the Luxembourg for nearly three weeks, but lodges in part of the old Hôtel du Luxembourg (ibid., p. 126): '. . . La Reine-Mère va s'établir demain pour quinze ou vingt jours dans son Palais du Luxembourg, pendant la durée de la foire; c'est pour ce motif et pour se purger qu'elle a fait tapisser les apartements du Palais neuf mais elle n'y peut pas coucher encore et habitera le vieux palais du Luxembourg; celui-ci est contigu au palais neuf et elle se rendra dans celui-ci par la galerie ou doivent venir vos tableaux'.

April 21 Proceedings threatened against de Brosse concerning the Luxembourg: '. . . au sujet d'une partie de sa construction pour laquelle il avait mal conseillé . . .'. (ibid., p. 156).

May 4 De Brosse reported as making various journeys to Limours, to provide drawings for work on the château belonging to Cardinal Richelieu (ibid., p. 162 and Cat. p. 225).

June–July Peiresc discusses with Rubens de Brosse's possible interest in buying a collection of antique medals (ibid., p. 192).

June 23 and June 27 Masonry and carpentry contracts for the Second Temple of Charenton-Saint Maurice. (Chap. X and Cat. p. 212).

June 26–August 23 *Procès Verbal* and *Expertise des travaux* at the Luxembourg on behalf of the Queen Mother on the one side and Salomon de Brosse on the other (Chaps. I and VII and Cat. p. 263 f.).

1624 *March 14* Contract signed by de Brosse for the building of the E. gallery of the Luxembourg (Cat. p. 264).

March 24 De Brosse resigns as contractor of the Luxembourg (ibid.).

April 14 De Brosse and Clément Métezeau asked to recommend masons for work to be done at the Louvre (Dumolin, 'Le Louvre de Le Mercier et de Le Vau', *G.d.B.A.*, 1928 (2), pp. 28 ff).

October 30 De Brosse represented by his son-in-law, Pierre le Blanc, at the drawing up of an agreement regarding the removal of builders' debris from the Luxembourg (Pannier, p. 271). Pierre le Blanc de Beaulieu married de Brosse's daughter, Madeleine. He accompanied de Brosse to Rennes in 1618 (ibid.).

December 14 Decree of the Conseil d'Etat on the proceedings between the Procureur Général de la Reine Mère and Salomon de Brosse over the construction of the Luxembourg (Pannier, p. 266, transcription). The details of the *Procès Verbal* are listed and the conclusion states that '. . . Tout considéré le Roy en son Conseil sans avoir esgard au renvoi requis par led. Brosse a ordonné et ordonne que les dictes parties escriront et produiront au principal tout ce que bon leur semblera dans huictaine pour ce fait et rapporté leur estre faict droict ainsy que de raison despens reservez. Faict au Conseil d'Estat du Roy tenu à Paris le quatorzième jour de décembre mil six cens vingt quatre'. The subsequent papers concerning the proceedings are lost (Chap. VIII and Cat. p. 264).

1625 *March 14* The Cathedral authorities of Orléans send to Paris to enquire whether de Brosse can visit them and provide plans and drawings for the transepts (Cat. p. 236).

June 26 De Brosse cancels a proposed visit to Orléans, being 'incommodé et destenu au lict de ses gouttes'. No assurance can be got from him about future activity (Chap. I and Cat. p. 236).

July 18 Because of de Brosse's 'grand incommodité' and illness, the authorities at Orléans ask for either Jean Androuet du Cerceau, or 'le sieur Brosse, filz' (ibid.).

August 6 Jean du Cerceau and Paul de Brosse sent by de Brosse to Orléans (ibid.).

1626 *March 26* The designs for the transept are sent to de Brosse in Paris (ibid. p. 237).

April 23 De Brosse returns the designs, expressing his disapproval and adds three of his own (ibid.).

December 8 Death of de Brosse in his lodgings at the Hôtel du Luxembourg.

December 9 Burial of Salomon de Brosse, 'ingénieur et architecte des Bâtiments du Roy, natif de Verneuil' in the Protestant cemetery, Rue des Saints Pères (Pannier, p. 107).

1626 *December 31–***1627** *February 15* Inventory (*Inventaire après décès*) made in de Brosse's lodging (publ. by J.-P. Babelon, Documents inédits concernant Salomon de Brosse', *B.S.H.A.F.*, 1962).

Château of Blérancourt

I ORIGINAL DOCUMENTS

Blérancourt is poorly documented, only three of the original contracts appear to have survived, of which only one concerns major construction-work. Although deeds concerning Bernard Potier and other members of the Potier family are numerous in the Minutier Central, few of these contain information of use in establishing the architectural history of the château.

PARIS, ARCHIVES NATIONALES,
MINUTIER CENTRAL

LXXXVI – 147 fol. 517 15 May 1600: Déclaration des biens. Marriage of Bernard Potier, Seigneur de Blérancourt, with Charlotte de Vieuxpont,
LXXXVI – 188 fol. 271 11 April 1612. Contract between Charles du Ry and Charlotte de Vieuxpont for the demolition of a tower and erection of the two pavilions flanking the court-façade of the château.
LXXXVI – 190 fol. 15 14 January 1614. Contract between Jacques François, 'maçon à Senlis', and Bernard Potier for 56 steps of Senlis stone for the 'trois pincipaux perrons du château de Blérancourt'.
LXXXVI – 197 fol. 200 23 August 1919. Contract between Barthélemy Tremblay,

sculptor, and Bernard Potier and Charlotte de Vieuxpont 'pour la salle du château de Blérancout et le fronton'.

PARIS, BIBLIOTHEQUE NATIONALE

B.N. MSS. fonds français 12115: Pierre Bergeron, *Voyages ès Ardennes, Liège et Pays Bas*, 1619. The original MS. of the published book.

PARIS, BIBLIOTHEQUE DE LA SOCIETE DE L'HISTOIRE DU PROTESTANTISME FRANÇAIS

816/10 (b) Papiers Charles Read. Letter of M. Marsy, Société de l'Histoire de Compiègne, 21 October 1872; other papers and MSS. notes of Read concerning Blérancourt.

II PUBLISHED SOURCES

Bruzen de la Martinière, *Dictionnaire*, 1739.
Tallement des Réaux, *Historiettes*, 1659/62, ed. Monmerqué, Paris, 1862.
Pierre Bergeron, *Voyage es Ardennes, Liège et Pays Bas*, 1619; various, incomplete printed

versions of this exist; it was publ. fully, with notes, by Michelaut, Liège, 1875.
M. Pette, 'Bernard Potier, Le Château, le couvent des Feuillants et l'hospice des Orphelins de Blérancourt', *Bull. Soc.*

Archéologique de Soissons, XI, 2e série, 1880.
C. Dessin, *Le Bourg de Blérancourt*, Editions du Guetteur de l'Aisne, 1926.

E. Coyecque, Catalogue du Musée de Blérancourt, re-ed. 1957 by 'Les Amis du Musée de Blérancourt' (Musée de la coopération Franco-Americaine).

III PLANS AND ELEVATIONS

Drawings

PARIS, BIBLIOTHEQUE NATIONALE

B.N.Est. Vª 428, de Cotte: Block-plan of the château and forecourt, with plan of the gardens (Pl. 89).
B.N.Est. Série H and Série B. Rés. Scattered through the volumes of the Série Hᵈ are seven drawings of Blérancourt. As this series is subdivided into various kinds of architectural details, within the division 'Architecture Civile', the drawings of Blérancourt have become separated from one another. One drawing, completely isolated in the Série B of the Réserve, undoubtedly belongs to this set and is by the same hand. All but one seem to have been made from the executed building, though the question of their origin is confusing (cf. Chap. V, p. 87, n. 4). All save one are in pen-and-ink only. They are all without a general scale, though the details of some are measured:
B.N.Est. Hᵈ 182, Détails d'Architecture, I (Entablements), fol. 2 *recto:* Three-quarter elevation of the lower part of one of the moat-pavilions; measurements of part of the basement inscribed.
B.N.Est. Hᵈ 182, fol. 2 *verso:* the dome and lantern of the same pavilion, almost the whole shown, but the lower part only roughly sketched in, partly in pencil only.
B.N.Est. Hᵈ 184, Détails d'Architecture, IV (Portes), fol. 17 *recto:* three-quarter elevation of the inner entrance-gate or *porte d'honneur*; the topmost element, which is cut off at the top, is repeated in pencil top right.
B.N.Est. Hᵈ 204, Architecture Civile, III (Habitations, Palais et Hôtels, France et Pays Etranger moins Italie), fol. 10 *recto:* three-quarter elevation of the two lower storeys of the central pavilion, *corps-de-logis*, court side. The elevation of both storeys is cut horizontally, and they are thus lowered to fit the paper (Pl. 98).
B.N.Est. Hᵈ 204, fol. 10 *verso:* three-quarter elevation of the attic storey and tympanum of the same façade (Pl. 99), intended to be placed above *fol. 10 recto:* measurements of various parts given on both drawings.
B.N.Est. Hᵈ 205, Architecture Civile, IV (Habitations, Châteaux de France), fol. 20 *recto:* three-quarter elevation of the two lower storeys of the central pavilion, *corps-de-logis*; probably a design for the garden front (Pl. 100).
B.N.Est. Hᵈ 205, fol. 20 *verso:* three-quarter elevation of the attic storey and tympanum of the same façade, intended to be placed above fol. 20 *recto*; both drawings are 'cut' as those on fols 10r. and *v*, in order to fit them on to the paper; measurements of various parts given on both drawings (Pl. 101).
B.N.Est. Série B 2 b Réserve: elevation of the first entrance-gate, forecourt side; one flanking pavilion and half of the other; the upper part of the gate cut by a drawing (upside down on page) of one ground-floor window-bay and half the main-door from the central pavilion of the *corps-de-logis*, court side; pencil-pen-and-ink with grey-brown wash (Pls 107, 116).

PARIS, LOUVRE

Dessins, RF 2027 Album attributed to le Père Derand: for this album, see Chap. V, pp. 78-79. The attribution to Derand is not tenable. None of the following drawings is of Blérancourt, but all apparently were made at the château. All are inscribed with its name. The signature 'Der' which appears on all five 'Blérancourt' drawings, and on nine others in the album, led to the attribution to Derand. All the drawings inscribed 'Der' are dated, and all the dates are between 1614 and 1616. It is very desirable that the author of this important album should be identified, but so far no researches in this direction have been successful. The pages of the album measure 27·5 x 41·8 cms.

Dessins RF 2027 fol. 3. Arched doorway in architectural surround showing Italian mannerist influence; inscr. 'à blérancourt 1614 Der'.

Dessins RF 2027 fol. 5 bis. Elevation of a tabernacle or possibly a small pavilion (no scale given); inscr. 'à blérancourt 1614 (or 1615, the last figure has been corrected) Der'. The plan of this structure appears on other folios but without the inscription 'blérancourt' (Pl. 86).

Dessins RF 2027 fol. 6. Arched doorway in elaborate architectural setting showing Italian and northern influences; inscr: 'à blérancourt 1615 Der'.

Dessins RF 2027 fol. 33. Rectangular doorway in architectural setting showing the same kind of influence as *fol. 3*; inscr. 'à blérancourt 1614 Der' (Pl. 85).

Dessins RF 2027 fol. 38. Elevation, with plan, of the door of the Cancelleria, Rome, not as engraved by Vignola, but as actually executed in 1589; inscr. 'dessigné à blérancourt 1615 (date 1614 corrected) Der'.

BLERANCOURT, MUSEE DE LA CO-OPERATION FRANCO-AMERICAINE

Cat. No. 2 (Pl. 6). Tavernier de Junquières: view of the château; *porte d'honneur* and main front, 1790; watercolour made for engraving in the *Voyage Pittoresque* by Laborde (Pl. 94).

LONDON, ROYAL INSTITUTE OF BRITISH ARCHITECTS

Drawings Library, Album of Jacques Gentilhâtre, fol. 25 *verso*. Pen-and-ink drawing of a pavilion with dome and lantern; based directly on one of the moat pavilions at Blérancourt. Gentilhâtre has almost caricatured it by the addition of rustication and du Cercesque detail.

BERLIN, STAATLICHE MUSEEN PREUSSISCHER KULTURBESITZ

Kunstbibliothek Hdz 2242. Pen-and-wash drawing of half the elevation of the outer gate and pavilions at Blérancourt, outer side. Showing urns instead of seated dogs above pavilion domes. This drawing appears from photographs to be close to the du Ry drawings of the Louvre 'de Brosse' album, R.F. 5946. Published and illustrated as by de Brosse in; *Die französischen Zeichnungen der Kunstbibliothek Berlin*, Berlin 1970.

Engravings

I. Silvestre. View, presumably of the garden-front, showing the moat-pavilions and *porte d'honneur* linked by a screen; inscr. 'Veuë et Perspective du Chasteau de Blérancourt basty par Messire Bernard Potier et Madame Charlotte de Vieuxpont Seigneur et Dame dudit lieu à 24 lieues de Paris, en Picardie. Israel excudit' (F. 62: 12) (Pl. 91).

I. Silvestre. View of the court-front (with *porte d'honneur* removed); inscr. 'Veuë du Chasteau de Blérancourt. Israel excud.' (F. 62: 13) (Pl. 92).

IV CHRONOLOGY AND NOTES

1600 *May 15* Ratification of contract and *Déclaration des biens* on the marriage of Bernard Potier, 'Seigneur de Blérancourt' with Charlotte de Vieuxpont. Charlotte brings Bernard the estate of Annebault in Normandy. Louis Potier de Gesvres et de Tresmes, father of Bernard, cedes to his son the château of Chaillot and the 'maison, terre et seigneurie de Blérancourt'. Blérancourt, and their hôtel in the Rue des Bourdonnais, Paris, are to be the couple's principal places of residence (Min. Cent. LXXXVI–147 and LXXVI–152).

1612 *April 11* Contract between Charles du Ry and Charlotte de Vieuxpont for building at Blérancourt, 'fault fouillir les tranchées pour les fondations de deux pavillons sur la face de l'entrée du chasteaux lesquelles fondations seront fouillées jusques à vif fonds et de mesme profondeur que celles du logis ja fondé . . . '. This must be a continuation of new work already begun. The contract includes the demolition of two towers to make way for these pavillons (Min. Cent. LXXXVI–188).

1614 *January 14* Contract between Jacques François, 'maitre masson à Senlis y demeurant, de présent en ceste ville de Paris', and Bernard Potier, seigneur de Blérancourt, and Dame Catherine de Vieuxpont, his wife; for the provision of stone steps for the principal staircase at Blérancourt and also for the three principal *perrons* (Min. Cent. LXXXXVI–190).

1614–1615 The author of the 'Derand Album' presumably at Blérancourt. One drawing inscribed 'dessigné à blérancourt 1615' (Louvre, Dessins RF 2027 fol. 38).

1619 *August 23* Contract between Barthélemy Tremblay, sculptor, and Bernard Potier and Charlotte de Vieuxpont, his wife. Tremblay is to execute the decorations of the ceiling of the 'grande salle' after designs by 'le Sieur Fremynetz' (Martin Fréminet); also to sculpt a figure of Minerva in stone to surmount the tympanum of the central pavilion of the *corps-de-logis* on the garden-side. (Min. Cent. LXXXXVI–197).

1619 *Summer* The château is nearing completion, according to a long description by Pierre Bergeron, who gives the names, including de Brosse's, of some of the artists employed there (Bergeron, *Voyage ès Ardennes, Liège et Pays Bas*, 1619: 'Je partis de Paris avec Monsieur et Madame de Blérancourt . . . le 18 juin 1619').

1661 Death of Bernard Potier, childless; 'Je donne à ma nièce de Tresmes, Anne-Madeleine Potier, qui a été nourrie avec feue Madame de Blérancourt, le reste de tous mes biens, meubles et immeubles . . .'. Blérancourt itself passed to the Gesvres branch of the Potier family (M. Pette *Le château de Blérancourt*).

1783 Blérancourt sold out of the family by the last Duc de Gesvres, passes into the possession of Jerôme-Joseph Genet (Cat. du Musée . . . de Blérancourt).

1792 *October 24* J.-J. Genet, self-styled 'Marquis de Blérancourt' declared an emigré. Inventory of the château drawn up by the Municipality. The château and contents declared a 'bien national', '. . . aussi la commission (municipale) n'a t'elle rien de précieux à consigner dans son procès verbal'. There is mention of 'une chapelle', 'une chambre des archives' and 'une orangerie', but the whole building is reported as being in total disrepair and in use as a wood and vegetable store (ibid.).

1793 Château sold as 'bien national', almost wholly demolished and the materials sold for building.

1815 J.-J. Genet tries to reclaim the château, but without success; '. . . Il voulait rentrer en possession de ce qui restait du château qui avait aussi été vendu et en partie destruit' (ibid.).

Post–1918 The ruins bought and restored by Miss Ann Morgan; foundation of the Franco-American Museum in the château.

Château of Blois,
Pavilion for Marie de Médicis

CHRONOLOGY, SOURCES AND NOTES

All references, unless otherwise indicated, are to Lesueur, 'Notes sur le Château de Blois au XVIIième siècle', *Mém. Soc. des Sciences et Lettres de Loir et Cher*, 1926, pp. 197 ff.

1617 *April 24*   Marie de Médicis is exiled to Blois after the murder of Concini. She is lodged in the S.W. range of the château.

June 30   The Queen consults with de Brosse about building a new pavilion for her use; '... La Royne Mère du Roy s'est faict représenter par Mre. Salomon de Brosse architecte ordinaire de leurs Majéstés le plan et devis qu'elle luy avoit commandé de dresser des besognes et ouvrages de maçonnerie ... qui sont à faire pour bastir et construire de neuf un petit pavilion que le Roy a eu agréable etre faict pour la commodité du logement de ladicte dame Royne ...' (B.N. MS. VC Colbert 91, 'Pièces pour le service de la Reine mère', 257v.–258v).

June–August   Contract signed on behalf of the Queen by M. de Saumery ('Intendant général des finances et bastiments au Comté

de Blois') with Jacques Bourg and Jacques Boyer, 'architecte' and 'maistre maçon' respectively.

August 1   The first stone laid. The pavilion was somewhere on the S.W. terrace (Golnitz, '*Ulysses Belgico-Gallicus*, 1631, pp. 259–260: 'In area arcis subtus ad pedem aedeficii novi a Regina Maria Medicea exstructi, visitur lapis circularis, cui crux incisa cum his verbis, 'ceste pierre a esté posée par la Royne Mère du Roy le 1 aoust 1617' ...'.

1618 *July 20*   Marie de Médicis pays Bourg and Boyer the 4,000 livres due.

October 31   Bourg and Boyer paid 600 livres and a further 454 livres for additional work, outside the contract, in accordance with a special *Mémoire* 'arresté par Salomon de Brosse'. Another 146 livres is paid to them for time lost when they were not allowed to work because of the noise they made before the Queen was up in the morning.

1635   De Brosse's pavilion is demolished to make way for François Mansart's wing at Blois.

Château of Bois-le-Vicomte

I ORIGINAL DOCUMENTS

Most of the original documents concerning Bois-le-Vicomte during the period of de Brosse's connection with it appear to have survived. There are in addition numerous documents dealing with the periods before and after Feydeau's ownership. Where relevant, these are quoted in the Chronology.

PARIS, ARCHIVES NATIONALES MINUTIER CENTRAL

CV – 215: 6 March 1619. Masonry contract between Antoine Feydeau, 'Intendant de la maison de la Reine Mère', and Jean Thiriot, master-mason of Paris; price 7 livres, 10 sols per thoise.

CV – 220: 21 November 1620. Masonry contract, between the same and the same, mentioning a 'plan et desseing' for the main gate by Salomon de Brosse; price 2,800 livres, plus 1,000 livres for the gate.

CV – 221: 13 March 1621; masonry contract, between the same and the same, for work on the château, on 'les deux pavillons de la basse-cour' and on the garden pavilions; price 7 livres, 4 sols per thoise.

CV – 222: 2 August 1621; Carpentry contract between Antoine Feydeau and Claude Molleur, master-carpenter of Paris, for the construction of two *dosmes* to the design of Salomon de Brosse; price 3,000 livres.

CV – 346: 3 June 1622; concerning the supplies of stone for a *pavier* at the château.

LI - 137: 2 October 1622; 'Mémoire de l'Estat des ouvrages de Massonerye qui est à faire pour Monsieur Feydeau pour la perfection de son chasteau de Bois le Vicomte'.

CV – 395: 12 April 1936; roofing contract for Bois-le-Vicomte, the Duc d'Orléans signing for Mlle de Montpensier as owner.

MELUN, ARCHIVES DEPARTMENTALES DE SEINE ET MARNE

Arch.Dép. 30. Z *Les monographies scolaires et communales* (MSS.), année 1899, Vol. XV, fols. 254–267.

II PUBLISHED SOURCES

A. N. Dézallier d'Argenville, *Voyage pittoresque des environs de Paris*, 1799 (last edition).

T. Lhuiller, 'Etude historique sur l'ancien château de Bois-le-Vicomte à Mitry-Mory', *Bull. Soc. d'Architecture de Seine-et-Marne*, IX, 1884, pp. 261–279.

J.-P. Babelon, 'Documents inédits concernant Salomon de Brosse', *B.S.H.A.F.*, 1962, pp. 141–156.

III PLANS AND ELEVATIONS

Drawings

Arch.Dép. 4 P 112, Commune de Mitry-Mory, Section F, Canton de Claye, Arrondissement de Meaux: 3 fols.; these are nineteenth century and show the site of the château and block-plans of it; part of a survey

dated 16 April 1785; also eighteenth-century technical drawings concerning the 'canal'.

Engravings

Gomboust, Plan of Paris; perspective view of the château in the border (Pl. 212).
Abbé Delagrive, Plan of Paris (environs); block-plan of the château; and plan of the lay-out of the 'canals' and park (Pl. 211).

IV CHRONOLOGY AND NOTES

1580 The château was built before this date, and was the property of Amery de Barbézières and Claude de l'Aubespine, his wife. (T. Lhuiller, op. cit., p. 261, says no château is recorded before 1585, which is incorrect: cf. Arch. Nat. Y121 Inv. 1702 fol. 282 *verso*: *Donation mutuelle*, Amery de Barbézières and Claude de l'Aubespine, 31 January 1580, in which mention is made of the château of Bois-le-Vicomte). This is the house which de Brosse and Thiriot altered and enlarged for Feydeau (Cf. also Min. Cent. XCIX–97, 2 July 1609, *Inventaire des biens de Amery de Barbézières*).

1614 *September 20* Guillaume de l'Aubespine leases to a Christophe Ganneron 'le portail de l'habitation et la basse-cour du château'; the lessor was to retain 'tous les logis hauts du principal corps-de-logis, et les pavillons ...' (Lhuiller, op. cit.).

1619 *January–February* Guillaume de l'Aubespine sells the château and estate to Antoine Feydeau, 'Tresorier de l'épargne, Intendant de la Reine Marie de Médicis dame de Montceaux' (ibid.).

March 6 Feydeau engages Jean Thiriot to demolish one pavilion 'quy est a costé du logis du costé de la bassecour' and rebuild it, to build 'de neuf' a chapel, to rebuild the

basse-cour and the surrounding buildings of the main forecourt; also to build a new main gate (Min. Cent. CV–215).

1620 *November 21* Feydeau signs a further contract with Thiriot for the completion of the 'corps d'hostel', the four pavilions 'aux quatre coings d'icelluy', and the work outlined generally in the first contract: 'plus il convient faire et parfaire la porte de l'entrée du château avec les deux culs-de-lampe ... couvertz en dosme ... de semblable façon et ordonnance que le plan et deseing de ce fait par ledict Sieur Brosse'. (Min. Cent. CV–220).

1621 *March 13* Further contract, for re-lining the moats and for building two pavilions at the corners of the basse-cour; also three pavilions at the three corners of the park (Min. Cent. CV–221).

August 2 Contract with Claude Molleur for two *dosmes* to be built 'suivant et conformément le desseing qui en a esté faict par le Sieur Brosse, architecte du Roy' (Min. Cent. CV–222; J.-P. Babelon, *Documents inédits*, p. 144).

1622 *October 2* The pavilion on the N.W. corner of the basse-cour still remains to be finished, also the re-lining of the moat beneath it. The lucarnes on the *corps-de-logis* have to be inserted. Seven stone urns are needed for the screens of the basse-cour and the fore-court, the *dosme* of the chapel and its wainscot (Min. Cent. LI 137).

1630 Feydeau sells Bois-le-Vicomte to Cardinal Richelieu (Lhuiller, op. cit.).

1633 Richelieu exchanges Bois-le-Vicomte with Gaston d'Orléans for Champigny (con-tract of exchange signed 1635) (Lhuiller, op. cit.).

1636 *April 12* The roofing of the château declared to have been in progress for nine years and not yet completed (Min. Cent. CV-395; this is stated in a contract for roofing signed on behalf of Mlle de Montpensier, daughter of Gaston d'Orléans).

1652 Mlle de Montpensier refuses, after the Fronde, exile at Bois-le-Vicomte, because it is in such a bad state (T. Lhuiller, op. cit., quoting Journal of Mlle de Montpensier).

1655–1687 The château was variously occupied or possessed by the Duc de Riche-lieu, lessee of Mademoiselle, by Mademois-elle herself, or by her creditors, by the Duc de la Meilleraye and his wife Hortense Man-cini, and, in 1668, by Barthélemy Hervart the financier and owner of the celebrated Hôtel Hervart in the Rue Plastrière. By inheritance after his death (1676) it passed through several owners to the Comte de Talleyrand Périgord (T. Lhuiller, op. cit.).

1787 *April 27* The Comte de Talleyrand Périgord sells Bois-le-Vicomte to the King (ibid.).

1791 *February 28* The château and land are sold as a 'bien national' (ibid.).

1816–1817 The buildings are demolished after having been pillaged by roving marauders ('la bande noire') (ibid.).

1884 One pavilion remained, to the right of the principal entrance (Lhuiller, op. cit.). This also has now completely disappeared.

Charenton, Protestant Temple

I ORIGINAL DOCUMENTS

The contracts listed below also serve as the CHRONOLOGY for this building.

PARIS, ARCHIVES NATIONALES
MINUTIER CENTRAL

CV – 330: 13 June 1623; masonry contract between Jacques Tardif, Pierre Marbault, Pierre de Launay, Ysaac Duysseau and Paul Chenevix ('disans avoir charge des ministres et antients de l'église pretendue refformée de Paris') and masons Daniel Mouret and Pierre Hureau.

CV – 330: 27 June 1623; carpentry contract between the same authorities and Jean de la Beaune, Claude Doublet, Pierre Régneau and Antoine Artault, master-carpenters.

II PUBLISHED SOURCES

A. N. Dézallier d'Argenville, *Vies des fameux architectes*, Paris 1788.

J. Pannier, *Salomon de Brosse*, 1911.

III PLANS AND ELEVATIONS

Drawings

PARIS, BIBLIOTHEQUE NATIONALE

B.N.Est. Ve 26f, Rés, Vol. I, fol. 81: exterior of the Temple; pen-and-wash; anon. late seventeenth century; inscr. 'Temple protestant à Charenton, detruit en ...' (date blank); probably derived from the engraving listed below anon. seventeenth-century engraving listed below. Section III.

PARIS, BIBLIOTHEQUE DU MUSEE DES ARTS DECORATIFS

Dessins A.8503: Treatise (MS.) by the architect Salvé, 1685; contains a copy of the plan of the Temple originally appended to the masonry contract of 13 June 1623; inscr. on the recto (by Salvé) 'Plan du Temple de Charenton par Salomon de Brosse, voir au verso la signature des entrepreneurs'; on the verso, 'Paraphé le seizième jour de juin 1623 par les 7 pnts Marbault, Hureau et Noretz, entrepreneurs'; this inscr. is all in the same hand, the signatures being copied by Salvé.

COPENHAGEN, ROYAL LIBRARY

MS Thott 434, 8° Watercolour from F. C. Deublinger of Speyer, *Liber Amicorum* (1648). This shows the interior of the Temple. The architectural details are not entirely accurate, particularly as regards the fenestration, but the general impression given is good. (Publ. M. D. Whinney, *Wren*, London 1971).

Engravings

J. Marot, 'Plan et Profil du Temple de Charenton du dessin du Sr. de Brosse. 'Veue en perspective du dedans du Temple de Charenton du dessin de Sr. de Brosse'. Both from the *Grand Marot* (Pls 214, 216).

Anon. seventeenth century: 'Le Temple de Charenton'; inscr. beneath with a vernacular verse rendering of Psalm 65 and 'ce Temple a esté relevé et rebasti tout de neuf par la permission du Roy, l'an mil six cens vingt et quatre'. (Pl. 215).

I. Silvestre, 'Veüe et Perspective du Pont et du Temple de Charenton' (F. 50: 8).

Château of Coulommiers-en-Brie

I ORIGINAL DOCUMENTS

This château is well-documented, although the early accounts (1613–1619) and the original drawings are lost. The principal published work on Coulommiers is the *Notice sur le Château Neuf et l'Eglise des Capucins de Coulommiers-en-Brie*, by Anatole Dauvergne, for many years librarian of the Bibliothèque Municipale of Coulommiers and an amateur historian who had access to original documents in private collections in the town. All references in the Catalogue to Dauvergne are to this article unless otherwise specified.

In 1959 Mme Hélène Titeux-Derottleur submitted a Diplôme d'Etudes Supérieures to the Institut d'Art et Archéologie in Paris, entitled *Le Château Neuf de Coulommiers (1617–1738)*. Of this she generously gave me a copy which has been invaluable. Mme Titeux transcribed the *Procès Verbal* of 1714 in its entirety, and gave me a copy of this. All references to 'T.-D.' are to Mme Titeux's Diploma Study. However, many of the contracts for Coulommiers were not known to Mme Titeux, nor was the mention of de Brosse and Mansart as architects in two of them. The existence of some of these contracts was indicated to me by Dr Peter Smith.

PARIS, ARCHIVES NATIONALES,
MINUTIER CENTRAL

XXXVI – 95, 3 January 1613, masonry contract between Catherine de Gonzague and Charles du Ry, Jean Coingt and Jean Gobelin, de Brosse named as architect.
XXXVI – 95, 25 May 1613: sculpture contract between Catherine de Gonzague and Nicolas Guillain 'dit Cambray' and Simon Guillain, father and son.
XXXVI – 96, 7 December 1613: carpentry contract between Catherine de Gonzague and Etienne de Fer; de Brosse named as architect.
CV – 513, 1 October 1614: carpentry contract between Etienne de Fer and Claude Chevin.
CV – 514, 2 January 1615: *Association* between Etienne de Fer and Claude Alexandre (carpentry sub-contract).
XXXVI – 119, 20 February 1627: contract between Catherine de Gonzague and Nicolas Borgny for construction of a conduit to bring water into the château.
XXXVI – 123, 27 May 1631: masonry contract between Henri, Duc de Longueville, and Charles du Ry; François Mansart named as architect.
VII – 23, 7 May 1634: *Déposition* by Henri, Duc de Longueville, of a *Déclaration* by his

mother, Catherine de Gonzague, dated 29 December 1618, reading as follows: 'Déclaration par Catherine de Ganzague écrite par sa propre main. ... Le Lieutenant de Coulommiers qui cest devant reçu les deniers que jemplois à mes bastimens a touché la somme de sinquante six mille cent soisante et un livre et en a employé sinquante cattre mil six cens sessants et quatorse livres tellement qu'il resterayt a me paier sinq cens catre vins dixel livres . . .'.

There are also contracts in the Minutier Central, not listed here, for the building and decoration of the Church of the Convent of the Capuchins, founded by Catherine de Gonzague in 1617, and built by Charles du Ry.

PARIS, BIBLIOTHEQUE DE LA SOCIETE DE L'HISTOIRE DU PROTESTANTISME FRANÇAIS

Papiers Charles Read, 816/10(a): MS. copies by Dauvergne of the building accounts for Coulommiers, 1619–1631, made in 1853–1854. They are for the following dates: 11 and 13 May 1619: 23 November 1619: 18 September 1620: 4 and 7 October 1621: 29 December 1621: 14 November 1622; 7 and 27 July 1623; 6 December 1623; 29 January 1625; 3 June 1625; 9 September 1626; 20 January 1627; 12 October 1629; 25 March 1631.

The total expenditure given by Dauvergne is 117,654 livres, 10 sols, 6 deniers. The covering notes for the copies states: 'Comptes rendus à Catherine de Gonzague Duchesse de Longueville et Dame de Coulommiers par son Intendant Denis de Beauvillain. Construction de Coulommiers 1619–1631. Signé Anatole Dauvergne'. (cf. below, Coulommiers, Bib. Municipale).

These are the copy-accounts which have been examined in detail by the author. The following names of masons, sculptors, etc., appear in them:

Charles du Ry; his son, Mathurin (named as in charge if his father is absent); Pierre Collot, sculptor; David de Villiers, sculptor; Timotée Noblet, sculptor; Claude Alexandre, carpenter; Etienne de Fer, carpenter; Claude Mollet, 'premier jardinier du Roy'; Michel Roger, 'maistre peintre-doreur a Paris'; Gaspard Silvint, joiner; Anthoine Cocquet, 'masson des fossés'; Jean Moreau, 'couvreur d'ardoises'; Charles de la Fontaine and Pierre Gilbert, leadworkers; Jean Saillet, blacksmith of Paris: Guillot, carpenter; and Ambroise Grand, 'tailleur de presses'.

MELUN, ARCHIVES DEPARTEMENTALES DE SEINE-ET-MARNE

557 bis, Série B: 'Procès verbal de la visite du château et de la terre de Coulommiers, 17–22 octobre 1714': examination and estimate of the cost of repair to the exterior and interior of the building, made on the orders of the owner, the Duc de Luynes. On the evidence of this report, the repairs were considered too costly and demolition was decided upon. The *Procès Verbal* is a most valuable source of information and a useful check on the descriptions made after the demolition.

COULOMMIERS-EN-BRIE, BIBLIOTHEQUE MUNICIPALE

MS. Paul Cazot, from the Clozier MS. (Vol. X): Copy of the *Mémoire sur la ville et château de Coulommiers* by Pierre-Nicolas Hébert, of which the original is, or was, in the possession of the Ogier de Baulny family, descendants of Hébert, and owners of his house and library (see below, pp. 216, 220). Dauvergne dates the *Mémoire* 1712, and believed that Hébert died in 1722. M. Roger Ogier de Baulny has proved from family papers that Hébert was born in 1691 and died in 1766 (T.-D.). His *Mémoire*, which refers to the château in the past tense, was unlikely to have been written when the author was only twenty-one; it evidently dates from after the demolition of the building, some time between 1738 and 1766.

MS. Paul Cazot, from the Clozier MS. (Vol. XII): Copy of *Mémoire sur les origines, etc., de la Ville de Coulommiers* by Jean-Baptiste Aubert de Fleigny, *c.* 1770. Fleigny was Mayor of Coulommiers in 1765. In Dauvergne's time the original MS. was still with the Fleigny family; its present whereabouts is unknown, though it is supposed to have been among the Ogier de Baulny papers in 1925 (T.-D.). There is a second copy in the Bibliothèque Municipale, made *c.* 1870.

MSS. Essais historiques et topographiques sur la ville de Coulommiers by Michel-Martial Cordier (1749–1824), written 1789 and annotated by the author in 1815. A copy of Cordier's MS. is in the *MS. Clozier-Cazot (Vol. I)*. Cordier was archivist to the Marquis de Montesquiou, last owner of the Coulommiers estate. Dauvergne supposes that Hébert, Fleigny and Cordier all made use of earlier sources now lost. Cordier follows Fleigny closely.

MSS. Documents intéressants à l'histoire de Coulommiers: Bound copies (16 vols) by Paul Cazot (1908–1910) after the original MSS. by, or collected by, Dr Clozier. These are the Clozier-Cazot MSS. referred to in the entries above.

MS. Compte rendu ... par Denis de Beauvillain à Catherine de Gonzague ... Dame de Coulommiers, 27 juillet 1623: the original of one of the accounts copied by Dauvergne and included in the copy-file (T.-D., however, states that she saw the original of this date in the Hébert Collection, Rue de Valentin, Coulommiers, in 1959).

MSS. (copies): Comtes rendus par Denis de Beauvillain à Catherine de Gonzague ... Dame de Coulommiers, 1619–1631 (*c.* 1853–1854). Writing to Charles Read in 1856, when sending him duplicate copies, Dauvergne states, 'J'ai remis toutes les liasses des plans et autres documents à Charles Ogier de Baulny'.

COULOMMIERS-EN-BRIE: HEBERT MSS., OGIER DE BAULNY COLLECTION

MS. *Mémoire sur la ville et le Château de Coulommiers*, by Pierre-Nicolas Hébert. Original from which the copy by Clozier-Cazot in the Bib. Municipale was made. Hébert MSS: At his death in 1766, P.-N. Hébert bequeathed to his family his library and a large number of MSS., plans and drawings concerning Coulommiers and the château. These remained in his house, 21 Rue de Valentin, and passed by descent to the Ogier de Baulny family. In 1960 they were in the possession of the Comtesse de Chirac (*née* Ogier de Baulny) who has since died. The contents of the collection have not been available for proper examination, and since the death of Mme de Chirac the collection appears to have been dispersed, although no exact information is available. Not only the contents of the library, but the room itself, remained virtually as Hébert left them in 1766. It is a regrettable loss if this fine eighteenth-century room and a collection of great local interest, have been dispersed. (cf. below, Section III, B.N.Est Vᵃ Grand Format).

II PUBLISHED SOURCES

Loret, *Muse Historique*, 1656, I, p. 11 (20 May 1650). Poem in praise of Coulommiers after a visit to Anne-Geneviève de Bourbon-Condé, Duchesse de Longuville.

L. Huygens, *Journal*, 1665, publ. by H. Brugmans, 'Châteaux et jardins de l'Ile de France d'après un Journal de 1665, *G.d.B.A.*, Sept. 1937, p. 104 ff.

Phélypeaux de Pontchartrain: 'Mémoires de la Généralité de Paris', 1669, ed. *Mémoires pour servir à l'histoire de France*, Serie 2, ed. 1887.

Piganiol de la Force, *Nouvelle description de la France*, 1718, III, p. 232.

H. Sauval, *Histoire et recherches des antiquités de la Ville de Paris*, 1724, III, p. 232, and IV, p. 50.

Rouget, *Généalogie des Longueville*, n.d., early nineteenth century.

L. Michelin, *Essais historiques et statistiques sur le département de Seine-et-Marne: Arrondis-sement de Coulommiers*, Melun, 1829–1844, ed. progressive, p. 1081–1432.

A. Dauvergne, 'Notice sur le Château-Neuf et l'Eglise des Capucins de Coulommiers', *Bull. Mon.*, 1853, p. 597 ff.

A. Dauvergne, *Notice* on the documents and plans concerning Coulommiers, *Bulletin du Comité de la langue, de l'histoire et des arts de France*, 1853–1854.

C. Read, 'Salomon de Brosse', extract from *La France Protestante*, II, 5e. fascicule, Paris, 1881.

Dessaint, *Histoire de Coulommiers des origines à nos jours*, Coulommiers, 1925.

III PLANS AND ELEVATIONS

Drawings

PARIS, BIBLIOTHEQUE NATIONALE

B.N.Estampes V^a 446 fol. 6: Topog. Seine-et-Marne: Plans of Coulommiers, the site of the former château and of the town and neighbourhood, by Dubray, 1770.

B.N.Estampes V^a Grand Format: Series of five plans and elevations of the Château of Coulommiers. These drawings, each of which is mounted on linen, were acquired by the Bib. Nat. in 1967, and apparently came from the 'succession Ogier de Baulny of Coulommiers'. (cf. *G.d.B.A.*, LXXI, February 1968, 'Chronique des Arts'. The number of drawings is given as four, not five). Their provenance is not published, but was indicated to me verbally by the Département des Estampes in 1968. Dauvergne saw at the house at 21 Rue de Valentin, 'six dessins colorés faits avec un soin extrême en 1712'. Writing to Charles Read, he says that, among Hébert's papers, he had found 'plusieurs plans du château de Coulommiers'. Dauvergne evidently did not see all the drawings then in the Ogier de Baulny collection; we know there were at least eight, and not all these are coloured (cf. nos. i and ii below). M. Hubert, late Archivist at Melun, informed

Mme Titeux that certain other drawings from the collection had, prior to 1960, been 'sold into England'. It has not been possible to verify this sale.

According to Dauvergne, all the drawings he saw were actually by Hébert, and he stated that on drawings connected with the château he had found 'la mention du nom de M. Hébert et la date' (Pap.Ch.Read). Neither of these is present on any of the B.N. series nor on those seen in the Ogier de Baulny collection, and although the linen backing may obscure original inscriptions on the verso, the drawings appear to have been backed before 1853. The date 1712 is certainly wrong.

Dauvergne asserts that five out of the six drawings he saw were 'relevés et minutieusement dessinés sur le monument même'. With the possible exception of nos. i and ii, which are almost certainly earlier in date than any of the others, this is untrue, the château having been demolished at the time of Hébert's *Mémoire* and of his making or collection of the drawings.

The majority of this series, therefore, possibly all of them, are retrospective, but they may derive from an early and valuable source now lost, indicated by Hébert in his *Mémoire*;

R

'Coulommiers fut commencé environ l'an 1613 sous la conduite et direction d'un nommé Charles du Ry, architecte normand d'Argentan, dont j'ai connue le petit-fils' (more probably his great-grandson). The drawings are as follows:

i Plan of the château: pencil-and-grey wash; inscription at bottom: 'Plan du Chasteau de Coulommiers'; scale: thoises; above the scale and inscription is a pencilled detail, left, of the plan of one of the quadrant arcades, and right, of the entrance-balustrade and the outline of the larger S.W. pavilion; between these, inscr. 'Antrée'; (0·54 x 0·77) (Pl. 118). This plan shows the château after 1631 when Mansart designed the new entrance-front and the staircase in the N. wing. It may belong to the period *c.* 1631–1640, or be connected with the *Procès Verbal* of 1714. The sheet, previous to its mounting, appears have been folded and bound. The draughts-manship is superior to that of any of the rest of the B.N. series.

ii Plan of the forecourt: (project)?; pen-and-ink, sepia with cross-hatching; inscr. on verso, 'Plan de Lavant-cour projettée du château de Coulommiers'; (0·52 x 0·77). The style of this plan, especially the use of a particular type of rough cross-hatching, suggests that it may be an original of Charles du Ry or closely copied from him (cf. below, Louvre, Dessins, RF 5946, fol. 25v.). Hébert in his *Mémoire,* Phélypaux (*Mémoires de la Généralité de Paris*) and Piganiol de la Force (*Nouvelle Description*) all state that the forecourt was only planned and never built; the expense seeming too great, it was abandoned by Henri II de Longueville. The site is now occupied by public gardens in front of the ruins of the château.

iii Plan of the château, the Convent and Church of the Capuchins, the gardens, park, canals and avenues of the estate: pencil, pen-and-ink and various colours; inscr. on verso, 'Plan coupe

du ch. de Coul. et du terrain des anciennes allées'; (0·60 x 0·214).
This plan was possibly copied from no. i, but it and nos. iv and v are all by another and cruder hand. The reference to 'anciennes allées' places the drawing in the retrospective category. Dauvergne says that one of the six drawings he saw was 'après un original qui appartenait au Seigneur de Coulommiers, M. le duc de Luynes' (*Bull. Mon.*). In his letter to Charles Read he says, 'Le plan que j'ai communiqué au Comité est une copie faite en 1712 de l'original qui existait aux archives de M. de Luynes. Il est long de près de deux mètres'. Drawing iii measures 214 cm. in length. Dauvergne give no source for his 'original' in the Luynes archives.

iv Perspective elevation of the château seen from the south: also part of the gardens, and a per-spective plan of the Capucin church. In-distinguishable coat-of-arms top l.h. corner, half cut away; pencil-pen-and-ink and various colours, including bright red to indicate brickwork; no inscr. (0·58 x 179) (Pl. 127). In his *Notice* of 1853–1854 to the Comité de la Langue, l'histoire et des arts de France, Dauvergne creates confusion between this drawing and no. iii. One of the 'plans', he says, is 'une copie de l'original présenté à Catherine de Gonzague qui se trouvait en 1712 dans les archives du Duc de Chevreuse'. As no. iv measures 179 cms. in length, it as well as no. iii could qualify for 'long de près de deux mètres'. However, neither iii nor iv can be a copy of de Brosse's original 'plan en élévation', mentioned in the 1613 contract (and the source of Phélypeaux's story of the deception of Catherine de Gonzague), for both show not de Brosse's original entrance-front but Mansart's. Dau-vergne's remarks therefore remain obscure, but may indicate sources of information available to him in the Hébert MSS. In drawing no. iv the central element of the *corps-de-logis* is covered by a quadrilateral dome with a lantern. The pilasters of the attic storey of the larger pavilions terminate in herms supporting the cornice, and all eight pavilions have mansard-type roofs. It was upon this drawing that Dauvergne seems chiefly to have depended for his descriptions and 'reconstructions' of the château.

v Elevation of the court-façade of the corps-de-logis, also part of the N.E. and S.E. pavilions and the N. and S. wings in section: scale, thoises; inscr. below; 'Face du chasteau de Coulommiers veu de la cour et coupe des deux elles faisant retour'; pencil-pen-and-ink, and various colours; (0·42 x 0·94). (Pl. 126).

Despite the crude draughtsmanship, which it shares with no. iv, this is probably a more accurate representation of the building. The smaller pavilions have pointed roofs, the larger ones the mansard-type. These latter may have been a modification made at a date later than that of the plaster relief in the Capuchin church, which shows the château with pointed roofs on all the pavilions. The *corps-de-logis* is shown without a dome. The section of the double S. wing presumably shows the interior as it was built for Henri II de Longueville, possibly by Mansart.

PARIS, LOUVRE

Dessins RF 5946: Parchment-bound album of architectural and decorative drawings, mostly pen-and-ink; inscr. 'Je suis à du Ry'; and 'Ce présent livre appartient à Charles du Ry architecte des bastiments du Roy travaillant pour Madame la duchesse de Longueville à son château de Coulommiers l'année que ledit chasteau a ésté commencé l'an 1613'. On verso of cover; 'Ce présent livre appartient à Charles du Ry demeurant à Verneuil sur Oyse' and 'Ce présent livre appartient à Charles du Ry demeurant à Coulommiers en Bry' and 'Charles du Ry'; (0·24·5 x 0·34·5).

Note : Pannier and Charles Read claimed to have read on the cover, 'Je suis à de Brosse mil six cent sept'. In order to 'bring up' the inscription, they employed chemicals whose subsequent action has destroyed the parchment. The inscription was said still to be visible in 1904 (H. Stein, *Extrait de l'Almanach de l'histoire de Seine-et-Marne*, 1904, p. 159). The attribution of the drawings to de Brosse made by Pannier rests solely on this fugitive inscription. The album may have belonged to him; he may have given it to his kinsman and collaborator du Ry, but there is no solid basis for the attribution to him of any of the drawings. Internal evidence points to du Ry as the author of nearly all; one other hand is possibly represented. Many of the drawings of Coulommiers must date from 1631 onwards, i.e., from after de Brosse's death. A series of drawings in the Kunstbibliothek of the Staatliche Museen preussischer Kulturbesitz in Berlin can probably also be attributed to Charles du Ry on the basis of R.F. 5946. For a discussion of one of these Berlin drawings. Cf. Cat: Blérancourt.

Folio 2 *recto*: part of the decoration above the cornice of the *corps-de-logis* (or of one of the pavilions?); on the same sheet a grotesque head and a pedestal. The two latter, in pen-and-wash, are in a different decorative style and possibly by a different hand (Pl. 123).

Folio 20 *verso*: façade of the central element of the *corps-de-logis* on the garden side. This corresponds with the plaster relief in the Capuchin church and with a drawing in the Hébert-Ogier de Baulny collection. No roof or dome shown here (Pl. 124).

Folio 21 *recto*: unfininished drawing of part of one of the smaller angle-pavilions, the ground and first floors. Upper floor lightly traced in pencil; no roof (Pl. 125).

Folio 25 *verso*: plan of the N.W. angle-pavilion (large), S. side, corresponding to the elevation of the fol. 29r. and showing the pavilion as remodelled by Mansart.

Folio 26 *verso:* Elevation of the above pavilion, W. side.

Folio 27 *recto:* Folio 28 *verso:* Four drawings of one of Mansart's entrance-pavilions; corresponding with the contract of 1631, the *Procès Verbal* and the existing ruins.

Folio 29 *recto:* elevation of the N.W. angle-pavilion, S. side; pen-and-wash; the same style as the pen-and-wash details on fol. 2r.; showing the façade as modified by Mansart.

COULOMMIERS, BIBLIOTHEQUE
COMMUNALE

Four Plans, 1787: annexed to M-M. Cordier's *Essais historiques* and probably executed by him; possibly from older plans now lost. They show the town of Coulommiers and the site of the château.

A. Dauvergne, watercolour: dated 1854; (0·60 x 0·45); showing part of one of Mansart's entrance-pavilions; in the frieze is reproduced the inscr. 'DAVID DE VILLIERS, BOURGUIGNON ET THIMOTEE SCULPST ANNI MDCXXV'. The date is wrong, the pavilion not having been begun until 1631. 'Thimotée (Noblet) is mentioned in the 1619–1631 accounts.

COULOMMIERS, MUSEE DES
CAPUCINS

Watercolour, perspective view of the château: executed 1853 by the pupils of the Ecole Communale of the town; this is based not on no. iv of the B.N.Est. series but on another perspective view once in the Hébert-Ogier de Baulny collection. (In the Arch. Dép. at Melun is a nineteenth-century photograph of yet another adaptation of this Hébert perspective, probably by Dauvergne. The original source-drawing is now lost. T.-D.).

COULOMMIERS, HEBERT DRAWINGS,
OGIER DE BAULNY COLLECTION

Note: the present whereabouts of the drawings listed below is not certain (information mainly T.-D.).

i Perspective view of the château of Coulommiers: pencil with colours; (resembling nos. iii, iv and v of the B.N.Est. series); (0·52 x 0·72); a cartouche in the top r.h. corner with a coat of arms (indistinct), and the following inscription: 'Elevation à vue d'oiseau du château de Coulommiers du costé du midy. Catherine de Gonzague Duchesse de Longueville commença à le faire bâtir en 1613; elle y dépensa plus de six millions en ce temps-là, sans toutefois l'achever entièrement. Du Ry, célèbre architecte d'Argentan en Normandie en eut la conduite et l'executa, dit-on, sur un dessin venu d'Italie. Marie-Charles Louis d'Albret, duc de Chevreuse, en ordonna la démolition en 1736'. This is obviously connected with B.N.Est. drawing no. iv. Both must have been in the Hébert-Ogier de Baulny collection in Dauvergne's day.

ii Drawing of the garden (east) front of the château: pencil-and-colour; framed and glazed and hung in the house, 21 Rue de Valentin, in 1960; 'Le deuxième dessin de Hébert possédé par la famille Ogier de Baulny est consacré à la façade Est et comprend le parti du 20 v. de l'album de dessins du Louvre, avec addition de deux figures manquantes', (i.e. from the top of the pediment). (T.-D.). The absence or presence of a dome is not indicated but the remainder of the text implies its absence.

iii Drawing of part of the court-façade, corps-de-logis: 'Nous avons également vu dans la bibliothèque de la maison d'Hébert un dessin qui n'est pas de sa main, représentant la demie-façade gauche du *corps-de-logis* principal sur la cour' (T.-D.).

Engravings

C. Chastillon: *Topographie Françoise*, 1614: print of the town of Coulommiers with a view, from the south, of the site of the future château.

J. Marot, *Petit Marot*:

i. Plan du Chasteau de Colombieres en Brie.

ii. Principale Entrée du Chasteau de Colombieres, comme estoit la pensée de l'architecte (Pl. 121).

iii. Le costé de dehors du Chasteau de Colombieres en Brie (Pl. 120).

iv. Profil du dedans de la cour du Chasteau de Colombieres en Brie (Pl. 122).

J. Marot, *Grand Marot*. Plan du château de Colommiers-en-Brie bâti par le Sieur de Brosses (Pl. 117).

Note: Mauban, *J. Marot*, 1944, p. 127: 'Outres les planches que nous avons décrites dans le Grand et le Petit Marot, nous noterons ici une grande planche (hauteur 0·23 sur 0·80) intitulée, veüe des aisles et des pavillons du château de Coulommiers, J. Marot fecit'. Bérand cite cette pièce comme très rare, et avant la lettre; nous ne l'avons jamais rencontrée'. It is interesting to speculate on a possible connection between this and drawing no. iii in the B.N.Est. series.

I. Silvestre:

i. Entrance and interior of the court, perspective view; to left, a half-elevation of a church-façade (F. 62: 17, and F. 203: 1–2).

ii. Perspective view of the S. and E. fronts (F. 62: 18, and F. 203, 1–2).

iii. Perspective view of the garden front (F. 203: –2).

Both show the *corps-de-logis* with a dome.

'F.A.P.': signature of the artist on a series of lithographs of the ruins of Coulommiers, dated 1817; published by G. Engelmann, Paris. The only accurate one is that showing the entrance to the *corps-de-logis* from the court (inscr. 'Ruines d'une des Portes de l'ancien château de Coulommiers, Seine-et-Marne')'.

A. Dauvergne/E. Sagot: Engraving, reproduced by Dauvergne, Bull. Mon., 1853; showing a three-bay, three-storey pavilion; purporting to be a copy of one of the Hébert drawings. This appears to be a mistaken adaptation from one of the perspective views. No pavilion at Coulommiers was three bays wide.

IV CHRONOLOGY AND NOTES

1613 *January 3* Masonry Contract for the 'Château Neuf de Coulommiers' between Catherine de Gonzague and Charles du Ry, Jean Coingt and Jean Gobelin, 'suivant le plan paraphé . . . en élévation que le Sieur de Brosse en a faict . . .' (Min. Cent. XXXVI-95).

March 20 Salomon de Brosse, Charles du Ry and Jean Gobelin make a survey of the site for the foundations (Albert de Fleigny, *Mémoire*. Piganiol de la Force gives the date as 'l'an 1613').

May 25 Contract for the statues for the exterior of the château, between Catherine de Gonzague and the Guillain brothers (Min. Cent. XXVI-95).

December 7 Contract for the roof-timbering, between Catherine de Gonzague and Etienne de Fer, 'suivant les desseings qu'en ont esté faictz par intention du Sieur de Brosse' (Min. Cent. XXXVI-96).

1614 *October 1* Sub-Contract for timbering between Etienne de Fer and Claude Chevin (Min. Cent. CV-514, 1 January 1615).

1615 *March 12* Survey and measurements made for the moat (Dauvergne).

1616 *October 4 Aveu et Dénombrement*—'Coulommiers-en-Brie à Catherine de Gonzague' (Min. Cent. CV–325); concerns the land only, no details of château given.

1622 *October 14* Payments made to Charles du Ry, Mathurin du Ry, David de Villiers and Bourgignon (Comptes Rendus, Dauvergne copy, cf. Sec. I.).

1626 *December 6* Death of Salomon de Brosse.

1627 *February 20* Contract for water-conduit to the château (Min. Cent. XXXVI-119). This may have some relevance to the 'salle des bains' at the W. end of the S. wing, mentioned in the 1714 *Procès Verbal.*

1629 Death of Catherine de Gonzague. Henri II, Duc de Longueville, continues the building. '... Henri II duc de Longueville, son fils le mit dans l'état où on le voit aujourd'hui. La cour et la chapelle sont restées à faire, ce Prince ayant été rebuté par l'excessive dépense qu'exigeoit ce somptueux édifice ...' (Piganiol de la Force, III, 232). The *Procès Verbal* shows that by 1714 the buildings of the court were generally habitable but the chapels were still unfinished and the forecourt never begun.

1631 *May 27* Masonry Contract between Henri de Longueville and Charles du Ry: certain parts of the N. wing to be completed for a visit of the King and Anne of Austria; a new entrance-front to replace the old one designed by de Brosse but scarcely begun. The new work was to be 'selon les dessins que sont demeurez ès mains du Sieur Mansart, architecte du Roy' (Min. Cent. XXXVI-123). The discovery, in 1965, of this contract confirms the persistent local tradition that Mansart was the Duc de Longueville's architect.

September 21 Visit of Anne of Austria to the château.

October 22 Visit of Louis XIII.

1655 Visit of Louis Huygens, who notes in his *Journal* '... la maison n'est pas encore tout-à-fait achevée par dedans, mais on y travaille tous les jours'.

1663 Death of Henri II, Duc de Longueville.

1714 *October 17* 'Procès Verbal de la Visite du Château et des terres de Coulommiers' carried out by the order of the Duc de Luynes (Melun, Arch. Dép. 557 bis. Serie B.).

1738 Demolition begun by the Duke's order and carried on by his son.

Henrichemont (Cher)

CHRONOLOGY, SOURCES AND NOTES

1605 *August 31* Charles de Gonzague de Clèves, Duc de Nevers and Prince de Boisbelle, sells the principality of Boisbelle to Maximilien de Béthune, Duc de Sully, for 42,000 livres. The principal source for the history of Henrichemont is Hippolyte Boyer, *La fondation de la Ville de Henrichemont*, Bourges, 1873. Unless other sources are indicated, information quoted is from this book. All contracts were passed with the Duc de Sully.

1608 *December 11* First contract for the new seat of the Principality, a town to be built for Sully and named Henrichemont (*Documents inédits, histoire, littérature, arts, XVI–XVIII siècles*, Fas. I, 1965, p. 3 (Internal publ. of papers in the Arch. Nat. Min. Cent., ed. E.-J. Ciprut.) This contract has not been traced, but is referred to in those of 5 February 1611.

December 24 Contract for the building of the town; the entrepreneurs named are Hugues Cosnier, Jonas Robelin, Claude Allaire and René Bénard. Within the walls of the town there are to be '. . . une église, ung temple, ung collège, seize corps-de-logis, une hostellerie et une Halle . . .'. Nothing else is to be built until these were completed, and any further buildings are to be 'in the same style and manner of architecture' (op. cit. ed. E.-J. Ciprut). Jonas Robelin and Hugues Cosnier were from Paris, Claude Allaire and René Bénard were local masons. The two pairs of entrepreneurs undertook to build one half of the town each. Cosnier was an engineer and

connected with the 1611 plan for the new walls and gates of the 'enceinte des fossés jaunes' in Paris, the extension northwards of the walls of the city (Dumolin, *Etudes de topographie parisienne*, II, p. 116).

1609 *November 16* Contract for 'portes-cochères, doors and window-bays; the portes-cochères are to be '. . . de semblable façon que ceux dans la Place Roialle de Paris . . .', and the window-bays '. . . . de semblable façon à celles de l'Arsenal . . .': (Min. Cent. III 487).

1610 *August 17* Contract with Jonas Robelin and Balthazar Huré for 'les deulx bondes de la chaussée de l'Etang du Vallon du Mansays proche la ville de Henrichemont . . . suivant le mémoire qu'en a été faict et dressé par le Sieur Salomon de Brosse ayant charge de la conduitte des bastiments et ouvrages qui se font en laditte ville . . .' (*Archives de Cher*, E.2313, fol. 169; publ. by Mme Gauchery-Grodecki in 'L'Architecture en Berry sous la règne de Henri IV et au début du XVII siècle', *Union des Soc. savantes de Bourges*, III, 1951/2, p. 90).

1611 *February 5* Two contracts (identical) one passed with Cosnier and Robelin, one with Bénard and Allaire; work is to be undertaken to complete the houses of the Grande Place of Henrichemont. Among other items, 'raccomoder les porteaux . . . et les enrichir et faire des parements par le dehors suivant le dessin qui en a été dressé par le Sieur de Brosse . . .' (op, cit. ed. E.-J. Ciprut, Min. Cent. III 490, transcription).

December 17 and 20 'Procuration pour ... rendre compte des ouvriers de l'enterprise pour la construction de la ville de Henriche-mont' (Min. Cent. III–491; cf. also Mallevoüe, *Les Actes de Sully*, 1600–1610, 1911, p. xix).

1613 *August 26* Inventory of Jonas Robelin, mason, deceased; 'Item ... une grande feuille de papier ... et le plan d'un édifice au dessous lequel plan est un compromis entre ledict deffunt et Charles Cornuat par lequel ledict deffunt et Cornuat se sont soumis au jugement des Sieurs de Brosse et Cosnier touchant le bâtiment duquel il est ques-tion ...'. Another item of the inventory refers to papers concerning Robelin's part in the construction of the arcades under two pavilions of the Place Royale in Paris (cf. contract of 16 November 1609) (Min. Cent. XXXIX–45, communicated by M. Louis-Henri Collard).

1624 *May 24* The entrepreneurs Hugues Cosnier and Alix Boulet, widow of Jonas Robelin, acknowledge receipt of 28,103 livres, 1 sol, part of the sum of 88,103 livres, 1 sol, still due to them from the total of 217,733 livres, 9 sols, which the Duc de Sully had been ordered to pay them by decree of the Parlement of Paris, 2 April 1624 (Actes de Sully, p. xx).

Château of Limours

CHRONOLOGY, SOURCES AND NOTES

The château was engraved by Gomboust for the border of his Plan of Paris, 1652. A small view exists by Chastillon of one of the rear corners, and there is an eighteenth-century view of the entrance-wing before demolition.

1539–1547 The château was built for the Duchesse d'Etampes (*Bull. Soc. Archéologique de Rambouillet*, XII, 1897; re-printing an eighteenth-century history of the château).

1547 Acquired by Diane de Poitiers for whom, sometime before 1561, Philibert de l'Orme designed a ballroom on the upper floor of the entrance-wing (ibid.).

1623 The château bought by Cardinal de Richelieu who commissions de Brosse to put the place in order (ibid. also *Correspondance de Rubens*, ed. Ruelens and Rooses, Antwerp, 1887–1909, III, p. 162; Peiresc to Rubens, 4 May 1623, '... causant un jour avec Monsieur l'Abbé des difficultés que le Cardinal de Richelieu avait fait subir à Monsieur Brosse, et qui cessèrent subitement aussitôt que le Cardinal eut conclu l'achat du comté de Limours où Monsieur Brosse fit plusiers voyages pour fournir les dessins d'une construction à éxécuter par lui dans le château ...').

1626 The château bought by Gaston d'-Orléans (*Bull. Soc. Archéologique de Rambouillet*, XII, 1897).

1651 *October 10* François Mansart working for Gaston d'Orléans at Limours (Dubuisson d'Aubenay, *Journal des Guerres Civiles 1648–52*, ed. G. Saige, 1883–1885; '... à Limours, trouver M. le duc d'Orleans qui y fait bâtir par le Sieur Mansart ...').

1775 The Comtesse de Brienne acquired the château. She subsequently destroyed the entrance-wing with de l'Orme's ballroom. The château was demolished in the nineteenth century. One sixteenth-century pavilion still exists intact, and there are vestiges of the entrance-pavilions across the valley.
Acknowledgment: All material in this entry has been communicated to the author by Dr A. J. Braham and Dr P. Smith.

Château of Montceaux-en-Brie

I ORIGINAL DOCUMENTS

The architectural history of this château is adequately documented despite the loss of all but two minor building-contracts. Neither of these, nor all the sources and chronology given in the catalogue, concern the time when de Brosse worked at Montceaux; but, for a proper understanding of his contribution, it is necessary to be familiar with the building-history of the château from 1547 to 1598.

PARIS, ARCHIVES NATIONALES, MINUTIER CENTRAL

XIX – 291 30 May 1557, Masonry Contract between Ambroise Perret, Robert Danvint, master masons of Paris and Montceaux respectively, and Philibert de l'Orme: construction of a pavilion and grotto in the garden.

XCVI – Répertoire March 1597, Building Contract between Gabrielle d'Estrées, Marquise de Montceaux, and Nicolas Lemercier.

XCVI – Répertoire 1598–1660 n.d. between Gilles Coppeau, Jacob Troublé and Gabrielle d'Estrées. Neither of the two XCVI – Répertoire contracts are in the files.

XXXIV – 13 30 May 1603, *Transport:* Jean Delorme makes over to his son Noël Delorme money due to him on a building at Montceaux ('in the lower garden') contracted for on 14 April 1600, still unfinished.

XXXV – 69 30 June 1614, *Association* of carpenters for work to be done at Montceaux (Document half-destroyed, little legible).

PARIS, ARCHIVES NATIONALES (MAIN ARCHIVES)

Arch.Nat. Série KK – 157 10 January 1596, *Brevet*, Henri IV, 'Lieutenants de la Robe Longue': Order for 10,000 écus, proceeds from tax on salt, to be paid to Mme la Marquise de Montceaux.

Arch.Nat. KK – 157 5 May 1599, Inventory: effects and papers, property of Gabrielle d'Estrées, Duchesse de Beaufort and Marquise de Montceaux, deceased (Published by Fréville, *Bibliothèque de l'Ecole des Chartes*, 1848, III, p. 148–171:).

Arch.Nat. KK – 193 17 June 1605, Deed of Transfer, Château of Montceaux, from César and Henriette de Vendôme, children of Henri IV and Gabrielle d'Estrées, to Marie de Médicis: price 300,000 livres.

Arch.Nat. KK – 107 1601, Papers concerning the acquisition of Montceaux by Marie de Médicis, letters-patent, etc.

Arch.Nat. Série KK – 193, Bâtiments de Marie de Médicis: papers of various dates as listed below.

Arch.Nat. KK – 193 1600 onwards, Letters of Marie de Médicis, some concerning Montceaux (Published in part by L. Batiffol, 'La vie intime d'une Reine de France', Vol. II, and 'Marie de Médicis et les arts', *G.d.B.A.*, XXXIV, p. 448.

Arch.Nat. KK – 193 1615–1620, Accounts of Florent d'Argouges, Treasurer to Marie de Médicis, for work on various buildings at

Montceaux; payments to masons etc., working under the direction of Salomon de Brosse; Sébastien Jacquet, Pierre Fourrault, Antoine Dufourmentel, Etienne Regnault, Gilles Coppeau, Jacob Troublé.

Arch.Nat. Série 01 –1709, Bâtiments Royaux (1621–1783): Maintenance; Letters etc. on the condition of Montceaux and other royal residences addressed to the Contrôleurs des Bâtiments, Lassurance, Gallant and Mollet successively.

Arch.Nat. 01 – 1709, fols. 291–301; *Mémoire* by the Directeur-Général des Bâtiments du Roi: concerning the condition of the buildings at Montceaux in 1783; containing a detailed description of exterior and interior.

PARIS, BIBLIOTHEQUE NATIONALE

B.N.MSS. Fonds Italien – 1746, fol. 162 ff., Despatches of the Venetian Ambassadors to the Court of Henri IV (1 March 1597–28 February 1598).

B.N.MSS. Fonds français 11424; 20 July 1599 and days following; Inventory of effects and papers of Gabrielle d'Estrées, Duchesse de Beaufort and Marquise de Montceaux, deceased: containing 'item ... papers in a casket'; record of payments made for work done on the buildings at Montceaux (1597–1598). Sums received by Du Cerceau (Jacques II), Salomon de Brosse, Rémy Collin, Nicolas Lemercier, Jean (Jehan) Delorme, Jean Taupin, Denis Le Moyne. (Published by Descloseaux, op. cit. below under II).

B.N.MSS. VC Colbert, 4, fol. 175: *Tutelle* of César de Vendôme and of his sister Henriette, 1599.

B.N.MSS. VC Colbert 90, fol. 155r., Salaries and appointments at Montceaux; leases of property in the village by Marie de Médicis.

B.N.MSS. VC Colbert 92, fol. 37v. Receipts for money paid for the building and decoration of Montceaux and for the salaries of those employed at the château ('gaiges d'officiers'), 1601–1610.

B.N.MSS. VC Colbert 87, Letters of Marie de Médicis 1604–1609.

B.N.MSS. VC Colbert 88, Letters of Marie de Médicis 1610–1612. (Published in part by L. Batiffol, op. cit., II.)

B.N.MSS. VC Colbert 92, fol. 114v.; Estimate of money to be paid to workmen to be employed on the buildings at Montceaux in 1612 (32,500 livres). Attached to this is a receipt dated 1612 for money received '. . . tant pour le bâtiment et décoration de nostre maison et château de Montceaux que pour les gaiges d'officiers ... depuis l'année 1601'.

Ibid, fol. 133v.; Estimate, building-work and salaries at Montceaux for 1613 (32,500 livres).

Ibid, fol. 143; Continuation of appointment: '. . . Salomon de Brosse, architecte et conducteur des bastimens ... de Montceaux'. Salary, 1,000 livres.

MELUN, ARCHIVES DEPARTMENTALES DE SEINE ET MARNE

Arch.Dép.134 F 22: Contract, 21 November 1623, Claude Bouthillier (signing for Marie de Médicis) with Nicolas Lemercier, for construction of a pavilion on the S.E. corner of the terrace at Montceaux.

Arch.Dép. G¹ 170, 1793: 'Vente du château de Montceaux comme Bien National'.

U⁶ 64, 1793: Description of the château of Montceaux by Cliquot, architect, preliminary to the above sale.

Various other documents.

VICENZA, MUSEO CIVICO

N.C. 42 Taccuino di Viaggio da Parigi a Venezia: Journal kept by Vincenzo Scamozzi the architect of his journey in 1600 from Paris to Venice with the Venetian ambassadors. Fols 7 and 8 contain a description of Montceaux.

MOSCOW

Original of *Brevet* by Henri IV, issued Paris, 26 June 1605, allocating 360,000 livres for the completion of the purchase of Montceaux, the money to be obtained at the rate of 72,000 per annum for five years through a charge on 'le droit forain et traite domaniale des provinces de Languedoc et Provence'. The Queen is noted as having already been allocated, above this sum, during six years past,

the sum of 216,000 livres, from similar charges, of which not all has been paid. Signed by Henri IV and by Potier ('Conseiller et Secrétaire d'Etat'). (Document communicated to M. Peyrot des Gachons at Montceaux as 'dans les archives de Moscou'; no further reference).

II PUBLISHED SOURCES

Philibert de l'Orme, *Instruction*, 1562–1563, published by A. Berty, *Les Grands Architectes de la Renaissance* as 'Mémoire justificatif de Philibert de l'Orme', Paris, 1860.
V. Scamozzi, *Taccuino di Viaggio da Parigi a Venezia 14 marzo–11 maggio 1600*, ed. Franco Barbieri, Fondazione Cini, Venice, 1959 (cf. above Sec. I).
Sully, *Les économies royales de Henry IV, 1570–1600 et 1601–1606*, ed. Amsterdam, n.d.
L. Huygens, *Journal*, 1665, translated by Henri Brugmans, Châteaux et jardins de l'Ile de France, d'après un journal de 1665, *G.d.B.A.*, XVIII, 1937, p. 103.
Phélypeaux de Pontchartrain, *Mémoires de la Généralité de Paris*, 1669. Ed. Boislisle, *Mémoires pour servir à l'histoire de France*, Série 2, Paris, 1887.
Bruzen de la Martinière, *Grand Dictionnaire Géographique*, 1729.

Dom Toussaint Duplessis, *Histoire de l'Eglise et Diocèse de Meaux*, 1731.
Abbé Expilly, *Dictionnaire Géographique*, 1762–1770.
Sully, *Mémoires*, (translation), London, 1773, from the French edition of l'Ecluse.
Bassompierre, *Journal de ma Vie*, ed. Chanterac, Paris, 1870.
T. Lhuiller, L'ancien château royal de Montceaux-en-Brie, *Mémoires de la Société des Beaux Arts*, 1884, VIII, p. 246, and separately by Plon, Paris, 1885.
L. Batiffol, Marie de Médicis et les arts, *G.d.B.A.*, XXIV, 1905.
L. Batiffol, *La vie intime d'une Reine de France*, Paris, 2 vols., 1931.
A. Descloseaux, *Gabrielle d'Estrées, Duchesse de Beaufort*, Paris, 1931.
R. Coope: The Château of Montceaux-en-Brie, *Journal of the Warburg and Courtauld Institutes*, XXII, 1959.

III PLANS AND ELEVATIONS

Drawings

PARIS, ARCHIVES NATIONALES

Arch.Nat. KK – 193, Plan of the château and forecourt with different floors indicated by flaps. Pen-and-ink: scale to 20 toises: dated 1727. In extremely poor state of preservation.

Displaced, and deposited for a reason and at a date unknown in the Archives du Service d'Architecture at the Château of Fontainebleau.
Arch.Nat. (ex. Arch. des Bâtiments Civils): Versement de l'Architecture, XXIII pièce 158: (i) 'Plan du château, capitainerie, village et parc de Montceaux'. Pen-and-watercolour:

scale in *perches*: inscribed 'Plan du Retz de chausée du Château de Montceaux' and with the names of buildings, woods, areas of the park, etc.; no date or signature; style resembling (iii) and (v).

(ii) 'Plan général du chasteau et des deux parcs de Montceaux'. Pencil, lightly inked in places, colour washes: scale to 20 toises; inscribed with notes on the condition of each area, e.g., 'jeu de longue paulme, à présent pré . . .'; no date or signature.

(iii) 'Plan du retz de chaussée du château de Montceaux'. Pen-and-ink and water-colour: scale to 20 toises; n.d. or signature. Note: this plan resembles in style those attributed to Mathis made in 1739, (cf. Melun, Arch.Déps. U⁶ 64) and may be the missing 'plan d'ensemble' from that set.

(iv) Plan of the château and forecourt, the different floors indicated by flaps; pen-and-ink; inscribed in pencil 'plan de Montceau', and having indications of the state of repair of the fabric, e.g., under the entrance-screen; *tombé*; n.d. or signature (Pl. 39).

(v) 'Plan des caves du château de Montceaux'. Pen-and-ink; n.d. or signature; style resembles that of (iii).

(vi) 'Plan des caves et du Retz de Chaussée de Lavant Cour du château de Montceaux'. To the r. the plan of the cellars, to the l. the ground floor, the latter is marked 'A-B' at its extremities and inscribed 'Plan des caves de laile AB'; ink-and-colourwash; n.d. or signature.

(vii) and (viii) Plans of the first and second floor and of the attics of the forecourt; style resembles that of (v); n.d. or signature.

Note: The *Bâtiments Civils* from whose archives these plans came were the *Bâtiments Royaux* of the ancient régime. The indications on the plans as to the condition (and maintenance?) of the fabric, grounds, etc., suggest that the set was made or collected for Colbert. Cf. *Collection de documents inédits sur l'histoire de France Série III, (Archéologie), I, Comptes de Colbert 1671, p. 546;* 'payé à Louis Vigneux,

le 17 Septembre 1671, pour parfaict paiement de 500 livres à luy ordonnez tant pour avoir levé les plans de Montceaux et d'Anguien (Enghien?) que pour son voyage, 3500 livres . . .': Montceaux, 100 livres'.

PARIS, BIBLIOTHEQUE NATIONALE

B.N.Est. Vᵃ 447. Block-plan of Montceaux. Pen-and-colour wash; dated in contemporary hand 1623, and in much later hand in pencil; 'Montceaux sur le bord de la Seine' (which it is not, but near the Marne). The earliest known plan of the château.

PARIS, LOUVRE

Dessins 33.029. Israel Silvestre. Drawing of the west front at Montceaux seen from the Trilport road beneath the second terrace: (preparatory drawing for the engraving in the series F.254).
Dessins 33.031. Ibid. Drawing of the east front at Montceaux and part of the forecourt: inscribed 'Veue du chasteau de Montceaux': (preparatory drawing for the engraving in the series F.254) (Pls 53, 54, 61). Cf. the note on the Silvestre engravings of Montceaux.

MELUN, ARCHIVES DEPARTMENTALES DE SEINE ET MARNE

U⁶ 64. Set of plans of Montceaux, the main château and the buildings of the forecourt; pen-and-ink with colour; legends and date 1739, in decorative cartouches; scale to 10 toise; attributed to Mathis, architect.
One plan of this series is attached to the 1793 *Description* by Cliquot in this file; it shows the whole property as well as the buildings. The remainder have been displaced and deposited at a date and for a reason unknown in the Archives du Service d'Architecture at the Château of Fontainebleau. The drawings at Fontainebleau are:
(i) Four plans of the main château: (a) cellars (b) first floor (c) second floor (d) attics.

(ii) Three plans of the executed wings of the forecourt: (a) cellars (b) first floor (c) third floor and attics.

All these 1739 plans were seen by the author and were in a good state of preservation in 1959.

MONTCEAUX, COLLECTION LEFOL

Two sheets of measured drawings of the surviving parts of the château, made in the nineteenth century; signed Lefol, and dated 1883. This M. Lefol was an architect residing at Montceaux, as is the present owner of the drawings, his grandson.

LONDON, ROYAL INSTITUTE OF BRITISH ARCHITECTS

Album of Jacques Genthilhâtre, mason-architect (b. 1578). This album or 'pattern-book' contains twelve certain drawings connected with Montceaux and several others which appear to be so. Most of the drawings were probably made, not from the building itself, but from projects for it made between 1597 and 1599. For Gentilhâtre, cf. R. Coope, op cit. *Journal of the Warburg and Courtauld Institutes*, 1959. The folio nos. and titles of Gentilhâtre's Montceaux drawings are:

20v. Staircase pavilion, principal *corps-de-logis*.
22r. Dome over the above pavilion.
39r. S.E. angle-pavilion and part of the screen (Pl. 42).
81r. Door of the N.E. moat-pavilion (Pl. 57).
83v. ?Dormer ?screen-opening, unidentifiable though inscribed 'Monceau'.
98r. Window from one of the moat-pavilions.
100r. Dormer-window: ?principal *corps-de-logis*.
100v. Detail of sculptured panel-decoration, moat-pavilions.
101r. Whole of the same panel.
106v. Lucarne.
142r. Chimney-piece (inscribed 'monceau' in later hand).

143r. Profile of chimney-piece, inscribed 'Montceaux' in later hand.
Drawings probably connected with Montceaux: folios 38r. 123r. 143r., and 144v.

WARSAW, MUSEUM NARODOWE

T 174 Inv.325 J. Rigaud, 'Vue du château Royal de Montceaux du Coté du village'; preparatory drawing for the engraving.
T 174 Inv.326 ibid., 'Vue du château de Montceaux du coté de la campagne'; (view from the forecourt to the east front); preparatory drawing for the engraving.

VICENZA, MUSEO CIVICO

N.C.42 Journal by Vincenzo Scamozzi (cf. above, Sec. II), fol. 5: a drawing, 'Castello di Monsiau', showing the east façade and the north wing in 1600.

Engravings

Israel Silvestre: (F.254: 1–4).
i. Bird's-eye-view of the château and forecourt.
ii. View of the château, east front (cf. drawings).
iii. View of the château, west front, and terrace (cf. above, Sec. II).
iv. View of the north front across the park.
Notes: Payments are recorded to Silvestre as follows (*Comptes de Colbert*, op. cit.): '30 Octobre 1769 à Silvestre pour deux planches qu'il a gravées l'une représentant le jardin de Diane à Fontainebleau et l'autre le jardin de Montceaux, 1000 livres ... 28 avril 1680 à Silvestre, autre graveur, pour deux planches qu'il a gravées représentant la vüe de Monceaux et l'autre du marais dans le petit parc. 1000 livres'.
Perelle, published by Mariette: View of Montceaux, forecourt and east front. Based on Silvestre?
J. Rigaud: i View of the east front.
ii. View of the south front (cf. above, under Drawings) (Pl. 55).

IV CHRONOLOGY AND NOTES

1547 Catherine de Médicis purchases the domain of Montceaux from Jean de la Guette and Marie Saligot his wife, daughter and heiress of Arthur de Saligot, Seigneur of Montretout and Montceaux (Lhuiller, L'ancien château royal de Montceaux-en-Brie'. p. 246).
The old manor-house demolished and the new château begun (Phélypeaux *Mém. de la Généralité de Paris*, I, p. 385).

1557 *May 30* Contract between the masons Ambroise Perret and Robert Danvint, and Philibert de l'Orme for the building of a garden-pavilion and grotto to de l'Orme's design (Min. Cent. XIX–291).

1558 Catherine in residence at Montceaux: 'Compte de Claude de Baune, Dame de la Royne ... ayant garde de ses coffres', publ. by M. H. de la Ferrière ('Introduction aux lettres de Catherine de Médicis' (*Coll. de docs. inédits sur l'Hist. de France*), quoted by Lhuiller, op. cit.).

1562–1563 Philibert de l'Orme refers to work done by him at Montceaux: '... à monsseau pour la Royne mère qui est la cause que je trouvay l'invention de charpenterye pour le jeu de paille-maille qu'elle vouloyt faire couvrir, là ou j'avoys dressé tant de belles inventions' (De l'Orme, *Instruction*, cf. Coope, *The Château of Montceaux-en-Brie*, p. 75 and notes 20, 21).

1562 onwards The court frequently in residence at Montceaux, indicating that some of the buildings were completed ('Notice sur un compte de l'écurie de la reine Catherine de Médicis', C. de Beaurepaire in *Précis analytique des travaux de l'Académie des Sciences, Belles-Lettres et Arts de Rouen*, 1879–1880).

1566 Publication of J. A. Androuet du Cerceau's *Livre de Grotesques* in which he says some of his examples of interior decoration are taken from Montceaux.

1589 Death of Catherine de Médicis. Montceaux held by her creditors.

1594 Henri IV negotiates with Catherine's creditors for the purchase of Montceaux for his mistress, Gabrielle d'Estrées, already installed at the château (Coope, op. cit. p. 72). The purchase was not completed until 1597.

1595 Letter of Marguerite de Valois to Henri IV referring to Gabrielle as 'Madame la Marquise de Montceaux'. (Coope, op. cit., p. 72, n. 5).

1596 *January 10* *Brevet* of Henri IV apportioning money from the levy on salt to be used for the building at Montceaux (Arch. Nat. KK–157, publ. Descloseaux, 'Gabrielle d'Estrées, Duchesse de Beaufort'). The details of the *brevet* appear in the inventory of Gabrielle's papers, made after her death: '... item; ung brevet du Xe janvier IIII^{xx} XVI signé Henry ... par lequel sa Majesté a accordé à madicte dame la somme de X^m esdus à prandre sur les deniers qui proviendront des lieutenants de robbe longue en tous les greniers à sel de son royaume ... et ordonne que tous les deniers ... soyent affectez pour les bastiments sans qu'ils puissent estre divertis ny employez ailleurs ...'.

1597 *March* Building contract between Nicolas Lemercier and Gabrielle d'Estrées (Min. Cent. Répertoire XCVI).

July First recorded payment for work on Henri IV's buildings at Montceaux, made to Nicolas Lemercier, 'entrepreneur de l'un des bastiments dudict Monceaux' (Arch. Nat. KK–157; Descloseaux, op. cit., p. 364; and Coope, op. cit., p. 78).

November Letter from the Venetian Ambassador to the Doge and Council, containing a reference to the start of building operations at Montceaux (*B.N.MSS. fonds Italien*, 1746, f. 162: and Coope, op. cit., o. 78) '... da questo si passo in altri propositi, come di

fabbriche, della quale mostra dilettarsi gran-
damente la Majestà Sua; e sapendo che si
compiace molto quella di monsèo, gia
principiata dalla Regina Madre e che hora si
continua, se ben con diversa architettura,
della quale è padrona Madama di Beaufort.
Il re ne riceve gusto, interrogandomi sopra i
particolari delli quali ne diedi quel conto che
bisognava, havendola veduto . . .'.

1598 *April* Payments made (for services unspecified) to 'M. du Cerceau' and Salomon de
Brosse; also for building to masons Rémy
Collin and Jehan de l'Orme, 'autres maçons
entrepreneurs des bastiments dudict Monceaux' (Arch. Nat. KK–157, d'Estrées' Inventory, cf. above, July 1597).

October A ballet danced before the King at
Montceaux by nobles and gentlemen from
Paris who are accommodated at Meaux, 'le
château n'étant guère logeable à ce temps
la . . .' (Bassompierre, *Journal de ma vie*,
p. 60 ff).

1599 *March 19* Contract between Etienne
Regnault, *maître couvreur*, and Gabrielle
d'Estrées for work on the roofs at Montceaux
(*Catalogue de la vente d'autographes faite par M.
Eugène Charavay*, 14 avril 1886, quoted by
Lhuiller, op. cit).

April 10 Death of Gabrielle d'Estrées in
Paris.

1600 *April 14* Contract passed for work on a
building in the lower garden at Montceaux,
between the Sieur Dubois, representing
Marie de Médicis and Jehan Delorme (Min.
Cent. XXIV–13, *Transport* of 30 May 1603
referring back to the original document).

March 18 Scamozzi visits and sketches
Montceaux during his journey with the
Venetian ambassadors: '. . . giognessimo a
Monsiau castello di Sua Maestà, e co' molte
fabriche fatte da nuovo ad instanza di
Madama la duchessa di Belfor: del quale ne è
il disegno passato; dove smontassimo e lo
vedessimo assai commodamente. La parte di

mezo contiene le scale in duoi rami come
ordinario della maggior parte delle magliore
case di Francia; a destra e sinistra duoi salotti
di tre fenestre, e poi una bella stanza; ma su
gli anguli una stanza, e picciolo camaretto,
che dicono gabinetto, co' scale secrete a
bando da un lato e una lunga galleria de piedi
120, larga p. 17 e alta 15, con 12 finestre o
lumi. D'intorno è una larga strada e negli
estremi due rottonde assai ornate; più abasso
sono i giardini molto lunghi e larghi; nella
quale altezza sono tutto oltre officine e
luoghi da servizio involto. Questa fabbricha
ha assai del buono e meglio sarebbe se non
havesse una picciola entrata, e due finestre da
lati assai ristrette'. *Taccuino di Viaggio* . . .
pp. 41, 42.

1601 Henri IV presents Montceaux to the
Queen: Sully *Mémoires*, II, p. 393: 'The King
made a promise to the Queen that, if she
brought him a son, he would present her with
the castle of Montceaux, "my wife", said he
in a letter to me, "has gained Montceaux by
giving me a son; therefore I desire you will
send for the President Forget, to confer with
him about this affair and take his advice concerning the security that must be given to my
children for the sum which I pay for Montceaux".' (Arch. Nat. KK–107, fol. 65).

1602 Building-work continuing at Montceaux: Sully, op. cit. III, p. 60: 'Henry was
detained a little time at Montceaux by a
fever occasioned by a cold he got in walking
late in the evening to see his masons at
work . . .'.

1605 *June 26* The King gives Marie de
Médicis 360,000 livres for the purchase of
Montceaux from his children by Gabrielle,
César and Henriette de Vendôme: Moscow,
Archives (cf. Cat, Sect. I): '. . . Le Roy . . .
désirant que la Royne acquire et fait achapt
de la maison, terre et seigneurie de Montceaux . . . sa Majesté a donné, accordé et
octroyé à ladicte dame la somme de trois cens
soixante mil livres a quoy se trouve monter

durant cinque années le tirement et surenchère de soixte. et douze mil livres par chacun an mis sur la ferme du droit forain et traite domaniale des provinces de Languedoc et Provence ...' (from the copy-document in the possession of M. Bernard Peyrot des Gachons). This gives the details of the solution found by Sully and Président Forget to the problem of how to raise the money: cf. above 1601. It is less than that recorded in the deed of acquisition (Arch. Nat. KK–107, f. 65).

1608 A further sum given by Henri for the buildings at Montceaux. Difficulties over the payment of the workmen by the mason-in-charge: Sully, op. cit., IV, p. 166 ff.: '... The Queen was delivered of her third son on the 26th of April ... the King ... allowed, at the request of this princess, that ten or twelve thousand crowns should be expended on buildings at Montceaux and sent me orders to that purpose. It is from these letters of his majesty that I collect these circumstances. This order he repeated when the Master-Builder, who had undertaken the work, informed him that he had been obliged, through want of money, to dismiss his men. I had given him an assignment upon a restitution of money to be paid by the nephew of Argouges, which he had not yet done. ... The King sent me orders to press him for payment and to advance the Master Builder the money out of other funds'. Sully added later (p. 292) that in this year 'some new embellishments were made at Fontaine-bleau and Montceaux'. The Master-Builder referred to may be de Brosse (Cf. below September 1608).

September 17 Marie de Médicis confirms Guillaume Condren de Boys, Superintendent of the château since 1599, in his post and, continuing the building programme at Montceaux, leases accommodation for her retinue in the village (B.N.MSS. VC Colbert 90, f. 155r).

Salomon de Brosse referred to by Marie de Médicis as being in charge of her buildings at Montceaux: B.N.MSS. VC Colbert 87, f. 284, letter to M. de Verdilly: 'M. de Verdilly, le Roy Monseigneur a fait expédier à Salomon de Brosse mon architect son (...?) pour la jouissance des privilèges attribuez à ses officiers et aux miens ... acquise de sa charge en mes bastimens de Monceaulx ... puisqu'il est à moy employé sur la roolle de mes officiers servans à Monceaulx continuellement occupé à mon service ...'.

1609 Marie de Médicis appoints a concierge, Claude Lemasson, for 'la grande basse-cour qui se construit à présent audict Monceaulx' (B.N.MSS, VC Colbert 90, f. 156r).

1610 Marie de Médicis to Marguerite de Valois: '... Vous trouverez à Monceaux tant de changements depuis que vous n'y êtes venue que vous ne le recognoistrez plus' (Quoted by L. Batiffol, *Marie de Médicis et les arts*).

October Louis XIII stays at Montceaux on the way to his coronation at Rheims. He hears Mass in 'la chapelle de la Galerie', and in the gallery also 'joue a la paulme' (B.N. MSS, fonds français (anciens) 4023–4027. Hérouard, *Histoire Particulière de Louis XIII*).

1611 Marie de Médicis sends to Rouen for twelve columns to decorate the altar of a new chapel at Montceaux (B.N.MSS, VC Colbert 90, f. 193v). There were, eventually, three chapels at Montceaux, one in the entrance-pavilion, one in the south range of the forecourt and one in the east range of the forecourt. The columns were most probably intended for the first (Coope, op. cit., p. 84 and n. 59).

1615 First year of the accounts kept by the Queen's treasurer, Florent d'Argouges, of sums spent during five years on the buildings at Montceaux, continued under the general direction of Salomon de Brosse. De Brosse specifically mentioned in the 1615 accounts as the designer of the *jeu-de-paume* (Arch. Nat. KK–193; Coope, op. cit., p. 81 and n. 45).

1616 *August 10* Louis XIII signs a *Brevet* granting 72,000 livres to his mother for work at Montceaux. (Arch. Nat. KK–193). This was no doubt already promised before the building programme was speeded up in 1615, when d'Argouges began his five-year account.

1617 *July* Particular mention in d'Argouges' accounts of work on the completion of the interior of the entrance-pavilion (Arch. Nat. KK–193).

December 22 Appointment of Bassompierre as superintendent at Montceaux; he is required to act as overseer for 'all embellishments and enlargements' to the château (B.N.MSS. VC Colbert 90 f. 104*r*). This seems to indicate that de Brosse, busy at the Luxembourg, could no longer supervise the work at Montceaux.

1618 The chapel in the entrance-pavilion referred to as 'la chapelle neufve du château' (Arch. Nat. KK–193).

September 23 The Turkish ambassador entertained at Montceaux (*Discours sur le sujet de l'ambassade du Grand Turc*, Paris, seventeenth century. Anon, n.d.).

1619 *November 5* Louis XIII and Marie de Médicis at Montceaux for ten days (Bassompierre, op. cit.; Arch. Nat. KK–193).

1623 *November 21* Contract between Nicolas Lemercier and the Queen-Mother to build a pavilion on the S.E. corner of the moat (Melun, Arch. Dép. 134 F22). Lemercier is instructed to follow exactly the style of the other moat-pavilions, designed for Henri IV in *c.* 1597.

Note: This is the last date of any importance in the building history of Montceaux. Although work there continued, it became more and more a matter of repair and maintenance. Lemercier's pavilion was the last new building of note undertaken, and it was never completed.

1642 Death of Marie de Médicis in exile. Reversion of Montceaux and its land to the Crown.

1783 Louis XVI gives Montceaux to the Prince de Conti. Conversion of one moat-pavilion (N.E.) into a hunting-lodge, the 'pavillon Conti' (Coope, op. cit., p. 72).

1793 Confiscation of all the Prince's property (ibid.).

1793–4 Almost total demolition of the main château. The Pavillon Conti, the S.E. moat-pavilion and the S. range of the forecourt survive.

Orléans, Cathedral of Sainte Croix

I   ORIGINAL DOCUMENTS

The original documents concerning de Brosse's connection with Orléans Cathedral (covering the restoration after the Wars of Religion and the building of the transept façades) are lost – destroyed in World War II. Copies of them were, however, made by Chanoine Chénesseau before he published his history of the Cathedral in 1921.

Although de Brosse was not finally responsible for the transept façades, the chronology of his negotiations with the Cathedral authorities is given here as being of interest both in his career and in connection with the activities of his immediate followers.

ORLEANS, ARCHIVES DEPARTMENTALES DU LOIRET

J.206, *Extraits de la Série C des archives du Loiret relatives à la Cathédrale:* copies by Chénesseau (15 notebooks).

II   PUBLISHED SOURCES

A. Chénesseau, *Sainte-Croix d'Orléans,* Orléans, 1921.

E.-J. Ciprut, 'Notes sur un grand architecte parisien, Jean Androuet du Cerceau', *Bull. Soc. Hist. Prot. Fr.,* CXIII, April–June 1967, pp. 149 ff.

III   PLANS AND ELEVATIONS

De Brosse's projects are all lost, and were so when Chénesseau published his history in 1921. Then surviving, but now destroyed, were two drawings: a project (elevation) for the transept façades, and a plan for the same (not corresponding to the elevation). On the verso of the elevation appeared the signatures Paul de Brosse, Jean Androuet du Cerceau, Charles du Ry, and the date 8 December 1625: Photos; Arch du Loiret, Série V 433; Repro. Chénesseau, op. cit., figs 61, 62; and Ciprut, op. cit., fig. 1.

IV CHRONOLOGY

Based on the lost documents in the Arch. du Loiret, Série C, as published by Chénesseau. The dates given are those of the *Ordonnances* and *Déliberations* of the Cathedral authorities, which do not in every case quote the exact date of the events they refer to.

1618 *August 4* De Brosse, 'one of the best experts in Paris', is consulted about the key-stones of the choir-vaults. He visits Orléans and submits drawings (C.419 and C.465).

1621 *March 15* De Brosse sends drawings for the exterior parapets of the choir and for 'les hautes dalles' (C.420).
Etienne Martellange submits a drawing for the transept façades: ibid. This is not approved, and the authorities direct that de Brosse be consulted (ibid.). A letter is sent to 'Le Sieur du Boys, Conseiller du Roy, trésorier général de France en la généralité d'Orléans ... "Monsieur, nous fault eslever les deux portaulx de l'Eglise Ste. Croix et pour cet effect nous fault l'advis et le desseing des meilleurs architectes de France car ici nous en manquons, nous vous prions de veoir Monsieur Brosse, et sçavoir de luy si'il ne passe poinct en ces quartiers dans peu de temps pour quelque aultre subjet, et en ce cas qu'il y passe le prier de nous veoir et nous donner son desseing. S'il n'a point d'occasion qui le puisse faire passer par icy, traicter avec luy quand il y poura venir exprès, et ce qu'il luy fauldra, c'est ce dont nous vous prions".' (ibid.).

1625 *February 20* De Brosse having done nothing, Théodore Lefebvre, 'grand voyer de la généralité d'Orléans', is paid 30 livres, as 'maistre architecte' for making a drawing for the 'façade de la grande croisée' (C.421).

March 14 Lefebvre's design proves unacceptable; it is decided to appeal again to de Brosse, and a letter is sent to du Boys in Paris (C.474) '... nous vous supplions de veoir Monsieur de Brosse et prendre de luy

le temps et la commodité pour venir jusques en ceste ville, ce que nous souhaittons au plustost. ... Vous sçaurez s'il vous plaist, de luy, la despense de son voyage, à laquelle il nous faudroit resoudre et s'il desireoit loger en quelque maison particulière ou aultrement'.

July 18 De Brosse having promised to come to Orléans fails to do so, 'incommodé et destenu au lict de ses gouttes'. Time pressing ('la saison se passe'), the Cathedral authorities decide to address themselves elsewhere (C.387). They send a letter to M. du Boys: '... Nous ne pouvons pas nous promettre de veoir icy Monsr. de Brosse, pour sa grande incommodité. Ce qui nous a fait resoudre de faire eslection de quelques aultres architectes qui puissent vacquer à notre desseing, raison pourquoy nous vous supplions de veoir Mr du Cerceau architecte et allié dud. de Brosse lequel on nous a dict estre fort recherché pour sa capacité et le resoudre à faire un voyage jusques icy; que s'il estoit aussy incommodé de quelque maladie vous verriez le sieur Brosse filz aux memes fins'. (ibid.).

August 6–8 Jean du Cerceau having replied immediately, arrives in Orléans on 6 August 'en compagnie de son cousin le Sieur de Brosse filz'. They take measurements and promise that one of them will bring drawings to Orléans in one month (C.387).

November 26 Neither of the architects having re-appeared, and no drawing having been received, the authorities call in experts to consult with du Cerceau or de Brosse; these experts are still waiting in Orléans (C. 474).

December 4–8 Jean du Cerceau and Paul de Brosse arrive in Orléans. They present a project which is not accepted. They prepare another 'sur le champ' and submit it then and there: C.387. The plan of the rejected design and the elevation of the second design are those which had been photographed before their destruction (Cf. Sec. II).

1626 *March 26* The collected projects of various architects (Lefebvre, Johannet, Martellange and the two designs by du Cerceau, Paul de Brosse and du Ry) are sent to de Brosse in Paris 'dans une boiste de fer blanche' (C.421).

April 23 The white tin box arrives back from Paris with de Brosse's unfavourable comments on the submitted designs and three drawings of his own: C.421. Finally, the authorities, strongly recommended thereto by Lemercier, choose the Gothic design by Martellange.

Paris, Hôtel Bénigne Bernard

Rue Coquillière

I ORIGINAL DOCUMENTS

The work done by de Brosse on this small town-house is well-documented; the documents would be even more valuable if we had some visual record of its appearance. Unfortunately none exists, except for the engraving of the door discussed in the text, Chap. IV, pp. 66-67.

PARIS, ARCHIVES NATIONALES,
MINUTIER CENTRAL

XXIV – 249 25 February 1614: masonry contract between Salomon de Brosse (signing as contractor) and Bénigne Bernard; for the enlargement of the *corps-de-logis*, new staircase, new entrance and other work.

XXIV–2543 October 1615 *Quittance:* de Brosse to Bénigne Bernard for payment for the above.

XXIV – 276 15 January 1618 *Quittance:* de Brosse to Bénigne Bernard for payment on a masonry contract (lost) of 17 May 1616 for extensions.

PARIS, ARCHIVES NATIONALES
(MAIN ARCHIVES)

Arch.Nat. K.576, Papiers de la Maison Savoie-Carignan: 5 October 1605; sale-contract of a house in the Rue de Grenelle-Saint-Honoré, mentioning the position of 'la maison de Mr Bénigne Bernard'.

Arch.Nat. S★ 1263, 1623, Censier de l'Archevêché: the hôtel recorded as the property of the widow of Bénigne Bernard.

Arch.Nat. Q¹★ 10995, Terrier du Roy, *c.* 1700, fol. 180 *verso:* Rue du Bouloi; site of Hôtel Benigne Bernard makes nos. 14 and 15; property of the Duchesse de Verneuil.

Ibid. Fol. 141: Rue Coquillière; (corner of the Rue Coquillière and Rue du Bouloi); no. 41 ('maison à porte-cochère') property of the Duchesse de Verneuil; nos. 39 and 40 are shops let by Mme. de Verneuil.

Arch.Nat. N.IV Seine 64, 1786, Rittman, Censive de l'Archevêché de Paris, fol. 23: Rue du Bouloi; Hôtel des Fermes (ex-Séguier) of which the Hôtel Bénigne Bernard now part.

Note: Further documents exist which have been verbally communicated to me; viz., Sale Contract, including the Hôtel Bénigne Bernard as part of a property purchased by Pierre Séguier, Chancellor of France; and *expertise* (valuation) dated 1639, of the Hôtel Séguier of which the Hôtel Bénigne Bernard forms part (with plan). No references were, however included in this information.

II PUBLISHED SOURCES

P. Le Muet, *Reigles des Cinq Ordres d'Architecture de Vignole*; *revues augmentées et reduites de grand en petit par Le Muet*, Paris, 1632, chez Melchior Tavernier; (called *Le Vignole Français*).

H. Sauval, *Histoire et recherches des antiquités de la ville de Paris*, 1724.

M. Dumolin, *Etudes de topographie parisienne*, Paris, 1929–1931.

E.-J. Ciprut, (Text of the *Quittance* of 15 January 1618), *B.S.H.A.F.*, 1955, p. 20.

J.-P. Babelon, *Demeures parisiennes sous Henri IV et Louis XIII*, Paris, 1965.

III PLANS AND ELEVATIONS

Drawings

PARIS, ARCHIVES NATIONALES

Arch.Nat. Q^{1*} 10995 fol. 137: block-plan of the site of the hôtel in *c.* 1700; Nos. 39, 40 and 41, Rue Coquillière, forming corner of the Rue du Bouloi.

Arch.Nat. N.IV Seine 164, fol. 23: block-plan of the Hôtel des Fermes (ex-Séguier) into which is incorporated No. 10 bis Rue Coquillière (ex-Hôtel Bénigne Bernard?).

Arch.Nat. F^{31} 80, Atlas Cadastral de Paris (1815–1850), Quartier de la Banque de

France, îlots Nos. 8 and 9: Rue du Bouloi. *Note:* To these can be added the plan mentioned above in Sec. I, dated 1639.

Engravings

P. Le Muet, Fig. XXXVII, p. 75; door (Vignola XXXIIII with pediment added), identifiable as the *porte-cochère* of the Hôtel Bénigne-Bernard (Pl. 83).

M.-E. Turgot, 'Plan de Paris', section 14 Place des Victoires et ses environs (Pl. 73).

IV CHRONOLOGY AND NOTES

1605 *October 5* Bénigne Bernard in possession of a house on the corner of the Rue Coquillière and the Rue du Bouloi (Arch. Nat. K.576. See F. Hamon 'L'hôtel de Hervart ...' *Revue de l'art*, 6, 1969, p. 80, n.4).

1614 *February 25* De Brosse, as architect and contractor, signs a contract with Bénigne Bernard, 'conseiller et maistre d'hôtel ordinaire du Roy, baron de Bones (Beaune) Sergues, des Mesmes et d'autres Lieux, demeurant à Paris, rue Coquillière ...', for the enlargement of Bernard's town-house already existing in the Rue Coquillière (Min. Cent. XXIV–249) 'Premièrement fault fouillir les tranchées et rigolles pō les fondãons d'ung alongement du corps-de-logis

quil convient fã attenant et aboutissant le grand corps-de-logis à pñt levé ... plus sera faict ung escalier dans le grand logis au lieu porté par le dessaing ... (et) pour l'entrée de la cour audict escallier se fera une alonge audict logis, de quelques quatre pieds ou environ ... dans lequel espace se fera ladicte porte ....'.

1615 *October 3* De Brosse is paid for the above work the sum of 16,000 livres (Min. Cent. XXIV–254).

1616 *May 17* Further contract for building at the hôtel ('ung petit logis ... bâti de neuf') next to the principal *corps-de-logis* (Min. Cent. XXIV–276 refers back to this contract).

1618 *January 15* De Brosse paid for the

above work the sum 7,000 livres (Min. Cent. XXIV–276).

1623 The hôtel in the possession of Anne Courtin, widow of Bénigne Bernard (Arch. Nat. S★ 1263).

1634 Pierre Séguier purchases the Hôtel de Bellegarde (formerly de Soissons), Rue du Bouloi (J.-P. Babelon, *Demeures parisiennes*, p. 272, under Rue J.-J. Rousseau, formerly Rue de Grenelle).

1639 By this date the Hôtel Bénigne Bernard appears to have become part of the Hôtel Séguier (Note below Sec. I).

1640 Sauval refers to 'La Maison de Nicolas de Mouy de Riberpré Marquis de Beauve, qui fait partie maintenant de l'Hôtel Séguier'. At this period and onwards, this hôtel, though separately occupied, belongs to the Hôtel Séguier.

1700 The hôtel is owned at this period by the Duchesse de Verneuil (Arch. Nat. Q¹★ 10995, fol. 180*v*.): where it is listed as 'appartenant à la Dame duchesse de Verneuil'. The adjoining Hôtel Séguier has become the Hôtel des Fermes (i.e. Hôtel des Fermiers Généraux, tax collectors).

Paris, Hôtel de Bouillon

(later de Liancourt), Rue de Seine

I ORIGINAL DOCUMENTS

Documents for de Brosse's work at the Hôtel de Bouillon are scarce. The buildings which were begun in 1635 for Roger du Plessis, Marquis and later Duc de Liancourt, are much more fully documented and are useful in identifying the earlier work. A list of the successive owners of the Hôtel de Bouillon (Liancourt) is given in *The Private Houses of Louis Le Vau* by Constance Tooth (thesis in the University of London, 1961).

PARIS, ARCHIVES NATIONALES, MINUTIER CENTRAL

XXIV – 245, 1 September 1612: Masonry Contract between Salomon de Brosse (signing as contractor) and Henri de Latour d'Auvergne, Duc de Bouillon, for the enlargement of the Hôtel de Bouillon, Rue de Seine.

XCVIII – 118, 11 April 1635: Masonry Contract between Frémin de Cotte and Roger du Plessis, Marquis de Liancourt, for demolition, rebuildings and enlargements at the Hôtel de Liancourt (formerly Bouillon).

XCVIII – 119, 13 July 1635: Masonry Contract, superseding that of 11 April, for more extensive changes in the building.

XLIII – 20, 10 December 1636: *Transaction* between Jeanne de Schomberg, wife of Roger du Plessis, and Frémin de Cotte, mason; settlement of a dispute over the contract of July 1635, to be negotiated between Louis Donon (for Jeanne de Schomberg) and Claude Monnard (for Frémin de Cotte), whose findings shall be judged by 'le Sieur Le Mercier architecte des bâtiments du Roi'.

XCVIII – 125, 2 May and 29 June 1637: Contracts for the construction of an aviary.

Note: E.-J. Ciprut, *Bull. Soc. Hist. Prot. Fr.*, 1964, November–December, p. 264, n. 39, states that on 17 June 1639, 'Robert Chuppin, maître charpentier, s'engageait à faire 'les ouvrages de charpenterie à l'hôtel de Mgr. Roger Duplessis, Marquis de Liancourt, sis à Paris à Sainct Germain des Prez suivant les plantz, desseings et marché faict avec le Sieur-Petit, mre. masson'. (No Min. Cent. reference is given).

II PUBLISHED SOURCES

C. Malingre, *Antiquités de Paris*, 1640.

J. Evelyn, *Diary*, ed. de Beer, 1955.

Tallement des Réaux, *Historiettes*, 1659–1662, ed. Monmerque, Paris, 1862.

Berty and Tisserand, *Topographie historique du vieux Paris*, 1866–1897.

C. Read, 'Salomon de Brosse, l'architecte d'Henri IV et de Marie de Médicis', Paris, 1881 (off-print of *Mem. Soc. Ant. Fr.*, XLI).

J. Guiffrey, 'La famille de Salomon de Brosse ... quelques mots de réponse à MM. Read

et Tisserand', *Bull. de la Soc. de l'hist. de Paris et de l'Ile de France*, 1882.

J.-P. Babelon, 'Documents inédits concernant Salomon de Brosse', *B.S.H.A.F.*, 1962.

—— *Demeures parisiennes sous Henri IV et Louis XIII*, Paris, 1965.

III   PLANS AND ELEVATIONS

Drawings

PARIS, ARCHIVES NATIONALES

Arch.Nat. F³¹ 78, Atlas Cadastral, 1815–1855, 10e arrondissement, Quartier de la Monnaie, Ilôt 7: a detailed plan which makes an interesting comparison with that of Marot, as it shows the hôtel with the exact interior disposition of that date, considerably varying from Marot's version.

Engravings

François Joannis: View of Paris showing the Louvre and Tuileries and the quarter on the opposite bank of the Seine; The garden-front of the Hôtel de Bouillon, as built by de Brosse is shown fairly clearly, with its two flanking pavilions. Signed and dated 1619.

J. Marot: *Petit Marot*, contains several plates of the Hôtel de Liancourt engraved *c.* 1640–1643:

i. 'Plan du rez de chaussée de l'Hostel de Liancourt Au faux-bourg St Germain à la rue de Seine'.

ii. 'Profil du dedans de la cour et du petit Jardin de l'Hostel de Liancourt' (Pl. 79).

iii. 'Profil du costé de la cour de l'Hostel de Liancourt' (Pl. 80).

iv. 'Elevãon de l'Hostel de Liancourt du costé qui regarde le Jardin' (Pl. 78).

v. 'Les mesures en grands volumes de l'Hostel de Liancourt'.

Note: A further plate, not in the *Petit Marot*, shows the street-front and bears the inscription: 'Veüe et Perspective de l'Hostel de Liancourt lors qu'il sera parachevé, du dessin de Mr Lemercier, architecte du Roy. Dessiné et gravé par J. Marot (chez Mariette)'. This is included in Mariette's 1727 edition of the *Grand Marot* (as vol. IV of his *Architecture Française*).

J. Gomboust: Plan of Paris, 1652; perspective view. Gomboust's representation of the Hôtel de Liancourt is one of his few major inaccuracies, and it bears little relation to the form the hôtel is known to have had at this date.

I. Silvestre: series of small engravings of the garden-front and the gardens of the hôtel:

i. 'Veüe de l'Hostel de Liancourt à Paris' (F.230–1).

ii. 'Veüe de l'Hostel de Liancourt du costé du Jardin à Paris' (F.230–2).

Abbé Delagrive: Plan of Paris, 1729; block-plan of the hôtel (Pl. 76).

Abbé Delagrive: 'Plan, Paris en 6 Quartiers', 1744; block-plan of the hôtel.

M.-E. Turgot: Plan of Paris, n.d. (before 1751); perspective view.

IV   CHRONOLOGY AND NOTES

1586 Two buildings on the site later occupied by the Hôtel de Bouillon united by the Duc de Montpensier into one house, named the Hôtel Dauphin (C. Tooth, Thesis cit.)

1610 Henri de Latour d'Auvergne, Duc de Bouillon, Prince de Sedan, buys the Hôtel Dauphin (ibid.).

1612 *September 1* Contract signed by Salomon de Brosse for the enlargement of the hôtel (Min. Cent. XXIV–245, publ. J.-P. Babelon, *B.S.H.A.F.*, 1962).

1613 *February 12* 'Mémoire des travaux de maçonnerie executés dans l'hôtel de Bouillon et verifié par Salomon de Brosse'; price of the work 868 livres, 14 sols, 6 deniers, and the work classed as 'travaux sans importance' (Pannier, p. 46 and n.1: *Catalogue de vente du libraire Dufossé, rue de Guénégaud*, March 1882; J.-P. Babelon, op. cit., who classes this as a quittance (original lost); cf. Guiffrey, *Bull. d'hist. de Paris*, 1882, p. 105).

February 28 Quittance, Salomon de Brosse to the Duc de Bouillon for work done at the hôtel (Pannier, J.-P. Babelon, op. cit.: Papiers C. Read); 'Je soubsigné, confesse avoir reçu de Mgr maréchal de Bouillon la somme de trois mille livres tournois par les mains du sieur Gérémie sur et tant moins des ouvraiges faits et à faire par moy marchandé pour le bâtiment que mondit seigneur fait faire en son hostel du fauxbourg Saint-Germain des Prés à Paris laquelle somme de trois mille livres je me tiens pour content et promets tenir conte sur lesdits ouvrages. Fait ce dernier jour de février mil six cens treize, de Brosse' (transcr. Pannier, p. 46; original lost).

June 28 Quittance, Salomon de Brosse to the Duc de Bouillon for the sum received for work on the hôtel (Pannier, J.-P. Babelon, op. cit.: Berty, *Topographie historique de Paris, le bourg Saint Germain*, p. 239, n. 2 (using notes by Charles Read): 'Sallomon de Brosse, architecte du roy et de la royne, demeurant rue des vieilz Augustins confesse avoir eu et reçu comptant de Monsiegneur le duc de Bouillon par les mains de Monsieur Lavasseur son secrétaire absent et des deniers dudit seigneur de Bouillon la somme de trois mille livres tournoys sur estant moings des ouvraiges de maçonnerye et autres ouvraiges par ledit de Brosse marchandés à faire pour ledit seigneur en sa maison sise ès faulxbourg Saint-Germain des Prés, lès Paris, dont et de laquelle somme de trois milles livres tournoys ledit Brosse est tenu pour content et a quité et quite ledit Seigneur de Bouillon, Lavasseur et tous altres ... Fait et passé à Paris, ès hostel et rue susdits, l'an mil six cent treize, le vingt huictiesme jour d'apvril ... de Brosse' (transcr. Pannier, p. 47; original document lost: 'Catalogue d'autographes de M. Charavay', March 1882, No. 374; cf. Guiffrey, *Bull. Hist.* Paris, 1882, p. 106).

1623 Death of the Duc de Bouillon; purchase of his hôtel by Roger du Plessis, Marquis de Liancourt. It becomes the Hôtel de Liancourt (C. Tooth, Thesis cit.).

1635 *April 11* Masonry Contract between Frémin de Cotte and Roger du Plessis for demolition, rebuilding and enlargements at the hôtel (Min. Cent. XCVIII–18). The staircase in the *corps-de-logis* is to be demolished, and replaced by another in the south wing. There is to be a new pavilion at the end of this wing, a cabinet on the garden-front to match one already built there; a gallery is to be created in the existing building by the demolition of internal walls, etc. The architect is named as Louis Petit.

July 13 A further Masonry Contract, superseding that of 11 April, naming Frémin de Cotte mason, Louis Petit architect and Jacques Lemercier to have a watching-brief over all (Min. Cent. XCVIII–119). More of the *corps-de-logis* is to be demolished and rebuilt, also the whole S. wing. The terms of this contract bring the hôtel more or less into line with Marot's engravings.

1636 *December 10* Following a dispute over the July 1635 contract, an adjudication is made by Jacques Lemercier, the architect (Min. Cent. XLIII–20).

1637 *May 2 and June 29* Contracts passed for building an aviary; the joiner is Jehan Limagne (Min. Cent. XCVIII–125: Peter Smith, *The Town Houses of François Mansart*, Thesis, University of London, 1965).

1640 Malingre writes, 'M. de Liancourt l'a divisé en plusieurs corps d'hostels, et l'accreu de quantité de salles, offices, galleries et courts' (II, p. 402).

1644 *March 1* John Evelyn visits the hôtel: 'I went to see the Count de Lion Courts Palace in the Rue de Seine which is well-built, towards his study and bed-chamber joins a little garden which, though very narrow is yet by the addition of an excellently painted perspective strangely enlarged to appearance; to this there is another part, supported by arches, in which there runns a Streame of water, which rising in the Aviary out of a statue seems to grow some miles, by being artificially continued in the painting . . . at the end of the garden is a little Theater which is made to change with divers pretty seanes. . . . We were lead thence to a pretty round cabinet, where was a neate invention for reflecting lights by lining divers sconces with thin shining plates of gilded copper. . . . In one of the rooms of State was an excellent Paynting of Pussine . . .'. (Diary, ed: de Beer, 1955).

1657–1659 Tallement des Réaux wonders if the hôtel will ever be completed (*Historiettes*, IV, p. 26).

1674 *August 11* Death of Roger du Plessis, Duc de Liancourt.

Note: The Marquisate of Liancourt later passed to the La Rochefoucauld family, and on Delagrive's 'Plan de Paris en 6 Quartiers' of 1744 the hôtel in the Rue de Seine is marked as the Hôtel de la Rochefoucauld. It was finally destroyed when the Rue des Beaux-Arts was built, and as far as is known no part survives in the block between this street and the Quai Voltaire.

Paris Hôtel de Bullion

Rue Plastrière, now J. J. Rousseau

I ORIGINAL DOCUMENTS

No description survives of the exterior of this hôtel, always more famed for its decoration than its architecture; only the contracts of 1614 and 1633 give some indication of its appearance. No engravings of it, other than those on the plans of Paris, have been identified. Documents concerning its decoration and 18th century history exist in the Archives Nationales and elsewhere, but are not relevant here.

PARIS, ARCHIVES NATIONALES, MINUTIER CENTRAL

XXXV – 191: 30 January 1614; masonry contract between Salomon de Brosse and Claude de Bullion; followed by receipt of 2 February 1614 for 3,000 of the 36,000 livres contracted for, signed by de Brosse.
LI – 170: 20 November 1633; masonry contract betwen Charles du Ry and Claude de Bullion.

PARIS, ARCHIVES NATIONALES (MAIN ARCHIVES)

Arch.Nat. Q^{1*} 10995 'Terrier du Roy, Censive c. 1700 fol. 152: No. 32, Rue Plastrière, 'Maison à Porte-cochère appellée l'Hôtel de Bullion, appartenant au Sieur de Bullion y demeurant, laquelle a sa bassecour par la rue Coqhéron au no. 3 et rue Coquillière no. 10' cf. also ibid. fols. 138 and 161.

II PUBLISHED SOURCES

G. Brice, *Nouvelle description de Paris*, ed. Paris, 1698.
H. Sauval, *Histoire et recherches des antiquités de la ville de Paris*, II, Paris, 1724.
A. N. Dézallier d'Argenville, *Voyage pittoresque de Paris*, Paris, 1749.
M. Charageat, *B.S.H.A.F.*, 1927, p. 179.

H. Dumolin, *Etudes de topographie parisienne*, II, Paris, 1930.
E.-J. Ciprut, *B.S.H.A.F.*, 1955, p. 120.
J. P. Labatut, 'Aspects de la fortune de Bullion', *Revue XVIIième siècle*, no. 60, 1963.
J.-P. Babelon, *Demeures parisiennes sous Henri IV et Louis XIII*, Paris, 1965.

III PLANS AND ELEVATIONS

Drawings

PARIS, ARCHIVES NATIONALES

Arch.Nat. Q¹★ 1099⁵, 'Terrier du Roy' c. 1700, fol. 149, Rue Plastrière: block-plan (Pl. 82).
Arch.Nat. N.IV Seine 64, 1786. Rittman, Censive de l'Archevêché de Paris, fol. 24; block-plan (Pl. 82).
Arch.Nat. F³¹ 78, Atlas Cadastral 1815–1850, 3e arrondissement, Quartier St Eustache, ilôt 8: plan of the ground-floor, after division of the hôtel into sundry dwellings.

Engravings

B. Jaillot, 'Nouveau plan de la ville et faux-bourgs de Paris ... 1713'; perspective-elevation, not complete and not accurate according to Arch.Nat. Q¹★ 1099⁵; no gallery shown.
Abbé Delagrive, Plan of Paris, 1729; block-plan, showing corps-de-logis, the adjacent property incorporated into the hôtel and rebuilt in 1633, but omitting the garden-gallery.
M. E. Turgot, Plan of Paris (before 1751); perspective-elevation; shown as four blocks surrounding courtyard-garden; (Pl. 73). Cf. Jaillot above.

IV CHRONOLOGY AND NOTES

1613 *September 6* Henriette d'Entragues, Marquise de Verneuil, sells to Claude de Bullion, 'Maître des Requêtes', for 69,000 livres, a house situated between the Rue Plastrière and the Rue Coqhéron (Dumolin, *Etudes de topographie parisienne*, II, p. 364).
The Marquise had bought the property two years earlier from Antoine Baudoin, who had built on the site between c. 1600–1610 (ibid.).

1614 *January 30* Masonry contract between Claude de Bullion and Salomon de Brosse for the addition to the existing *corps-de-logis* of two blocks, one large pavilion, a gallery, various offices and a wall with a *porte-cochère* on to the street (Min. Cent. XXXV–191, fols. 30–34; cf. E.-J. Ciprut, *B.S.H.A.F.*, 1956, p. 120ff.). The contract was for 36,000 livres.

February 2 De Brosse receives 3,000 livres on account for this contract, with which to start the work (Min. Cent. XXXV–191). (The *quittance* for the remainder of the sum is missing).

1632 Claude de Bullion becomes 'Surintendant des Finances' to Louis XIII.

1633 *November 20* Masonry contract between Claude de Bullion and Charles du Ry for the demolition and rebuilding of a house next door to the Hôtel de Bullion as an extension to the same. 'Une sallette, une garde-robbe, une gallerie autour de laquelle se continuera un pavillon dans lequel y aura un grand cabinet et un petit à chancun estaige ...' (Min. Cent. LI–171).

1634–1635 Decoration of the gallery of the hôtel by Blanchard and Vouet (J.-P. Babelon, *Demeures parisiennes*, pp. 200, 213–220, 237 n. 44 and 272).

1724 *July 15* Auguste Léon de Bullion bequeathes the hôtel to his nieces, the Duchesses de Laval and de la Vallière. (Dumolin, op. cit. II, p. 388).

1776 *December 30* The hôtel, having remained in the family for 160 years, is sold by Guy-André-Pierre de Montmorency, Duc de Laval, husband of Jacqueline-Hortense de Bullion, to Marie-Louis-César Roulleau for 44,000 Livres (ibid.).

1781 *October 10* Roulleau sells the hôtel to

Claude Belliard de Bélissard, 'architecte du Roi' (ibid.).

1786 The hôtel is divided into a number of small dwellings (ibid. and Arch. Nat. F[31] Quartier St. Eustache, ilot 8). (To-day the building no longer exists).

Paris, Hôtel de Fresne

(Rue Saint-Honoré)

I ORIGINAL DOCUMENTS

PARIS, ARCHIVES NATIONALES,
MINUTIER CENTRAL

XLII – 48 fol. 87: 29 March 1608: Masonry contract between Claude Pouillet and Pierre Forget de Fresne.

II PUBLISHED SOURCES

Fauvelet du Toc, *Histoire des Secrétaires d'Estat*, Paris, 1668, pp. 186 to 192.

H. de Luçay, *Des origines du pouvoir minis-* *térial en France, les Secrétaires d'Etat*, Paris, 1881, pp. 31–35.

Paris, Hôtel du Lude

(Rue du Bouloi)

I ORIGINAL DOCUMENTS

The recently-discovered contract of 1618 gives the first good description of the important features of this hôtel, but no visual representation of it as it is portrayed therein is known.

PARIS, ARCHIVES NATIONALES, MINUTIER CENTRAL
XIX – 385: 30 September 1618; Masonry contract between Jean de Fourcy (authorized by François de Daillon, Comte du Lude) and Antoine Petit, master-mason, for work to the designs of Salomon de Brosse.

PARIS, ARCHIVES NATIONALES, (MAIN ARCHIVES)
Arch.Nat. Y 163, 'Insinuations du Châtelet':

24 December 1622; Timoléon de Daillon and Marie Feydeau, his wife; 'donation mutuelle'.
Arch.Nat. Z¹J 261: 5 May 1643; 'Prisée des ouvrages de couverture' for the replacement of slates; 'toisé par expertz Fuzier et Bernard'.
Arch.Nat. Q¹* 1099⁵, 'Terrier du Roy, fol. 179, c. 1700 Rue du Bouloi', Censive. 'no. 2, maison à porte-cochere appartenant au Sieur de la Reynie'.

II PUBLISHED SOURCES

H. Dumolin: *Etudes de topographie parisienne*, II, Paris, 1930.
E.-J. Ciprut: 'Nouveaux documents sur de

Brosse, architecte du Roi', *Bull. Soc. Hist. Prot. Fr.*, October–December 1964, p. 253 ff.

III PLANS AND ELEVATIONS

Drawings

PARIS, ARCHIVES NATIONALES
Arch.Nat. N.IV Seine 64, 1786. Rittman, Censive de l'Archevêché de Paris, fol. 23.
Arch.Nat. F³¹ 80, Atlas Cadastral, 1815–1850. Quartier de la Banque de France, îlôts 8–9: Rue du Bouloi.

Engravings

Gomboust: Plan of Paris, 1652; perspective-elevation; four blocks round a court; *porte-cochère* on to the Rue du Bouloi; 'l'Ovalle' not shown.

T

B. Jaillot: Plan of Paris, 1713; Hôtel de la Reynie shown as a single block; cf. Gomboust.

Abbé Delagrive: Plan of Paris, 1729; block-plan 'Hôtel de la Reynie', as altered showing the property next door which de la Reynie incorporated into the hôtel.

E.-M. Turgot: Plan of Paris, 1751; shows the two adjacent blocks and, clearly, the *porte-cochère* on to the Rue du Bouloi (Pl. 73).

IV CHRONOLOGY AND NOTES

1609 *December 8* Thibault de Laveran sells an hôtel, Rue du Bouloi, to François de Daillon, Comte du Lude, for 31,500 livres: (Dumolin, *Etudes de topographie parisienne*, II, 1930, p. 421). Laveran possibly obtained the house from the du Plessis-Richelieu family; it was the reputed birthplace of the Cardinal, and was formerly the Hôtel de Losse.

1611 *December 23* After considerable complications concerning the purchase, it is completed, Daillon furnishing the necessary 'Decret volontaire' (ibid.).

1618 *December 30* Jean de Fourcy, 'surintendant des bâtiments' (authorized by François de Daillon) signs a contract with Antoine Petit, master-mason, for the alteration and enlargement of the Hôtel du Lude to the designs of Salomon de Brosse (Min. Cent. XIX–385, publ. E.-J. Ciprut, *Bull. Hist. Soc. Prot. Fr.*, October–December, 1964, p. 253). The principal *corps-de-logis* on the Rue du Bouloi is to be rebuilt with a large *porte-cochère*; inside the courtyard, joined to the old walls, there is to be a circular structure with a dome ('l'ovalle appellée coppole'), and in one corner of the courtyard there is to be a new staircase from the cellar to the attics.

1619 *December 27* Death of François de Daillon. He is succeeded as Comte du Lude by his son Timoléon (Dumolin and Ciprut, op. cit.).

1622 *December 24* Having married in April of the same year, Timoléon de Daillon and Marie Feydeau make a 'donation mutuelle des biens', including the Hôtel (ibid.).

1643 *May 5* Repairs to the roof of the hôtel carried out for Henri de Daillon, Comte du Lude (son of Timoléon, deceased). They concern the roofing on the *corps-de-logis*, the pavilion 'a costé du dosme', and part of that over the staircase (Arch. Nat. Z¹ J 261, publ. Ciprut, op. cit.). From this document we learn that the 'coppole' was beside one of the pavilions 'donnant sur la cour'.

1655 The adjacent property ('maison de Jean le Bossu') comes into the family. It is called the 'Petit Hôtel du Lude' (Dumolin, op. cit.).

1677 *January* Gabriel-Nicolas de la Reynie buys the hotel and adjacent property. He alters the whole (ibid.).

1709 *June 14* Death of G.-N. de la Reynie. Inventory of the hôtel (ibid., p. 425).

1808 *April 19* Sold by the then owner, François-Antoine Rubit, for 265,175 francs, to Pierre Louis Guénin (ibid., p. 425).

1880 Sale of the hôtel to the Compagnie des Chemins-de-fer Paris-Lyon-Mediterranée, who pulled it down and rebuilt on the site (ibid.).

The singularly complete list of owners existing for this hôtel and discovered by M. Dumolin makes it worth entering into this chronology, although after 1677 it would appear that little of the original building was left unaltered.

Paris, Hôtel de Soissons

Of the long and complicated history of this hôtel very little is relevant here, but see Chap. IV, pp. 60-63.

No original documents concerning de Brosse's employment by the Comte de Soissons have so far come to light, and chronology within this brief period is non-existent. This catalogue entry, therefore, refers only to published sources, drawings and engravings which concern the period *c.* 1606-1612, and that part of the building (in which Soissons apparently lived), bordering the Rue du Four and the Rue des Deux-Ecus.

II PUBLISHED SOURCES

H. Sauval: *Histoire et recherches des antiquités de la ville de Paris*, II, Paris, 1724.
J. M. B. de Saint-Victor: *Tableau historique et pittoresque de Paris*, II, 2nd ed., Paris, 1822-1827.

J.-P. Babelon: *Demeures parisiennes sous Henri IV et Louis XIII*, Paris, 1965.

III PLANS AND ELEVATIONS

Drawings

PARIS, ARCHIVES NATIONALES

Arch.Nat. Q¹⋆ 1099⁵, Terrier du Roy, fol. 123, *c.* 1700 Rue des Deux-Ecus: block-plan showing entrance to courtyard from the street (Pl.74).
Ibid, fol. 125 *verso* (Censive No. 26): 'Maison à porte-cochère appellée l'Hotel de Soissons … appartenant a M. le Prince de Carignan'.

PARIS, BIBLIOTHEQUE NATIONALE

B.N.Est. Vª 29: drawing of the *porte-cochère*; inferior draughtsmanship; doubtless copied from another drawing, possibly Louvre RF 5946, fol. 13ᵛ.
B.N.Est. Vª 230ᵈ: plans concerning the transformation of the Hôtel de Soissons into the Mint; the entrance in the Rue des Deux-Ecus is marked 'Principalle entrée' and shows plan of doorway.
B.N.Est. Vª Grand Format 814 and 815: ibid.
B.N.Est. Vª 441: ibid. Robert de Cotte.

PARIS, LOUVRE

Dessins, RF 5946 Album 'de Brosse', fol.
13*v*.: the door of the Hôtel de Soissons; copy
of the Stockholm drawing? Almost certainly
by Charles du Ry.

STOCKHOLM, NATIONALMUSEUM

CC 1572 *recto:* the door of the Hôtel de
Soissons; (Pl. 75) pencil-and-wash with
remains of gilding; unsigned; possibly an
original by de Brosse, but there is no way to
prove the attribution. On the *verso* there is a
drawing of dormers; formerly believed to
refer to Bullant's work at the hôtel for
Catherine de Médicis, these can be certainly
identified with the early seventeenth-century.
Place Royale (des Vosges).

Engravings

Gomboust: Plan of Paris, 1652; section 5;
showing the block on the Rue des Deux-
Ecus in perspective elevation where the
porte-cochère cannot be seen.

B. Jaillot: 'Nouveau plan de la ville et faux-
bourgs de Paris', 1713; perspective elevation
(derived from Gomboust?).

Abbé Delagrive: Plan of Paris, 1729; block-
plan; entrance on to the Rue des Deux-
Ecus shown.

M. E. Turgot: Plan of Paris, before 1751;
the courtyard bordering the Rue des Deux-
Ecus shown in perspective elevation; *porte-
cochère* hidden (Pl. 73).

I. Silvestre: 'Vue de l'Hostel de Soissons, bâti
par Catherine de Médicis et conduit par Jean
Bullant, architecte du Roi' (F. 52: 10); this
representation is not relevant to the part of the
hôtel where de Brosse worked, but is too
well-known to be omitted.

J. Marot: 'Porte de l'Hostel de Soissons'; a
variation on the Stockholm drawing; the
voussoirs no longer break the entablature; the
keystone is altered to a console which does;
door-panels no longer bear the cipher of
Charles de Soissons and Anne de Montafié,
as in the Stockholm and Louvre drawings;
the royal arms appear above the door in place
of those of Soissons; (This engraving, to be
found in B.N.Est. V^a 230^d, is not listed by
Mauban).

Paris, Palais de Justice

(Salle des Pas Perdus)

There is no scarcity of documents concerning the Palais de Justice, one of the principal public buildings of Paris. Not many of these, however, throw much light on the architectural history of the Grande Salle in the period succeeding the fire of 1618. Only those few which are relevant to this, therefore, are listed below. The original contracts, which would have been an invaluable source of knowledge about this much restored and rebuilt work, are lost.

I ORIGINAL DOCUMENTS

PARIS, ARCHIVES NATIONALES,
MINUTIER CENTRAL

LXVI – 37: 30 March 1618; *Association* between Jean Gobelin on the one side, and on the other Charles Benoist, Jehan Girard, Jean Pasquier (master-masons) and Louis Coullon (master-carpenter) for the demolition and reconstruction of the 'grande salle du Palais . . .'.
LXVI – 37: 3 August 1618; Undertaking given by Louis Chabannes, boatman, to Paul de Brosse, 'stippulant pour son père', and Jehan Gobelin, to carry away all the debris from the demolition of the Grande Salle.
LXVI – 37: 28 September 1618; Agreement between Paul de Brosse, 'stippulant pour son père', and Jehan Gobelin on the one side, and ? de la Garde, boatman, on the other, concerning the transportation of stone for the rebuilding of the Grand Salle.

CV – 335: 5 May 1619; Annulment of articles of association on behalf of Charles Benoist and Jean Girard

PARIS, ARCHIVES NATIONALES,
(MAIN ARCHIVES)

Arch. Nat. X 1937 Régistres du Conseil: 12 November and 13 December 1622.
Arch. Nat. X^{1a} 1912 Régistres du Conseil: September and October 1620.
Arch. Nat. X^{1a} 8649 Ordonnances de Louis XIII: 5 September 1617 to 18 September, 1622.
Arch. Nat. E 60^A Conseils du Roi –Finances: October and November 1618.
Arch. Nat. E 78^A ibid.: January and February 1624.
Arch. Nat. U 997, Bâtiment du Palais de Justice, réparations et reconstructions; mélanges.

II PUBLISHED SOURCES

C. Malingre: *Les antiquités de Paris*, Paris, 1640.

H. Sauval: *Histoire et recherches des antiquités de Paris*, Paris, 1724, Vol. III.

A. N. Dézallier d'Argenville, *Vies des fameux architectes*, Paris 1788.

J. M. D. de Saint-Victor: *Tableau historique et pittoresque de Paris*, Paris, 2e ed., 1822–1827, Vol. I (1st. ed. 1808–1811).

Sauvan and Schmit: *Histoire et description du Palais de Justice, de la Conciergerie et de la Sainte-Chapelle*, Paris, 1825.

H. Bonnardot and others: *Paris à travers les âges* . . . Vol. I (*Le Palais de Justice et le Pont Neuf*), Paris, 1875.

H. Bonnardot: *L'Incendie du Palais de Justice de Paris en 1618: relation de Paul Bontray*, Paris, 1879.

H. Stein: *Histoire du Palais de Justice et de la Sainte-Chapelle de Paris*, Paris, 1912.

M. Gallet: Bulletin du Musée Carnavalet (Coll. Historique de la Ville de Paris), June 1963, pp. 2–4.

III PLANS AND ELEVATIONS

Drawings and model

PARIS, ARCHIVES NATIONALES,

Arch.Nat. Q^{1}★ 1099^{1}, Terrier du Roy, fols. 67, 76 and 84: plans, of which no. 84 is full-page and important; dated *c.* 1770.
Arch.Nat. III Seine 725^{1} and 725^{2}: plans of the barrel-vaults over the Salle; eighteenth century.

PARIS, BIBLIOTHEQUE NATIONALE

B.N.Est. Rés. V^{e} 53g (Paris): pièces:
1020: 'Élevations des bâtiments anciens qui formoient l'enceinte de la Cour du Mai du Palais'; Thierry; 1777; water-colour.
1023: Cour du Mai after the rebuilding, 1780's; anon; pen-and-ink and water-colour.
1030: Cour du Mai, early nineteenth century; anon; water-colour.
1031: Interior of the Salle, de Brosse's work rebuilt by Antoine; early nineteenth century; anon; pen-and-wash.
1032: View of the E. façade of the Salle; anon; pen-and-wash; dated 1815.
B.N.Est V^{e} 53h, Rés. (Paris) fol. 107: plan of the Cité with important early plan (?. seventeenth century) of the Grande Salle and adjacent buildings (Pl. 189).
B.N.Est. V^{e} 84 Dessins de Couture, architect: sundry plans, made after the fire of 1777; the following are relevant to de Brosse's Salle:
fol. 41: The E. and part of the N. façades (plan).
fol. 53: plan; '2e étage des requettes de l'hôtel'.
fol. 60: 'Profil projetté pour faire passer les eaux . . . entre les deux grands combles de la salle'.

PARIS, MUSEE CARNAVALET

Model Room
Model: Jacques-Denis Antoine, architect; showing his rebuilding of de Brosse's Salle after the fire of 1777; wood, with white-painted interior; marked, 'La Grande Salle et le depôt des Archives du Palais de Justice, Reconstruits par Jacques-Denis Antoine en 1784' (Pl. 194).
Dessins D 2987 and D 2997: by Thomas de Thonon(?); watercolour; showing the buildings of the Cour du Mai before the reconstruction of the 1780's.
Réserve des Dessins, Grand Format: by Thomas Froideau; view of the Buildings of the Cour du Mai after the fire of 1777; pen-and-ink; inscr. 'Veüe d'une partie du Palais prise du Bureau des Finances, dessiné le 10 mai 1777'; this drawing is the basis of many contemporary and later drawings and engravings of the scene (Pl. 191).

Engravings

Jacques I Androuet du Cerceau: interior of the medieval Salle; publ. *Les Plus Excellents Bastiments*, Vol. II, 1579.

Perelle: The buildings of the Cour du Mai; *c*. 1650–1660.

Gomboust: Plan of Paris, 1652; includes view of the W. elevation.

Boisseau: Perspective view of the same; seventeenth century (Pl. 188).

Abbé Delagrive: Plan of Paris; 1729.

M.-E. Turgot: Plan of Paris; before 1751.

Thierry: View of the demolition of the buildings in the Cour du Mai, 1777.

Desmaisons: View of the Cour du Mai in 1782, as reconstructed after the fire of 1777.

Legrand and Landon: Plates for various editions of *Description de Paris*; the Ile de la Cité under Napoleon.

Sauvan and Schmit: Plates for their publication of 1825; (Pl. 193), see Sec. II.

J. M. D. de Saint-Victor: Plates for the publication of 1822–1827; see Sec. II.

Note: The Bib.Nat. Dép. des Estampes (Vᵃ 225 to Vᵃ225f) contains many engravings (plans and elevations) concerning the Grand' Salle in the nineteenth century. Most important (Vᵃ 225) are engraved plans of Paris in 1754, 1830, 1835, 1870 and 1880. Also plans, etc., of the architects Duc and Dourmey (restoration of the Salle in the 1840's), and Daumet (restoration of the Salle after the fire of 1870). Most of these engravings are to be found in various publications, but are usefully collected here for comparison.

IV CHRONOLOGY AND NOTES

1618 *March 7* The medieval Grand'Salle of the Palais de Justice is destroyed by fire: (Malingre, *Antiquités de Paris*, I, p. 126) 'L'an 1618, le sept mars sur les deux heures après minuit … la grand'chambre fût brulée en moins de demie heure'.

March 30 An *Association* formed between Jean Gobelin and four master-craftsmen for the reconstruction of the Salle (Min. Cent. LXVI-37).

April 18 Letters-patent of Louis XIII authorizing the rebuilding of the Salle and directing the Procureur-Général to choose an architect (Arch. Nat. U.997, regd. 23 April 1618): 'Louis … etc. … Nous ayant faict représenter les plans et desseings d'aucuns architectes les plus experimentez pour servir à la réfection de la Grande Salle … que nous voulons faire rebastir le plus tôt qu'il se pourra selon la magnificence, grandeur et dignité du lieu le plus auguste de nostre royaume …'. At the same time, the building should, the King says, cost 'le moyant des deniers qu'il soit nécesaire'.

August 3 The demolition either under way or about to start; arrangements for the disposal of the rubble signed by Paul de Brosse on Salomon's behalf (Min. Cent. LXVI-37).

September 28 Further arrangements for the transport of stone to the site, signed by Paul for his father (Min. Cent. LXVI-37).

1619 *May 5* Annulment of the articles of association on behalf of Benoist and Jean Girard, Jean Gobelin. (Min. Cent. CV-335): '… (qu')icelluy Gobelin fasse lesdictz ouvraiges et resfection de ladicte salle … selon et ainsy que l'adjudication luy en a esté faict et à Me Salomon de Brosse …'.

June 19 The King directs that the Procureur-Général sees to the raising of money for the Grand'Salle by the public auction of land on the eastern boundaries of the Faubourg Saint-Germain-des-Prés (Pannier, p. 74).

1620 *September 2* The Cour du Parlement discusses the above (ibid.).

1622 *November 12* Work well under way as the Grand'Salle is used to celebrate the annual Mass of the Parlement (ibid.).

1623 *November* The Grand'Chambre being 'occupée par des massons', the annual Mass is held elsewhere (ibid.).

1624 *January 18* Henri Colin, 'maître des oeuvres et bastiments du Roi', is in charge of the work (ibid., and Arch. Nat. E–78 A fol. 112r). This Colin is possibly a son or other relative of the Rémy Collin who worked at Montceaux (see p. 232, (1598)).

1630 *April 30* The King directs that a new building be erected alongside the Grand'Salle (in the Cour du Mai), which could contain several 'stone shops' (Arch. Nat. U.997): 'Un nouveau bastiment depuis la Cour joignant la Conciergerie jusques au Perron Royal servant à monter à la Grande Salle ... la hauteur ... dudict bastiment ne pourra excedder l'imposte des arcades de ladicte salle et sera sans aucune cheminée afin de conserver les jours et les croisées de ladicte salle suivant le dessin qui nous en a esté presenté'.

1640 *February 14* Apparently no progress was made with this; the King now signs letters-patent relative to the erection of a gallery alongside the Grand'Salle (ibid. and H. Stein, *Histoire du Palais de Justice*, p. 58): '... une nouvelle galerie le long de la grande Salle, dite Galerie Dauphine ...'.

1730 *May 26* The architect Boffrand plans attics for document-storage to go above the Grand'Salle (Arch. Nat. U. 997).

1761 *April 29* One of these attics is already built (ibid.): 'Détail de ce qu'il en couteroit pour la construction d'une gallerie qu'on pourroit pratiquer dans un des combles qui est au dessus de la Grande Salle du Palais

semblable à celle qui est dans l'autre comble ...'.

1777 *May 9 and 10* During the night the Palais de Justice burned. The Grand'Salle badly damaged but not destroyed (H. Stein, op. cit., p. 66 ff): 'Mais comme la grande salle et la grande chambre s'en sauverent, on plaid, quinze jours après, comme si de rien n'était, et on reprit les grandes affaires du Maréchal de Richelieu et des édits qui occupèrent tous, alors'.

1777–1787 Rebuilding of the Cour du Mai after the fire. Jacques-Denis-Antoine restores the Grand'Salle (M. Gallet, *Bulletin du Musée Carnavelet*; J.-P. Babelon, 'Le Palais de Justice et la Conciergerie' (*Série Les Guides du temps*, p. 66). Antoine also rebuilt the stair in the new building which replaced the Salle Dauphine. This blocked de Brosse's S. range of windows.

1812 Collapse of part of the floor of the Salle into the Salle des Gardes of the Conciergerie (Sauvan and Schmit, *Histoire et description du Palais de Justice*). Restorations follow.

1836 Further restorations proposed to the Grand'Salle 'avec diverses modifications' (H. Stein, op. cit., p. 86).

1840 *May 26* The above scheme approved by the King, but Huyot, the architect proposed, dies (ibid.).

1852 Construction of the present E. façade of the Salle and of the stair at the E. end (ibid., p. 90). The architects were Duc and Dourmey.

1858 Restoration and consolidation of the barrel-vaults (ibid., p. 92).

1871 *May 24* A great part of the Grand' Salle is burned, and the vaults collapse.

1875 *November* The Grand'Salle is re-opened after its final reconstruction by the architect Daumet (ibid., p. 93).

Paris, Palais du Luxembourg

I ORIGINAL DOCUMENTS

The architectural history of the Luxembourg is not difficult to establish, despite the loss of all the original contracts made with de Brosse. Only minor contracts of the 1630s survive, together with the record of the transfer of the direction of the building-work from de Brosse to Marin de la Vallée in 1624. The record of an examination of the whole fabric made in 1623 provides valuable early information regarding the appearance of the exterior and the arrangement of the interior of the building before the alterations of the eighteenth and nineteenth centuries.

PARIS, ARCHIVES NATIONALES, MINUTIER CENTRAL

LXXXVI – Répertoire: 232 and 233: 'Avril 1625, Marché; Reine-Mère; Marin de la Vallée'. '1 Avril 1626, Marché Reine-Mère; Marin de la Vallée'. '1 Juin 1626, Marché; Reine-Mère; Marin de la Vallée'. The Répertoire (daybook) contains this record of contracts between Marie de Médicis and Marin de la Vallée. The contracts themselves, however, are missing from the bound files. (In one case there are traces of cut pages in the file. It is probable that these documents bearing the valuable signature of the Queen, were extracted and sold before the files were deposited in the Minutier. Cf. the history of the contract now preserved in the Bib. du Sénat, given below):

PARIS, ARCHIVES NATIONALES, (MAIN ARCHIVES)

Arch.Nat. Série o¹: In this series, for the dates 1605–1687 there are various documents, none of which is important for the architectural history of the Luxembourg, both the plans and drawings contained in it are listed in Section III below.

Arch.Nat. Série KK – 193 and 194: Household accounts of Marie de Médicis, not solely concerning the Luxembourg.

PARIS, BIBLIOTHEQUE NATIONALE

Bib.Nat.Mss: Ms. fr. 18202: 'Arrêt du Conseil d'Etat, entre le Procureur Général de la Reine Mère et S. de Brosse', 14 December 1624; concerning the *Procès Verbal* of 1623; publ. in full by Pannier, p. 264 ff. For the *Procès Verbal*, see below under Bib. de l'Arsenal.

B.N.Est. Papiers de Cotte, Hᵈ 135ᵉ: Notes relevant to the plans and drawings listed in Section III below.

PARIS, BIBLIOTHEQUE DE L'ARSENAL

MS. fr. 5995: 'Procès Verbal des visites et mesures des ouvrages du Pallais du Luxembourg commencé le 26 juin 1623 en vertu d'une ordonnance rendue entre le Procureur

Général de la Reine Mère Marie de Médicis et l'architecte entrepreneur des bastimens dud. Pallais'.

PARIS, ARCHIVES DE LA BIBLIOTHEQUE DU SENAT

Receuil Factice No. 2, Arch. P. 1: 'Documents relatifs à l'histoire du Palais du Luxembourg':
14 March 1624: Contract, Marie de Médicis and de Brosse; construction of the E. gallery.
26 March 1624: Contract, Marie de Médicis and de la Vallée; de la Vallée replaces de Brosse as contractor. (This document was purchased by the Bib. du Sénat in 1904 at a sale of autographs at the Hôtel Drouot.)

1 June 1626: Contract, Marie de Médicis and de la Vallée; terrace and balustrade within the courtyard in front of the principal *corps-de-logis*.
23 July 1626: Record of the advice of Salomon de Brosse and Alessandro Francini on points arising from the above contracts and estimates.

FLORENCE, UFFIZI, ARCHIVIO DI STATO

Arch.Mediceo 5953 6 c 27, 28: Letters of Marie de Médicis to her aunt, the Grand Duchess of Tuscany, October 1611 (publ. in full by Pannier, p. 258 ff.).

II   PUBLISHED SOURCES

Malingre: *Antiquités de Paris*, 1640.
Richard Symonds, *Notebooks*, 1649. The part of these notebooks in which the Luxembourg features, has been published by O. Millar 'An Exile in Paris: The Notebooks of Richard Symonds' in *Studies in Renaissance and Baroque Art*, Phaidon, 1967, p. 157 ff.
G. Brice: *Description de la Ville de Paris*, 1st. ed. 1685, other important editions 1706 and 1725. Between these three early editions there are important differences in the descriptions of the Luxembourg.
J. F. Blondel, *Architecture Françoise* 1752–1753, Vol. I, Book I and Vol. II, Book III. The latter contains a detailed analysis of the Luxembourg. (The *Architecture Françoise* was reprinted, Paris, 1904, ed. Gaudet and Pascal).
A. N. Dézallier d'Argenville, *Vies des fameux architectes*, Paris 1788.
C. Percier and P. L. F. Fontaine: *Parallèle entre plusiers Residences de Souverains*, Paris, 1833.
A. de Gisors: *Le Palais du Luxembourg, origine et description de cet édifice*, Paris, 1847.
D. L. M. Avenal: *Lettres du Cardinal de Richelieu*, Paris, 1853–1877.

C. Ruelens and M. Rooses: *Correspondance de Rubens et documents épistolaires concernant sa vie et ses oeuvres*, 1887–1909, Vols. II and III.
A. Hustin: *Le Palais du Luxembourg, ses transformations, son agrandissement, ses architectes, sa décoration, ses décorateurs*, Paris, 1904.
L. Batiffol: Marie de Médicis et le Palais du Luxembourg, *Revue de l'Art Ancien et Moderne*, *XVII*, 217, 1905.
A. Hustin: *Le Luxembourg, son histoire domaniale, décorative et anecdotique, des premiers siècles à l'année 1611'*, Paris, 1910.
G. Hirschfeld: *Le Palais du Luxembourg*, 1931. (In the series 'Petites monographies des grands édifices de France' this excellent monograph, which contains a valuable chronology, is extremely rare, but one of the most useful publications concerning both the general and the architectural history of the Palace).
A. Blunt: 'A Series of Paintings, illustrating the History of the Medici Family, executed for Marie de Médicis', *Burl. Mag.*, CIX, September 1967, pp. 492–498: October 1967, pp. 562–566.

III   PLANS AND ELEVATIONS

Drawings

PARIS, ARCHIVES NATIONALES

Arch.Nat. N.III Seine 108: Site of the Luxembourg in 1605; plans of properties which were acquired at the start of and during the building of the Palace. Rep. by Hustin, *Le Luxembourg*, 1904, p. 3.

Arch.Nat. N.III Seine 12095: File inscribed in late-eighteenth or early-nineteenth century 'Paris 31 Section, Citoyen Chalgrin architecte. Une liasse de plans du Palais du Luxembourg dont 7 collés sur toile un petit carton blanc de plans du Luxembourg'. Among these plans are Soufflot's project for the alterations and enlargement of the Luxembourg in 1776. The others are probably by Chalgrin. Soufflot's plans are inscribed 'Plan du Premier/Second étage du Palais du Luxembourg avec les additions et changements convenables pour le rendre logeable'. Three elevations in pen-and-colourwash are by Soufflot: (i) Proposed new entrance-screen, street elevation: (ii) Proposed new entrance-screen, court elevation; (iii) Proposed new wing for the garden-front, between the two projecting pavilions: these projects were never carried out. Also plans by Soufflot of the first and second floors of the entrance-pavilion.

Arch.Nat. N.III Seine 156, 222 and 724: contain various plans by Chalgrin signed and dated 1778 and 1779.

Arch.Nat. N.III Seine 1206: Further plan, signed by Soufflot, and dated 1776; the principal *corps-de-logis* and the plan for extending it towards the garden; inscr. 'Plan du rez-de-chaussée du Palais du Luxembourg avec les additions et changements convenable pour le rendre logeable'. Also in this file is a plan of 1744 showing the alterations made in the interior disposition of the building between 1733 and 1736; cf. Chronology. (Both *N.III Seine 1205* and *1206* contain sundry other eighteenth-century plans).

Arch.Nat. N.III Seine 657, 724, 1096, 1101, 1206 and 1306; N.II Seine 149, 156, and 122: all contain late eighteenth and early nineteenth century plans of the Luxembourg.

PARIS, BIBLIOTHEQUE NATIONALE

B.N.Est. Vᵃ 264: Plans in pencil-and-colourwash of the ground, first and second floors of the entrance-pavilion, and an elevation in section of the same, all made before Chalgrin's alterations; and an elevation, partly in pen and partly in pencil, of the entrance-pavilion and two bays of the entrance-screen facing the Rue de Vaugirard; made before the piercing of the screen by Chalgrin. The similarity in style of drawing and in the use of colour in these plans to that in Soufflot's drawings in Arch. Nat. N.III Seine 1205 suggests their attribution to that architect. The pen-and-pencil elevation of the pavilion and screen is probably also by him. Soufflot's B.N. drawings are invaluable as a record of de Brosse's entrance-pavilion in its original state. (Pls 139, 140, 169).

B.N.Est. Vᵃ 419 j (f.13): Anon. XVII Century. Block-plan in pen-and-wash of the whole palace with its dependencies and parts of the gardens, showing the Fontaine Médicis in its original position (Pl. 135).

B.N.Est. Vᵃ 443: Plans by Robert de Cotte (cf. Orig. Docs. B.N.Est. Hᵈ 135e, *Papiers de Cotte*): (i) plan inscr. 'Plan schématique du Palais et des Jardins avec les sources d'eau': (ii) a similar plan; both in pen and colourwash; (iii) plan of the ground floor with flaps for the entresols; (iv) plan of the first floor, with flaps for the south pavilions showing the entresols; (v) plan of the second floor, with flaps for the third floor in the S. pavilions, and showing the long gallery of the E. wing attic; (vi) plan of the attics.

B.N.Est. U b 9 Série Vues de France: Drawing by Etienne Martellange showing the W. façade of the W. gallery and part of the Petit Luxembourg from the Rue de Vaugirard; inscr. 'Palais du Luxembourg, 1635'.

PARIS, LOUVRE

Dessins RF 7123: Drawing in pen, with light colour-washes attributed to de Brosse by Pannier and others. The attribution cannot be supported in the absence of any other certain drawing by the architect. Part of the *corps-de-logis* on to the courtyard is shown, including half of the central entrance, the S.E. angle-pavilion and part of the E. wing in section. Numbered details of the cornice and terrace-balustrade; inscr. 'face du Luxembourg dedans la cour'; scale in pieds; the sheet carries an old page number 122 and measures 47·5 x 34·5 cms. It should be noted that in this drawing, as in the executed building, there is no triangular pediment on the north face of the pavilion flanking the *corps de logis*, where it rises above the wing. In this it differs from both Marot's and Blondel's plates where pediments (without seated figures above them) are shown on this part of both flanking pavilions. This may indicate not only that in this particular Blondel based his rendering upon Marot, but also that the drawing was made from the fabric itself. (Pl. 149).

PARIS, ECOLE DES BEAUX ARTS

Anon. fr. XVI à XVII siècles Coll. Lesafouché fol. v: drawing of the doors of the entrance-pavilion; inscr. (probably later hand) 'Porte de l'entrée principale du Palais du Luxembourg les principaux ornements comme les mascarons les enfants et les boulles sont de bronze Doré en partie couleur de bronze antique'. The door has the cipher 'M. and H.' at the top and 'H' in the panels, also the lily of France and the Medici *palle*. Sauval, (III p. 7) says that the doors were by Mercier.

LONDON, SIR JOHN SOANE'S MUSEUM

Volume of drawings by John Thorpe: Plans of the ground and first floors of the Luxembourg, the ground floor inscr. 'Queene Mother's Howse fabor Sct Jarnins alla Paree altred pr J. Thorp', 1621. There are indications, particularly in the vestibule or tribune behind the principal staircase of the *corps-de-logis*, that in some places at least Thorpe drew out the real plan of the Luxembourg and, partly erasing it, superimposed his own version, for an English country-house. In 1621 he could have seen the copy of de Brosse's plan; Marie de Médicis is said to have sent copies to several European courts for the consideration of their principal architects. Cf. 'The Book of Architecture of John Thorpe in Sir John Soane's Museum', ed. by Sir John Summerson in *Walpole Soc.* Vol. 40, 1966, pp. 78 and 79 and pls 58 and 69 (orig. Thorpe fol. nos. 123–124 and 127–128).

STOCKHOLM, NATIONALMUSEUM

Drawings CC 273: Plan in ink; in certain details this differs from all other plans, viz., the steps from the courtyard terrace to the *corps-de-logis* entrance are semi-circular, the orders are omitted in places, e.g., on the exterior of the tribune on the garden-front and on the entrance-pavilion; inscr. in relevant places, 'Grande Cour', 'Terrasse', 'Gallerye' and 'Jardin'.
Drawings CC 90: Elevation in pen-and-wash of half the entrance-pavilion, the east side of the screen and the N.E. pavilion; above the entrance-pavilion is the plan of half its top-floor in pencil; as in CC 273 there are differences from the executed building and the drawing is after the *Petit Marot* plate of this elevation. The dome of the entrance-pavilion is shown without ribs, and without the fish-scale patterning of the leads.

NEW YORK, PIERPONT MORGAN LIBRARY

MS. 1955. 12: Volume of plans of the Royal Residences made for the Marquis de Marigny, *Intendant des Bâtiments* to Louis XV; contains a plan of the Luxembourg, with flaps; inscr. 'Rez de Chaussée du Palais du Luxembourg avec les entresoles'; this plan is particularly useful for its rendering of the disposition of the principal staircase.

Engravings

J. Marot: *Petit Marot:* One plan and four elevations of the Luxembourg; inscr. (i) 'Plan du Palais d'Orléans à Paris'. (In the 2nd ed. (*c.* 1738) by Mariette, the words 'du dessin du Sr. de Brosse' are added to this description) (ii) 'Elevation de l'entrée du Palais d'Orléans à Paris'; (iii) 'Elevation du grand Escalier du Palais d'Orléans'; (iv) 'Profil du Palais d'Orléans bastie par la Roine Marie de Médicis'; (v) 'Elevation du Palais d'Orleans du coste du Jardin'. An engraving by Marot of the Fontaine Médicis was published as pl. 210 in Jombert's *Les Délices de Paris et des environs* in 1753 (Pl. 173). J. F. Blondel published nine plates of the Luxembourg in his *Architecture Françoise* (1752–53), Vol. II, Book III; one general plan, three floor-plans, four elevations and one plan and elevation of the Fontaine Médicis. (For the latter cf. Chap. VII, p. 132, n. 66). Blondel states (op. cit. p. 52, note C, and Mauban repeats this assertion,

op. cit. p. 214) that his elevations are those engraved by Marot, and that he considers the latter to have been partly from de Brosse's drawings and partly from the unfinished building. In fact the elevations published by Blondel, though certainly based on Marot's, are not directly reproduced from them. Blondel's plates are larger and differ in certain —though largely unimportant—particulars. (For differences cf. p. 119, n. 25 and p. 124, n. 38). Plates from Blondel rather than from Marot have been used here (Pls 136–138 and 141–144) to illustrate the Luxembourg because of their greater clarity, especially for purposes of reproduction.

Silvestre, Aveline, Poilly and others: made engravings of the Luxembourg in the seventeenth, eighteenth and nineteenth centuries. Silvestre shows several views of the gardens, Fontaine Médicis, etc. (F.48,11: F.54,2:F 116, 1–5: F. 117, 1–11).

Percier and Fontaine: publ. engraved plans of the Palace in their *Parallèle*, showing the building as it was after Chalgrin's alterations and before Gisors'.

Nineteenth century: very numerous engravings and lithographs were made after the alteration to the S. front made by Gisors.

IV CHRONOLOGY AND NOTES

1611 *October 6* Marie de Médicis writes to her aunt, the Grand Duchesse of Tuscany, telling of her decision to build a palace in Paris, and requesting a plan, elevation and perspectives of the Palazzo Pitti, Florence (Pannier, p. 258 ff., published in full): 'Ma tante. Estant en volonté de faire bastir et accomoder une maison à Paris pour me loger et voulant en quelque chose me regler sur la forme et le modelle du Palais de Piti (lequel Jay tousiors estimé pour l'ordre de son Architecture et grandes commoditez qui y sont) Je vous fais celle cy pour vous dire que J'auray à singulier plaisir que vous m'en faciez faire

le plan en son entier avec les eslevations et perspectives des bastiments tant du costé de devant ledict Palais qu'au derrière d'icelluy du costé des terrasses, vous priant de me les envoyer à la première occasion, ensembles les mesures et proportions des courtz, terrasses, salles, chambres et autres stances ('stanze') de ladicte maison pour m'en ayder et servir en la structure et decoration de la mienne. . . . A Fontaynebleau le VI jour Doctobre 1611. Ma tante vous me feres bien plaisir/ de menvoyer le plan et les/dessin gs du palais de Pitty dont ie me/veux servir pour l'ordre et orn/e ment de ma maison . . . Marie'. (The last lines added in the Queen's own hand). And (Pannier, p. 259): 'Ma Tante. Je vous ay escrit depuis quelques jours ença et faict savoir le desir que j'ay de faire bastir une maison à Paris, et que mesmes ayant tousiours estimé le palais de Piti à cause de l'ordre de ses bastimens. Je desirois que vous m'en envoyassiez le plan avec les eslevations pour le faire imiter en ce que Je trouveray plus à propos. Mais comme Jay du depuis advisé que pour avoir une entière intelligence du modelle de lad. maison et des mesures et proportions de toutes les pièces et stances qui en dependent, et que pour me servir plus utillement de ce desseing pour la structure et ornement de la mienne, Il est besoing d'envoyer sur les lieux une personne qui soit bien entendu et experimenté en telles affaires, Je vous ay déspéché ce porteur nommé Métezeau Architecte du Roy monsieur mon filz avecq celle cy que Je vous fais de rechef, pour vous prier d'avoir agéable qu'il voye et considère particulièrement ledict Palais de Piti en tous les endroictz de son ediffice tant par le dedans que par le dehors d'icelluy, en sorte qu'il me puisse fidellement rapporter tout ce qui est de l'art et architecture de ladicte maison avec les mesures et proportions de ce qui en deppend pour l'effect de dessus. M'assurant bien que si pour cela ledict Métezeau a besoing de vostre faveur et assistance vous la luy despartirez à ma recommandation, en quoy vous me ferez ung singulier plaisir, Priant Dieu Ma Tante qu'il vous ayt en sa Ste. and digne garde, A Fontynebleau le XIIIIe. Jour d'octobre 1611 Vre vien bonn' et affnee niepc. Marie' (Florence, Uffizi, Archivio Mediceo, 5953, 6c, 27/28). The architect sent to Florence was Louis Métezeau.

1612 Marie de Médicis purchases the Hôtel de Luxembourg from François de Pinay-Luxembourg.

1615 De Brosse takes up residence in the Rue de Vaugirard (Min. Cent. XXIV–249, 25 February 1614: Contract for the Hôtel Bénigne Bernard; the architect is described as living in the 'rue des Viels Augustins, paroisse Saint-Eustache': Min. Cent. XXIV–254 3 October 1616: *Quittance* for the above; the architect is 'demeurant à Saint Germain des Prés': Min. Cent. XXIV–276, 15 January 1618: in a further contract for the same Hôtel, de Brosse is 'demeurant . . . rue de Vaugirard'). In 1616, Paul de Brosse is described as living in his father's house 'en l'hostel du Lucenbor' (Chronology and Notes p. 199).

1614–1616 Various payments for the building-works. By 1616 work on the roof is particularly mentioned (Arch. Nat. KK–193/4, Comptes de Marie de Médicis).

1616 *September 1* De Brosse's workmen at the Luxembourg join rioters pillaging the Hôtel of the Maréchal d'Ancre, Rue de Tournon (Bassompierre, *Mémoires*, ed. Petitot, II, p. 123): '(Ils) prient des pièces de bois du devant du Luxembourg que l'on bâtissoit encore, pour rompre la porte dudict logis . . . et quantité de maçons du Luxembourg s'y etant joints ils entrèrent dedans'.

1620 Guillaume Berthelot, sculptor, starts work on the decoration of the Palace (Arch. Nat. KK–194/5, *Correspondance de Rubens*, II, p. 351).

1621 Marble brought from the Valois Mausoleum at Saint-Denis for use as paving and for the terrace-balustrade in the court (G. Brice, *Description de la Ville de Paris*, p. 55).

1622 *March* Letter to Florent d'Argouges, Marie de Médicis' treasurer, from Cardinal Richelieu enquiring about the progress of the building (Arch. du Ministère des Affaires Etrangères, Fonds de France, 776, f. 64).

April 3 D'Argouges replies, '. . . le pavillon sera pret à couvrir . . .' (ibid.). The pavilion referred to was that in the N.E. corner on the Rue de Vaugirard. In the *Procès Verbal* of 1623 it is referred to as 'le pavillon commancé'.

April 7 Peiresc writes to Rubens about the measurements of the Long Gallery in the W. wing, which is complete except for the interior decoration, door-cases, chimney-pieces, etc. (*Correspondance de Rubens*, II, p. 372): 'nous nous sommes rendus chez M. Brosse avec lequel nous avons pris les mesures exactes des espaces reservés dans la galerie pour les tableaux ... quant aux trois autres champs du fond, M. Brosse me promet d'en faire le dessin la semaine prochaine avec les mesures des portes qui doivent y venir. Il fera de même pour les quatres petits champs à l'entrée, mais pour ceux-la il demande quelque temps; il doit d'abord faire le dessin de la cheminée pour savoir quels espaces resteront libres sur les parois ...'. The correspondence on this subject and de Brosse's procrastination in the affair occupy ten months of the year 1622.

May 26 Peiresc writes to Rubens that Marie de Médicis has ordered eight statues from Guillaume Berthelot, '... qui doivent être posées autour du dôme surmontant le portail de son Palais' (ibid., II, pl 419): '... Elles doivent représenter Les Femmes Illustres. M. Berthelot et l'abbé m'ont demandé de désigner ses héroines; j'ai choisi Olympia mère d'Alexandre-le-Grand; Bérénice, mère de Ptolemée-Philadelphe; Livie, femme d'-Auguste; Mammée, mère d'Alexandre Sévère; Ste. Hélène, mère de Constantin; Ste. Clothilde, femme de St. Clovis; Berthe, mère de Charlemagne et Blanche, mère de St. Louis ...'. The relevance of this programme to the Queen-Mother is obvious; Peiresc asks Rubens' advice on it, but he suggests (ibid. III, p. 11) Allegorical rather than Queenly figures. The statues were of bronze and have now gone, stone figures having taken their place.

June 9 De Brosse involved with the fittings of the W. Gallery, doors, etc. (ibid. II, p. 437): 'Il m'a été impossible d'obtenir les mesures de M. Brosse, celui-ci rejetta sur les difficultés du lambris qu'il voudrait placer dans les panneaux, il cherche à lui trouver l'ornamentation indispensable qui s'adapte le mieux autour des portes mais je ne laisserai en repos qu'il n'ait terminé cette affaire ....'.

July 26 Letter from Florent d'Argouges to Cardinal Richelieu relevant to the finances of the building and exonerating de Brosse from suspicion of malpractice (Arch. Min. Des Affaires Etrangères, Fonds de France, 776, f. 245, and *Correspondance de Rubens*, III, p. 156, 21 April 1623). D'Argouges writes, '... Pour ce qui est du Bâtiment si vous n'ordonnez que deux mil livres à M. Brosse par semaine il faudra qu'il retranche la moité de ses ouvriers, ce n'est pas le moien duser de la dilligence que vous m'avez commandé par toutes les lettres qu vous avez plu m'écrire. J'ay veu la distribution par le même de deux mil livres que je luy fournis et je vous assure qu'il ne met rien à sa bourse ....'.

1623 *February 3* Marie de Médicis spends three weeks at the Luxembourg but sleeps in the old Hôtel du Luxembourg, the implication being that the Palace is not yet properly habitable (See this date, Chron. de Brosse, Cat. p. 201).

April 21 Peiresc writes to Rubens; he fears that proceedings will be instituted against de Brosse for bad technical advice, bad financial management and for unwarranted delay in the building programme (*Correspondance de Rubens*, III, p. 156): 'Un Procès était à craindre contre Monsieur Brosse, au sujet d'une partie de sa construction pour laquelle il avait mal conseillé, et que la construction de l'autre galerie était en retard, faute de vingt mille écus qui manquaient pour payer la maison d'un particulier dont on avait besoin pour jeter les fondements ...'.

June 26–August 23 These charges are brought and result in an examination and evaluation of the work done; two experts for de Brosse and two for Marie de Médicis. For de Brosse the experts were Jean Autissier, 'juré du Roy ès oeuvres de massonnerie', and Christophe Gamard, 'maître maçon, bourgeois de Paris'; and for the Queen, Pierre Saintôt and François Boucherat, 'bourgeois de Paris'. The text of the *Procès Verbal* survives, bound and complete (Paris, Bib. de l'Arsenal, MS. Fr. 5995).

1624 *March 14* Contract for building the E. Gallery, signed by de Brosse: (Bib. du Sénat, Recueil factice No. 2, Arch. P. 1. cf. Min. Cent. Répertoire LXXXVI).

March 24 De Brosse resigns as contractor and architect in charge of the Palace (Hirschfeld, p. 13 and Pannier, p. 59).

March 24 Marie de Médicis signs a contract with Marin de la Vallée for the completion of the Palace. De Brosse referred to as 'préceddant entrepreneur dudict pallais' (Bib. du Sénat, R. Fac. No. 2, Arch. P.1.: Hustin, p. 16 n. 2 published this document in full). It seems from this document and from the fact that immediately previously de Brosse had signed the contract for the E. Gallery, that even as late as 1626 his advice was sought on a detail of construction; and that de la Vallée fulfilled the rôle of contractor and overseer, without designing any important part of the Palace.

December 14 De Brosse referred to as 'cy devant architecte du Pallais' (Arrêt du Conseil d'Etat, B.N.MSS. Fr. 18202: Pannier, p. 264 ff; Cf. Chronology and Notes, p. 201).

1625 *April* Contract between Marin de la Vallée and Marie de Médicis (Min. Cent. Répertoire LXXXVI, No. 232). Document missing and not among those at the Bib. du Sénat.

1626 *April* Contract between Marin de la Vallée and Marie de Médicis (Min. Cent. Répertoire LXXXVI, No. 233). Document missing as above.

June 1 Contract between Marin de la Vallée and Marie de Médicis for the construction of the courtyard-terrace (Min. Cent. Répertoire LXXXVI, No. 235: document in Bib. du Sénat, R. Fac. 2 Arch. P. 1).

June 23 Salomon de Brosse and Alessandro Francini advise Marin de la Vallée on the above contract (Bib. du Sénat, ibid.).

December 8 Death of Salomon de Brosse.

1631 Marie de Médicis leaves the Luxembourg for the last time. From this date until 1646 the building is abandoned.

1646 *March 15* By an *Acte de Partage* Louis XIV cedes the Luxembourg to Gaston d'Orléans and it becomes the 'Palais d'Orléans'. Gaston was already living there, and the children of his second marriage were born in the Palace.

1660 *February 2* Death of Gaston d'Orléans.

1660–1733 The Palace occupied by Gaston d'Orléans' widow and his daughter Mademoiselle de Montpensier. The method by which the Palace was divided up between these ladies is of interest (Hirschfeld, p. 29 ff.), as we learn from it a certain amount about the interior and the uses of parts of the building, viz., 'Madame la Duchesse d'Orléans (prit) l'aile droite; le grand portail et ses terrasses, le dôme sur le grand portail ou etait le trésor des chartes, la cour et sa terrasse, le grand escalier, la chapelle, le passage sous l'escalier pour se rendre au jardin restaient en commun . . .'. Apart from this statement there has never been any indication of what use was made of the first floor of the entrance-pavilion, nor does this explain its later elaborate restoration and alteration by Chalgrin. The description of the passage under the staircase corresponds with the plan in Vol. II of the Marigny Album, in the Pierpont Morgan Library, New York.

1685 First edition of the *Description de la Ville de Paris* by Germain Brice. (Brice's passages on the Luxembourg are important, especially in the edition of 1725 which has a more detailed description of the first floor of the entrance-pavilion).

1693 *April 5* Death of Mlle de Montpensier. ('La grande Mademoiselle').

1694 Mlle d'Alençon, Duchesse de Guise, sister of the late Mme d'Orléans (d. 1672), gives the Palace to Louis XIV.

1715 Philippe d'Orléans, the Regent, installs his daughter, the Duchesse de Berry, in the Palace (Brice, op. cit.).

1733–1736 Considerable restoration of the building. The windows on the first floor cut down to the entablature of the Order on the ground floor, and balustrades inserted (Blondel, *Architecture Françoise*, II, p. 50).

1750 A museum of painting installed in the E. Gallery. The Luxembourg administered during the last years of Louis XV by the Marquis de Marigny (brother of Mme de Pompadour), 'Gouverneur des Maisons Royales', for whom the book of plans of the *Maisons Royales* in the Pierpont Morgan Library was drawn.

1776 Soufflot proposes various alterations to the Palace (Cf. Cat. Section III, i).

1778–1779 Proposed alterations by Chalgrin (ibid.).

1804 Chalgrin begins his alterations, and builds the new great staircase, the new Assembly Hall in the place of the old staircase, pierces the entrance-screen and alters the first floor of the entrance-pavilion.

1834 Alphonse de Gisors, architect to the Senate, begins the major alterations which left the Palace as it is today.

V

Paris, Church of Saint Gervais

I ORIGINAL DOCUMENTS

The contracts listed below also serve as the Chronology for this building.

PARIS, ARCHIVES NATIONALES,
MINUTIER CENTRAL

XXVI – 33: 23 April 1616; masonry contract between the churchwardens, the master mason Claude Monnard, and the master carpenter Claude Molleur; also signed by Clément Métezeau, possibly as surety, possibly as overseer.

XXVI – 47: 4 March 1622; further masonry contract, signed by Claude Monnard.

Note: In December 1618 a joinery contract was signed for the erection of a screen in the church, to the design of Métezeau: Min.Cent. XIX – 385, 15 December 1618. In January 1628 Claude Monnard contracted to build the stone organ-loft which houses the celebrated organ used by Couperin: Min.Cent. XXVI – 53, 23 1628.

II PUBLISHED SOURCES

G. Brice: *Nouvelle Description de Paris*, all eds., Paris, 1684–1725.

H. Sauval: *Histoire et recherches des antiquités de Paris*, I and II, Paris, 1724.

J. Piganiol de la Force: *Description de Paris*, Paris, 1736.

A. Daviler: *Cours d'Architecture . . .*, Paris, 1750.

J. F. Blondel, *Architecture Française*, Vol. II, Book IV, Paris, 1752–53 (Reprinted Paris, 1904).

A. N. Dézallier d'Argenville: *Voyage pittoresque de Paris*, Paris, 1755.

——, *Vies des fameux architectes*, Paris 1788.

H. Dumolin: *B.S.H.A.F.*, 1933, I, p. 45.

Dumolin and Outardel: *Les Eglises de France; Paris et la Seine*, Paris, 1936.

L. Brochard: *Saint-Gervais*, Paris, 1938.

P. du Colombier: 'Autour des Métezeau', *Bibliothèque d'Humanisme et Renaissance*, III, 1943.

L. Brochard: *Saint-Gervais, histoire de la paroisse*, Paris, 1950.

Michaux: *Histoire et description de Saint-Gervais*, Paris, Plon, n.d.

Boinet: *Les églises parisiennes*, I, Paris, 1962.

III PLANS AND ELEVATIONS

Drawings and Model

PARIS, BIBLIOTHEQUE NATIONALE

B.N.Est, Ve 53ᵉ, No. 452: drawing of the west front; pencil and wash, eighteenth century anon.; (Apparently made from the wooden model).

PARIS, SAINT GERVAIS

Baptistery Chapel: wooden model of the façade made for the churchwardens in 1615; noted by Sauval (I, p. 453) as then in the Lady Chapel; now forming retable of the altar.

Engravings

J. Marot: *Grand Marot* 'Portail de Saint Gervais, à Paris, du dessein du sieur de Brosses'.

Mariette, *Architecture Françoise* I, (Paris 1727). Pl. 5. 'Elevation du Portail de l'Eglise paroissiale de S. Gervais scise près la Place de Greve a Paris bati en 1616 sur les dessins de Jacques de Brosse'. Pl. 6. 'Profils en grand des principaux membres d'architecture du Portail de l'Eglise de S. Gervais'. These two plates from Mariette appear in Blondel, *Architecture Françoise* (1752–53), Vol. II, Book IV, (between pp. 117 and 118), with slightly different inscriptions on the plate of the Orders. (Pl. 182).

Rennes, Palais du Parlement de Bretagne

(now Palais de Justice)

I ORIGINAL DOCUMENTS

Many documents survive from the long period during which the Palais at Rennes was under construction; comparatively few of these, however, deal directly with its architectural history. The greatest gap in our knowledge of this history is caused by the loss of de Brosse's original *Devis descriptif* of 1619. Documents concerning the interior decoration of the building are not listed, as this work was carried out after 1655 and not to designs by de Brosse (but cf. A. Mussat, op. cit., Section II).

RENNES, ARCHIVES DEPARTEMENTALES, ILLE-ET-VILAINE

Arch.Dép. Titres concernant le Palais de la Ville de Rennes, Liasse 250: Letters-patent of Henri IV, 3 July 1609; construction of a new building for the Parlement authorized.
Ibid.: 'Devis et estat général de touttes choses utiles et nécessaires pour la construction du Bastiment du Pallays'; Germain Gaultier (1614–6115).
Ibid: Submissions by Gaultier concerning the proposed building (part of a collection of papers, plans, etc., mostly lost, deposited with the Parlement, cf. Arch.Dép. Arrêts du Parlement, Liasse Palais).
Arch.Dép. Titres concernant le Palais de la Ville de Rennes, Liasse 251: 'Supplique des bourgeois de Rennes', 1618; signed Gilles Martin, Sindic; request for the commencement of building operations.
Ibid.: Description of the laying of the first stone (15 September 1618).
Ibid.: Instructions by Gaultier to Hervé Pellan, master mason, January 1619.

Ibid.: Register of workmen employed during and after 1618.
Ibid.: 'Comptes de Gilles Mérault et Georges Chauvet, commissaires l'an 1618'.
Arch.Dép. Série Bᵉ XI (ex Arch. de la Ville de Rennes): Commission of Germain Gaultier as 'conducteur de l'oeuvre du pallais', October 1618; signed by Gaultier.
Ibid.: 'Devis du Pallais dressé par Corbineau, architecte nommé pour en faire la conduite', 1624.
Ibid.: *Mémoire* by Corbineau; work still outstanding on the N. wing, 1627.
Ibid.: 'Estat des ouvrages de massonerie . . . (etc.) . . . à faire pour rendre le palais de Rennes en perfection . . .': estimate of work outstanding drawn up by Pierre Hardy, signed by the Commissioners on 2 March 1636.
Ibid.: 'Devis pour la construction et pour continuer . . . le corps du bastiment du palais du costé des pères Cordeliers . . .': unsigned, dated 30 March 1640.
Ibid.: 'Copie du marché fait avec Tugal

Caris pō la continuation du palais neuf du costé des R. P. Cordeliers', 28 April 1640.
Parchment-covered notebook, 'I*er Registre*': 'pour servir à . . . MM (les) commissaires . . . pour aviser ce qui se doit faire pour le bastiment du Palais, commencé le 10 Septembre 1617'; years 1614–1624; annexed to Titres concernant le palais . . . de Rennes, Liasses 250 and 251.

Arch.Dép. F.306: MS. 'Journal d'un Bourgeois de Rennes . . . XVII siècle'.
Note: In addition to the above documents use has been made of the various sources contained in the Registres Secrets, Arrêts du Conseil du Parlement and other official papers fully listed by Bourde de la Rogerie and Nitsch and d'Harcourt, cf. Section II.

II   PUBLISHED SOURCES

M. H. Bourdonnay: *Le Palais de Justice de Rennes*, Rennes, 1902.
H. Bourde de la Rogerie: *Germain Gaultier, architecte et sculpteur et les premiers projets du Palais du Parlement de Bretagne*, Rennes, 1930.
G. Nitsch and Xavier d'Harcourt: *Le Palais*

de Justice de Rennes et la Cour du Parlement de Bretagne, Rennes, 1930.
A. Mussat: *Quelques précisions sur la décoration intérieur du Parlement de Bretagne*, (see Chap. IX, note 19).

III   PLANS AND ELEVATIONS

Drawings

RENNES, ARCHIVES DEPARTMENTALES, ILLE-ET-VILAINE

Arch.Dép. Titres concernant le palais . . . liasse 250: sketch by Gaultier for the timbering of one of the pavilions, *c.* 1614–1615.
Ibid.: (recorded, but lost ex liasse 250): original plans made by de Brosse, August 1618, signed by the commissioners and deposited with the Parlement; three separate sheets; ground floor, first floor, attics; fully annotated by the architect; photographed, and reproduced by Pannier 1911 (Pls 196–198 in present work).
Arch.Dép. C 315, Fonds Intendance de Bretagne: File dated 1724. Drawings by Jacques V. Gabriel connected with his alterations of 1726:
i Plan of ground floor, S. end of building, showing terrace and *perron* removed and new staircase in place in the courtyard; inscr. by

Gabriel and dated 'ce huitième may sept cens vingt cinq Gabriel'.
ii S. façade before the alterations; inscr. accordingly (Pl. 200).
iii Project for the alteration of the S. façade; inscr. accordingly and dated 'fait à Rennes le 19 novembre 1724'.
iv Alternative project for the above; unsigned and undated; this was the one executed by Gabriel.
Arch.Dép. C 315: A further series of drawings made at the time of the installation in the Palais of the Tribunal Civil; drawn by G. Richelot, signed by him and by the Prefect of Ille-et-Vilaine, and dated 27 December 1838 (Pls 205, 206 are from this series).
Ibid.: Nineteenth-century perspective reconstruction of the S. front and the W. façade before Gabriel's alterations; signed Dennieul and inscr. 'Palais de Justice de Rennes dans son etât ancien . . . d'après les plans de l'époque.

Engravings

Only one engraving of the Palais made before Gabriel's alterations to the S. façade is known. This forms the frontispiece to a *Thèse en action* spoken by the pupils of the Jesuit College at Rennes on the occasion of the

return of the Parlement from exile on 1 February 1690. The only extant example recorded is in the Musée Archéologique de Rennes (cf. Pannier, op. cit., p. 221, n. 1) (Pl. 199).

IV CHRONOLOGY AND NOTES

1609 *July 3* Letters-patent issued by Henri IV concerning the building of a new Palais, 'pour bastir ung palais Royal et y établir le Parlement'. The town of Rennes is authorized to impose a tax of 3 deniers on each 'pot de vin breton ou de cidre et un sol sur chaque pot de vin non breton', sold in the town, and one-third of this is to be devoted to the building expenses (Bourde de la Rogerie, Germain Gaultier, p. 17; Arch. Dept. Titres ... Liasse 250).

July Germain Gaultier arrives in Rennes. He is appointed 'conducteur des oeuvres de la ville (ibid.).

1613 *November 2* Commissioners appointed to choose the site of the new Palais (ibid.).

1614 *October 31* Plans are submitted by Gaultier and a colleague, Thomas Poussin, but are not accepted (Arch. Dép. F. 306, publ. de la Bigne, *Mélanges d'histoire et d'archéologie bretonnes.* I).

1614–1615 Gaultier prepares two further plans known as 'le grand dessin' and 'le petit dessin' (cf. below) (Bourde de la Rogerie, p. 19). He also draws up his 'Etat et devis' for the proposal building (Arch. Dep. Titres .... Liasse 250; trnscr. by Bourde de la Rogerie).

1615 *June 16* Gaultier presents a scheme for the roof-timbers of two pavilions of the Palais, together with sketches (ibid.).

1617 *September 28* Gaultier's 'petit dessin' adopted; the alignments, etc., are ordered to be made; 'Architecte, Gaultier, Arpenteurs Cerin et Symon Brundeau ... pour tenir

l'ordre du Bâtiment'. It is also decided to buy twelve columns for the principal façade and steps for the *perron* in front of it (Arch. Dép. 1er Régistre', fols. 1–3 *verso*).

1618 *March 4* A decision is reached in Council to send for Salomon de Brosse, and this is ratified by the representatives of the townspeople (ibid., fol. 6 *et seq.*).

July 26 Lettre-de-cachet of Louis XIII ordering de Brosse to proceed to Rennes (Bourde de la Rogerie, p. 20).

August 8 De Brosse arrives at Rennes (ibid).

August 14 De Brosse appears before the commissioners: 'Le procureur syndic exposa que le Sr de Brosse depuis qu'il est en ceste ville auroit vu les plans dudit Palays qui auroient esté cy-devant faicts par Germain Gaultier maistre architecte, tant du grand que du petit desseign'. These plans examined, and also 'celuy faict par ledict Sieur de Brosse depuis qu'il est en ceste ville. Et ayant le Sieur de Brosse représenté le plan par luy faict, et veu ceulx qui ont esté cy-devant faictz ... et sur le tout délibéré, les dicts sieurs commissaires ont arresté que ledict sieur de Brosse fera ung aultre plan en la forme qui luy a été prescripte, pour estre Jeudy prochain représenté en la Cour et icelluy veu, y estre ordonné et chiffré (Arch. Dép. '1er Régistre', fol. 7 *verso et seq.*; Bourde de la Rogerie, pp. 20 and 21).

August 16 De Brosse is officially nominated 'Architecte du Palais du Parlement'. He presents the 'aultre plan' which is approved.

'Et fut ordonné que . . . ledit Palais sera construit et basty . . . suivant ledit plan qui demeura au greffe de ladite Cour, sera chiffré par les commissaires députés pour la direction dudit bâtiment duquel sera fait description et devis, ledit de Brosse appelé en présence des députés de la communauté de Rennes' (Transcr., Bourde de la Rogerie, p. 21; Arch. Dép. Série B, Fonds du Parlement, titres du Palais). De Brosse is further ordered to make copies of the plan for the Procureur-Syndic.

August 22 De Brosse declares that the King needs him in Paris and has recalled him. He leaves Rennes, after receiving 1,000 livres in payment for his services (Bourde de la Rogerie, p. 22).

August 23 The Parlement pays to Jean Saiget, 'hoste de l'hostellerie de la Harpe', 260 livres for the accommodation of de Brosse and his retinue (ibid.).

August 24 The Procureur-Syndic presents copies of de Brosse's plans to the representatives of the townspeople: (ibid., p. 21, n. 3).

September 15 The first stone of the building is laid by Germain Gaultier (Arch. Dép. Liasse 251; G. Nitsch, Le Palais de Justice de Rennes, p. 16).

October 4 Letters-patent of Louis XIII, continuing for nine years 'le debvoir d'un sol et liard pour pot (de vin) afin de donner moien de bastir ung Pallais audit lieu pour loger notre dict Cour, duquel Pallais le Sieur Des Brosses, nostre architectre a réglé l'architecture . . .' (Nitsch, p. 16).

October 9 Official commission of Gaultier as conductor of the work. He is to be paid 50 livres a month personal salary. He is asked to present his accounts for work done concerning the Palais, from 1615 up to 8 August 1618 when de Brosse arrived in Rennes: (Arch. Dép. Série Be XI).

1619 *January* Gaultier's journey to Paris to consult de Brosse (Bourde de la Rogerie, pp. 28–29, and n. 1, p. 29).

March 15 Gaultier arrives back in Rennes. Drawings and *devis* are deposited with the Parlement and copies are made for Gaultier (Arch. Dép. Régistres des commissaires; Bourde de la Rogerie, p. 29, n. 1).

1620 *June* Gaultier's second journey to Paris to consult de Brosse (Bourde de la Rogerie, p. 30 and no. 1).

1624 *January 6–7* A vault under construction collapses; '. . . il tomba une des voutes du Pallais, celle du coin devers la Tour le Bart' (Arch. Dép. F.306). Gaultier was severely injured, and the Président de la Cour, de Brie, asked the Procureur Syndic to start looking for a new architect. Gaultier protests and delay is accorded 'jusque à ce que ledit Gaultier soit ouy de bouche' (Bourde de la Rogerie, p. 31 and n. 3).

March 6 The commissioners go to the Palais where experts pronounce on why the vault collapsed (ibid.).

March 11 Death of Germain Gaultier: (ibid.).

March 22 Jacques Corbineau is called before the commissioners as a candidate for succession to Gaultier (ibid., p. 32).

March 26 Jacques Corbineau is sworn in as conductor of the work and also succeeds Gaultier as 'conducteur des oeuvres de la ville'. He is also made to promise to follow the plan made by de Brosse (ibid. and n. 2).

1625 *September* Cordineau's *devis* (Arch. Dép. Série Be XI). (The date of this *devis* is given by Bourde de la Rogerie on p. 32, but no source for it is quoted. The *devis* has an old inscription on the cover, '1624 Devis du bâtiment du pallays dressé par Corbineau architecte nommé en 1624 pour en faire la conduitte'. However, Bourde de la Rogerie is not often inaccurate.)

1627 *January* *Mémoire* drawn up by Corbineau about work remaining to be done in parts of the N. wing (Arch. Dép. Série BᵉXI: 'Mémoire de ce qu'il est à faire pour rendre regnable le -?- qui fut faict le dixhuictiesme jour du présent moye de janvier mil six cent vingt sept au corps de logis du pallais Royal de Rennes du costé du Septentrion . . .'. Plague breaks out in Rennes; building is brought to a standstill on the Palais (Bourde de la Rogerie p. 33).

1628 Despite the difficulties, early in the year the commissioners put the completion of the N. wing out to tender. This was 'la charpente nécessaire au corps-de-logis dépendant dudit oeuvre, du costé du septentrion prest en état de recevoir la charpente' (Nitsch, p. 21–22).

March 2 Julien Gaunarry, 'charpentier', receives the contract (ibid.).

July 3 The work for the roofing with slates is put out to tender; 'l'adjudication des travaux de la partie septentrionale' (ibid).

1628–1634 The plague continuing, work is dropped and the Palais remains unfinished and roofless (ibid. and Bourde de la Rogerie p. 33).

1634 *March 24* The Parlement orders that the contract for finishing the building be put out to tender; '. . . à qui voudroit entreprendre la construction de tout ou partie de ce qui reste à faire pour l'accomplissement dud. bâtiment suivant le plan qui en a esté faict tant pour les murailles et voultes que charpente . . .' (Nitsch, p. 22).

1636 *February 19* Apparently this appeal went unanswered. Further efforts made to find contractors (ibid, p. 22).

February 29 Louis de Keraly, 'conseiller à la cour de Rennes', sends word from Paris that he has found 'le Sieur Barbier' who, with Guillaume Mathurin, Jean Dury and Pierre Hardy, will undertake the contract. They arrive and are interviewed (ibid., p. 23 and Bourde de la Rogerie, p. 33).

March 10 The offer and propositions of Pierre Hardy (working with 'Duris', i.e., Jean, the son of Charles du Ry) are accepted. The Parlement negotiates with Hardy to finish the work completely within six years (Arch. Dép. Série Bᵉ XI *Estat de ouvrages . . .* Pierre Hardy).

1640 *March 30–1642 April 30* The four outer and inner walls being ready for the roof, a contract is signed by the Parlement with Tugal Caris (now 'architecte du Palais'), Bonaventure Pelletier, 'charpentier de la ville de Nantes' and 'un nommé Malateste, charpentier' (ibid. Devis pour la construction . . . Tugal Caris. Nitsch, p. 24).

1643 *April 15* Trouble over the roofing of the N. end of the building; decision to raise pavilions (Nitsch, p. 24).

1647 *November 26* Parlement re-affirms that the original drawings be adhered to (ibid., p. 24).

November 26 Order of the same date that the terrace shall now be built between the pavilions, '. . . suivant led. premier dessin': (ibid., p. 24).

1648 *April 4* Trouble about the roof; the money is not forthcoming to buy the roof-timbers. Pierre Corbineau, now architect-in-charge, is forced to suspend work (ibid., p. 25; Bourde de la Rogerie, p. 33).

1650 *December 14* A request submitted to the Parlement by P. Corbineau that something be done to protect the unroofed building (Nitsch, p. 25).

1651 *February 16* Orders given by 'Maître Gabriel Constantin et François Grimaudet, conseillers', that suitable measures should be taken (ibid).

November 9 Nothing having been done, Corbineau complains to the Parlement; the walls are still uncovered and 'peuvent dépérir par le rigueur de l'hyver'. A *procès verbal* is ordered on the matter (ibid., p. 26).

1652 *September* Work held up by 'malversa-tions' concerning the tax on wine levied for the building-work (ibid., p. 26).

1655 The Parlement at last moves in to the still unfininished building (ibid., p. 26; Mussat, Quelques précisions. . . .).

1726 Jacques V. Gabriel called in to modify de Brosse's main façade; he removes the *perron* and terrace, erects a covered stair in the court, and arranges the basement of the main façade in the manner existing to-day.

1790 *February* Suppression of the Parlement and institution of a 'Cour Souveraine Pro-visoire'.

1804 The 'Cour d'Appel' installed in the first floor.

1836 Installation of the Tribunal Civil and the official naming of the building as The Palais de Justice.

1838 Alterations made to the buildings to accommodate the Tribunal (Arch. Dép. C.315, Drawings of Richelot).

Château of Verneuil-sur-Oise

I ORIGINAL DOCUMENTS

There is only one very unimportant document concerning Verneuil in the Archives Nationales. The papers preserved in the Condé Archives at Chantilly are only helpful for the appearance of the château after 1600, and all the documentary sources are secondary to the writings, drawings and engravings of Jacques I Androuet du Cerceau.

PARIS, ARCHIVES NATIONALES,
MINUTIER CENTRAL

XIX – 384: 5 September 1617; *Promesse,* Adam Lefebvre, carpenter, to Dame Catherine Henriette de Balzac, Marquise de Verneuil, to carry out work on the floor of her room at the château.

CHANTILLY, MUSEE CONDE, ARCHIVES

CC¹2: 6 February 1575; 'Contrat d'aquisition faicte par M le duc et Mme la duchesse de Nemours de M et Mme de Boulainvilliers de la terre at seigneurie de Verneuil' (old copy of a deed registered at the Châtelet before the notaries Paulmyer and Frémont).

CC¹8: 3 February 1615; *Aveu et dénombrement*: Henriette de Balzac to Louis XIII, voluntary declaration of possessions at Verneuil.

CC¹16: 16 July 1707; *Aveu et dénombrement:* Henri-Jules de Bourbon, Prince de Condé, to Louis XIV; voluntary declaration of possessions at Verneuil.

II PUBLISHED SOURCES

Jacques Androuet du Cerceau: *Les Plus Excellents Bastiments de France,* I, 1576.

H. Sauval: *Histoire et recherches des antiquités de Paris,* Vol. II, Paris 1724.

G. Macon: *Chantilly, les archives, le cabinet des titres,* Vol. IV, Paris, 1929.

I. Toesca: 'The drawings by Jacques Androuet du Cerceau the elder in the Vatican Library', *Burl. Mag.,* XCVIII, 1956.

A. Ploix: *Verneuil, château royal oublié,* Paris, 1957.

R. Coope: 'History and Architecture of the Château of Verneuil-sur-Oise', *G.d.B.A.,* LIX, May–June 1962.

R. Cazelles: 'Plans du château de Verneuil-sur-Oise au XVIIe siècle, *G.d.B.A.,* LXXIV, December 1969.

III PLANS AND ELEVATIONS

Drawings

PARIS, ARCHIVES NATIONALES, (MAIN ARCHIVES)

Arch.Nat. N – 111 Oise 34 and 54:
Arch.Nat. N – 11 Oise 50:
Arch.Nat. N.III Oise 148 and 179:
All these are general plans of the neighbour-hood with block-plans or other summary in-dications of the château, its gardens and canals.

PARIS, BIBLIOTHEQUE NATIONALE

B.N. Cartes et Plans: Plan by Dubois, 1723; publ. Ploix, op. cit., 1957, pl. II.

PARIS, LOUVRE

Dessins, R.F.5946, 'Album de Brosse', fol. 14 *recto*: part of the entrance-front (S. pavilion) deriving both from du Cerceau (*Les Plus Excellents Bastiments*, the *Second Design*) and the Cooper Union drawing, New York (see below).

CHANTILLY, MUSEE CONDE, ARCHIVES

Unclassified file, inscr. 'sans interêt' (prob-ably part of the papers confiscated during the Revolution, taken to Vincennes, and returned to the Condé family at the Restoration); plan of the ground and first floors of the château (development of the *Second Design*); inscr. 'à vaniour' (Pls 16, 17).

LONDON, BRITISH MUSEUM

B.M. C 99[a], Ducerceau, Vols. III and IV: nine drawings, Ducerceau nos. 39–47; inscr. as follows:
39. 'Plan du Chasteau neuf de verneil pres Senlis'.
40. 'Cecy est le plan du Chasteau de Verneuil avec le circuit des jardins, allees, galleries, canaux, que la veuë des par(c)s co(mm)e il se veoit . . .' (Pl. 14).
41. 'Ce portraict est pour monstrer l'elevation du Chasteau neuf que le viel de Verneuil pres Senlis avec les jardinages et autres lieux'.
42. 'Face du devant du Chasteau de Verneuil en laquelle est la principalle entree'.
43. 'Face du costé de la court ou est l'entree dudit Chãu de Verneuil'.
44. 'Face de la Gallerie dans la court du Chasteau de Verneuil En laquelle au second estage sont aucunes effigies des plus notables qui ont regne la monarchie des Assiriens et sont les figures de sept piedz de hault'.
45. 'Les six figures de la Monarchie des Assiriens qui sont mis en la gallerie du Chasteau de Verneuil'.
46. 47. Four other drawings of chimney-pieces intended for the *salle* and other parts of the interior.

LONDON, ROYAL INSTITUTE OF BRITISH ARCHITECTS

Drawings Library, Gentilhâtre Album, fol. 14 *verso*: drawing of an angle-pavilion and part of the garden-front (*Second Design*) from du Cerceau, *Les Plus Excellents Bastiments*, I, inscr. 'Vergneulle'.

ROME, VATICAN LIBRARY

MS. Barberini, Lat. 4398: 'Plan du chasteau de Verneuil'; drawing by or from the circle of the elder du Cerceau; possibly the earliest project for the château.
Ibid: Elevation of the court-façade; N. wing, with the Assyrian kings; directly derived from B.N. no. 44 and *Les Plus Excellents Bastiments* pl. 55.

NEW YORK, COOPER UNION MUSEUM

Prints and Drawings (uncat.) ex Destailleur and Decloux colls.: Elevation of the entrance-front of Verneuil; derived, with important variations, from the *Second Design* (*Plus Excellents Bastiments*); 4·29 x 5·49 cms.; anon.; late sixteenth or early seventeenth century (Pl. 21).

Engravings

J. Androuet du Cerceau: ten plates (not corresponding to the B.M. drawings) in *Les Plus Excellents Bastiments*, I, 1576:
pl. 47: 'Le plan du bastiment neuf.'
ibid.: 'Le plan du bastiment neuf comme il est de present (viz. the *Second Design*; double-spread (Pl. 15).
pl. 48: 'plan du Bastiment de verneul tant du viel logis que du Nouveau Encommance Avec Les Jardrins, Allées et contenu aussi partie de commancement de la closture du parc'.
pl. 49: 'Desseing de Lelevation de verneul tant du viel logis que du nouveau Encommance avec Les Tardins allees et canaux' (elevation of pl. 48).
pl. 50: 'face du dehors du coste du parc laquelle na este parachevee'; (entrance-front) (Pl. 18).
pl. 51: 'Ce desseing avoit este arreste pour la face de la terrace qui eust este devant le logis neuf' (façade of 'the garden pavilion') (Pl. 19).
pl. 52: 'face dans la court opposite a celle de dehors du coste du parc laquelle na este parachevee'.
pl. 53: 'La monstre du bastiment du coste du parc qui est lentree' (*Second Design*) (Pl. 20).
pl. 54: 'La monstre du bastiment du coste du vallon qui est opposite de lentree' (*Second Design*).
pl. 55: 'Gallerie dans la court' (N. wing).
pl. 56: 'Verneuil, Fontaine pour le jardin'.

I. Silvestre: Three views of the château all based on the *First Design* and bearing no relation to the building as executed:

i   'Veuë et perspective du Chasteau de Verneuil à douze lieux de Paris appartenant à très haut et très puissant Prince, Monseigneur Henry de Bourbon, Evesque de Metz, Prince du S. Empire, Abbé des Abbayes de Saint Germain des Prez lez Paris, Thiron, etc'. (F.62(9)).

ii   'Veuë de l'entrée du Chasteau de Verneuil' (F.62(10)).

iii   'Veuë du Chasteau de Verneuil du costé des parterres' (F.62(11)).
No. iii is interesting, for it purports to show the garden-front of the *First Design*. This was not engraved, or, as far as is known, drawn in large by du Cerceau. Silvestre has enlarged and adapted the small elevation from du Cerceau's perspective view (B.M.41); clearly he never visited the château, although it still stood throughout the ownership of Henri de Bourbon (son of Henriette d'Entragues and Henri IV).
Aveline: 'Veuë et perspective du Château de Verneuil', 1692 (entrance-front) (Pl. 22).
Poilly: 'Veuë et perspective du Chasteau de Verneuil' (entrance-front).
Aveline's and Poilly's representations correspond in general to the descriptions of 1615 and 1707 (cf. above Sect. I).
Dupont: Pair of engravings of the ruins of Verneuil, dated 1776; from 'Voyage pittoresque de France par une Société de gens de lettres, province de Valois et Comté de Senlis,' Paris, 1789 (publ. *Méms. de la Soc. Académique de l'Oise*, II, 1852); also B.N.Est. Vᵃ 144 (cf. Pl. 23).

IV CHRONOLOGY AND NOTES

1568 Philippe de Boulainvilliers inherits Verneuil from his father (Chantilly Arch. Série CC¹; cf. Ploix, *Château royal oublié*, p. 8). A medieval manor, recently rebuilt in more modern style, existed on the property: (Coope, *G.d.B.A.*, LIX, p. 292).

c. **1568–1575** Jacques I Androuet du Cerceau employed by Boulainvilliers to design and build a new château on a site above the old manor (Du Cerceau, *Les Plus Excellents Bastiments'*, I, 1576).

1568 Arrival of Jehan de Brosse, 'maître architecteur', at Verneuil. In this year he is recorded as resident at Verneuil and as buying land there (Chantilly Arch., *Acte du Terrier de Verneuil*, publ. Pannier, p. 26).

1575 Boulainvilliers, having run into financial difficulties, sells the property to the Duc and Duchesse de Nemours. The new château consists only of foundations and the un-unfinished N. wing (Chantilly Arch., CC¹2 (copy); Coope, op. cit., p. 294).

1576 Publication by du Cerceau of the first volume of *Les Plus Excellents Bastiments de France*, containing the designs made for Verneuil for Philippe de Boulainvilliers (the *First Design*) and the modified plans and elevations made for the Duc de Nemours (the *Second Design*) (du Cerceau, op. cit.).

1576–1585 Building on the modified programme continues at Verneuil (Coope, op. cit., p. 294–295. *Note:* owing to misunderstanding on the author's part of the calendar-reforms in France, the dates in the *G.d.B.A.* article were given wrongly. The sale of the property to the Duc de Nemours was in 1575 and not 1576 N.S.). During this period de Brosse was training at Verneuil in the du Cerceau *atelier*.

1585 Death of the Duc de Nemours. Probable year of du Cerceau's death. Work ceases at the château during the following years of religious strife in France. The parts probably completed by this time were the main buildings of the château, the *corps-de-logis*, wings and pavilions (Coope, op. cit., p. 295).

1600 *June 3* Letters-patent of Henri IV raising the title of Verneuil to a Marquisate in favour of Henriette de Balzac d'Entragues, to whom the King had given the château and property (Chantilly Arch., publ. Ploix, op. cit., pp. 70–75 (reproducing original documents, pl. VI).

*c.***1600–1616** De Brosse working for Henriette d'Entragues at the château. He finishes the entrance-pavilion, builds the screen, the forecourt and gates in the wall surrounding the estate. 'La marquise de Verneuil . . . a continué le magnifique château de Verneuil' (Sauval, II, p. 311; Coope, op. cit., pp. 313–315; Cazelles, *G.d.B.A.*, LXXIV, December 1969, pp. 361–364).

1609 Disgrace and retirement to Verneuil of Henriette d'Entragues (Ploix, op. cit., p. 101).

1617 *December 20* 'Acte de foi et d'hommage' by de Brosse for the Seigneurie of du Plessis Pommeraye near Verneuil, in lieu of money owed to him, 'a cause des advances et frais par lui faictz et qu'il pouvoit prétendre en conséquence des bastiments qu'il a faict faire audict lieu de Verneuil. . . .' De Brosse also lent the Marquise considerable sums of money (Chantilly Arch., Châtellerie de Creil; see also Pannier, op. cit., pp. 117–118, and *Pièces Justificatives*, pp. 252–255). De Brosse is referred to as 'entrepreneur desdicts bastiments de Verneuil'.

1633 Death of Henriette d'Entragues, Marquise de Verneuil; she is succeeded by her son Henri de Bourbon, created Duc de Verneuil in 1652 (Ploix, op. cit., p. 9).

1705 The château and estate bought by the Prince de Condé; the archives removed to Chantilly (ibid.).

1734 Demolition work begun on the château.

APPENDIXES

Catalogue of other works sometimes attributed to Salomon de Brosse

I

Aqueduc d'Arcueil

THIS aqueduct, which in part followed the course of a Roman prototype, was constructed to bring the waters of Rungis to the Luxembourg and its neighbourhood, and was begun in 1613. Louis XIII laid the first stone, and the work was completed in 1623.[1] Three-quarters of the water was destined for the Palace and its gardens, the remainder by the Queen's consent for a few privileged inhabitants of the neighbourhood.

There is a representation of the Aqueduct in the border of Gomboust's plan of Paris, and another in an engraving made in 1705 after a drawing by Guéthard.[2] The 1705 engraving shows the massive construction pierced only at fairly widely-spaced intervals by arches, and supported by buttresses used in their upper stages as a Doric 'order', their capitals supporting a string course with modillions.

One 'château d'Eau' was recently recorded at Fresnes,[3] and other fragments are to be found along the course of the Aqueduct.

Sauval attributed the Aqueduct to de Brosse: '. . . Jaques de Brosse, l'un des plus habiles architectes de son tems, qui a donné les dessins du Palais du Luxembourg, de l'Aqueduc d'Arceuil et de plusieurs autres grands bâtiments . . .'.[4]

Pannier, though without citing Sauval,[5] gives the work to de Brosse, and in

1. Journal of Jean Hérouard, quoted by Pannier, p. 68 and n. 3, for the laying of the first stone. Dézallier d'Argenville (*Vies des fameux architectes*, Paris 1788, p. 332) attributes the aqueduct to de Brosse but dates it rather early as he states that it was 'entirely completed' by 1624.

2. Repro. Engr. by Silvestre, Pannier, p. 69. (F. 167).

3. Hautecoeur, I, p. 592: '. . . il est fait de pierres bien appareillées; un dôme sur un plan carré contient un lanternon'.

4. II, p. 454; part of his description of the W. front of Saint Gervais.

5. He cites (p. 241, nn. 1 and 3) L. Vaudoyer, *Magasin pittoresque*, 1845, p. 77, and Ch. Lucas, *Grande Encyclopédie*, t. XIII. On p. 67, n. 2, he writes: 'Nous avons utilisé . . . un . . . *Mémoire manuscrit sur les fontaines et Aqueducs de Paris* (Recueil Ameilhon, Tome XI, Bibl. de l'Arsenal Ms. 3937, fol. 37 sqq)'. Pannier quotes as follows in his text: 'Celui de tous les entrepreneurs qui demanda le moins fut Jean Coing, maître maçon à Paris . . . l'ouvrage lui fut adjugé le 18 octobre 1612. Dès le 11 décembre suivant Jean Coing reçut l'Ordre de se trouver à l'Hôtel de Ville avec les Sieurs Pierre Guillain, Francine, Metheizeau et Cosnier pour se transporter avec MM le prévot des marchands et echevins à Rungis . . .'. Pannier adds that Jean Gobelin took over in 1614.

so doing seems to follow an established tradition. Hautecoeur, however, states that Louis Métezeau and not de Brosse was the architect, giving as authority a document of 1644: 'On y lit que Louis Métezeau est architecte de l'Aqueduc et que les plans ont été dressés par Francine'.[6] The entrepreneur was Jean Coing, and, after he died in 1614, Jean Gobelin. The appearance of these two members of de Brosse's 'team' in the affair may be significant.[7]

In view of the late date of the 1644 document in the history of the aqueduct and of the respectable tradition that de Brosse was its architect, the attribution can perhaps be left open until more nearly contemporary or conclusive information is available. The confusion between de Brosse and Métezeau as architects of the W. front of Saint Gervais may be recalled in this context; also, Sauval's attributions should not be discounted without definite contrary evidence.

6. Hautecoeur, I, p. 592 and nn. 9 and 10, citing Mousset, *Les Francines*, 44, and Bertin, *Mémoires pour servir à l'histoire de Paris*, XXVIII, 1901, p. 10. The document on which Hautecoeur bases his attribution is an entry for 9 July 1664 in the 'régistre des commissaires du Roi pour les fontaines de Rungis', which was discovered by M. Tesson.

7. See above n. 5.

II

Château of Liancourt

THIS château was probably built (or rebuilt on the site of an older one) by Roger du Plessis, Duc de Liancourt, and his wife Jeanne de Schomberg,[1] the owners of the house in Paris upon which de Brosse had worked when it was the Hôtel de Bouillon. The château was nearly completed in 1637 when it was visited and described in detail by the brothers Godefroy.[2]

Silvestre engraved the buildings and the celebrated garden in a splendid series of plates made in 1656.[3]

Like the Hôtel de Liancourt in Paris, the château passed into the family of la Rochefoucauld; it was pulled down by the orders of the Duc de la Rochefoucauld in 1803.

There is no firm evidence as to the designer of this château. As shown by Silvestre the gallery, 'face du costé du jardin à fleurs' is reminiscent of Lemercier at the Palais Cardinal. As Lemercier was the architect probably responsible for the rebuilding of de Brosse's Hôtel de Bouillon for the Duc de Liancourt, the attribution to him seems reasonable on the grounds of style and on the supposition that, if he worked for the owners in Paris, he is likely to have done so at Liancourt.

Monsieur E.-J. Ciprut however, following his discovery of Paul de Brosse's activity at Liancourt in 1628, deduced that the latter was brought in after his father's death in 1626 to complete a work begun by Salomon de Brosse.[4]

On 3 March 1628 Paul de Brosse signed a contract to complete the work at Liancourt; he was to 'percer' the doors and windows of the chapel and the 'deux pavillons dedans' (presumably those flanking the entrance-pavilion). He was also to erect the balustrades of the terrace 'du parterre de derrière'.[5]

1. Cf. P. de Cossé Brissac, *Châteaux de France disparus*, Editions Tel, 1947, p. 79.

2. Jean Tremblot, 'Liancourt (Oise) en 1637 (d'après la description de Denis II Godefroy)', *B.S.H.A.F.*, 1918/19; publ. separately Paris, 1920. The original Godefroy manuscript, a journal of travels in 1637, is in the Bibliothèque de l'Institut.

3. F.230, series 3–8.

4. *Bull. Soc. Hist. Prot. Fr.*, CX, October–December 1964, p. 260 ff.

5. Ibid. On the same day Paul also signed a contract to rebuild completely the village church at Liancourt at the Duc's expense – his only known completely independent commission. The church remains as he built it.

We know from the Godefroy description that there was a chapel in the entrance-pavilion,[6] and may presume this to have been the one completed by Paul. At first glance this pavilion – the only part of the château as engraved by Silvestre to do so – does somewhat resemble de Brosse's style, and the arrangement is of course that of the entrance-pavilions at Verneuil, Montceaux and Coulommiers.

The stylistic resemblance is, however, superficial, for on closer examination it appears merely derivative. The style is also very unlikely for a late work by de Brosse, which one would presume this to be.[7] It appears to be modelled on such early works at Montceaux and may possibly have been by Paul de Brosse rather than Lemercier. This tentative suggestion is supported by an apparent dissonance between the style of the pavilion and the rest of the building. It must be remembered, however, that the only visual evidence is Silvestre's representation.

Neither the style of the entrance-pavilion as engraved by Silvestre nor its interior arrangement, nor the intervention of Paul de Brosse in 1628, seems sufficient grounds for the attribution of any part of Liancourt to Salomon de Brosse.

6. Tremblot, op. cit.,: '. . . y ayant seulement au milieu, et immediatement au dessus de la grande porte-cochère, une chapelle, en forme de petit pavillon qu'on gagne par la traverse d'un balcon qui sort de la galerie couverte'.

7. Charles du Plessis, father of Roger, died in 1620, and in that year the new Marquis de Liancourt – he was not yet a Duke – married Jeanne de Schomberg. Any building on a large scale done for Roger du Plessis would almost certainly be after this date. (He did not buy the Hôtel de Bouillon until 1623).

W

III

Château of Ognon: the Gloriettes

THE château of Ognon has disappeared, save for one medieval tower incorporated into the nineteenth-century building now standing on the site.[1] A considerable amount remains, however, of the original lay-out of the park and of the buildings and statues with which it was adorned. Part of this park was created for François de la Fontaine, Seigneur d'Ognon, in the early seventeenth century.

François de la Fontaine was one of Marie de Médicis' friends; he lent her large sums of money and thereby ruined himself, being forced to sell Ognon in 1632, in which year he died.

The park contains two garden-pavilions which, stylistically, obviously date from the period of François de la Fontaine's ownership; these are the buildings known as the 'Gloriettes' of Ognon.[2] They stand on terraces, half-way up each side of a flight of balustraded steps in an avenue known as 'le mail'. Built entirely of stone, they are square, each side being pierced by a large plain arch with a triple keystone. There are Doric or Tuscan pilasters at the corner of each face (owing to the absence of the balustrade which must once have existed, and the dilapidation of the entablature, the capitals have disappeared). Surmounting the pavilions are ridged, square domes of the Verneuil type and rusticated lanterns each with four arched openings and small ridged cupolas. On the two principal faces of each pavilion is an *oeil-de-boeuf*, and one of these is still decorated with the original urn over its entablature.[3]

On the balustrades which flank the staircase itself (they are also carried round the terrace on which the pavilions stand) are four stone statues of women holding flowers.

The Gloriettes have such strong stylistic affinities with de Brosse's work that their attribution to him, suggested by Mlle Marguerite Charageat,[4] is completely

1. For the history of the château and its owners, cf. Marguerite Charageat, 'Le château et le parc d'Ognon', *La Gazette illustrée des amateurs de jardins*, 1935, p. 1–19, and Ernest de Ganay, *Châteaux et manoirs de France*, 1938, IV, p. 29 ff.
2. E. de Ganay, op. cit., illustrates these, pls 44 and 45.
3. Or was, in 1938, when the pavilions were photographed for Ganay.
4. Op. cit., above, n. 1.

convincing, though it must at present rest on style alone in the absence of any documentary evidence.

Mlle Charageat supports her suggestion by pointing out that the style and handling of the statues on the balustrades corresponds so closely with that of the original stone statues made by Berthelot for the Luxembourg,[5] that they must be by him. She thus establishes a link between the Palace and the Gloriettes. She believes that the statues may have been a gift to François de la Fontaine from Marie de Médicis.

The nearness of Ognon to Verneuil, and to de Brosse's own house at Mont-laville (it was only a few miles distant in the Forêt d'Halatte); the relationship of François de la Fontaine with Marie de Médicis; the presence of Berthelot's statues, all support the attribution of the Gloriettes to de Brosse. But it is above all their style which suggests their origin. Their links with Verneuil, Montceaux and Blérancourt are obvious. These pavilions have excellent proportions and a robust classical simplicity which gives them a grandeur which has nothing to do with size – they are, in fact, very small in scale. They could well be de Brosse's ultimate development of the Verneuil style.[6]

5. Which Mlle Charagent examined in a store at the Luxembourg. She does not specify for what part of the attic of the palace the statues she saw were destined, and her account here is slightly confusing. However, her attribution to Berthelot is perfectly convincing.

6. I suggest a date *c.* 1620–1623 for the Gloriettes on general style, but also for another important reason: if they are de Brosse's work, he has here for the first time that we know of, made each pilaster reach right up to the edge of the face of the building and meet the one on the returning face.

IV

Paris, Collège de France

ON 28 September 1610 Louis XIII laid the first stone of the Collège de France, which had been founded by Henri IV shortly before his death. The building proceeded slowly, and only one of the three *corps-de-logis* envisaged was completed. In 1640 Malingre wrote, 'des trois costez il y en a déjà un bien advancé'. 'Déjà' seems a curious qualification for a building whose first stone had been laid thirty years previously. In 1774 a complete reconstruction was ordered and was carried out by Chalgrin.

Malvoüe (*Les Actes de Sully*, 1600–1610, ed. 1911, p. 170) says, 'Sully, le Cardinal du Perron, le Président de Thou et un conseiller au Parlement avaient visité cet emplacement le 23 décembre 1609. Il semble que les plans et devis des constructions avaient été dressés par Salomon de Brosse . . . et dont le nom 'Brosse' sans autre indication, se trouve mentionné dans le présent acte comme auteur de la mise à prix de 25 livres la thoise de maçonnerie'.

Mallvoüe prints part of the *devis* for the building from the *marché et devis* of 5 April 1610: 'Marché passé avec Claude Monnart, maître maçon en suite des adjudications des 10 et 16 février 1610, moyennant le prix de 14 livres par thoise'.

At the end of this extract he gives a list (p. 172) of all the entrepreneurs who tendered for the contract. Besides 'Brosse' (without, as he says, any Christian name given) there are among the names those of two of de Brosse's associates, Jean Coign (Coulommiers, 1613; Palais de Justice, Paris, 1619) and Claude Monnart (St Gervais, 1616). 'Brosse', at 25 livres per toise, put in the most expensive tender. As we have seen, Monnart obtained the contract at 14 livres.

Monnart having been chosen, there is no evidence save that of the style of the building to suggest that de Brosse had anything further to do with the project, Mallvoüe does not support his assertion that the architect provided the 'plan et devis'. The style, however, is interesting, and in several ways supports an attribution to de Brosse.

The appearance of the Collège is known from the *devis* published by Mallvoüe and from an engraving by Chastillon in his *Topographie Française* of 1641. The two agree remarkably well.[1] In fact, since we know from Malingre that only one of the

1. Chastillon's engraving is inscribed 'Le Grand Collège Roial basti à Paris du Regne de Henri le Grand 4e du nom Roy de France et de Navarre, 1612'.

three wings was built by 1640, Chastillon must have based some of his engraving on the *devis* or on drawings.

The building occupied three sides of a court, the entrance was through a gate in the screen running parallel with the street. Part of the *devis* reads as follows: '. . . (les) faces qui regardent la court (et) la rue seront au premier estaige[2] ornez d'arcades faictes d'espace en espace, et chacun desdits espaces ou trumeaux sera orné de deux pilastres portés sur piedestaux le tout naissant d'une saillie ou plinthe qui sera sur ledict rez-de-chaussée. Et regnera au partour desd. logis lesd. pillastres portant ung architrave, frize et cornice s'erigera ung autre ordre de pillastres accouplez aussy de deux en deux et posés directement sur ceulx dembas, qui sera continué par tout ledict deuxième estaige . . .'.

The walls were brick, the arcades, pilasters, window surrounds, parapet and lucarnes stone. The screen, shown by Chastillon, but not mentioned in Mallvoüe's transcription, continued the design of arcades and coupled Ionic pilasters.[3] The entrance-gate is specified in the *devis*: '. . . se fera ung portail portant pareil ornement tant par devant que par dehors, chargé de son frontispice'. Chastillon shows the *portail* flanked by double pilasters, and surmounted by an unbroken triangular pediment.

The use of superimposed orders on the façades of the Collège is interesting. Blérancourt, with its superimposed Doric pilasters, and the Collège may have been designed at almost the same time; (from the 1612 contract for Blérancourt, we know that at that date de Brosse's château was already begun). Coulommiers, with its superimposed orders of coupled columns, followed in 1613. Outside de Brosse's work the superimposed order is rare at this date in France. It is worth noticing, in connection with de Brosse's known usage, the placing of those (single) pilasters at the Collège which occur on the outer corners of the street-façades of the flanking *corps-de-logis*. This is shown clearly by Chastillon, and supported by a seventeenth-century drawing in the Bibliothèque Nationale.[4] The rhythm of double and single pilasters on these façades is like that of Rennes, built nine years later.

2. It is clear from the sense of the rest that the ground floor is meant.

3. The order is not specified in the *devis*, but is shown by Chastillon.

4. B.N.Est. V^a 259 h: contains various plans and drawings: fol. 1, 'Plan du Collège Royal dit des trois evesques à Paris en l'Université 28 mai 1664'; fol. ii, ditto, first floor; fol. vi, Plans (by Chalgrin?) showing the old and new projects; fol. vii, Drawing (by Chalgrin?); pen and colour-wash, showing the street façade of one of the wings; this corresponds with Chastillon's engraving, except that there are no lucarnes above the cornice.

General Bibliography

A. F. Blunt, *Art and Architecture in France, 1500–1700*, London, 2nd edition, 1970.

A. F. Blunt, *Philibert de l'Orme*, London, 1958, Volume I in the series *Studies in Architecture*.

R. Blomfield, *A History of French Architecture, 1494–1661*, London, 1911.

H. von Geymüller, *Les Ducerceau, leur vie et leur oeuvre*, Paris, 1887.

L. Hautecoeur, *L'histoire de l'architecture classique en France*, Volume I (in two parts), Paris, 1943.

A. Mauban, *Jean Marot, architecte et graveur parisien*, Paris, 1944.

J. Pannier, *Salomon de Brosse, un architecte français au commencement du XVII siècle*, Paris, 1911.

C. Read, *Salomon de Brosse, l'architecte de Henri IV et de Marie de Médicis*, Paris, 1881, offprint from *Mém. Soc. Ant. Fr.*, XLI.

H. Sauval, *Histoire et recherches des antiquités de la ville de Paris*, Paris, 1724.

A. Venturi, *Storia dell'Arte Italiana*, Volume XI, part 2, Milan, 1939.

These works are referred to, throughout the text and notes, simply by the name of the author in each case, except in that of the two works by A. F. Blunt, which are distinguished as *Art and Architecture* and *Philibert de l'Orme*.

Note. Serlio's 'True Sixth Book': References throughout the text to the manuscript identified by Professor Rosci as the 'True Sixth Book' of Serlio have been made in that form. A full reference to Professor Rosci's *Il Trattato di Architettura di Sebastiano Serlio* (ed. Brizio, Milan, 1966), in which he traces the history and provides a critical analysis of this collection, will be found in Chapter II, p. 19 and note 7.

Index

Brosse, Salomon de Chronology, *passim*, 197–202
Bullant, Jean, 6, 11, 19, 20, 32, 34, 37, 48 n., 54, 60, 88, 92, 189, 200
Bullion, Claude de, 68, 198, 245, 246
Buontalenti, Bernardo, 79–80, 103, 132, 133
Burlington, Richard Boyle, 3rd Earl of, 185 n.

Capranica: Santa Maria del Piano, 52
Caprarola, Villa Farnese, 24, 27, 61, 77, 151, 176
Caris, Tugal, 162, 177 n., 272
Cassel, 9
Cataneo, Pietro, 45
Catherine de Médicis, 19, 38, 60, 231
Catherinot, Nicolas, 137 n.
Cazelles, Raymond, 40 n., 274
Censive de l'Archevêché, xxiv 238, 249
Chalgrin, Jean-François, 100, 115, 131, 265, 282
Chambord, Château de, 25 n., 83 n.
Champigny, Château de, 183, 211
Chantilly: Châtelet, 33
Charageat, Marguerite, 284–5
Charenton: Protestant Temple, 6, 183–7, 201, 212–13
Charles IX, 27
Charleval, Château de, 20, 23, 26, 27, 28, 29, 31, 34, 158
Charleville, 44, 45, 139 n.
Chastel, André, 19 n., 25 n., 28 n., 56 n.
Chastillon, Claude, 32, 221, 225, 282, 283
Chénesseau, A., 146 n., 235, 236
Chenonceau, Château de, 25 n., 28
Chilly-Mazarin, Château de, 139 n.
Cigoli (Ludovico Cardi), 103
Ciprut, E-J., xxi, 4 n., 11 n., 12 n., 24 n., 70 n., 110 n., 134 n., 139 n., 148 n., 151 n., 183 n., 198, 199, 200, 223, 235, 239, 245, 249, 280
Coing, or Coingt, Jean, 214, 221, 278 n., 282
Colbert, Jean-Baptiste, 228
Colin, Henri, 256
Collard, Henri, xxi
Collin, Rémy, 7, 12, 50, 51, 145 n., 151 n., 232, 256
Collot, Pierre, 103
Condé, Louis, Prince de, 40, 277
Conti, Louis François, Prince de, 51, 55

Coope, R., 26 n., 35 n., 39 n., 41 n., 228, 274, 277
Corbineau, Jacques, 162–74 *passim*, 271, 272
Corbineau, Pierre, 162
Cordier, Michel-Martial, 216
Cormatin, Château de, 107
Cornon, Raymond, xxi, 166 n.
Cosnier, Hugues, 45, 223–4
Cossé Brissac, P. de, 280
Cotte, Robert de, 32, 73 n.
Coulommiers: Capuchin Church, 96, 97 n., 98, 147 n.
Coulommiers, Château de, 2 n., 5, 13–14, 18, 43, 64, 70, 73, 85, 88, 93–109, 110, 111, 112, 115, 117, 118, 128, 129, 138, 147, 150 n., 171 n., 173, 175, 176 n., 188, 190, 198, 214–221, 281
Couture, Thomas, 150 n.
Couzy, Helène, xxi
Coyecque, E., 75 n., 76 n., 83 n., 204

Dauvergne, Anatole, 96 n., 100, 101, 214, 217
Delagrive, Abbé, 64 n., 67 n., 70, 179, 180, 210, 242, 246, 250, 252, 255
Della Porta, Giacomo, 141
Derand, François, 78, 146, 147 n., 204
Deschamps, Christophe, 71 n.
Descloseaux, A., 228
Dessin, Charles, 75 n., 204
Diane de France, Duchesse d'Angoulême, 32
Diane de Poitiers, 225
Dimier, L., 80 n.
Dinsmoor, W., 20 n., 22 n.
Domenico da Cortona, 25 n.
Donon, Jean de, 135, 136, 138
Du Cerceau, Baptiste Androuet, 3, 5, 7–8, 19, 29, 32, 34, 38, 71, 72, 84 n.
Du Cerceau, Jacques I. Androuet, 3, 4 n., 7, 8, 18, 19, 20–33 *passim*, 39, 41 n., 46, 47, 53, 55, 70, 84 n., 85, 87, 91, 94, 101, 105, 107, 108, 117, 119, 143, 147, 151, 152, 156, 175, 189, 190, 193–4, 197, 255, 274, 276, 277
Du Cerceau, Jacques II Androuet, 3, 4, 5, 8, 9, 32, 34, 35, 37, 49, 61 n., 71 n., 90, 118, 129, 139, 161 n., 183, 184, 185, 198
Du Cerceau, Jean Androuet, 5, 6, 7, 10, 11, 12, 15, 62, 71 n., 133, 145, 202, 235, 236, 237
Du Colombier, Pierre, 15 n., 18 n., 135 n., 137 n., 138 n., 266

Plates

1. Philibert de l'Orme. Anet. Frontispiece

2. Philibert de l'Orme. Anet. Cryptoporticus. Detail

3. Lescot. Louvre. Square court

4. Jacques I du Cerceau. Drawing. Louvre. Square court. Detail

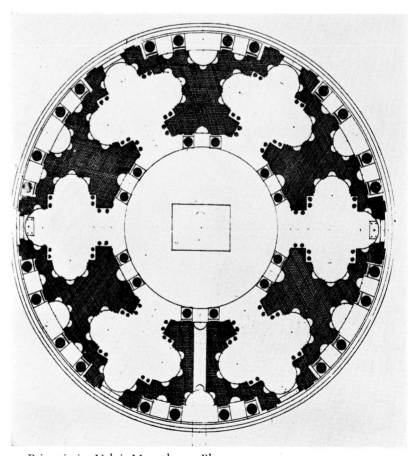

5. Primaticcio. Valois Mausoleum. Plan

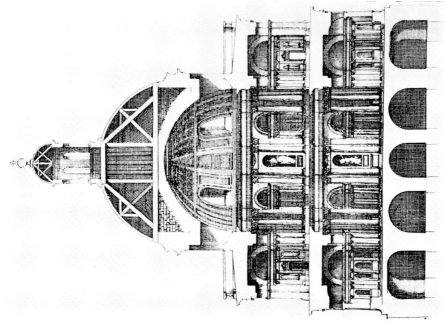

7. Primaticcio. Valois Mausoleum. Section

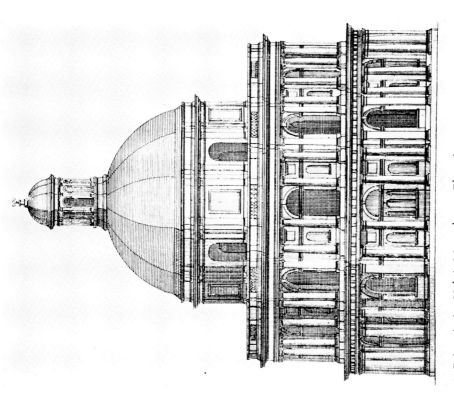

6. Primaticcio. Valois Mausoleum. Elevation

8. Serlio. Fontainebleau. Entrance to the Grand Ferrare

9. Serlio. Ancy-le-Franc

10. Bullant. La Fère-en-Tardenois. Entrance to the Gallery

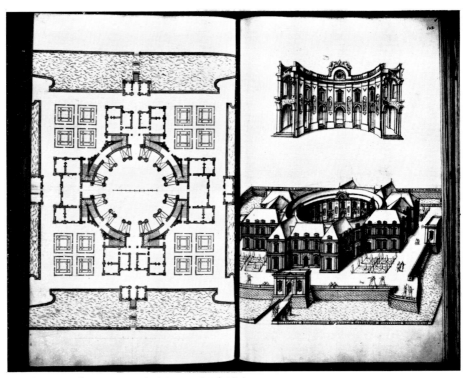

11. Jacques I du Cerceau. 'Bâtiment à Plaisir'

12. Grosbois. Principal Façade

LELEVATION DE TOVT LE CONTENV DV CLOZ

VI

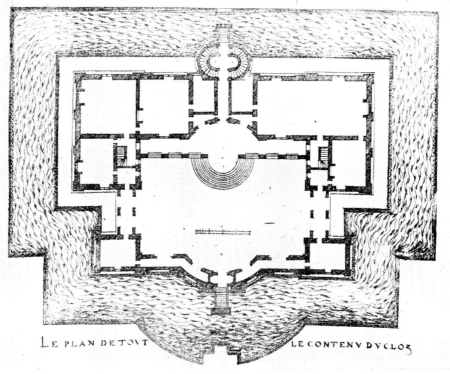

LE PLAN DE TOVT   LE CONTENV DV CLOZ

13. Jacques I du Cerceau. Design for a Château

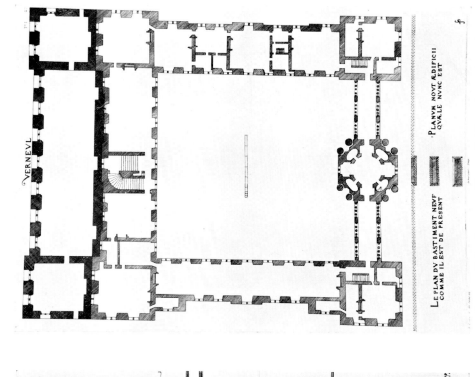

VERNEVL

15. Jacques I du Cerceau. Verneuil. Plan. Second Design

Cour du Chasteau

14. Jacques I du Cerceau. Verneuil. Plan. First Design

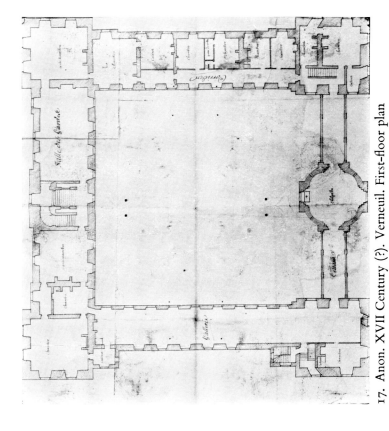

17. Anon. XVII Century (?). Verneuil. First-floor plan

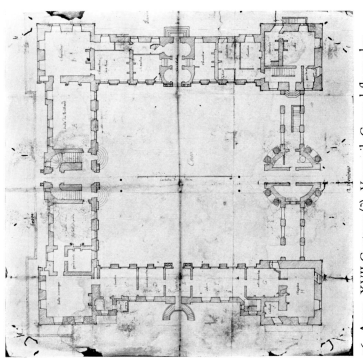

16. Anon. XVII Century (?). Verneuil. Ground-floor plan

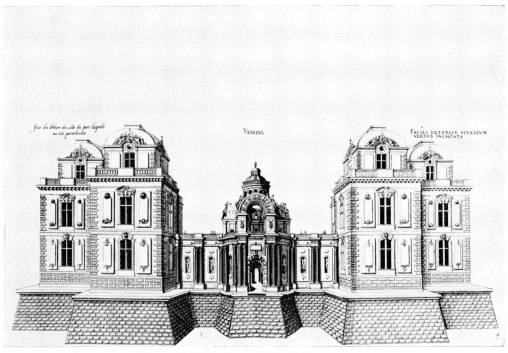

18. Jacques I du Cerceau. Verneuil. Main Front. First Design

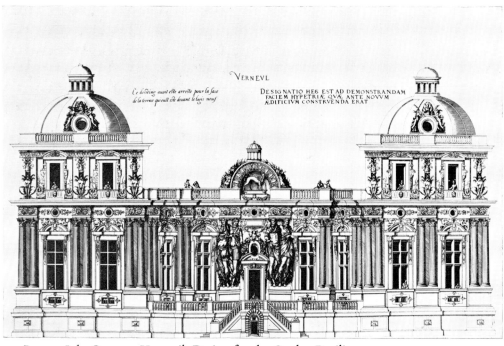

19. Jacques I du Cerceau. Verneuil. Design for the Garden Pavilion

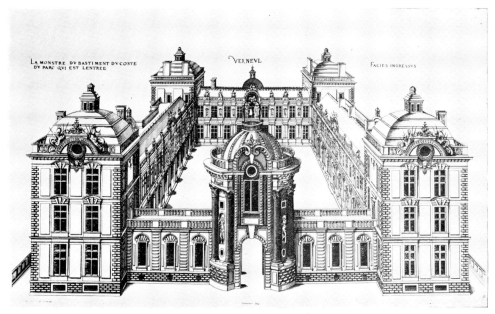

VERNEVL

FACIES INGRESSVS

20. Jacques I du Cerceau. Verneuil. Main Front. Second Design

21. Anon. Early XVII Century. Drawing. Verneuil. Main Front

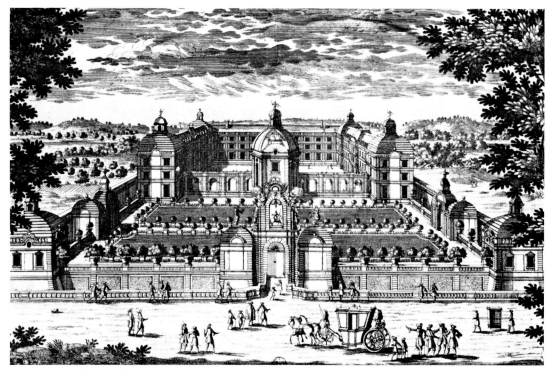

22. Aveline. View of Verneuil

23. Dupont. View of Verneuil in ruins

24. Jacques I du Cerceau.
    Design for a Gate

25. Verneuil. Porte Henri IV

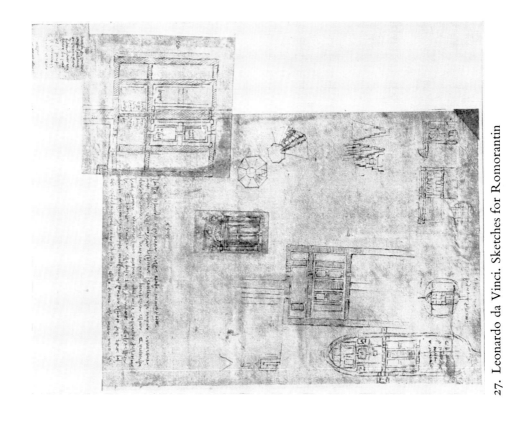

27. Leonardo da Vinci. Sketches for Romorantin

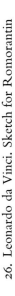

26. Leonardo da Vinci. Sketch for Romorantin

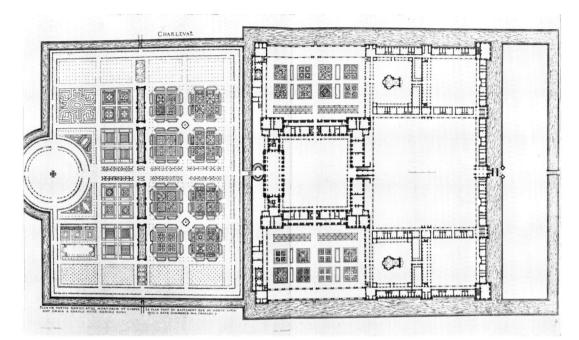

28. Jacques I du Cerceau. Charleval. Plan

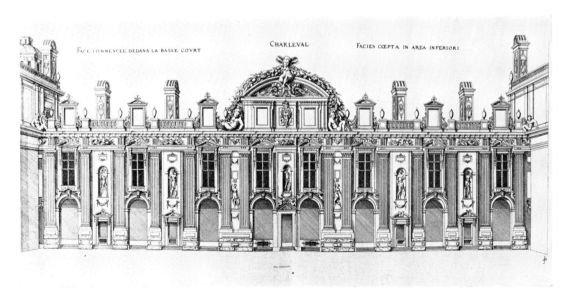

29. Jacques I du Cerceau. Charleval. Elevation

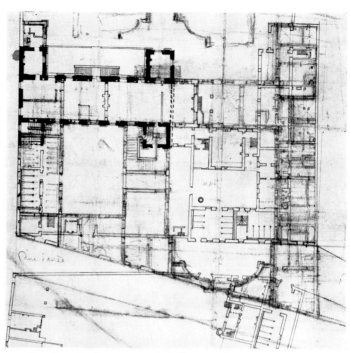

30. Baptiste du Cerceau. Hôtel d'Angoulême. Plan

31. Baptiste du Cerceau. Hôtel d'Angoulême.
Detail

32. Baptiste du Cerceau. Hôtel d'Angoulême. Detail

33. Baptiste du Cerceau. Hôtel d'Angoulême. Detail

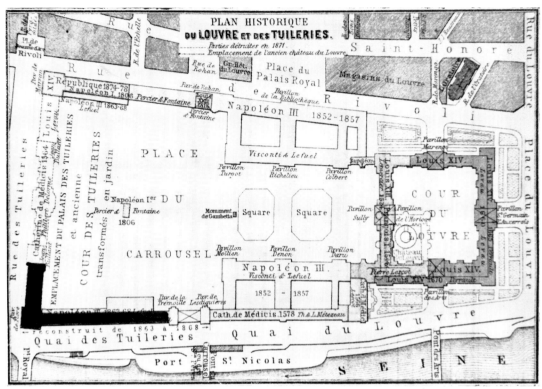

34. Louvre. Historical Plan (showing work by Jacques II du Cerceau in black)

35. Jacques II du Cerceau. Tuileries. Pavillon de Flore and Petite Galerie des Tuileries

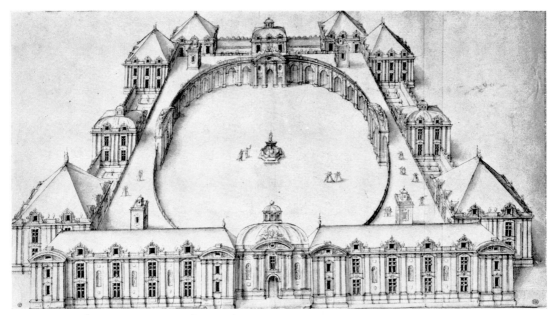

36. Jacques I du Cerceau. Design for a Palace

37. Jacques II du Cerceau. Louvre. The Grande Galerie before demolition

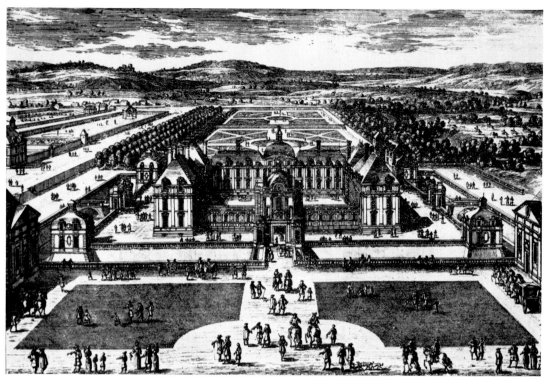

38. Perelle. View of Montceaux

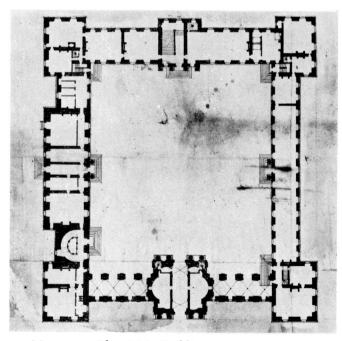

39. Montceaux. Plan. Main Buildings

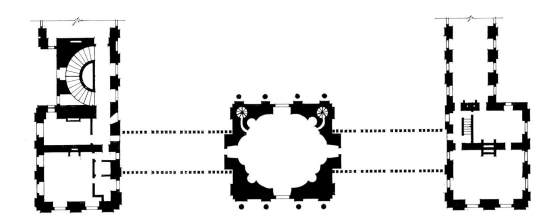

40. Montceaux. Plan. Detail. Entrance Front. First floor

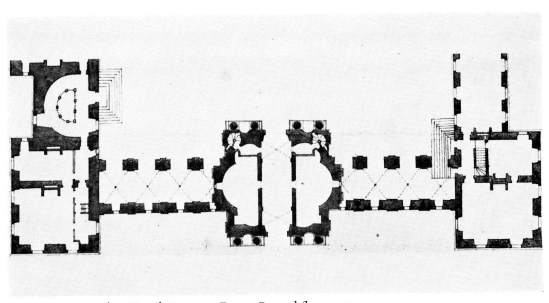

41. Montceaux. Plan. Detail. Entrance Front. Ground floor

43. Jacques II du Cerceau (?). Montceaux. N.W. Pavilion

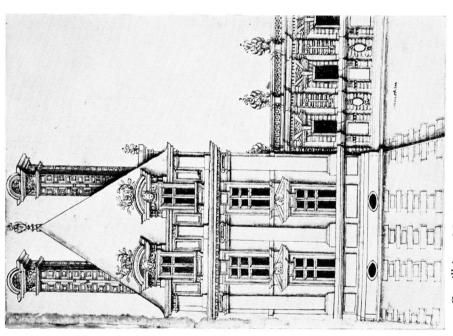

42. Gentilhâtre. Montceaux.
Entrance Screen and S.E. Pavilion

44. Jacques II du Cerceau. Tuileries. Pavillon de Flore

45. Henrichemont. Aerial View

46. Henrichemont. Grande Place. Aerial View

47. Henrichemont. A *Porte-cochère*

48. Henrichemont. 'Maison du Procurateur Fiscal'

49. Salomon de Brosse (?).
Montceaux. S. Wing.
Entrance from the court

50. Salomon de Brosse (?). Montceaux. S. Wing. Entrance from the court. Detail

51. Salomon de Brosse (?).
Montceaux. S. Wing.
Entrance from the Court.
Detail

52. Jacques II du Cerceau (?). Montceaux. *Corps-de-Logis*.
Main Door

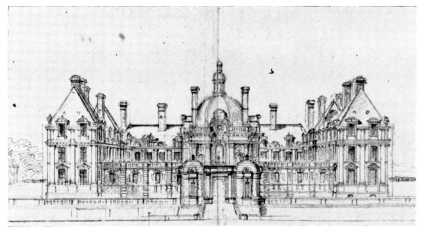

53. Silvestre. View of Montceaux. Main Front. Detail

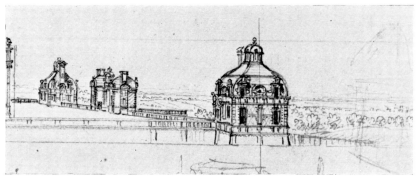

54. Silvestre. View of Montceaux. 'Pavillon Conti'. Detail

55. Rigaud. Montceaux. View from the South

56. Salomon de Brosse (?). Montceaux. 'Pavillon Conti'. Detail

58. Salomon de Brosse (?). Montceaux. 'Pavillon Conti'. Door

57. Gentilhâtre. Montceaux. 'Pavillon Conti'. Door

60. Salomon de Brosse (?). Montceaux. 'Pavillon Conti'. Door. Detail

59. Salomon de Brosse (?). Montceaux. 'Pavillon
Conti'. Decorative Panel

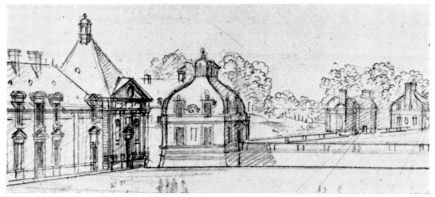

61. Silvestre. View of Montceaux. Detail. Forecourt.
Chapel and part of the S. Range

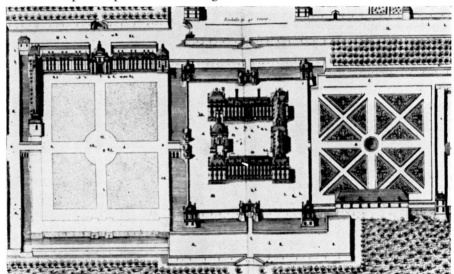

62. Silvestre. Montceaux. Bird's-eye view

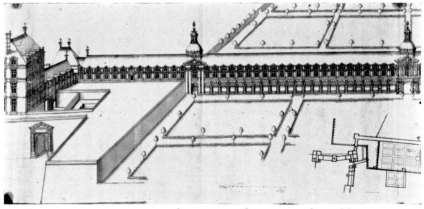

63. Anon. Late XVI Century. Blois. Design for Henri IV's Buildings

64. Rémy Collin. Fontainebleau. Entrance to the Cour des Offices.
Detail

65. Montceaux. Forecourt. S.Entrance

66. Montceaux. Forecourt. Chapel. Detail

67. Montceaux. Forecourt. Chapel and part of the S. Range

68. Montceaux. Forecourt. Chapel

69. Montceaux. Entrance Pavilion

70. Montceaux. Entrance Pavilion and
    part of the Screen Arcade

71. Jacques II du Cerceau (?). Montceaux. *Corps-de-Logis*. Façade

72. Montceaux. Entrance Pavilion Chapel. Interior. Detail

73. Turgot. Plan of Paris. Detail

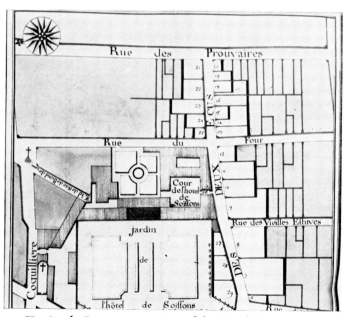

74. Terrier du Roy. *c.* 1700. Site of the Hôtel de Soissons,
Rue des Deux-Ecus

75. Anon. XVII Century. Hôtel de Soissons. Door. Drawing

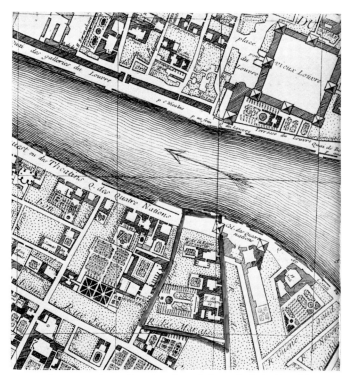

76. Delagrive. Plan of Paris. Site of the Hôtel de Bouillon,
Rue de Seine

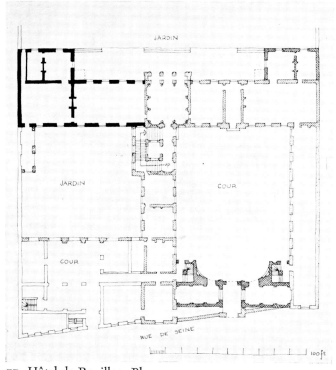

77. Hôtel de Bouillon. Plan

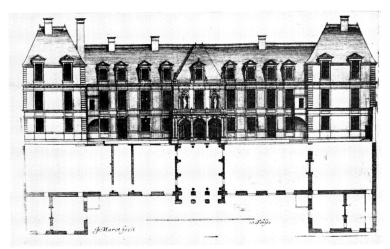

78. Hôtel de Bouillon. Garden Front. Plan and elevation

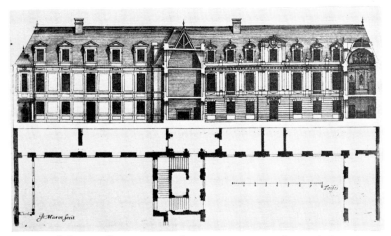

79. Hôtel de Bouillon. Main and Service Courts. Plan and elevation

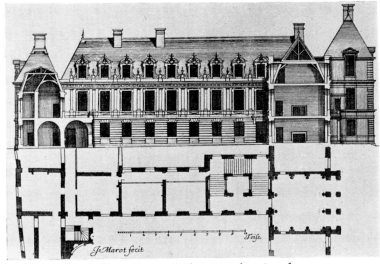

80. Hôtel de Bouillon. Plan and Elevation showing the
Entrance Front in Section

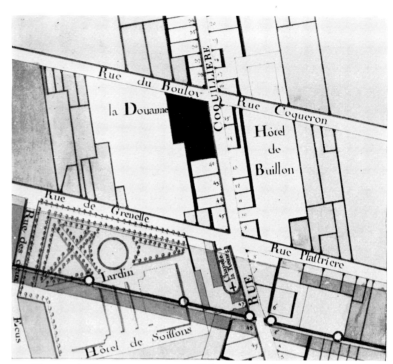

81. Terrier du Roy. *c.* 1700. Site of the Hôtel Bénigne Bernard,
Rue Coquillière and Rue du Bouloi

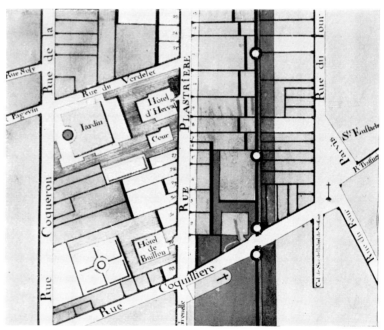

82. Terrier du Roy, *c.* 1700. Site of the Hôtel de Bullion,
Rue Plastrière

84. Salomon de Brosse (?). Verneuil. Parish Church.
Door in N. Porch

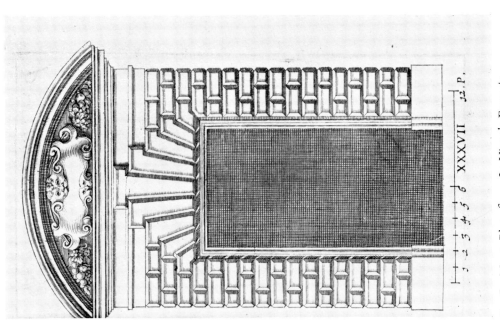

83. Le Muet. Plate from *Le Vignole Français*.
Door of the Hôtel Bénigne Bernard

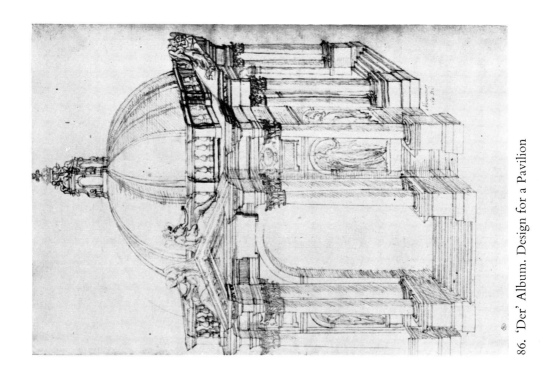

86. 'Der' Album. Design for a Pavilion

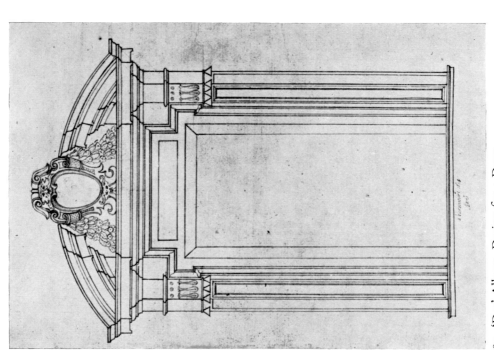

85. 'Der' Album. Design for a Door

88. Fréminet and Tremblay. Fontainebleau. Chapel of the Trinity. Ceiling Decoration

87. Fréminet. Fontainebleau. Chapel of the Trinity, Design for the High Altar

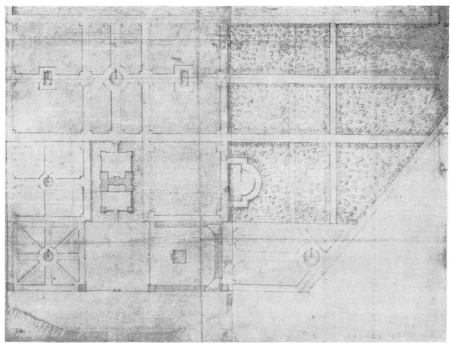

89. Blérancourt. Plan and part of the general lay-out of the Gardens

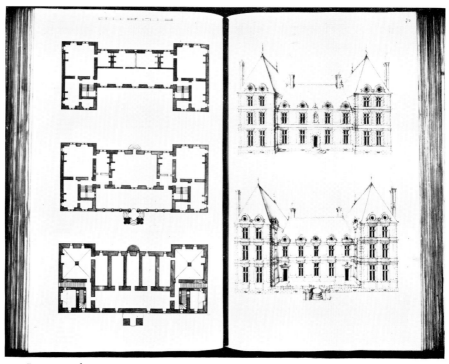

90. Jacques I du Cerceau. Design for a Country House

91. Silvestre. View of Blérancourt

92. Silvestre. View of Blérancourt

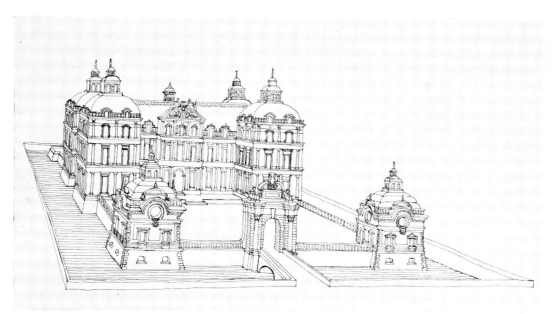

93. Blérancourt. A Reconstruction. Drawing

94. Tavernier de Junquières. View of Blérancourt

95. Blérancourt. S.W. Pavilion. Ground floor

96. Blérancourt. S.E. Pavilion. Ground floor. Reconstruction

97. Blérancourt. Court Façade. Central Element. Reconstruction

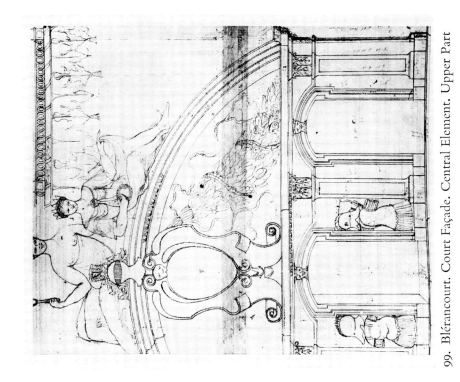

99. Blérancourt. Court Façade. Central Element. Upper Part

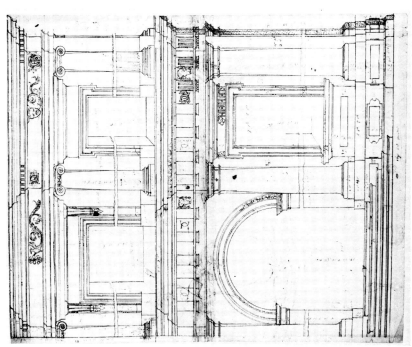

98. Blérancourt. Court Façade. Central Element. Lower Part

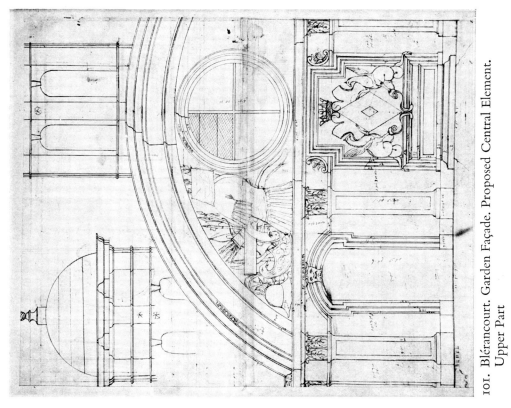

101. Blérancourt. Garden Façade. Proposed Central Element.
Upper Part

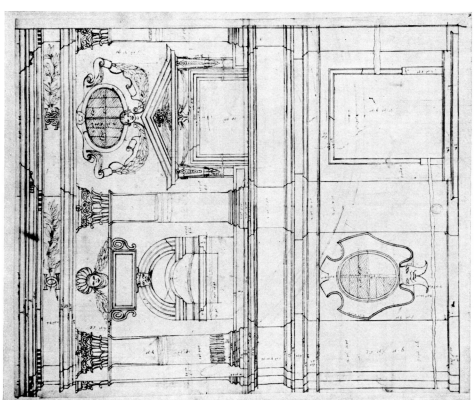

100. Blérancourt. Garden Façade. Proposed Central Element.
Lower Part

103. Blérancourt. S.E. Detached Pavilion

102. Blérancourt. S.W. Pavilion. Window

104. Blérancourt. *Porte d'Honneur*

105. Blérancourt. *Porte d'Honneur*. Detail

106. Blérancourt. *Porte d'Honneur*. Detail

107. Blérancourt. Court Façade.
Central Element. Detail

108. Montlaville-sous-Verneuil. House of Salomon de Brosse. Detail

109. Blérancourt. S.E. Detached Pavilion. Detail

110. Blérancourt. View of the detached Pavilions and the *Porte d'Honneur*

111. Jacques I du Cerceau.
Design for a Gate

112. Blérancourt. Part of the Substructure

113. Blérancourt. Main Gate and Pavilions

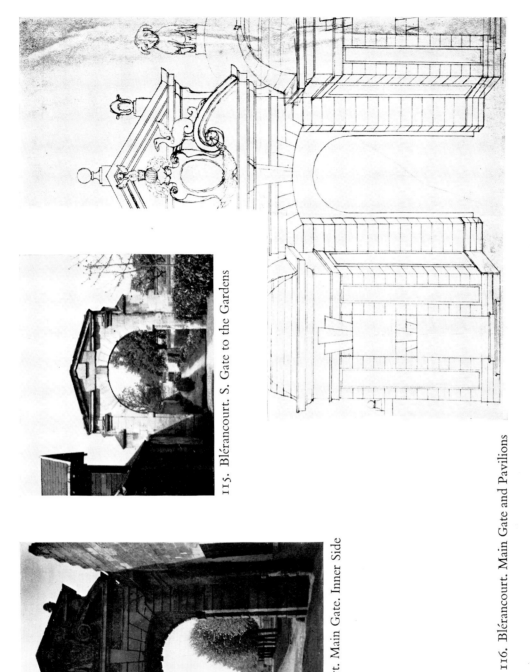

114. Blérancourt. Main Gate. Inner Side

115. Blérancourt. S. Gate to the Gardens

116. Blérancourt. Main Gate and Pavilions

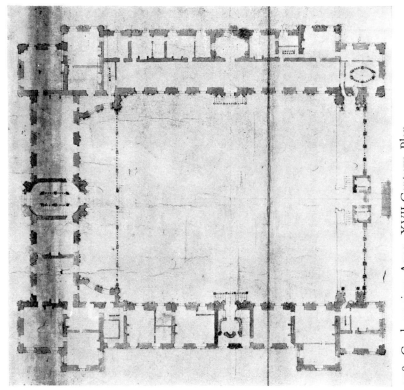

118. Coulommiers. Anon. XVII Century. Plan

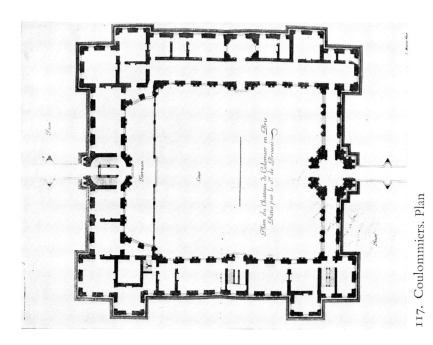

117. Coulommiers. Plan

119. Coulommiers. Capuchin Church. Plaster Relief. Landscape. Detail

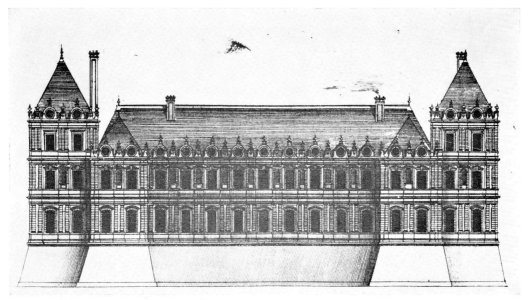

120. Coulommiers. N. Wing. Exterior

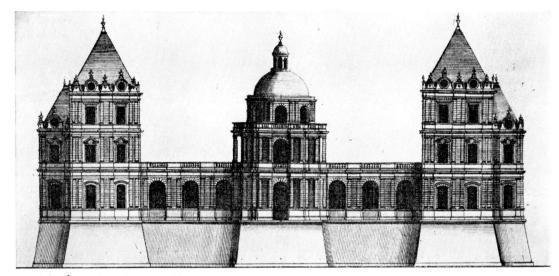

121. Coulommiers. Entrance Front

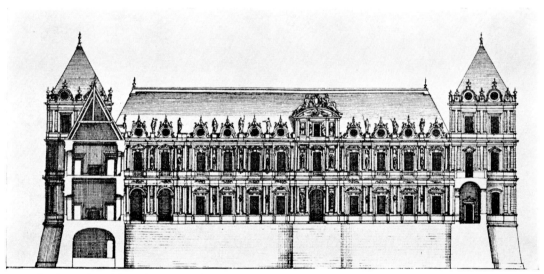

122. Coulommiers. Elevation on to the Court

123. Charles du Ry. Coulommiers. Decoration

124. Charles du Ry. Coulommiers.
Garden Front. Central Element

125. Charles du Ry. Coulommiers. Part of Exterior

126. Anon. XVII Century. Coulommiers. *Corps-de-Logis*. Façade

127. Anon. XVII Century. View of Coulommiers

128. Coulommiers. Quadrant Arcade.
Detail

129. Coulommiers. *Corps-de-Logis.*
Ruined Arch of the Main Entrance

130. Coulommiers. Quadrant Arcade

131. Mansart. Coulommiers. Entrance Pavilion. Decoration. Detail

132. Mansart. Maisons-Lafitte. Decoration. Detail

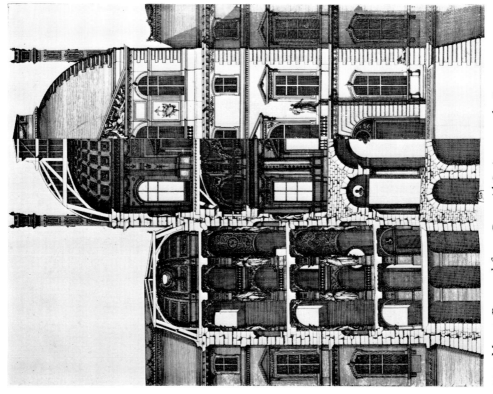

134. Marot. Proposal for a Caryatid Staircase at the Louvre

133. Unknown Architect. Cormatin. Main Staircase

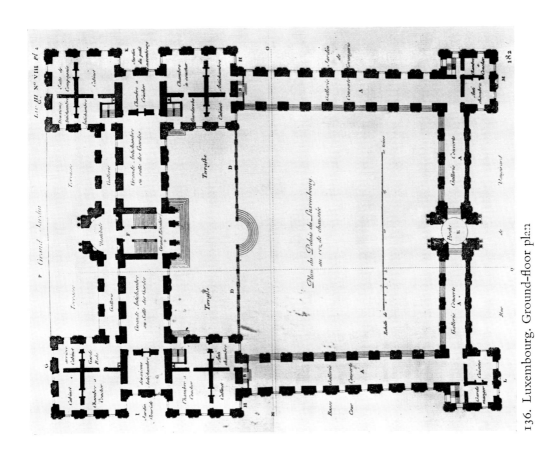

135. Anon. XVII Century. Luxembourg. General plan

136. Luxembourg. Ground-floor plan

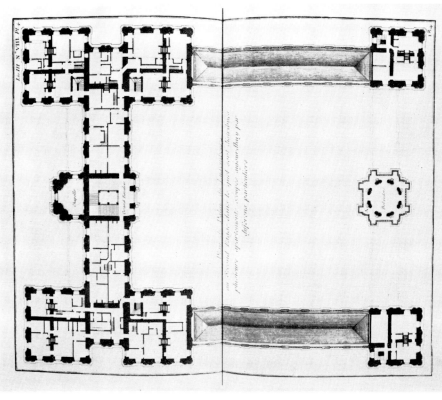

138. Luxembourg. Second-floor plan

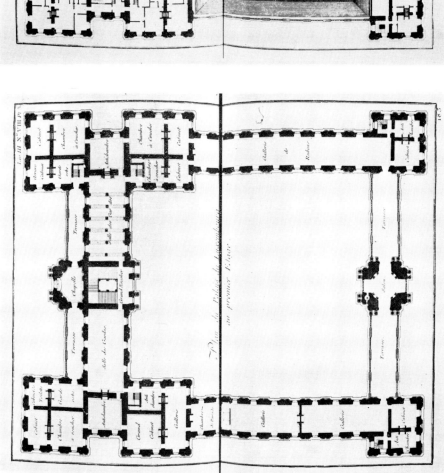

137. Luxembourg. First-floor plan

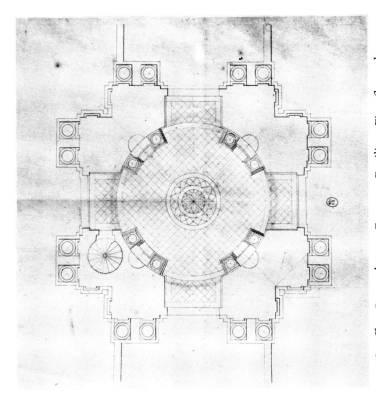

140. Soufflot. Luxembourg. Entrance Pavilion. First-floor plan

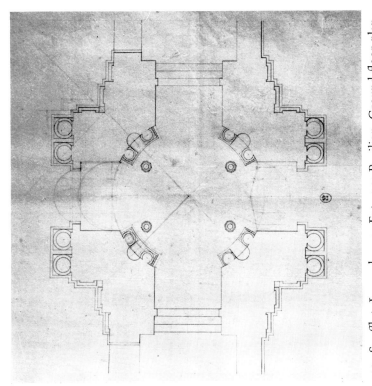

139. Soufflot. Luxembourg. Entrance Pavilion. Ground-floor plan

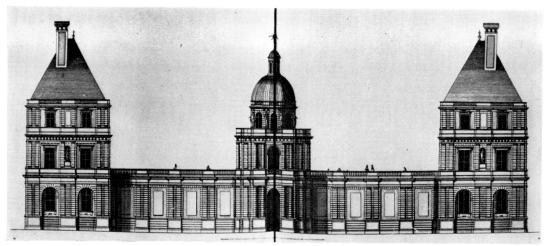

141. Luxembourg. Entrance Front

142. Luxembourg. Section

143. Luxembourg. S. Front

144. Luxembourg. *Corps-de-Logis*

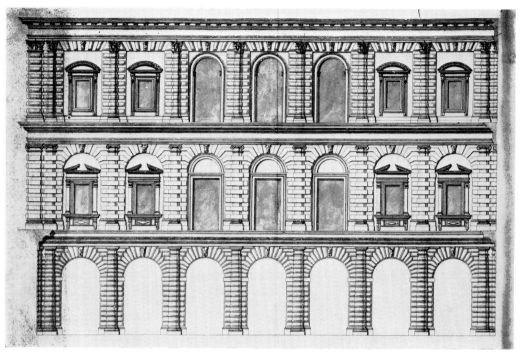

145. Anon. Drawing. Florence. Pitti Palace. Façade of Ammanati's Court

146. Florence. Pitti Palace. Ammanati's Court

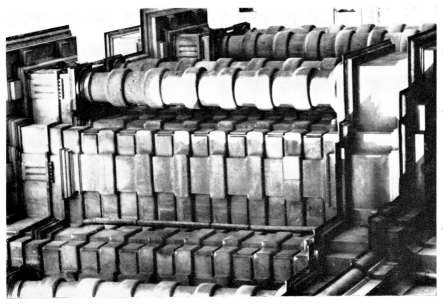

148. Luxembourg. Entrance Pavilion. Detail

147. Florence. Pitti Palace. Ammanati's Court. Detail

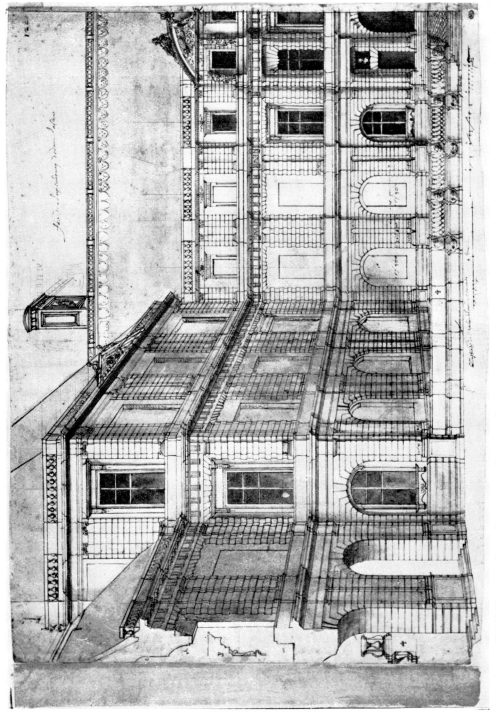

149. Anon. XVII Century Drawing. Luxembourg. The Court. Detail

151. Luxembourg. Entrance Front

150. Luxembourg. Entrance Front

152. Luxembourg. Entrance Pavilion.
Drum of the Dome. Detail

153. Luxembourg. Entrance Pavilion.
Screen and N.W. Pavilion

154. Luxembourg. *Corps-de-Logis*. Part of the Original Structure

155. Luxembourg. N.W. Pavilion

156. Luxembourg. East Façade

157. Luxembourg. East Façade. Detail

159. Luxembourg. East Façade. Detail

158. Luxembourg. East Façade. Detail

160. Luxembourg. E. Façade. One of the Double Pavilions

161. Luxembourg. S. Façade. Central Element

162. Luxembourg. S. Façade

163. Luxembourg. Court and *Corps-de-Logis*

164. Mansart. Blois. Orléans Wing. Court Façade

165. Luxembourg. *Corps-de-Logis*. Detail

166. Luxembourg. Court. E. Façade. Detail

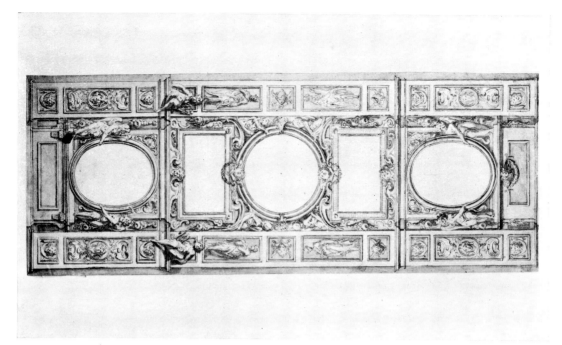

167. Anon. Early XVII Century. Design for a Ceiling

168. Luxembourg. Entrance Pavilion. First floor. Detail

169. Soufflot. Luxembourg. Entrance Pavilion. Section

170. Luxembourg. Entrance Pavilion.
Ground floor. Detail

171. Luxembourg. Entrance Pavilion. Ground floor. Detail

172. Luxembourg. Entrance Pavilion. Ground floor. Detail

Grote de Luxembourg

Iean Marot fecit

173. Luxembourg. Fontaine Médicis

174. Luxembourg. Fontaine Médicis. Detail

175. Buontalenti. Florence. Pitti Palace. Garden Grotto

176. Saint Gervais. West Front

177. Unknown Architect. Late XVI Century. Le Mesnil-Aubry. Church.
West Front. Detail

178. Unknown Architect. Early XVII Century. Paris. Saint Etienne-du-Mont.
W. Front

179. Saint Gervais. W. Front seen from the S. Side

180. Saint Gervais. W. Front. Detail

181. Saint Gervais. The Porch

Plan inferieur de
l'Ordre Dorique
du Portail
de Sᵗ. Gervais.

182. Saint Gervais. W. Front. The Orders

183. Saint Gervais. W. Front. Detail

184. Saint Gervais. W. Front. Central Door. Detail

185. Philibert de l'Orme. Anet. Entrance. Detail

186. Saint Gervais. W. Front. Detail

187. Saint Gervais. W. Front. N. Door. Detail

188. Boisseau. Paris. The Palais de Justice and the Sainte Chapelle. Engraving

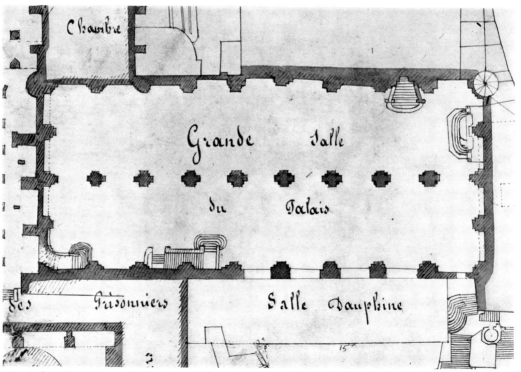

189. Palais de Justice. Salle des Pas Perdus. Plan

190. Salle des Pas Perdus and Palais de Justice. XIX Century

191. Froideau. Palais de Justice. The Cour du Mai after the Fire of 1777

192. Jacques I du Cerceau. 'Interior of an Antique Temple'

193. Salle des Pas Perdus. Interior

194. Antoine. Wooden model of the Salle des Pas Perdus

195. Salle des Pas Perdus. The Interior Today

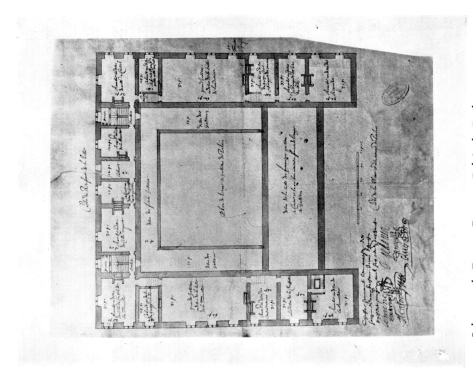

197. Salomon de Brosse. Rennes. Palais du Parlement.
Attic-floor plan

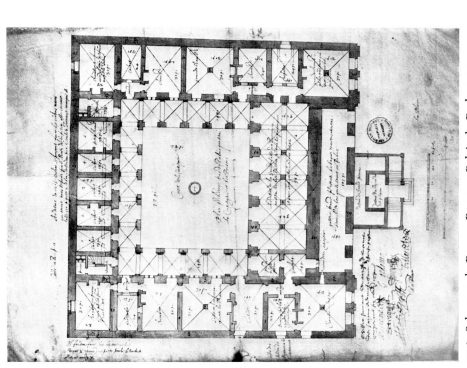

196. Salomon de Brosse. Rennes. Palais du Parlement.
Ground-floor plan

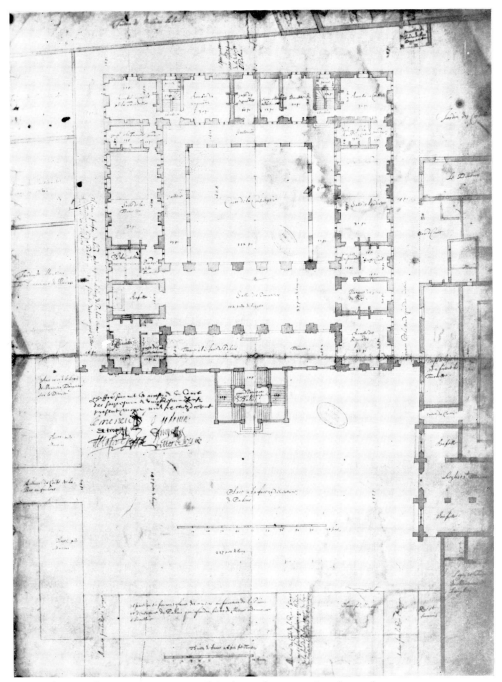

198. Salomon de Brosse. Rennes. Palais du Parlement. First-floor plan

199. Rennes. Palais du Parlement. Engraving of 1690

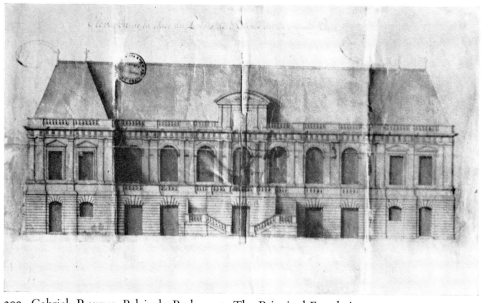

200. Gabriel. Rennes. Palais du Parlement. The Principal Façade in 1724

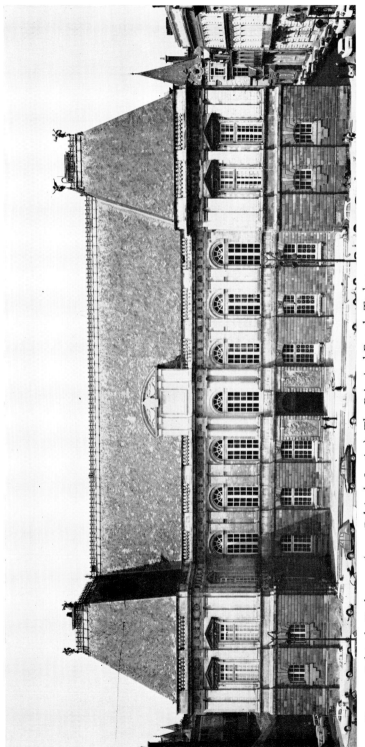

201. Rennes. Palais du Parlement (now Palais de Justice). The Principal Façade Today

202. Rennes. Palais du Parlement.
    E. Façade

203. Rennes. Palais du Parlement. S.W. Angle

204. Rennes. Palais du Parlement. Aerial View

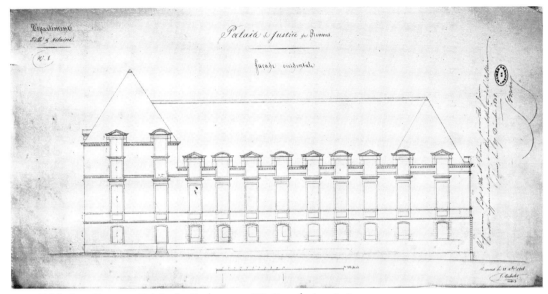

205. Richelot. Rennes. Palais du Parlement. W. Façade in 1838

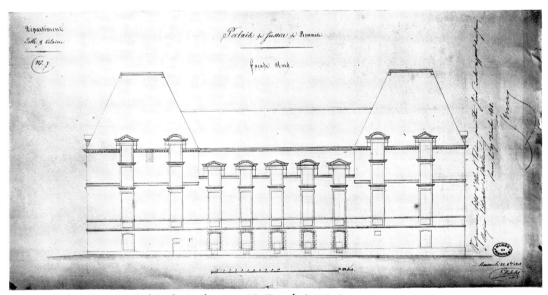

206. Richelot. Rennes. Palais du Parlement. N. Façade in 1838

207. Rennes. Palais du Parlement. Courtyard. Detail

208. Rennes. Palais du Parlement. Interior of the Grande Salle des Procureurs

209. Rennes. Palais du Parlement. Principal Façade. A Window

210. Salomon de Brosse and Michel Lasne. Engraving in Honour of Pope Gregory XV

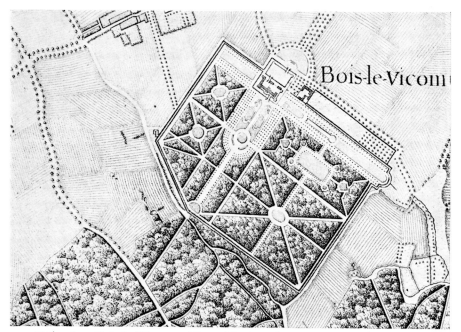

211. Delagrive. Bois-le-Vicomte. Plan of Paris and Environs. Detail

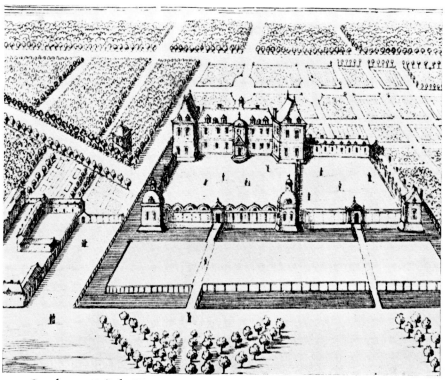

212. Gomboust. Bois-le-Vicomte

213. Brécy. Calvados. Garden Balustrade and Pavilion

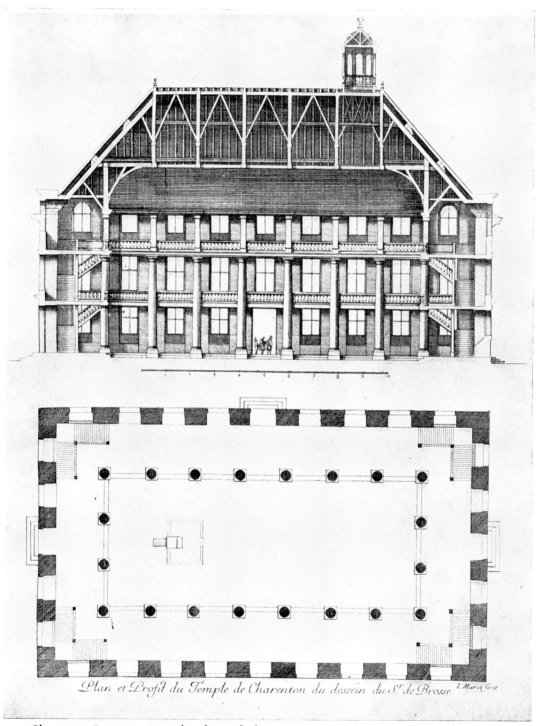

Plan et Profil du Temple de Charenton du dessein du Sr de Brosse. I. Marot fecit

214. Charenton. Protestant Temple. Plan and Elevation

215. Anon. Engraving. XVII Century. Charenton.
Protestant Temple. Exterior

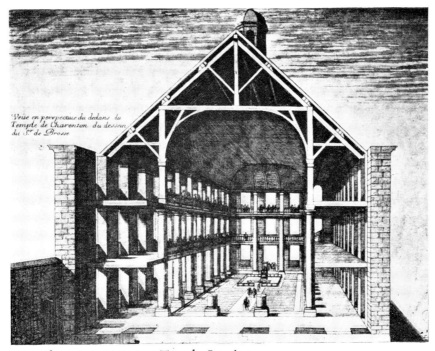

216. Charenton. Protestant Temple. Interior